TELEVISION

The Next Ten Years

STANFORD

The Institute for Communication Research

1962

This report has been prepared and published by the
Institute for Communication Research, Stanford University, Stanford, California,
pursuant to a contract with the United States Office of Education,
Department of Health, Education, and Welfare.

Library of Congress Catalog Card Number: 62-13346

A report and summary

of major studies on the problems

and potential of educational television,

conducted under the auspices of

the United States Office

of Education.

EDUCATIONAL

EDUCATIONAL TELEVISION

THE NEXT TEN YEARS

CONTENTS

FOREWORD

For many reasons this has seemed a highly desirable time to take a hard look at educational television and at the problems and potentialities in its future.

For one thing, the number of noncommercial educational stations has now grown large enough to have a substantial impact. At this writing there are 56 educational stations operating. In the whole history of ETV only one station has failed—56 successes, one failure. This is an astonishing success figure for stations which have no commercial income and depend entirely on financial support from communities, school systems, colleges, and universities. Up to this time, the educational stations have proved hardier than anyone except "dreamers," as they were then considered, would have predicted ten years ago. And thanks to this hardiness, they are now numerous enough to make a real difference in the television opportunities offered Americans.

In the second place, instruction on television has now been tried and observed widely enough to let people judge its potential. The third year of the widespread program sponsored by the Fund for the Advancement of Education to try out television in schools has been completed. As a result of this and other programs, several millions of children have had part of their schoolwork by television. In Chicago, an entire junior college curriculum is on television. In a university like Penn State, a substantial number of courses are being taught by closed-circuit television, and this teaching is accompanied by well-designed testing to find out where and how television teaching is effective. One of the best features of the introduction of instructional television has been the research which has been built into a great many of the early trials. Later in this book, the point is made that more than four hundred experiments have been conducted on the effectiveness of teaching by television. Although much more research is needed, we are now in position to say something about what instructional television can do and what it can't, and what hope it holds for education.

In the third place, there are important stirrings in the field. A very large number of educational systems and institutions are deciding whether and when to enter instructional television, closed circuit or open. The question of channel allocations is in the air again, and with it the question of where education can find room for its projected needs. A number of additional stations are in the planning or construction stage, and determined efforts have been made to acquire a VHF channel for educational television in the nation's largest metropolis. A number of plans are on paper for new state networks of educational stations, and for several regional networks—steps that are expected by many observers eventually to lead to a national interconnected educational network. Educational television's present "network" headquarters—the National Educational Television and Radio Center, which distributes its programs by mail—has taken some notable forward steps and is now providing block programming for three evenings a week. While NETRC thus serves the needs of community programming better, the schools and colleges are seeking a way to exchange instructional programs so as to share master teachers and production costs with each other. It is clear that there is a ferment in educational television, and important developments are just around the corner.

In the fourth place, in the midst of all the enthusiasm for better programs on the community stations, for the early successes of teaching by TV, and for the projected plans, still a row of formidable problems has become apparent. One of these we have mentioned: the scarcity of desirable channels. Another is finance. Still another is programs, which is closely tied to finance. Another is manpower. Yet another is the problem of sharing instructional and community programs.

Aware of these problems and of the striking developments underlying them, the Educational Media Branch of the United States Office of Education, and notably Dr. C. Walter Stone, director of the Branch, decided in late 1960 that the time was ripe to look into the future of educational television. The Office therefore commissioned four studies. One of these was designed to survey the plans of educational institutions, systems, and communities for the use of educational television, to estimate the channel allocations these plans would require if carried out, and to make engineering studies as to how these needs might be met. This study was contracted to the National Association of Educational Broadcasters, and the results of it are summarized in this volume in a report by Vernon Bronson.

The Office contracted a second study to personnel at the University of Nebraska. This was to survey the needs and plans of educational systems and institutions for exchange of teaching materials on television, and to make recommendations as to how the indicated needs could best be met. This study also is reported in this volume in the chapter by Wesley Meierhenry and Jack McBride.

A third study was assigned to the Institute for Communication Research, at Stanford. The task was to look at the future of educational television in a more general way than either of the other studies. It was to consider the problems of financing educational television, of raising program quality, of training adequate manpower, of the future instructional uses of television, of designing and equipping schools for television, and so on. Reports from this study fill the greater part of this volume. They include the papers by Asheim, Hall, Schramm, Lasswell, Seldes, Head, Gitlin, Gunn, Hudson, White, Nelson, Maloney and Donner, Town, and Carpenter and Greenhill.

The fourth contract was placed with the National Educational Television and Radio Center, and provided for a study of the audiences of eight educational television stations in six different situations throughout the country. This study, under the research direction of Wilbur Schramm, was the last to be contracted, and analysis of the voluminous data is not yet complete. The study will later be published separately. Pending that publication, an appendix note by Schramm summarizes in this volume some of the available findings of the study.

Finally the Office asked its Education Media Study Panel to hear testimony on the problems and potential of television from a number of distinguished and informed citizens, and on the basis of that testimony and the three studies to make some recommendation concerning "the next ten years" of educational television. Those recommendations are the first item in the pages that follow, and the testimony before the panel is represented in the selections by Brish, Hechinger, Revelle, Fletcher, and Lerner.

This volume was put together to make it possible for educators, television people, and everyone else interested in the future of educational television to share the conclusion of specialists concerning what ETV can be and do, and how it can solve the problems which stand between it and its destiny.

In addition to knowing of the important policy papers in the first part of this volume, the reader should be aware how much hard-to-get information on educational television is gathered into certain papers in the book. For example, the paper by Professors Carpenter and Greenhill is a veritable textbook on equipment and facilities which will repay the attention of every educator who is using or thinking of using instructional television. The paper by Dean Town is an extremely useful introduction to the complicated scientific problems of spectrum and channel analysis—indeed, one of the few places where a nonscientist can find a readable exposition of those problems. Mr. Nelson's paper contains more detailed information on the cost and financing of educational television than is anywhere else available. The report of the Nebraska survey contains quite remarkable data on the amount and kind of televised instructional material that is being recorded in this country. The paper on what we know

about the effectiveness of televised teaching brings together the results of
more research than has ever before been assembled; more than half of this
research has not yet been published. Therefore the volume has certain
qualities of a reference book as well as a challenge to policy. Speaking
for the authors and the sponsors, may I say that we hope it will prove both
informative and challenging.

WILBUR SCHRAMM

Stanford University, September 1961

I. RECOMMENDATIONS

—By the Television Advisory Panel of the United States Office of Education, Department of Health, Education, and Welfare

A NATIONAL POLICY FOR
EDUCATIONAL TELEVISION

The Educational Media Study Panel was established in 1960 as an official advisory group to the Commissioner and the U.S. Office of Education. The membership of the Panel has included the following representatives from business, industry, and education:

Cyril M. Braum, Engineering Consultant, National Educational and Radio Center

LeRoy Collins, President, National Association of Broadcasters*

Leland Hazard, Vice-President and General Counsel, Pittsburgh Plate Glass Company*

Richard B. Hull, Director Telecommunications Center, Ohio State University

Herold C. Hunt, Professor of Education, Harvard University

Kenneth E. Oberholtzer, Superintendent of Schools, Denver, Colorado

John R. Richards, Director, Coordinating Council for Higher Education, State of California

William E. Spaulding, President, Houghton Mifflin Company

Graham T. Winslow, Chairman of the Board, Massachusetts Council for the Public Schools

The Panel was asked to study the new and rapidly growing developments in the communications and educational media field and to make recommendations to the Commissioner which would be useful in developing sound national policy. The need for such a panel and study arose from new technological advances, and from the expanded and intensive research and utilization which have resulted from the implementation of Title VII of the National Defense Education Act.

As a result of inquiries and surveys encouraged by the Panel, it became apparent that of all the new media of communication, educational television presented the most immediate and significant national problem.

In less than ten years educational television has reached a point where more than 60 broadcasting stations are now on the air, serving schools by day and homes by night. A program center in New York serves as "network" headquarters for these stations, enabling them to exchange their own best programs, and furnishing other program materials on video tape and film. Between two and three hundred closed-circuit television sys-

* Mr. Collins and Mr. Hazard attended the early meetings of the Panel, but were no longer members at the time these recommendations were approved. At the time of his appointment to the Panel, Mr. Collins was Governor of Florida.

tems have been installed by local public schools, school districts, colleges, and universities, for direct systematic instruction and to share superior teaching and educational resources. Heralding the day when the best teaching may be shared even more widely, an airplane is now flying over central Indiana, broadcasting televised class lessons to schools in parts of six states.

The audiences of educational television are no longer mere handfuls. In cities where educational stations are in operation and well established, nearly one out of four adults is a regular viewer. The number of school children who have received some teaching by television is now in the millions.

Apparently, an even more explosive period of growth lies ahead. At least 40 new stations are in some stage of preparation. Several hundred educational institutions are now making plans for extending the use of closed-circuit television. Following the lead of Alabama, Oklahoma, Florida, North Carolina, and Texas, nearly a dozen states are planning state-wide educational television networks. In the Middle West and in New England, plans are being drawn for regional networks. A national "live" network, connecting educational stations by cable or microwave may not be far in the future. The possibility of an educational communications satellite, instantaneously relaying programs for national and hemispheric coverage, is a foreseeable reality.

This growth, development, and impact of educational television, with the immediate problems and concerns which it has raised, motivated the Panel to sharpen the focus of its study, and to concentrate its initial attention upon television. To this end, Panel members proceeded to obtain summary reports on the background, development, and present status of the various uses of television in education, consulted with key research authorities conducting special studies in the field, and heard testimony and statements offered by more than a dozen national leaders, including such authorities as Arthur Adams, George V. Allen, C. Scott Fletcher, Frederick Ford, Fred Hechinger, Francis Keppel, Harold Lasswell, Max Lerner, Ralph McGill, Roger Revelle, Wilbur Schramm, Gilbert Seldes, Carleton Sprague Smith, Frank Stanton, and others.

Out of these reports and hearings, a number of questions were raised, and certain suggestions and conclusions were drawn. The major questions, issues, and guidelines which emerged from the discussions held were identified by the Panel as follows:

1. WHAT IS THE GROWTH CURVE OF EDUCATIONAL TELEVISION LIKELY TO BE?

The number of stations serving their communities with cultural, artistic, and public service programs has increased steadily, and the rate shows no sign of slackening. Furthermore, recent surveys show that the audiences for these stations have increased substantially in the last two years. More and more schools and colleges are indicating that instructional television is part of their future plans. A large number of school officials believe that, ten years from now, television will carry some part of the teaching of the great majority of school children in this nation, and that it will be used increasingly for direct instruction in the large colleges and universities. It is also expected that television will make available at home to students of whatever age, a large part of the college curriculum. Thus education may become easily available at any time in life.

The growing proportion of leisure time in our society, and the increasing complexity of the knowledge a citizen must have about the world in which he lives, point to a constantly growing need for educational television broadcasting services in the community. By the same token, the population explosion and the rising costs of buildings and services, as well as the generally greater demands for educational quality, suggest a constantly growing need for direct instructional television in the schools. A medium with so much potential, with so many needs to meet, and so many plans being made for it, is likely to continue to grow for a long period of time. (The vital importance of educational television to national defense efforts is not stressed in this report, but argues for more adequate service.)

2. HOW CAN THE PROGRAMS OF EDUCATIONAL STATIONS BE IMPROVED?

Distinguished programming costs money. At the present time, the total program cost of educational television stations nation-wide, is about equivalent to the cost of one network series on commercial television. The total annual budget of most educational stations is far less than the cost of a single commercial TV "spectacular." Only a small number of non-commercial stations have the equipment necessary to originate and produce "remote" telecasts of events outside the studio. The educational stations do not have a "live" network nationally, and therefore many timely programs are unavailable to them.

However, money alone will not necessarily produce outstanding and distinguished programs. There are two additional requirements—talented writers, producers, performers, and program managers; and a clear and viable policy as to what audience is being served. Better financing for educational stations will help to bring in talent; but the policy is relatively independent of financing, except in the sense that money is required to implement any policy to the degree that it should be implemented.

The present audience of educational television includes a large proportion of highly educated persons, professional men and women, and persons who are influential in forming public opinion and determining the cultural tone of their communities. This is a tremendously potent group of people. However, educational television, as it grows in resources and skill, can appeal increasingly to larger audiences. It should be possible in time to furnish at least some cultural and intellectual stimulation on occasion to a very high proportion of the total audience. For the most part, the cultural and intellectual capabilities of the American people have been underestimated by the mass media. The challenge to educational television is to develop in its programs the skill in writing and production, and the understanding of the audience, required to serve these capabilities.

In seeking to stimulate thought and discussion at a high level among its viewers, educational television has a great potential ally. This is the existing structure of community learning activities—organized discussion groups, study groups, vocational interest groups, and the like. If educational television can create a series of programs to feed and stimulate these groups, it will then be in position to supplement its direct effect with active learning experience, to enrich the work of the existing groups, and to increase the impact of its broadcasts.

3. HOW CAN TELEVISION CONTRIBUTE MOST TO EDUCATION?

Television is a channel for conveying whatever is put into it. Instructional television, or television designed for direct use in the classroom, must depend importantly upon classroom teacher guidance for determination of its content, presentation, and effective utilization. But while instructional television may change some of the things the classroom teacher does, the major change will be in the direction of freeing a teacher for more productive use of his time (e.g., working with individuals), rather than restricting him.

The spectrum of instructional uses of television is not completely known. It is clear that there are some teaching acts it can do superlatively well. It can let a large number of students look into a microscope at the same time, or watch surgical procedures from close at hand. It can let a class watch an activity that would be spoiled by direct observation. It can share great teaching and great demonstrations. But, there are also some things it cannot do. It cannot conduct a seminar discussion efficiently. It cannot give specific and direct personal help. These uses and limitations are clear, but, how much longer the list may be is not now known.

It is clear that there are some ways of using television which make for better learning than others; some ways of putting school materials on television which result in better teaching than others; some ways of combining television with other learning experiences in school that are more effective than others. But, preoccupation with television sometimes obscures the fact that it is only one of the teaching resources available to the modern school. The modern teacher has books, guides, periodicals, films, tapes, slides, records, laboratory equipment; some have language laboratories; and soon many of them will have programmed self-instructional materials. The basic question, therefore, is not simply how to use television alone, but rather how to combine it most effectively with other learning experiences and resources.

Experience indicates that the most effective uses of television have been in situations where it has been combined carefully with other activities in a total learning situation; and where students were strongly motivated to learn from it. This challenges educators to make a broad review and restructuring of what happens in the classroom. Television can share the best teaching and the best demonstrations; self-instructional materials can conduct drill expertly and give the student a new freedom to work at his own best rate. A teacher who has these devices working for him may not have exactly the same duties as before, but his duties will be no less important. The student who has these devices working for him will not spend his day exactly as before, but his learning opportunities will be no less, and probably considerably more.

A school where these new devices are in use may find itself bursting out of old patterns. Instead of classes of 35 alternately being lectured to, studying, and reciting, it may assemble groups of several hundred to watch the television lecture or demonstration, but devote a greater proportion of its teacher time to individualized instruction. Instead of waiting his turn for class drill, a student may follow his own drill schedule with self-instructional materials or language laboratory.

The well-planned television program can motivate students, guide and sharpen their reading by providing background and demonstrations, encourage responsibility for independent learning, arouse curiosity and develop new insights and the excitement of discovery. The medium is so flexible that it need never be used merely to promulgate the old lecture method and the idea that good teaching is "telling." In the richness and versatility of television the classroom teacher will be faced with a new challenge. The teaching required to meet the individual interests, needs and problems of his students, and to encourage them in their individual learning experiences will call for all his talent. He will be devoting his time to the kind of teaching that has satisfaction, rewards, and excitement far beyond those of routine group instruction.

The possibility of being able to arrive at a new and more efficient distribution of student activities and teacher responsibilities, in which the talents of both and their time in the classroom will be more efficiently used, is the great hope for a "breakthrough" that instructional television holds out. Without the new devices now available, this greater flexibility would be immeasurably more difficult to achieve. Now that the amount of learning that takes place in our schools has taken on new importance, it is fortunate that these new tools are available to encourage a fundamental review of classroom practices and procedures.

4. HOW CAN THE STRENGTHS IN EDUCATIONAL TELEVISION BE SHARED?

Many of the practices of educational television do not take advantage of the fact that it can serve the nation as a whole. The shape of the future in educational television clearly includes a national and perhaps several regional centers for the exchange and evaluation of television teaching materials. It also includes a gradual and increasing interconnection of educational broadcasting stations. Some state networks exist, more are being planned. Plans are also being made for regional networks. Undoubtedly, these developments are preludes to a nationally interconnected educational network. Until we do have a nation-wide interconnection of educational stations, and a national system of production, evaluation, and exchange of instructional television materials, educational television will not be able to work at its full strength for the public good.

5. WHAT SPECIALLY TRAINED MANPOWER WILL EDUCATIONAL TELEVISION NEED?

Expert and imaginative personnel are essential, if noncommercial educational stations are to realize their potential. The educational station must have employees familiar with the content of educational and cultural materials. Courses in these areas should become part of the college preparation of production personnel for educational television; and the educational stations should operate their own in-service training programs, perhaps in conjunction with neighboring schools and colleges.

One of the urgent needs of all television, commercial or noncommercial, is for a pool of creative talent (writers, directors, performers, technicians). To the extent that its finances permit, educational television should take the lead in seeking out such persons, encouraging the training of more of them, and giving them an opportunity to use their talents in the medium. One of the requirements for attracting such talent, and for attracting excellence in general to educational television, is the ability to pay adequate salaries. If educational television can strengthen its financial basis so as to be able to offer higher salaries, it will be in far better position to offer the kind of excellent and professional program service that is necessary to the fulfillment of its objectives.

In the schools, more and more teachers will need to become familiar with the skills of teaching on and/or with television. This will require in-service training programs, summer courses, workshops, and new opportunities for gaining experience with television.

Television programs which are to be conceived and developed as part of a total systems approach will require, for a new order of collaboration among subject-matter and curriculum experts, talented persons enjoying a very high degree of skill in the analysis of teaching techniques to meet specific objectives, experienced teachers, writers, artists, directors, and imaginative technicians. Every individual serving on such a team must become highly sensitive to the potential values of television as a medium and to the subtleties of teaching and learning intended to achieve clearly defined objectives.

Numerically, the greatest need in the schools will be for a large number of classroom teachers able to make television a part of the total learning experience of students, and able to weave it into classroom activities. Colleges, universities, and particularly schools of education can be of great help in developing this skill; and the schools themselves can profitably share their experiences in utilizing television.

6. HOW CAN EDUCATIONAL TELEVISION BE FINANCED ADEQUATELY?

Compared to the present cost of educational television, the bill for the kind of service needed will be large. Compared to the cost of commercial television, or of organized education, the bill will be small. The capital cost of the first 56 noncommercial educational stations has been about 29 million dollars. Their annual operating budget is around 15 millions. They are furnished programs by the National Educational Television and Radio Center, for which the present annual budget is 3.6 millions. The schools and colleges have installed between 200 and 300 closed-circuit television systems, at an estimated capital cost of around 11 millions and an annual operating cost of around 4 millions.

Looking ahead ten years, we can anticipate a doubling of the number of educational stations, at additional capital costs of about 30 millions, and additional operating costs of another 15 millions. In some combination of closed-circuit and low-power transmitters, the schools may spend as much as 50 millions more in capital costs to develop instructional television facilities; and the annual cost of operating these installations more fully than the present installations may run to 150 millions.

The present levels of annual expenditure for the national program center and the local noncommercial stations are insufficient for the quality of program service required. In the past, the operating funds of the noncommercial stations have come, in various proportions, from five sources, according to the type of station represented (commonly, school or university, state network): (1) membership contributions from the public, (2) contributions from business, industry, and other civic groups, (3) foundation grants, (4) contracts for the production of programs, (5) tax funds from school systems, universities, colleges, and other educational groups. The support of the national program center has come from three sources: (1) foundations, (2) production contracts, and (3) business and industry. The continuing support of *all* these sources for both the stations and the network will be *most* important. However, financing is now the chief factor limiting the quality and amount of service educational television is able to provide. Unless the financial barrier can be breached, unless the amount of support can be increased to a substantial degree, the bright promise of educational television will remain no more than a promise.

7. WHAT CHANNEL ALLOCATIONS WILL EDUCATIONAL TELEVISION NEED TO DO ITS JOB?

Most television in the United States is presently in the VHF (Very High Frequency) band which provides 12 channels, and requires rather wide separation of stations on the same channels. VHF channels are in short supply in most of the cities and metropolitan communities of the nation. In many cities there is no VHF channel for education. This is the case in some of the largest communities of the nation. For example, there is no VHF channel presently available to education in Los Angeles, Baltimore, Washington, Cleveland, Columbus, or Detroit.

There is still a great deal of room available in the UHF (Ultra High Frequency) band, which offers more channels than VHF but smaller areas of coverage. Only a small percentage of the receiving sets now in use are equipped to receive UHF. Therefore, if a new station is added in the UHF band, in a community where the existing stations operate in VHF, the new station cannot be received until new television sets are purchased or UHF converters are installed.

These matters are exceedingly important to educational television because of its expected expansion. If it is indeed the case that the number of educational stations will double in ten years, and that there will also be a large, though as yet undetermined, number of low-power stations serving schools, colleges, and universities, then the problem of finding and allocating channels will be a very complex one, and the solution to the problem is bound to be most difficult. It is clear that the nature and magnitude of anticipated future needs should be made immediately known to the Federal Communications Commission; and that these recommendations should concern the full use and reservation of education's fair share of *all* spectrum resources.

8. WHAT GUIDANCE DO EDUCATIONAL INSTITUTIONS NEED ON TELEVISION FACILITIES?

No one can predict with confidence either what equipment will be available for television ten years hence, or what institutions will be using it. However, it appears quite certain that technical developments will come quickly, and that every stage and part of education is a potential user of educational television. Therefore, in planning new buildings, the best guideline is to provide for the possible future use of television in *any* building where teaching is to be done; and to try in general to design such buildings with a maximum of flexibility for different sizes of viewing groups, and different uses of television, not all of which are yet foreseen. If it is true that television and other new developments open the door to a considerable revision of classroom organization and activities, then physical facilities should be kept as flexible as possible until the nature of these changes becomes apparent. In selecting television equipment now, or in designing and arranging rooms for viewing or production, the educational administrator and the television director have expert advice available and should make use of it.

* * *

In summary of these facts and findings, the Study Panel suggests the following general guidelines:

(1) If educational television is to continue to grow in importance and use both in the home and in the school, long-range plans for its growth and development are needed *now*.

(2) If the medium is to reach its full potential, there must be increased and continuing efforts to develop new and improved techniques of programming for both in-school and out-of-school audiences, to encourage and support greater creativity, and to raise the cultural and informational values of the service to a new level.

(3) If the medium is to fulfill completely its promise of aid to the educational system, the better and more effective ways of utilizing it must be identified; particularly there must be new patterns of educational planning and curriculum design which will relate all media and learning resources in a common effort to fulfill optimum learning requirements. Research can profitably move into these problems.

(4) Improvement in the school and community services of educational television is closely related to financing. The promise of the medium cannot be fulfilled unless the financial support of educational television stations, programs, and services is broadened and expanded. A continued growth is called for in local community financial support, and, in addition, some form of local and state tax-based support, and some form of federal

aid or assistance for the development of new stations, programs, and national and state educational television services.

(5) The need for sharing new and superior programs grows in importance as such programs are created. The organization of state and regional educational television networks is therefore a desirable development, looking toward the ultimate establishment of a national "live" interconnected network. As a source of production and exchange for such a service, the present national educational program service and video-tape "network" need to be strengthened, in order that the qualitative improvement of this important supply of programs may be continued.

(6) In order to share instructional television materials, regional and national centers for the production, evaluation, and exchange of such recordings are needed. So that this exchange may proceed efficiently and with fairness to all, a study of the problems of recording, distribution, teacher rights, compensation, and residual uses of educational and instructional television programs and materials is also needed at the first possible moment.

(7) Healthful community development of educational television will require not only that it serve its present basic audiences more effectively, but also that it finds the means of broadening its audiences and extending its services; and that it become closely identified with the learning activity and experience of the entire community.

(8) The quality of educational television will be no higher than the quality of the men who make its programs and operate its stations and services. The combined efforts of schools, colleges, universities, educational and commercial television stations will be needed to develop the creative talent and professional personnel required to plan and produce the highest quality programs for educational use.

(9) Another crucial personnel need will be for teachers expert in using television and other new media in their classrooms. Workshops, seminars, training programs, and publications will be needed for the in-service training of teachers in this skill. A major effort by colleges and universities will be needed to prepare their students who will enter the educational profession to be able to make effective use of the new media in their teaching.

(10) The future development of "open-circuit" educational television is limited by the channels available to carry its signals. It is imperative, therefore, that every effort be made to reserve the necessary spectrum resources required by the anticipated growth and development of educational television.

(11) Schools and school administrators will be well advised, in the design of school buildings and in the purchase of technical equipment and

facilities, to provide for the planning, installation, and future use of educational television and the other new media.

RECOMMENDATIONS

The Educational Media Study Panel believes that educational television has a unique and significant role to play in both the extension and improvement of the educational and cultural environment necessary to the fulfillment of our national interests. Therefore, the panel offers the following specific recommendations to the Commissioner and the Office of Education, for consideration in relation to national policy:

A. The opportunities afforded by television must become more readily available for education (from classroom cables to relay stations in outer space).

The advent of television and, indeed, the whole complex of newer communications media (from video tape to satellites) has given American citizens unparalleled opportunities to advance in their ability to record and communicate ideas. These new communications resources must now be harnessed to serve the ends of education in a time when American school and college programs must now find new and improved ways to cope with spiraling enrollments and increasing shortages of adequate classrooms and able teachers, as well as the new educational needs created by the explosions in new knowledge and by the changing world conditions which threaten national survival.

We recommend that the federal government take the steps necessary to assure for every American the opportunity to receive ETV signals; and more specifically to reserve those parts and amounts of the broadcast spectrum and related electronic resources necessary to guarantee nation-wide transmission and reception of the full range of educational television services.

B. Educational television *programs* must be produced in sufficient number and quality to meet critical educational needs in both the present and the future.

Two broad philosophies have thus far governed the growth of television in the United States: (1) the concept of a competitive free-enterprise, entertainment-centered program service based on popular appeal, containing significant but limited segments of news, public affairs, and cultural offerings supported by advertising revenue; (2) the concept of an alternative, noncommercial educational television service whose programs, directed at audiences of mature adults and out-of-school children, would emphasize most what commercial systems tend to emphasize least and, additionally, would serve as a distributor of instructional materials conceived within the framework of formal education, and directed to enrolled students. These two philosophies are complementary rather than opposing, and result in differences in emphasis and depth at given times in given programs, in types of audience, and in potential audience size.

But the needs of America for television cannot be met by the present commercial and educational television systems. Nor can the massive new problems of education await solution by traditional methods which utilize only existing facilities. Realization of the goal of equal educational opportunity for all now rests increasingly on the national ability to use effectively electronic technology for educational purposes.

We recommend public as well as private support of a new, vigorous, and coordinated national effort on the part of American schools, colleges, communities, government agencies, and other interested groups to encourage the production of more and better educational television programs addressed to the needs of our time.

C. Sound *research* and experimentation are keys to quality in ETV.

The new media and devices now available to education hold as much promise for improvement of instruction as did the invention of the book. This promise will never be fulfilled unless we continue through study and research to deepen our understanding of their use.

Until recent years, the so-called newer media (i.e., films, radio, filmstrips, etc.) have most frequently been considered "aids" or have simply been regarded as devices incidental to the traditional processes of education as carried on in a classroom. Today, television is regarded not only as a medium in its own right, but as a device which uniquely can transmit sound, live images, film, print, and charts, and thus can serve as a distribution system for all other media. More importantly, it provides a new kind of linkage from one classroom to another, to laboratories, and to any part of the world outside. The results of research completed during the past decade underline the need for continuing and expanding programs of research and development directed toward realization of new levels of teaching and learning which utilize more efficiently the instructional and communications media.

We recommend a continuing nation-wide program of research and evaluation which will help to identify and increase both the worth and efficiency of ETV.

D. A new reservoir of *manpower* must be recruited and trained for ETV.

The increasing shortage of skilled ETV personnel and other media specialists is not confined to administrative and managerial areas but extends to every aspect of ETV efforts. It embraces every type of communications engineering from the transmitter to the video-tape recording room and culminates (acutely) in the area of talent—the skilled teacher of subject matter, the analyst of public and world affairs, the performing artist, the creative producer, and writer. A comprehensive approach to the problems posed would involve a personnel inventory of experienced and potentially gifted individuals in media fields, systematic "crash" programs to re-train individuals who might be recruited to the new field, and long-range plans for developing individuals in what has become a new professional service field. Without such a systematic and comprehensive approach on a national basis, it will be impossible to produce the personnel needed to mount a major attack on education's problems using the media.

We recommend that a nation-wide talent search and training effort be launched by schools, colleges, and stations to create and keep in full supply a reservoir of personnel qualified to serve in all "departments" of educational television.

E. A new plan for increased *financial support* must be established to provide the dollars needed for ETV.

Despite Educational Television's impressive record of growth in its first decade (with some 60 stations now on the air and several hundred closed-circuit installations), no adequate local, state, regional, or national plan of financing new stations or for expansion of existing facilities has yet been developed, nor has an adequate plan been put forward to meet the costs of operation.

If educational television is to fulfill its role in providing a new dimension for cultural and educational opportunities, a new kind and amount of financial support must be provided.

We recommend that financial support for educational television be provided from both public and private funds at the local, state, and national level, to ensure that the necessary new stations may be built, and that the facilities may be operated and programmed to the fullest degree in the public interest.

CYRIL M. BRAUM
RICHARD B. HULL
HEROLD C. HUNT
KENNETH E. OBERHOLTZER

JOHN R. RICHARDS
WILLIAM E. SPAULDING
GRAHAM T. WINSLOW

November 15, 1961

II. TELEVISION'S FUTURE PLACE IN EDUCATION

Is instructional television here to stay? What do the schools and colleges who have had most experience with it, now think of it? What do we know about the efficiency of learning from television? About the educational levels and subjects where it can be most effectively used? These are the kinds of questions considered in the following papers.

A SURVEY OF INFORMED OPINION ON TELEVISION'S FUTURE PLACE IN EDUCATION

Reported by Lester Asheim

Dr. Asheim is Dean of the Graduate Library School, University of Chicago

THE QUESTION with which this report is concerned is this: what role will television be playing in education ten years from now? It is an important question to which, unfortunately, no one really knows the answer. But if the best we can do is guess, then the best guesses are likely to come from those who have been working with teaching by television or who—because of their research interests, their foundation connections, or some other professional concern with formal learning—have already had to think seriously about television in education.

The method of "research" upon which this survey is based, therefore, has been that of personal interviews with a few of the people whose guesses are, within the framework of the above assumption, more informed than most. The panel of experts whose opinions were solicited for this report were

Vernon BRONSON, Director, Survey of the Needs of Education for Television Allocations, National Association of Educational Broadcasters, Washington, D.C.

Lee CAMPION, Associate Director, Technological Development Project, National Education Association, Washington, D.C.

William G. CARR, Executive Secretary, National Education Association, Washington, D.C.

Clifford G. ERICKSON, Dean, Television Instruction, Chicago City Junior College

Clarence FAUST, President, Fund for the Advancement of Education, New York

John FRITZ, Director, Audio-Visual Instructional Materials Center, University of Chicago

John GARDNER, President, Carnegie Corporation of New York

Donald GRASSMEYER, Co-ordinator of Recorded Televised Instructional Materials, University Television, University of Nebraska, Lincoln

Carl HANSEN,* Superintendent of Schools, Washington, D.C.

William HARLEY, President, National Association of Educational Broadcasters, Washington, D.C.

Francis KEPPEL, Dean of the Graduate School of Education, Harvard University

Jack McBRIDE, Director of Television and Station KUON-TV, University of Ne-

---

* Schedule conflicts did not permit a personal interview, but several written reports which summarize Dr. Hansen's position were made available to this reporter.

braska, and W. C. MEIERHENRY, Assistant to the Dean, Teachers College, University of Nebraska; Co-Directors, Study of the Use and Distribution of Recorded Televised Instruction

Lloyd S. MICHAEL, Supervisor, Evanston Township High School, Evanston, Illinois

Wanda MITCHELL, Head, Department of Speech, Evanston Township High School, Evanston, Illinois

KENNETH E. OBERHOLTZER, Superintendent, Denver Public Schools, Denver

Thomas POLLOCK, Dean, Washington Square College, New York University

John W. TAYLOR, Executive Director, Chicago Educational Television Association and WTTW (Channel 11), Chicago

Paul WITTY, Professor, School of Education, Northwestern University, Evanston, Illinois

John H. WORTHINGTON, Midwest Program on Airborne Television Instruction, Chicago

The report is a sincere attempt accurately to reflect ideas and predictions which were voiced in the interviews. In the writing of the report, however, it became necessary to select, rearrange, and synthesize; and the interpretation of the reporter may well have done injustice to some of the respondents. While all have had an opportunity to read this report and comment on it, the writer is acutely conscious that while the hands are the hands of the experts, the voice is the voice of Asheim.

Let us start with certain assumptions:

education in the United States is, among other things, one of the most important tools for the preservation of the ideas and ideals which we like to think of as distinctively and characteristically American;

those ideas and ideals face a period of serious crisis and threat in the years ahead;

the traditional methods of education are likely to be increasingly inadequate to meet the stresses and strains of the times.

If these assumptions are correct—and there would certainly seem to be a consensus among the students and critics of American education that they are—then steps must be taken, and must be taken now, to re-evaluate our aims and commitments, and to explore the means—any means—that give promise of improving the quality of our education. One of the means which, in the eyes of many, seems to hold potentialities of real value to education is television.

That television as a mass medium of entertainment, information, and commercial enterprise is here to stay seems fairly clear; that it has a real contribution to make to the education of Americans is not so unanimously accepted. Television as a tool of education has had enthusiastic supporters and violent opponents; it has become a vital part of some school systems, and has been unequivocally rejected by others; it has been seen as a solution to many of our major problems of education, and as just another complication in an already complicated field. If we believe the enthusiasts, we as a nation should bend every effort to assure that television assumes a predominant place in the educational scene; if we believe the dim viewers, the sooner we discard these misguided efforts to force television upon educators, the better for all concerned. In view of the importance of education in the world of today, it seems important to weigh these pros and cons with some care; the pressures of the times deny to education the luxury of making a costly error—either of commission or omission. Can we afford to commit our educational system to the large-scale adjustments necessary to put television into active use in education? Can we afford not to? The following discussion may help to throw some light on this pressing problem.

Perhaps it would be best to begin with some of the major objections to television in education, since these raise basic questions about the medium which should be used to test any of the claims made for it. The objections cited in this study are not just the inertia and resistance that greet any change regardless of its merits, although there is plenty of that kind of resistance among educators. The arguments mentioned here are based upon the experience of men who have studied or used television, and cannot be dismissed as mere ignorance of either its practical or its theoretical values.

Perhaps the most important question raised has to do with the nature of the learning experience itself. There are those who feel that much of the value of teaching lies in the continuing process, not just in fragments of it as represented by the television lessons. Thus even the so-called "master teacher" may not project the real values of his teaching just because he records some of his lectures. (Witty) The student wants to be known by his teacher, and he wants to know that he is known; this kind of personal relationship, built up through time, is as important as a brilliantly conceived and planned lecture crammed with facts. Information-acquisition is not enough in education, and there is a danger that educational television lends itself to being nothing more than this. (Fritz) If ETV instruction becomes standardized, unfocused, and fragmented, it will not be a good learning experience. And the use of television in the classroom cannot be justified if it reduces the quality of education. Its justification lies either in its ability to provide equally good education at less cost or to offer a better learning experience than our present methods of teaching can supply.

One of the important aspects of the good teaching situation is the opportunity for face-to-face exchange which it provides. The attempts to build some kind of talk-back system into television teaching have not been particularly successful, and they decrease in efficiency as the size of the audience increases—which is precisely where one of the major benefits of using television is supposed to lie. (Taylor) Many experiments have discovered that students are reluctant to use the talk-back opportunity, and in Evanston Township High School (where students and teacher were already well related and where use of the talk-back equipment was more readily accepted than in most experiments) it was found that the topnotch student liked the talk-back system the least. (Michael) Thus the critics of educational television are not yet convinced by anything they have thus far seen that the face-to-face experience, which they consider essential to good teaching for most subjects and at most levels, can be adequately provided by the mechanical devices ETV is using at the present. "The good teacher is sensitive to the way her pupils react to what she is teaching. As she senses their comprehension, she reviews, repeats, asks questions, explains more fully, inspires and motivates. These indispensable elements in teaching cannot be packaged, because they are products that can never be separated from the process." (Hansen)

The adaptation of televised lessons to the needs of different schools and different teaching situations is very difficult. A lecture or demonstration on kinescope or tape is often too far below the level of some students, too far beyond the level of others; unless it is screened and adapted it is not likely to be as useful as the classroom teacher's own focused presentation. This is not merely a matter of the level of the content per se; it is related to a basic mechanical problem in the use of ETV: the fact that television goes at a fixed rate and that children learn at different rates. (Keppel) Yet TV teaching, if it is to be curriculum-centered, virtually requires that the classroom teacher follow the curriculum lead of the TV teacher. Thus the content is often ill-adapted to local needs, and the initiative is taken away from the classroom teacher—who should be the person who knows best the needs of her particular students. The typical situation in the use of direct teaching by television is that the teacher is told to use it; she does not choose to do so herself. (Campion) This often leads to resentment or indifference to the TV lesson, and it was unanimously agreed by all the respondents, proponent and opponent alike, that the classroom teachers' attitude can make or break the effectiveness of educational TV.

Student reaction to ETV is also thought to be an unknown quantity by many educators. In Washington, D.C., the schools found an initial interest followed by a "phenomenal" decline in interest in a very short time. In Witty's survey of viewers' preferences, no educational television program ever showed up among the ten top favorites of children, teachers, or parents. More than that, the expectation among many students and other viewers has frequently been based on commercial television standards; "teachers are expected by their constituents to have video know-how [that is, the slick style of announcers, panelists, and other professional performers] as well as teaching skill. Lacking it, after the novelty wears off, they lose their following." (Hansen)

Finally, the temptation in educational television is strong to re-use kinescope and tapes unimaginatively, about the way educational films have been used in recent years. (Fritz) The television receiver is fast becoming merely a film projector rather than a source of vital and fresh, on-the-spot television. (Hansen) In view of the difficulties of financing (costs still are high), the technical difficulties of using and maintaining the machines, and the elaborate planning that must go into paving the way for television in teaching, the use of television will be worth the effort only if it can offer something considerably more than low-level occasional "enrichment."

The advocates of educational television acknowledge the pertinence of these questions, but do not consider them to be unanswerable. Concerning teaching method, it is acknowledged that some kinds of subject matter and some levels of instruction are less well adapted to television techniques than are others. It is acknowledged also that, so far, the emphasis has been on the mere recording of lectures and demonstrations, because this is easiest to do, while discussion and other techniques are harder to manage. But more imagination in the use of television, and adaptation of technique and methods to the medium, are possible to make it useful and effective in any subject matter. (Mitchell) It is encouraging that, as Harley points out, generally those who have used television have had their apprehensions dispelled.

The opposition to television—because it does not provide feedback, discussion, or participation—is based, according to Meierhenry, on a failure to use television properly, and not on faults inherent in the medium itself. In fact, it is his belief that the whole new movement toward personalization and humanization of teaching will be aided by television rather than harmed by it, and we shall return to this point later. In any case, much of the criticism against use of television assumes that television will provide the total teaching situation, whereas the present direction in television use is toward a combination of classroom and television teacher, cooperating as a team. If television itself cannot provide the face-to-face exchange where that is essential, the savings from mass techniques can make possible the creation of more face-to-face situations where they are needed. (Taylor)

The standardization and conformity feared by some educators is no more serious a threat from television than it has been from the textbook. (Faust, Worthington) Libraries of tapes and kinescopes make it possible for the individual instructor to choose what he wishes to use, and even to use only a part of the tape if that better fits his needs. (Mitchell) None of the respondents anticipates a national syndicate which will impose the same content uniformly throughout the nation. Regional associations of schools are being formed, but on a voluntary basis, and each school may choose to accept or reject from what is made available. With this kind of voluntary pooling of resources, conformity is avoided; the only restriction is upon mediocrity, and "in the present state of the world, we cannot afford to tolerate mediocrity any longer." (Harley)

Finally, several of the respondents are quite willing to accept the "enrichment" role of television. Educational television is seen by some as a teaching adjunct rather than as a substitute for good live teaching, and "a good wide reservoir of teaching materials can enrich the program while keeping the focus on live teaching." (Witty) Even so, educational television is not likely to be confined to occasional enrichment alone. "Enrichment is justification enough for the use of television in teaching, but the drift is toward direct teaching, rather than just enrichment" (Campion) with greater imagination and sophistication in its use developing with experience.

Quite apart from the defenses against specific objections that have been cited above, there seems to be quite general consensus on certain incontrovertible strengths of educational television. First, television, by sharing the good teacher, makes it possible to have a good teacher in every subject in every school. The good teachers will be shared on a nation-wide basis—but not simultaneously; flexibility and local choice can be maintained through the use of television tape. (Pollock)

Second, one of television's greatest contributions is its distribution factor: it can be used in schools and areas where facilities and skills are not available. (Campion) Thus underprivileged schools can take advantage of laboratory equipment, demonstrations, and teaching skills—in such subjects as foreign languages, sciences, and art, for example—which they couldn't possibly have on their own. (Faust) Nor is it only the so-called "underprivileged schools" which can benefit from the facilities and skills provided by educational television; good teaching personnel are in short supply throughout education, and even the best schools can use ETV to some extent to make up for this shortage. (Witty)

Third, educational television is definitely superior in providing close-up views which the live demonstration cannot supply. Similarly, it provides intimacy of communication with the teacher as well; where more than 60 to 70 students are involved, television is actually more intimate and personal than the live classroom situation. (Faust, Pollock)

Fourth, television has been a spur to the re-evaluation of our aims and commitments; (Fritz) and has been remarkable as a catalyst in bringing groups together across county and other traditional lines that used to separate them. ETV has triggered more cooperation than has any other educational device. (Harley) Thus it seems to have a particular power to stimulate and motivate in the direction of improvement in education which marks it as unique among the many innovations that have at one time or another been introduced into the educational scene.

Fifth, educational television can free the teacher for more individual work with students by releasing him or her from a number of current responsibilities. (Worthington) As Keppel puts it, educational television may finally provide the device that spares the teacher the necessity of "taking the kids' boots off." Thus freed from time-consuming but nonproductive activities, the teacher can move in the direction of more personalized and humanized teaching, as Meierhenry suggests. Certainly the role of educational television's relation to independent study should be explored, (Faust) for television may be especially beneficial in the teaching of exceptional students of all kinds: the slow learner, the very bright, those with highly specialized interests. (Witty)

It should be noted that among the special benefits claimed for ETV by the respondents in this study, the claim is seldom made that it will save money. While it is true that television introduces some efficiencies, and may thus be said in a way to be an economy measure, all were agreed that, as McBride put it, "Money saving is not the real justification. The criterion should be the improvement of education. The use of large classes, for example, is of value, not because it saves money but because large-class instruction by television makes it possible for the classroom teacher to concentrate on small classes and personalized attention to the students. The result is not the elimination of teachers, but their redeployment."

Whether it is the basic justification for television teaching or not, there are economies possible. The Chicago experience with TV College has shown that the full cost of TV operation compared with the cost of resident instruction reveals a break-even point somewhere around 675–680 full-time student equivalents. "Every full-time equivalent thereafter is served for $\frac{1}{9}$ to $\frac{1}{5}$ of the cost of a full-time equivalent on the campus. Thus we are able to say that a doubling of TV college enrollments over the next ten years in Chicago would probably represent not more than a 12 percent to a 25 percent additional outlay. This I believe is a very high leverage." (Taylor)

For most initial experiments with ETV, however, schools may find that they will have to spend more rather than less. But since the money is spent in order to do a better job, they get more for their money, which is one way of saying that it is cheaper. (Michael, Taylor)

A specific example was supplied by Worthington. Air-borne television, if it is to be put on a permanent basis, would require about $2 million per year for a minimum program; $5 million for a medium program; $10 million for a very good one. Thus, to provide the best teacher, the greatest variety of content, etc., to a million students in a six-state region, the cost would come to about $5 per year per student; less for a larger audience. This is not too much to pay for what you get. But there will be no reduction in the number of teachers employed; the saving is in the use of the teachers' time and abilities. And to get the same coverage at the same quality level through land-based ETV would cost about three times as much to establish and slightly more than the air-borne system to maintain. Thus it is that one can claim savings even though more money is spent; the real contribution is in making things possible that could not otherwise be supported at all.

Because of this emphasis upon the improvement of teaching, the advocates of ETV feel that it is much more than a stopgap device, despite the present use of it in many instances to deal with current crises in particular localities. If television is used to promote the trend toward differentiated, individual instruction; if it enhances the quality of instruction and makes good teaching more widely available—then educational television will have a lasting benefit for education and a permanent role to play in education of the future. There is the danger, however, that "for the short run, the mass characteristics of television may divert attention from the more generic problems of education" (Fritz) and the best development of ETV will be sidetracked. The full development of educational television's potential depends upon the conviction of administrators that ETV really meets their needs. (Bronson)

At this point, it may be well to explore some of the best present and potential uses of television in different areas of education. This survey was designed to cover, not only formal education through the schoolroom, but education in all of its aspects; and the respondents—usually reflecting their own experience and special competence—spoke of the educational use of television in many different contexts.

In elementary and secondary schools.—Organized instructional programs have already proved very successful in many instances, particularly in those subject areas where there is a serious shortage of teaching personnel (languages, for example). On the other hand, informal, free-choice, out-of-school programming in the evenings has not proved successful with children. (Oberholtzer) If this is to be a part of education by television in the future, it will have to discover some other approach than that presently employed.

More and more, classroom teachers are beginning to recognize that confined teaching (the small class; the single teacher for all subject matters) is going to be eliminated, (Bronson) but at the secondary level it is very likely that a great variety of different groupings will be tried: small classes, large-class presentations, individual use of television (especially in laboratory situations), etc. In other words, educational television will introduce college-type techniques at the secondary school level. (Campion) Single-unit schools like Evanston Township High School have found that the most promising potential of television lies in a library of tapes and kinescopes which can be used and re-used, like library books, by individual instructors for their own individual purposes. (Mitchell) Multi-unit systems and voluntary regional associations will probably move in the direction of tapes also; not necessarily original lessons, but tapes of broadcasts from open-circuit systems. With such a library of tapes, the problem of the "bell schedule" can be resolved, and the regional cooperation will make possible a much greater wealth of resources for classroom use. (McBride)

There is reason to believe, also, that the use of educational television can speed up education; in Hagerstown it has been demonstrated that college mathematics can be introduced at the high school level. (Worthington) The difficulty is that at the moment teachers do not seem to know what to do with the gain; when a class gets ahead of its schedule, the present tendency is to stop to review and otherwise fill up the time until the normal schedule is reached for the next step in the content. Educational television might introduce greater flexibility and more imagination into scheduling to take advantage of these gains.

Other possibilities, if school systems have their own equipment, will be the use of television in such areas as group guidance, instruction in library use, physical education, driver training, and other such subject matters where extremely large group presentations are feasible (and are probably employed, in any case), and where detailed and close-up demonstrations can be made more effectively than in a large classroom with a live presentation. (Michael) Distribution of films to individual classrooms via CCTV is an important use. (Mitchell) There are likely also to be many noninstructional uses of closed-circuit television in the schools: simultaneous availability of a student's record for all teachers involved in a telephone conference; information for students during registration immediately apparent on the television screen, etc. (Mitchell) This is one way that Dr. Keppel's concern with "taking the kids' boots off" can be met by television.

With all these several possibilities for the improvement of teaching in the schools, "any new school going up today should have studio and equipment for closed-circuit origination, as well as for outside pickup. Closed circuit is an excellent tool for magnification, and the system should be so established as to make possible the origination of a telecast from any classroom, the library, the principal's office. . . . In the future such closed-circuit systems could tie in more than one school, although this is not a likely development in the next few years." (Campion)

In colleges and universities.—So far, colleges and universities have demonstrated less imagination than have the schools in the use of educational television. (Faust) At present, television merely distributes the regular lecture or laboratory demonstration to a larger number. While this is useful, it does not really raise the level of teaching. But much more sophisticated uses of television are possible (the multiple screen, for example), and it may be that exposure to one's peers on the television screen will motivate instructors to make a more professional presentation of their material. (Campion)

The most institutionally revolutionary aspect of television use is the extension of the campus. (Gardner) "The compelling needs of the world today are such that universities will have to take greater responsibility to inform the whole citizenry and expand their services beyond their campuses. This is supplementary and specialized, however, rather than the presentation of material that can substitute for on-campus degree programs." (Harley) But this too is coming. European universities have long since supplied the model: independent study at the student's own pace; lectures by outstanding authorities; examination as the basis for award of the degree. If the content is of the same high quality, and if the same demonstration of mastery of content is required through examinations, there is no reason why the TV degree should not be the equivalent in every way of the residence degree. (Taylor) Before this is widely accepted, however, there are hurdles to clear: the long, traditional resistance to nonresident substitutes for campus work; the fear of "popularization"; the difficulty of convincing administrators that TV-lecturing is an academic activity comparable to publication and research when promotions and pay rises are awarded. But Meierhenry believes that the "extension" stigma is already beginning to lessen and that there will probably be increasing use of nonresident avenues to the college degree.

Some of the resistance to large-scale credit instruction by television is prompted by the fear of some college and university administrators that such course work may well reduce the amount of resident tuition that will be available. Why should the student pay high tuition when he can get the same thing so much less expensively? Both Taylor and Erickson feel this fear is unfounded; the potential residence audience is likely actually to be increased by this exposure to solid-course content on ETV. Erickson points out particularly that television instruction often helps people over emotional blocks against residence college work; "it sensitizes people to college. Thus television is a vestibule to the classroom for many . . ."

But is there not the possibility that the use of educational television will be seen by many administrators as a confession of weakness? In order to achieve academic responsibility, will a school have to get rid of its educational television courses as soon as possible? (Keppel) So long as television is seen as a device to be used primarily to fill up shortages; to provide "master teachers" to those schools whose faculties are not adequate to the full teaching task; to make available laboratory and experimental facilities that many schools can't afford, this confession-of-weakness concept might well prevail. Equally important is the university's or college's idea of its public image. The small college—which prides itself on its small classes, its high-quality faculty, the individual attention each student receives—will resist the use of educational television. (Pollock) Thus the rate and scope of acceptance will be different for different categories of schools, and the urban universities are more likely to use it than are the small prestige schools. (Keppel) This could make a difference in the future use of ETV at the college level; snob appeal might militate against it. The hope lies in the emphasis that is placed on the quality of the educational experience. (Pollock)

For the improvement of teaching.—One of the major impacts of educational television may be on teaching method. Teaching by television is different from other teaching: it imposes a sharper discipline upon method; it increases the use of a variety of devices as teaching aids; it introduces innovations that can affect all teaching, in the classroom as well as on the screen. (Meierhenry) Particularly valuable is the opportunity it provides for self-evaluation for those whose teaching presentation is taped and made available for viewing by the teacher himself. (Erickson) And it is at its best in the team-teaching situation, where each teacher stimulates the other, learns from observing the other, and is motivated to try to equal or excel the other in strong and careful lesson planning and effective presentation. (Mitchell) Through the use of a television teacher for some of the content, the classroom teacher can learn along with the students, but without loss of prestige in their eyes. Thus content and method both are upgraded by participation in televised team teaching.

Such general improvement in teaching, derived from the teaching experience itself, is a useful by-product, but it should not be the primary value sought. Better education for the students, not just valuable experience for the teacher, should be the goal. (Campion) But educational television is also an excellent device in formal teacher training itself. It is especially valuable in providing opportunities for the observation of classrooms and teaching method in practice, and there is every probability that there will be increasing intra-school, intra-building, closed-circuit use of this technique. (Fritz) Television could show how different groups learn differently, thus actively guarding against conformity and stereotyping in teaching method. (Witty) Research on teaching method can be enriched, particularly since television makes possible the preservation on tape of different kinds of teaching method, or of identical methods employed for different kinds of classes and content. (Oberholtzer) And the ability of television to reach large groups with detailed content makes it a promising device for use in teacher-training workshops—particularly on the subject of teaching by television itself. One such workshop is already being planned for air-borne transmission. (Worthington)

One real reservation should be voiced, however, about the improvement in teaching method which is supposed to accrue, almost automatically, when the classroom teacher observes the "master teacher" on television. The classroom teacher, it is true, is assisted in covering core content by the TV teacher, and some new teaching methods may be suggested by the television presentation. But this does not do a lot to make her a better *original* teacher; there is a point of diminishing return in watching someone else teach. (Campion) Equally important is the fact that the television teacher often pitches his presentation above the level of the classroom teacher's competence, showing the latter at a disadvantage and exposing him or her to student questions that he cannot answer. This kind of embarrassment doesn't necessarily motivate improvement; rather it increases tensions and the fear of threat to the classroom teacher's authority. Resistance rather than learning may derive from this experience; the dynamics of the individual situation are not taken into account in the more optimistic predictions. (Fritz)

Thus one of the most important needs of the immediate future is a clearer definition of the respective roles of the classroom and television teacher. (Campion) For one thing, it should be understood that the television teacher is the expert on planned preparation for short-period presentation; the classroom teacher is the expert on utilization—how best to use this concentrated material in discussion periods. These are different kinds of competences; hopefully they should not cause rivalries and conflicts. (Worthington) But there are many other important questions to be resolved as well. What is the purpose of television in the classroom— to give the classroom teacher a chance to work with individuals? to give a better presentation of content than is possible by the classroom teacher? to provide a release period for the classroom teacher to plan and prepare her own work? to make it possible for the classroom teacher to present only once to a much larger group the content which she now repeats in more than one class? The goals will differ for different subject matters and for different levels. (Campion) Keppel suggests that the next ten years may be needed adequately to define this distinction of roles.

In adult education.—As suggested in the discussion of college and university use of television, out-of-school programming is an increasingly important aspect of education in the United States. Even now, where the option is offered for taking educational television courses with or without college credit, there is a steady ratio of about 90 percent who take them without credit as compared with 10 percent who seek the credit. This does not count the purely "bonus" audience of casual viewers who form a significant part of any television audience. Informal education is the aspect that is usually thought of when "adult education" is mentioned in connection with educational television.

"There are terribly exciting possibilities for educating everyone everywhere through the medium of open-circuit television." (Gardner) Particularly promising are the prospects for meeting the problems of those who are functional illiterates or only slightly better than that. (Witty) But since an informed electorate requires continuing education after formal schooling is completed, the literate audience is also a target for such programming—especially those who, for one reason or another, have not been able to pursue all of the formal schooling they might have wished to have. For many adults, the problem of travel time is decisive in determining whether additional schooling can be taken, and television reduces the travel-time barrier. (Meierhenry)

There are other possibilities. Vocational training (in such subjects as bookkeeping, accounting, shorthand, business law, etc.) is particularly well adapted to television instruction. In-service training, especially in business and for mass re-training for automation, and on both open- and closed-circuit television, is a potential field for further development. Informal discussion groups on civic and social issues can very readily be organized around television programs. Co-operation with specific associations concerned about special problems of public interest—lip reading, care of the eyes, etc.—has great possibilities. (Oberholtzer) And going beyond the boundaries of our own country, television—and especially airborne television—can make a real contribution to adult education in underdeveloped countries by by-passing one of the major hurdles, the necessity to teach reading first before any other kind of education can be begun. (Worthington) In the long run, then, educational television, like the printing press and other great revolutionary developments in communication, will spread knowledge outside the realm of formal education. (Pollock)

In parent education.—Strictly speaking, parent education is one aspect of adult education, but it is distinctive enough to deserve special attention in this report. An important field for development of educational television for parents is in those areas where children's habits are really established by parent imposition rather than by the schools—health, education, dental hygiene, and the like. Thus open-circuit telecasting will probably show increasing emphasis on child rearing and other content touching upon the parent-child relation. (Fritz)

As the educational level of parents rises, there is likely to be increased interest in the quality and content of children's education, and this should be exploited. Open broadcast of actual classroom content is important in that it serves to educate parents as well as the students, permitting them to see what education is and what it does. (Worthington) "The involvement of parents may represent an important push in learning." (Oberholtzer)

Preschool possibilities.—Some of the uses of television with parents suggest that there might well be guided instruction for parents to use with their children to prepare them for school and perhaps speed up the coverage of classroom content. Certainly it is possible now to teach reading via television, so that first-graders could begin with a basic reading ability already established. (Taylor) Not all educators welcome this application of television, however; Keppel fears that "in the present state of the American family, I am afraid that this would lead to chaos even worse than that which now exists in the early years of the schools," and Campion believes less gloomily that the "basics" might better be held for the individual instruction of the live teacher. The real potential of preschool educational content on television lies in providing a background about people, places, and things which would equalize experience for all children. Thanks to television, there need not be so many "underprivileged" children whose limited experience and environment handicap them in their early years of formal schooling.

Anyone who has been in the educational field for very long will recognize many of the brightest promises of television as essentially the same promises that were held out for educational radio and educational film. As a matter of fact, there are educators—William Carr is one—who see no particular advantage claimed for television, except for the showing of live news events at the moment they are occurring, which cannot as readily be had, and often better, through the use of educational film. Indeed, educational film is sharper and clearer than television, can employ color, can range far more widely, and has the advantage of being available for preview and planned use. In many of the suggested uses of television, it is not at all the live telecast that is envisioned, but a taped or kinescoped record of it, which reduces the television screen to the status of a projector for filmed content. The key question then is: what reason is there to believe that television will be any more successful than film or radio has been in revolutionizing and improving American education? Both film and radio were as enthusiastically hailed when they first appeared; both have been relegated to a very minor role as incidental "enrichment" in those classrooms that use them at all.

The proponents of television cite several advantages which television has over film for classroom use. For one thing, the room need not be darkened, thus permitting note taking and reducing the discipline problem. TV is less costly for comparable time coverage. The trend in teaching is to take the mechanics and the machine out of the classroom, and TV sharply reduces the amount of mechanical and machine manipulation. But more than that, television and film are two quite different media, with different effects and different effectiveness, and this is true even when television is used only as a system of distribution for tapes or kinescopes. (McBride) Somehow there is a greater immediacy about the television presentation; Campion suggests that this may be because in the film audio is secondary whereas it is primary in TV. Thus TV can more readily be used as a classroom lesson whereas film is primarily an illustration for the lesson rather than its central focus. Some of this difference in approach is historical: for one thing, it was the commercial film people who first went into educational film work, and they brought to it the techniques and the values of the commercial film. In television, on the other hand, it was the radio people who first came in, bringing with them their emphasis upon the audio aspect of the presentation. But even more important, educational television began early, as film did not, to look at the medium as a tool of education rather than as a mere adaptation of an entertainment device. In other words, one of the advantages that television has over the film is that its users and backers have learned from the errors of the past; the mistakes that created blocks against the use of the film are not being committed with the new medium.

Above all, ETV came at just the right time, when it is no longer possible or desirable to maintain the status quo in many areas including education. (McBride) The introduction of ETV coincides with a period of emergency in education, represented by the wave of enrollments and the consequent teacher shortage, by international tension which has focused attention on weaknesses in our educational system, by a popular demand to "increase educational productivity," (Taylor) and by a widespread hospitality to innovation in almost all fields. This crisis situation works in favor of any dramatic innovation that seems to give promise of solving some of the problems—and television thus has an opportunity that film and radio didn't have. It is possible that wider use of film, which really

became available in good technical form by the middle 1930's, was inhibited by the fear in those Depression years that use of films might put
some teachers out of work. (Keppel) Thus, ironically, television may
stimulate more interest in the use of film for educational purposes than
film was able to generate on its own, (Witty) for one of the characteristics
of the crisis, and of the present trends in television use, is the willingness
to use all kinds of devices and approaches, to combine all aspects of education that can be helpful in increasing the quality of education at all levels.
The big contribution of educational television is that it "will break the
lock step at the elementary and secondary levels." (Taylor)

The several possibilities for use of television which have here been
suggested raise the question: which is better, more promising, more likely
to be the more widely used—open- or closed-circuit television? The respondents seem agreed that both closed and open circuit will increase in
the years ahead. Closed circuit will probably catch up and overtake broadcast use of television because it is much less costly, and because it can be
better tailored to the individual institution's needs. (Harley) Closed
circuit is excellent for special subjects, for a single high school in a community, within described jurisdictions where close cooperation and planning exist between the classroom and the TV instructor. It is likely, in
many school systems, to be the channel through which open-circuit telecasts, recorded on tape, will be viewed by the students.

Open circuit, on the other hand, is most promising for adult education
uses, for larger school systems, and for reaching the rural residents, the
home-bound, and the older person. Open circuit may be used to a limited
extent in the classroom—especially for some occasional event of importance (the inauguration, a major speech of national significance, etc.)—
but not nearly so widely as in informal adult education.

In view of the many uses of open-circuit television, could not much of
the educational material be handled on commercial television—as indeed
much of it now is? Could not the proportion of educational content be
increased, and commercial channels be used to serve wherever open-circuit
programming is to be used? The majority of the respondents, while ac-
knowledging the excellent educational programs that have appeared on
commercial television, the helpfulness of the networks in providing study
materials, and the cooperation that many local stations have extended to
educational programming, were nevertheless convinced that educational
television will have to be over and above the normal programming of the
commercial stations, and on stations of its own. "The job is too big to
hitchhike on commercial facilities," Harley says. "Education needs even
more channels than are now available; it needs access to the 'prime' hours
as well as to the commercially unprofitable ones, and it needs primary

commitment to educational content." McBride makes a similar point: "The need is greater than commercial television can handle, especially where a conflict between commercial and quality considerations occurs. Educational television stations will serve a function in broadcasting like that served by university presses in publishing." This last point is particularly pertinent, for much of commercial television's "educational" content is embedded in a format designed to serve other purposes first, and educational aims only incidentally. The discussion programs, for example, on which educators have appeared as guests to discuss matters of some importance, have frequently failed to achieve a very high level of educational content. "One of the drawbacks in commercial discussion programs is this, that the educator is forced to play someone else's game on somebody else's field according to someone else's rules." (Gardner) Faust elaborates the point: "You have to pretend that the question asked by the master of ceremonies is important . . ."

More importantly, there is a danger that open-circuit telecasting of classroom content may put education up to popular referendum. Can courses in the social sciences, literature, biological sciences be as complete, as outspoken, as critical before a general audience as they should be in the closed classroom? The privacy, the lack of outside supervision, the primacy of educational objectives which characterizes the classroom make it possible to pursue knowledge for its own sake, to experiment with teaching method, to make mistakes and benefit from them. This must not be lost. (Gardner, Faust) As yet, there is no evidence that open-circuit television teaching has been inhibited by audience considerations; as a matter of fact, Sunrise Semester and the experiments in Wisconsin are outstanding examples of undiluted, university-level content on the open air which have met with audience approval. (Pollock) But the potential danger is there: could social science classes treat the United Nations without interference in the Los Angeles area, or literature classes deal with the modern novel equally thoroughly in all sections of the country?

But ETV has much to learn from commercial television in skill of production and technical competence, and, even more importantly, in the evaluation of impact and effects. (Mitchell) In any case, ETV should not be the only kind of telecasting there is; commercial has its own values. As must always be recognized, much that appears on commercial television is useful for educational purposes. Attempts to guide student viewing of particular commercial programs to serve the ends of the classroom have been hampered without study aids, outlines, and guides, but commercial television has been pretty good in cooperating and supplying materials, and there is every likelihood that this will continue and increase. (Mitchell)

Does that mean, then, that the impact of educational television will influence commercial television to improve its content? It is a hope of the educators, but a far from sanguine one. It is possible that ETV will eventually create an appetite for better programming, especially as increasing longevity, more education, and early retirement create a larger audience for serious content. But this is not a matter for the next ten years; Taylor suggests that 40 to 50 years is a more probable figure. These comments were made before Newton N. Minow's speech to the National Association of Broadcasters. Whether his forthright declaration may actually make a practical difference in the long run is a point on which the critics of commercial television are not yet in agreement.

There are some ten-year predictions, however, that the respondents were willing to risk. By 1971, and barring quite unforeseen and unforeseeable developments, the situation will probably look like this:

Not every school, rural and urban, will have television by 1971, but probably every *major* school, college and university will have at least one closed-circuit system, and there will not be many school children who will not have had some television in their educational experience. (Erickson, McBride, Meierhenry, Taylor, Worthington)

In general, a wider use of television in teaching can be expected, although there will be some subjects and some levels that will use it more than others. Demonstration, laboratory and observation kinds of uses will probably be the most widespread. (Campion, Fritz, Oberholtzer)

Although this increase in use can be expected, educational television will probably reach a plateau very soon. Other technological developments (teaching machines, for example) will appear to challenge it, and in the competition among devices and methods the proper place of each will be more clearly defined, with no one of them seen as the universal panacea for education's many problems. (Campion, Harley)

One certain development will be the use of ETV to provide teaching and demonstration in specialized subject fields (the sciences, for example) where teachers or equipment are in short supply. (Campion, Oberholtzer)

While there may be some instances of "total teaching" by television, particularly in the more routinized subject matters, the major use of television for more conceptualized content will be supplementary. This will not be only "enrichment" in its narrower sense; there will likely be some large-group instruction as well. But television will be seen as an instructional tool, not as a replacement for good teaching. (Fritz, Michael, McBride)

Some adaptation of the Stoddard Plan will be typical: part of the day utilized in the large television class, and the rest in smaller-than-usual groups for discussion and socialization. The exact proportion in television and non-television classes is not yet determined, and certainly it will differ for different kinds of subject matter and at different levels. But the future will probably see something like 20 minutes out of the hour given to television at the elementary and secondary levels, and 30 minutes at the college level. (Meierhenry, Worthington)

One very probable development is the use of closed-circuit television to distribute taped programs, derived from open circuit. In this area, "a revolution is afoot." (Erickson)

The greatest changes will be apparent in teaching method. ETV will spearhead the movement toward the better use of instruction materials of all kinds, with the emphasis, not on the gadget, but on communication. There will be a tendency for the discussion groups to be even smaller than the present classroom, with ability groupings to facilitate the discussion. The emphasis on ability groupings will lead to greater attention to the most able students, with greater reliance upon independent study and the development of responsibility for learning in the learner himself. The classroom teacher will not be replaced, generally speaking, except for certain highly specialized content where a specialist is required to present the core content; the emphasis will be on team teaching, with the consequent influence upon teaching method which the shared "master teacher" can introduce. (Bronson, Michael, Oberholtzer, Worthington)

There will be an increasing recognition of superior teaching ability, and differential in salaries in school systems will begin to be based upon this kind of talents. At the college level, teaching ability will begin to be considered, along with publication and research, as a basis for academic recognition. (Bronson)

Although in 1971 the normal road to the college degree is still likely to be residence instruction, it is not impossible that as much as 50 percent of the college degree program will be available for credit via television. The traditional insistence on classroom instruction will begin to crumble as the conviction grows that demonstrated mastery of the subject matter should be the criterion, no matter how the mastery is acquired. (Erickson, McBride, Taylor, Worthington)

Air-borne television may already be obsolete by 1971, with ETV from satellites accomplishing the kind of umbrella coverage air-borne is now pioneering. (Taylor, Worthington)

Technical developments will open many new possibilities which will be something more than just the adaptation of devices designed for other purposes. Such current developments as the approved use of translators for original transmission, or as pickups to beam the program to an even wider area, suggest some of the possibilities. (McBride, Worthington)

The local grass roots will prevail, however, even in the use of air-borne. The local school, quite rightly, wants control over content and its use; anything coming from outside must be adapted and screened to be most effective. Pooling of resources at the local level, and state and regional networks, will provide the wealth of materials from which to choose, but national syndication (except for some in-service and general education at the adult level where there is agreement on certain standard content) is not a major probability in the classroom situation. (Erickson, Fritz, Michael, Pollock, Taylor)

The developing pattern will be that of cooperation between the state system of higher education and the school system, with legislative support. Already state plans are being built into ETV legislation. (Bronson, Harley)

The wide audience served by regional systems and air-borne television will represent a potential market for better and more carefully chosen text-

books and other materials supporting ETV. Thus television could well be
an important factor in improving textbook publishing. (Erickson)

School buildings will be much more flexible and adaptable, with portable soundproof partitions and similar features designed with ETV in
mind. (Bronson, Campion)

By 1971, school administrators will have learned not to use a Rolls-
Royce where a Rambler will do. Tape, produced at some central spot and
"bicycled around," or telecast widely via air-borne, can be extremely inexpensive per user if the costs are shared. Thus the production center may
well be the solution to the present impossibly high line charges and the
other time-staff-money problems that seem to be hurdles today. (Campion)

One thing on which both opponents and proponents of educational
television are agreed: the changes are going to come about much more
rapidly in the future, if for no other reason than the increasing exchange
of ideas through meetings, publications, and other channels of communication within the profession. The traditional "fifty-year lag," that presumably occurs between the introduction of a new idea in education and
its actual adoption by a majority of the schools, will be much reduced.
Thus the ten-year predictions made here are not too unrealistic. But this
speed-up could be harmful if ETV is rejected too quickly because of wide
public exposure of the natural mistakes that occur during a period of experimentation. This could frustrate the best development of the medium.
(Carr, Fritz, Oberholtzer, Worthington)

There are many problems to be solved before the optimistic view of
1971 can become a reality. Some of these are technical: good reception
on a large screen has not yet been attained; an inexpensive tape recorder
has not yet been developed; sufficient usable channels to meet the growing
need have not yet been created; machines need constant checking and
rechecking; and there is not enough technically trained personnel to do
the job. (Bronson, Michael, Mitchell, Oberholtzer, Pollock) Some of the
problems are psychological: administrators find it difficult to dissociate
themselves from immediate budgetary limitations to plan ahead sensibly
on a long-term basis; many vested interests (county agents, for instance,
as well as classroom teachers who have developed their own teaching
methods) feel threatened and oppose the changes that educational television would bring; administrators don't want to give up their administrative controls despite their glowing verbal support of cooperation; colleges are reluctant to admit that they do not have teachers who are competent to handle the subject matter. (Bronson, Meierhenry, Mitchell,
Michael) And there is the interesting and knotty question of residual
rights: Is the teacher entitled to royalties when his telecasts are re-used,
or used by other schools? What are the relative rights of the teacher and
the sponsoring agency in recorded materials? Do the entertainer's replay
rights carry over into educational television, especially where commercial
television is used? Will commercial film makers, television stations, and

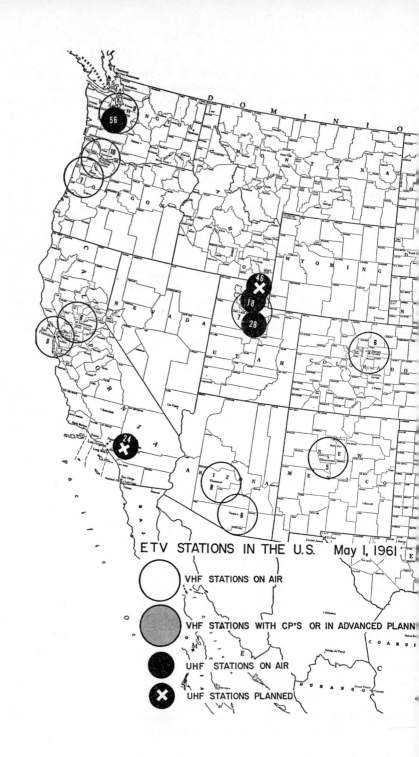

ETV STATIONS IN THE U.S.   May 1, 1961

○ VHF STATIONS ON AIR

● VHF STATIONS WITH CP'S OR IN ADVANCED PLANN

● UHF STATIONS ON AIR

❌ UHF STATIONS PLANNED

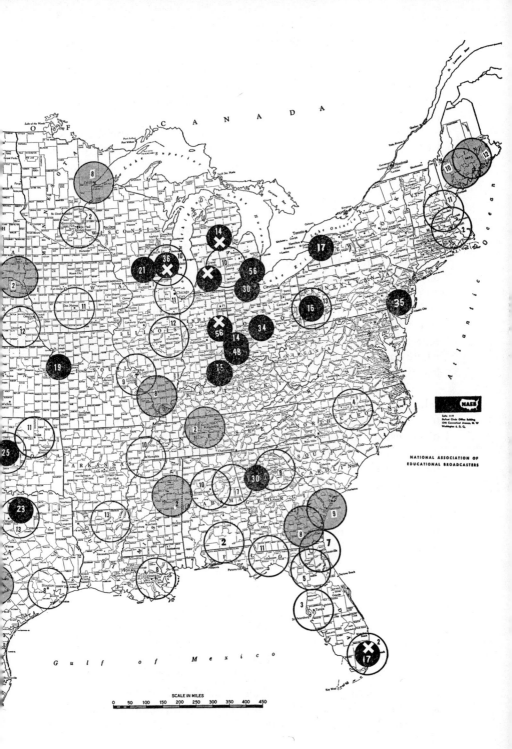

NATIONAL ASSOCIATION OF
EDUCATIONAL BROADCASTERS

SCALE IN MILES
0   50   100   150   200   250   300   350   400   450

others who could supply the variety of materials needed for enriched programming demand royalties so prohibitive as to tie the hands of the educational telecasters? This kind of jurisdictional questions could upset many
of the best-laid plans for ETV.

The problems define the needs. The engineers can probably keep up
with most of the technical requirements—multiplexing, microwave, tape
recording, low-power translators and transmitters, etc.—so long as the
need is made manifest. (Harley, Taylor) More and more regular support,
both public and private, is essential if the potential of ETV is to be realized;
this need should be recognized by foundations, government, and other
sources so that creative people will not have to continue to spend their
time on money raising and budgetary problems. (Fritz, Witty) The key
decision rests with the Federal Communications Commission, which is
obviously becoming aware of the requirements and seems favorable to a
more liberal allocation of channels for educational use. So long as ETV
is held to ultra-high-frequency channels its best contribution is being
thwarted. (Campion, Erickson, McBride, Oberholtzer) And finally, research is needed on the very topic with which this report is concerned:
where and how can educational television be best used to improve the
learning process? (Mitchell)

All of the arguments, pro and con, and all of the problems and proposed
solutions, can probably be summed up succinctly as follows: Educational
television is an instrument of great potential value in improving the quality
of education in all subject matters and at all levels—*if* it will be used
creatively and imaginatively. Experimentation should be on a pluralistic
basis; we should aim for a variety of subject matters and a variety of
approaches rather than to decide in advance where and how it is likely
to be best used. (Gardner) Local schools and educational stations should
use the best from all sources, but they should be encouraged to initiate
their own programs and not be content just to be outlets. (Pollock) The
proponents of ETV envision just such variety and originality; the opponents of ETV condemn it because it has not thus far demonstrated such
qualities.

Above all, educational television should not be allowed merely to
duplicate present educational methods, continuing on a larger scale all of
the blunders of the present. (Worthington) A typical defense of ETV
that it does the same things as traditional teaching with similar results is
irrelevant; the concern should be with good *television* teaching, not with
parallels and comparisons. The problem is one of taking proper sights on
a rapidly moving target (Gardner) and of finding the right questions to
ask. (Faust) If educational television meets this kind of challenge, it will
be particularly attractive to the good young teachers who are concerned

with moving somewhere. Any new job description will catch on if it introduces excitement, interest, and a chance to exert influence to combat the flatness of life and the low ceiling for growth, typical particularly of elementary and secondary school teaching. (Keppel) Television teaching could represent such a job description.

The temper of the time is favorable; the need is great; the tools seem promising. Television, and the more imaginative use of all educational devices which it promotes, could improve our chances to realize the long-held dream of good, universal education. The next ten years will be decisive in establishing whether ETV really can fulfill its exciting potential.

ETV, A MAJOR RESOURCE
By Joe Hall

Mr. Hall is Superintendent of Schools in Miami, Florida, where extensive use has been made of instructional television.

IT IS THE PURPOSE of this paper to review from the standpoint of a school superintendent the development and future possibilities of educational television, both in the school and in the community.

A group of public-spirited citizens of the Greater Miami area began to work in 1951 to develop community interest in the establishment of an educational television station. Their hard work and persistence was rewarded in 1954 when the Board of Public Instruction of Dade County was granted a Channel 2 permit by the Federal Communications Commission. WTHS-TV signed on the air on August 12, 1955, as Florida's first ETV station. For two years the station programmed for five or six hours during the evenings with educational films, a selected list of live local programs, and a rather limited signal of 9,000 watts. Even within these limitations the channel quickly validated itself as a community service and Dade County school personnel began to wonder more and more if—and how—this device might be put to work to help with the problem of improving the learning of boys and girls.

The Dade County School System had experienced a phenomenal growth in school population from a school system of 88,000 in the 1952–53 school year to 136,000 in the 1957–58 school year for an increase of 54 percent during the five-year period. Increases such as this were not uncommon throughout the State of Florida and adequate funds were not available to meet the need for classrooms. The 1957 session of the legislature gave serious consideration to requiring twelve-month operation of schools with a rotating vacation schedule whereby one-fourth of the pupils would be on vacation at any one time.

In a report requested by the Dade County Board of Public Instruction the superintendent listed some advantages and disadvantages of various ways of dealing with the oversize school population. The twelve-month four-quarter school year plan was compared with double sessions or the use of an extended day having overlapping sessions in the noon hours. It was felt that this last plan supported by educational television seemed to offer the greatest promise.

An additional reason for beginning instructional television was the national shortage of trained instructional personnel caused by the large annual growth in school population and the relatively small numbers of college students choosing teaching as a profession. The employment of some thousand well-prepared teachers each year in the local school system presented increasing difficulties. Tied closely with this was the obvious need for sharing or spreading the influence of outstanding teachers to large numbers of boys and girls and other teachers.

This situation created a need favorable to the exploration of educational television. However, the real impetus behind the decision to utilize television was a sincere desire on the part of the school people to explore this medium as a way of improving the learning of boys and girls.

In Dade County during the first year of the television project (1957–58) there were nine participating schools: three elementary schools, three junior high schools, and three senior high schools. Seven thousand students were involved. The results of this first year revealed a slight advantage for the experimental as compared to the control groups. The findings were generally non-significant, but the comparisons of academic growth showed greater than normal gains.

Since the achievement of the classes during the first year showed promise that television could increase the learning of boys and girls, and since the experiment was effecting substantial economies in classroom space, it was decided to increase the number of participating schools in the second year to a total of ten elementary schools, twelve junior high schools, and six senior high schools. Eighteen thousand five hundred students were involved. The testing of TV and non-TV students during this year again confirmed that TV students in large classes were achieving as well or better than non-TV groups.

During 1959–60, the third year of the television project, a total of twenty-eight schools and thirty thousand boys and girls was involved. They represented classes in fifteen elementary schools, ten junior high schools, and thirteen senior high schools. Test results have indicated that boys and girls have continued to learn well with the help of television and that many of the problems in classroom management have been solved.

So it is that now we are in the fourth year of our in-school television project. This year 50,000 boys and girls in our county include in their schedules one class taught with the help of television.

Elementary schools involved in the project are so organized that one-half of the pupils in the fifth and sixth grades work in small classes for one-half of the day, while the other half is in the large classes. During the time that the pupils are in the small classes they participate in the regular work of the fundamental skills—reading, writing, spelling, language, and arithmetic. These classes are smaller in number than the normal elementary class. This reduction in class size is made possible without increasing costs by having the pupils in larger classes for the other part of the school day. While they are in large classes, they participate in the subjects of conversational Spanish, social studies, and science. It is here in the large group containing from 150 to 200 pupils that the children receive their daily telelesson in American history. They also receive a varied schedule of telelessons designed to inspire and stimulate direct teaching in Spanish, science, and literature (1).

This year 45 additional elementary schools are participating in the fifth and sixth grade Spanish, science, and literature television lessons on a different plan from that of the regular elementary TV project schools. The elementary children on the modified plan attend the telelesson in a central viewing area with their teachers. They then return to their regular classrooms for follow-up or related activities. Whereas most of our telecourses are offered as daily major resources and provide direction for the content, the elementary offerings in Spanish, literature, science, and speech improvement might be considered supplementary or enriching in nature for the schools on this limited program.

The junior high schools utilize television as a resource in teaching seventh grade science, eighth grade United States history, ninth grade civics, and ninth grade science. The size of the classes varies from 300 to 600 students in each receiving room.

The participating senior high schools utilize television as a resource in teaching tenth grade English, tenth grade biology, eleventh grade English, and eleventh grade American history. The average size class in the senior high schools is 320, although some are considerably larger.

The plan of operation in the junior and senior high schools calls for a team of teachers assisted by a teacher aide. For instance, this team of teachers at the junior high level often consists of a seventh grade science teacher and an eighth grade history teacher. They share the services of one teacher aide. The science teacher is in charge of the television science class. That is, he is responsible for the children during the telelesson and for preparing and directing the classroom portion of the lesson. During the science telelesson the history teacher assists the science teacher. During the history class the history teacher is in charge and the science teacher is in the role of an assistant. The teacher aide's functions are to take attendance, set up the equipment and release the teachers from the nonprofessional tasks in order to permit them to devote their full time to teaching. The television classroom teachers, in addition to being responsible for teaching one large class and assisting in another, are required to teach one regular size class. Thus, the teachers under this plan are occupied in the classroom three periods a day. The other three periods are allotted to the additional planning, grading, and counseling entailed in teaching the large groups.

All of the televised lessons are five days a week (except for examination days) and of 27 minutes duration with a comparable amount of time for the classroom portion of the lesson.

Our driver-training course is somewhat different and so interwoven with the ETV program that it deserves special treatment here. The standard driver-training course requires six hours of behind-the-wheel instruction and 30 hours of classroom instruction. We believe that we have developed a plan which will enable us to provide such instruction in an economical manner. Our plan works as follows: during the homeroom period of 15 minutes for three days each week for a semester of 18 weeks, direct teaching is provided to all tenth grade pupils in a given school. In many cases this number will exceed a thousand in a particular school. This provides for 12 of the 30 hours of classroom instruction. For the other 18 hours of classroom instruction, pupils are drawn from their physical education classes and given classroom instruction in smaller groups.

For the behind-the-wheel, six-hour requirement, 10 to 15 cars are utilized with two pupils in each car. The area for training is set up in the general nature of an obstacle course on which there is no street traffic. The automobiles are provided with equipment which restricts their speed. The instructor is provided a loudspeaker and gives directions to the cars from a central location not in a car. The pupils in a period have a full half hour behind the wheel. For the 12 periods necessary for this six hours of instruction, the pupils are drawn from physical education classes.

Television supports the extended school day in a number of junior and senior high schools. In these schools one-third of the students and teachers begin classes at 7:30 a.m. and complete their six periods at 2:15 p.m. Another group begins at 8:30 and completes its school day at 3:15. The final one-third of the student body arrives at 9:30 and finishes at 4:15. This means that the total population is in the building for the four periods between 9:30 a.m. and 2:15 p.m. It is here that the large TV classes, conducted in the auditorium, relieve much of the load on school facilities.

No student at the secondary level receives more than one-half hour of television instruction per day, unless he is in the tenth grade and is assigned to the driver-education instruction for three homeroom periods each week.

Our schools are now planning their third daytime instructional program for summer. Eight different areas will be taught over television with an approach which combines both remedial and the broadening aspects. Pupils have found that participation in the summer telecourses is a good way to strengthen themselves in the areas in which they have had difficulty during the regular school year and to acquire additional knowledge in areas in which they have not had the opportunity to study.

With the beginning of the public Junior College in Dade County in September 1960 there was demand for time for courses of junior-college level. The only time available on Channel 2 was from 3:00 to 5:00 in the afternoon. This time is being utilized by the Junior College but is regarded as less satisfactory than would be hours earlier during the day. Efforts are now being made to obtain a second channel in order that these needs may be met.

With the facilities available in the school there are many other types of activities involving all or a part of the 7,000 and more instructional personnel in the school system. In-service training programs of great variety are conducted in specialized areas; faculty meetings of the air involving all personnel are provided. Similarly, general information about the various programs in the schools is presented to the general public on this open circuit high-frequency station.

Station WTHS-TV is a nonprofit, VHF, school-owned and operated, open-circuit educational television station functioning under the jurisdiction of the Dade County Board of Public Instruction. The many telecasts which constitute the heavy back-to-school schedule of live telelessons are originating from two studios. The power of the station signal has been increased from 9,000 watts to 100,000 watts.

Most of the schools use auditoriums or cafeterias as television classrooms. These large areas are equipped with television sets at the ratio of one set for each 50 students. In the elementary schools which use cafeterias for the large television classrooms, care is exercised to schedule the instructional periods early in the morning and late in the afternoon to avoid any conflict with the serving of lunch. For the best acoustical effects in these large rooms, it is important to beam the sound directly to the viewers. This is done by detaching the television speakers and remounting them in a frontal position aimed straight ahead and slightly downward.

The TV sets are 21-inch table models of a standard make mounted so that the center of the screen is 5'8" from the floor, approximately the height of an average teacher. The sets are tilted on the mounts so that the face of the screen is perpendicular to the line of vision of the students. Where possible, the sets are mounted in such a manner that they do not have to be moved about the room. In some schools permanent shelves are built for the stationary sets along the wall. For the sets located in the front of the room and in the seating area, special mobile stands are constructed complete with roller casters and shelf space for storing materials. For better classroom control, all television sets in a given room are attached to a common switch permitting them to be turned on or off simultaneously. Each large classroom is equipped with an overhead projector. The classroom teachers use lapel microphones with 50-foot cords to permit freedom of movement. In addition to the standard telecasting equipment used by the station, a warning clock is shown preceding each telelesson. This permits the teachers in the classrooms to time accurately for the reception of the telecasts.

Maintenance and repair of television sets and the antenna systems are provided by the maintenance department of the Dade County Board of Public Instruction. The service is prompt and efficient. Minor surface adjustments of the sets are made by the classroom teachers.

By employing television in the teaching of large classes certain economies have been effected. This current year we have utilized the savings in teaching personnel to pay the full operating cost of the television station and to provide educational services in the form of specialized personnel such as remedial reading teachers, counselors, and additional librarians. To provide for the number of pupils that we now have in our buildings in the established pattern for education without the large television classes, which are employed in a limited number of our schools, would require an immediate capital outlay of at least four million dollars. If our present rate of growth continues, we believe as we involve other schools that the amount of capital saving in schoolhouse construction will be increased far beyond this point.

If American education is to develop within our boys and girls skills, knowledge and attitudes which will perpetuate our society and strengthen the material and moral fibre of the nation, then we must pursue excellence, keeping in mind these goals. It would seem logical that one way excellence could be achieved would be to improve the effectiveness of the already proven effective medium of television as an educational resource. We hope to approach this task in the future by working on at least four major components: (1) physical facilities for transmission and utilization, (2) materials for greater program impact, (3) curriculum planning for wider acceptance and greater goal achieving efficiency, and (4) personnel and talent identification and training both in the studio and utilization areas.

As school people we are interested primarily in television's utilization to improve educational processes and their final product. However, we realize that only through technology was it made possible for us to bring the whole spectrum of audio-visual devices to bear on education through this medium. Therefore, it might be well to consider the future and the miracles which are already being wrought for our use. Educational television within the foreseeable future will offer color with all the implications that it has for teaching. Bulky receivers will likely become a thing of the past. Large screen, thin receivers mounted on floating aluminum railing will permit the teacher to position the television receivers easily and quickly in any part of a room or auditorium. It will be possible to let studio teachers know immediately the broad reactions of students to the salient questions, issues or proposals being presented. Desk buttons can reflect at least such general reactions as approval, disapproval, agreement, disagreement, clear and unclear. Within seconds computers can relay this information to studios, and teachers may be guided. The reaction panel would be sensitized on the request of the studio teacher.

The function of ETV stations will probably be modified. Air-borne stations, regional and national ETV networks and international satellite relays will make it possible for the stations to select from programs of remarkable quality and unlimited variety. These then may be recorded and transmitted for local utilization to accommodate schedules as required within a given system or, with careful planning, schools may want to select their own programs from the different sources of origin available. Closed circuitry is almost certain to become more widely used. Technology now assures us that it is possible to have all the film in a given library or center catalogued and arranged in cartridges so that selection may be made for instantaneous relay and reception by manipulating a keyed panel in an individual classroom.

Educators are interested and hopeful concerning current experimentation in TV-classroom designs. It is likely that the TV classrooms of the future will vary greatly in capacity and shape. This will be true because of the variety of ways in which TV will be employed. Some small TV classes for exceptional children will require the intimacy of a laboratory study. Other uses of television will make feasible, even desirable, classrooms which will accommodate a thousand students. However, it seems safe to say that all of these areas should have in common good acoustics, no-glare provisions, adequate lighting for instructional purposes, desks with writing surfaces, good ventilation, and provision for easy ingress and egress.

It is likely that all large schools will have individual video-tape recorders or at least play-back mechanisms. This could mean that ETV stations will also become duplicating centers for tapes which will be bicycled on schedule throughout a given school system so as to permit use at any time of a given day and thereby break through the rigidity problem sometimes posed by open-circuit schedules.

So much for the future of facilities and equipment. These and more things will come—not all at once anywhere and much sooner in some places than others. In fact, some of them are already possible, indeed, are already being used on a limited basis. Technology is coming faster than will be comfortable for many of us. This has the clearest implications for teacher-training institutions as well as school administrators who are responsible for in-service training of teachers.

Those involved in in-school and community programming are the first to admit that the quality, although generally good, leaves much to be desired.

Studio teachers the nation over, whether they are recording for tape networks or doing live telelessons, are handicapped by a lack of visuals to do the job with the precision and impact that is being demanded of them. A studio teacher of U.S. history may spend hours previewing five or six 30-minute films of different vintage, searching for a two-minute segment which will vividly illustrate a point in what she hopes will be an unforgettable manner. At last she discovers what she thinks will do only to find that it may not be cleared for television because of copyright problems. If it is cleared, this film which was made for a large screen, when reduced to the 21-inch classroom (receiver) screen will leave much to be desired. A teacher with inadequate art help may labor for hours over a three-dimensional visual to be used fleetingly one time during the year. A studio science teacher may be able to dominate one end of the studio for an afternoon to set up a science experiment which may or may not go off well.

Should we not mount an effort to obtain adequate visuals for studio teachers with the same enthusiasm that we now work to obtain adequate textbooks and equipment for the classrooms? Many of those concerned with the problem are proposing that private and public educational agencies join to produce professionally short film clips of not more than two or three minutes duration which illustrate to near perfection the crucial areas in history, science, language, and arts. It has been said that a hundred of these clips could be well directed just to the electricity units of junior high science. Hundreds of others should be made for crucial decisions in American history. National experts should be video-taped talking succinctly and directly to specified points in which they are authorities. These clips should be made available for rapid distribution on demand from any part of the country. They should be made for television and cleared from their inception. Here we are not talking about a piecemeal or amateur job that might be done by an over-busy studio but a dedicated effort of national proportions to provide materials of such quality that any studio teacher of ability could put together a lesson which would draw from her worst critics the remark that, "this lesson really exploited the medium."

Short film or video-tape clips of top quality seem to offer the greatest potential as highly portable visuals. The television potential is far too dramatic—even too expensive—to put teachers before the cameras without adequate tools of the trade to offer maximum impact. Technology will likely continue to provide improvements for the studio such as technamation and visamatic devices. Rear screen and remote pickup for mobile units will likely become standard equipment. The controlling factor for gauging what is effective in the studio will continue to be the measurement of how effective it is in the classroom in terms of pupil achievement.

School superintendents and administrators now recognize that innovations in education are never widely accepted unless the curriculum planning for the content and implementation is carried out on a wide coopera-tive base among all the instructional personnel involved. Planning is the key word here. The joint planning among school people for educational television has already done much to improve the curriculum in many school systems. The future will likely see this planning intensified and broadened even further. Subject-area supervisors, receiving teachers and school ad-ministrators all must have a voice in deciding what is to be taught and—to a degree—how it is to be taught. These decisions help set the stage for later evaluation and improvement as the work moves along. As the ex-change of video tapes among the various school systems of the nation assumes substantial proportions, curriculum planning for television will also become a wider cooperative sphere. Here we find ourselves in hearty agreement with Wiles, when he says that co-planners make co-advocates (2).

Who will be the future studio teachers? Many of the same ones who are teaching on-camera today, because most of them are doing a good job. However, as the influence of the studio teacher grows it is likely that the search for talent will increase. Why shouldn't a modern school personnel department make a short sound-on-film clip of every teacher in action? Although time consuming, it might be time well spent when searching for a really effective studio biology teacher to preview every one of the film clips of certificated biology teachers searching for leads to the one in a hundred or one in a thousand whom we hope to share with the many. Teacher-training institutions will be called into this picture also. Schools of education are even now exploring the desirability of setting up courses treating with methods and techniques of studio teaching. It would seem logical that if we are to specialize, that there must be training for the specialty.

Who will be the producer-directors of educational television lessons and programs? This person whose position has been called that of "the newest engineer in American education" will increase in importance. More will be demanded of him as a full-fledged partner of the studio teacher and talent.

Therefore, those presently doing this work will likely seek additional training. The ones coming into the profession may find themselves better equipped if they have a minor in education and a major in television-film production. It might be well to induce certain interested and talented class-room teachers to pursue graduate work in television production and return-ing to the school system as producer-directors. Presently employed pro-ducer-directors who have commercial backgrounds may be well advised to obtain additional training in the form of selected courses in education. It is likely that this position will develop an identity and usefulness unique in the profession.

Who will be the television classroom teachers of the future? They will likely be the teachers we have today and others from the same general sources with the difference that they shall have had more preparation in how to use television effectively as a resource in teaching boys and girls. School systems have only begun to train their teachers in the methods of teaching with the help of television. Schools of education are cooperating in conducting summer workshops and in-service credit courses in how to use television as a resource. It is likely that future teacher-training curriculums at the undergraduate level will require work in the use of this medium. Television itself offers a real opportunity for administrators to acquaint the teachers with educational television and its utilization. It might be concluded that any competent classroom teacher can use quality ETV to advantage. Additional training will be provided to telescope the development of effective utilization.

What will be taught by television? There appear to be few, if any, limitations as to what is possible in this area. As improved techniques become available and the relationship between the team, which includes the studio teacher and the classroom teacher, is improved, much more can be done. It seems evident that there can be little or no decrease in the number of personnel required in the individual schools. The nature of the work which they do and the service which they render, however, will probably be considerably changed as improvements are made. The possibility of assisting students in certain aspects of homework has had little exploration but offers a potentially fertile field. Likewise, the nature of the in-service training programs will probably be considerably changed to make more effective the utilization of the professionally trained educator's time.

Although the advent of the in-school television project became the center of much interest in our country, the citizenry seemed equally interested in continuing and improving the evening community television program. The Community Television Foundation of South Florida as a pioneer body in the support of educational television for the community and the Board of Public Instruction as licensees of the station were in a position to do this. It was felt that there needs to be no limit to the amount persons can learn, if properly motivated, and that educational and cultural programs should be continually made available to the general public. Therefore, the evening adult program of our ETV station was developed with equal enthusiasm and in close cooperation with the in-school daytime program.

What of the future of the after-school or evening community programs? In looking to the future here, we in Dade County are talking about such things as station personality, programming purpose, and source of programs.

Those concerned with the station's personality for the community program will insure that the station will reflect the community by first involv-

ing the community. This is already being done across the nation in our
ETV stations and the pattern will probably be accented in the future.
Sound planning will call for program committees which represent a true
cross section of the community; committees, the members of which will
not act as rubber stamps because they will have ideas of their own about
raising the cultural level of the community by obtaining programs of such
quality that the general public will say, "This is something that we can't
do without." A station having developed the genuine community side of
its personality will then take on an identity to a degree compatible with
its locale. For instance, in Miami Channel 2 has and will continue to have
a Latin touch. Geography and community interest dictate an interest in
Latin America, its language, art, and music. Time, facilities, and local
talent to respond to this interest are available.

As stations mature they will likely develop flexible but more definite
concepts of their function in the community. Some of the persistent purposes may be: (1) to raise the cultural level of the community by providing quality programs in music, literature, and drama, (2) to provide accurate information in depth, (3) to provide a continuing source of learning
by offering formal adult educational experiences both in the form of credit
and noncredit telecourses and "how to do it" series, (4) to help prepare
children for their first formal school experiences by offering entertaining
but valid preschool programs aimed at building attitudes and early skills
desirable for the very young.

Every indication is that we shall continue to obtain programs of ever
better quality from sources such as our National Educational Television
and Radio Center. These programs will continue to be dedicated to areas
of broad interest and needs common throughout the country. Technology
will likely make available programs from other nations and over a national
educational microwave. However, local programs will continue to identify
the station as a community function and asset.

No segment of educational television has improved more directly in
quality than the community programming. Uniformity of growth of quality has been assured in all the ETV stations by the "package" of filmed and
video-taped programs which has come from the National Educational Television and Radio Center. This source and the steady increase of know-how
at the local level hold the brightest promise for the future in this phase of
the media.

As the quality of community programming improves, citizens are demanding that the station stay on the air six and seven days a week twelve
months of the year. Most community stations which have not been able
to have such schedules are looking forward to the day when they may serve
their communities on a time basis similar to commercial stations. They
ask, "How can we be the true alternate station unless we are on the air?"

ETV in terms of substantial utilization is an infant, certainly less than ten years old. Yet, no innovation has marched so quickly and confidently into the field of learning. It moves into the future of American education as a major resource.

REFERENCES

1. Stoddard, Alexander J., *Schools for Tomorrow: An Educator's Blueprint.* New York: The Fund for the Advancement of Education, 1957.
2. Wiles, Kimbal, *Supervision for Better Schools.* New York: Prentice-Hall, 1950.

WHAT WE KNOW ABOUT LEARNING FROM INSTRUCTIONAL TELEVISION

By Wilbur Schramm

The author is Director of the Institute for Communication Research, Stanford University.

THERE CAN NO LONGER BE any doubt that students learn efficiently from instructional television. The fact has been demonstrated now in hundreds of schools, by thousands of students, in every part of the United States and in several other countries. The list of subjects which schools and colleges have been able to teach effectively by television includes: arithmetic, algebra, geometry, calculus, accounting, consumer mathematics, physics, chemistry, biology, physiology, general science, engineering, psychology, sociology, anthropology, government, history, economics, electronics, humanities, art, music, philosophy, literature, spelling, physical education, reading, writing, social studies, health and safety, driver education, Spanish, French, German, Russian, English, typewriting, and slide rule. Over all this list, the conclusion of testers, school administrators, teachers, and students alike has been that the average student is likely to learn about as much from a television class as from ordinary classroom methods. In some cases he will learn more, and in some less, but over-all the conclusion has been "no significant difference."*

Now that we have approximately four hundred scientifically designed and statistically treated comparisons of ITV and classroom teaching, however, it is time to review that verdict. Do the early conclusions stand up under this massive testing? Under what conditions, for what students, and in what areas of subject matter, does instructional television teach best, and in which ones least? What do teachers and students think of classes by television? What does instructional television do to morale and to motivation? How does it interact with mental ability? This is the kind of question which is going to concern us in the following pages.

Much of the research on instructional television is not in the journals.

---

* See, for example, the two excellent reviews by Kumata (53 and 56 in the list of references appended to this paper), and the insightful article by Carpenter (19). There is also a useful review by Finn (35).

It exists in the form of mimeographed reports. The Ford Foundation, the Fund for the Advancement of Education, the United States Office of Education, and a number of school officials and researchers have made their collections of these reports available to us. As a result, we have been able to assemble 393 cases in which instructional television has been compared with other classroom teaching, 32 cases in which home instruction by television has been compared with classroom teaching, and 14 cases in which military instruction by television has been compared with face-to-face teaching, with what seemed to be adequate design, controls, and statistics. These experiments are not the only ones that have been made, but they are the only ones now available to us. They do not include, for example, any results from the massive Hagerstown project, on which significance figures have not yet been released. But in any case, these represent a much larger sampling of results than has ever before been put together, and on the basis of them we can speak with somewhat more confidence than before about instructional television.

THE BASIC DATA

1. ON LEARNING FROM TELEVISION

The following table sums up the result of the 393 comparisons in schools and colleges. "+TV" means that television was significantly superior (at the .05 level or better) to ordinary classroom teaching; "n.s." means not significant—no difference between television and face-to-face teaching at the .05 level; and "—TV" means that television was significantly inferior to ordinary classroom teaching at the .05 level or better. Thus the first box of the table should be read: In experiments on teaching mathematics in the third through sixth grades, television was significantly more effective in 14 cases, there was no significant difference in 21 cases, and in 3 cases television was significantly less effective than was ordinary classroom teaching.

This table tells us that the early conclusions do stand up. Instructional television is at least as effective as ordinary classroom instruction, when the results are measured by the usual final examinations or by standardized tests made by testing bureaus. This begs the question of whether the "intangibles" of televised teaching are as beneficial as those of ordinary classroom teaching, and this is a question which we must consider before we come to the end of this report. But employing the usual tests that schools use to measure the progress of their students, we can say with considerable confidence that in 65 percent of a very large number of comparisons, between televised and classroom teaching, there is no significant difference. In 21 percent, students learned significantly *more*, in 14 percent, they learned significantly *less*, from television.

School Level		Math.	Science	Social Studies	Humanities History Lit., Arts	Language Skills	Health, Safety	Total	
3d–6th	+TV	14	8	12	0	14	2	50	+TV
grades	n.s.	21	14	11	0	36	4	86	n.s.
	−TV	3	1	1	0	10	1	16	−TV
7th–9th	+TV	4	9	0	2	0	3	18	+TV
grades	n.s.	11	8	1	7	0	1	28	n.s.
	−TV	2	3	0	0	0	0	5	−TV
10–12th	+TV	0	3	3	4	1	1	12	+TV
grades	n.s.	10	7	17	17	6	0	57	n.s.
	−TV	5	3	0	9	4	0	21	−TV
College	+TV	0	1	1	0	0	1	3	+TV
	n.s.	4	26	24	11	12	7	84	n.s.
	−TV	0	1	4	3	1	4	13	−TV
Total	+TV	18	21	16	6	15	7	83	+TV
	n.s.	46	55	53	35	54	12	255	n.s.
	−TV	10	8	5	12	15	5	55	−TV

Total = 393*

It is clear that televised instruction has been used with greater success in the grades than in high school or college. This can be illustrated by figures derived from the preceding table:

	TV More Effective	No Significant Difference	TV Less Effective	N
	(Percent)	(Percent)	(Percent)	
Grades 3–9	33	56	11	203
High school	13	63	24	90
College	3	84	13	100

The results for grades two through nine are significantly different from those for high school and for college, as are also the differences for grades three to six and grades seven to nine taken separately.

Turning again to the large table, we can see that some subject-matter areas have apparently been taught by television more effectively than others. Mathematics and science, for example, have been outstandingly successful, and so have social studies. History, humanities, and literature have been less successful. Language skills and health and safety have been in the middle—neither so successful as the most effective subjects nor so ineffective as the humanities group. Many of these numbers are too small to show up on tests of significance, but nevertheless both science and social studies are significantly different from the humanities group. Other differ-

* 3d–6th grades different from 10th–12th, p = .001. 7th–9th different from 10th–12th, .01. 3d–9th different from 10th–college, .001. Both 3d–6th and 7th–9th different from college, .001. Science different from humanities, .01. Social studies different from humanities, .05.

ences must be considered only trends, although highly indicative and suggestive.

In several cases, there appear to be interactions of importance between subject matter and grade level. Televised language skills have been somewhat less effective than other televised subjects at the early elementary school level, although still over-all as effective as classroom teaching. Mathematics has been more effectively taught by television in the early grades than in high school. Televised social studies have been somewhat less effective in college, and the humanities group also appears to have been taught less effectively on television at the higher grade levels.

Thanks to the Chicago City Junior College study (32) and the San Francisco State College study (28) we are able to make some comparisons of televised instruction for students at home versus ordinary classroom teaching. The 32 such comparisons now available to us, all on the college level, may be tabulated as follows:

	Math.	Science	Social Studies	Humanities	Language Skills	Total
+TV	1	4	2	1	2	10
n.s.	2	4	8	1	6	21
−TV	0	1	0	0	0	1
					Total	32

It must be remembered that these home students are, in large part, adults who have been unable to finish their college education because they are home-bound. They are consequently highly motivated, and grateful for their opportunity to study by television. When the home-TV students are compared with students taught by television in the classroom, they have almost always done better. However, the unusually high motivation of the home students, and the rather negative attitudes of the classroom-TV students (who were assigned to an experimental section and deprived of the personal contact which other resident students had with the instructor) lead us to discount these latter comparisons, and not to record them here.

There are also a number of studies of television in military training. We have at hand 14 experimental comparisons of television vs. face-to-face teaching of military trainees. In six of these, the groups taught by television learned significantly more; in four cases, there was no significant difference, and in four the television group learned less.

2. Student Attitudes Toward Instructional Television

Students in grade school typically think they learn more from televised classes, whereas high school and college students are more doubtful. When students in various school systems were asked, "Do you think students learn more, the same, or less from a TV class?" they answered as follows:

	Florida Elem.	No. Carolina Elem.	Nebraska High School	Cincinnati High School	Kansas City High School	Florida High School
N =	(670)	(533)	(254)	(277)	(300)	(2014)
	(Percent)	(Percent)	(Percent)	(Percent)	(Percent)	(Percent)
More	72	77	35	30	57	31
Same	22	13	35	37	31	40
Less	6	10	30	33	12	29

This question was not often asked in the same way in college experiments, and therefore the results cannot be compared exactly. However, the general attitudes of college students toward ITV are, if anything, less favorable than those of high school students. Students of psychology and chemistry at Penn State (18) rated the amount of learning about the same for televised and classroom instruction, but students in *non-TV class* rated psychology *as a subject* somewhat higher than did TV students. At Miami University only two attitude comparisons in 10 were favorable to TV (59), and only one of these was significant; whereas three comparisons were significant in the direction of classroom teaching. Seven out of the 10 responses became less favorable to TV as the course progressed. In a Purdue calculus class the attitude toward ITV worsened as the course went on (29). San Francisco State and the Chicago Junior College (32, 28) both found that the students they assigned to classroom TV were more negative toward the course than were ordinary classroom students, and more negative toward teaching by television than were students who viewed the class at home.

There is a great deal of material on the morale and attitudes of TV students which we cannot refer to here, except by saying that, in general, elementary school children are enthusiastic over television classes, high school students are much less so, and college students are equivocal or even in some cases unfavorable. If now we add home-TV students (who are, for the most part, adults taking a course by television that they could not take in residence) we have a U-shaped distribution of attitudes: The attitudes of grade school children, at one end, and adult home students, on the other, very favorable; the attitudes of high school and college students in the lower parts of the U.

We do not mean to say, however, that there is a simple relationship between age or grade level and attitude. Rather, there is considerable evidence that attitudes tend to be specific to subjects and teachers.

For example, in Jefferson County, Kentucky, almost 100 percent of the children preferred the televised science class to the regular class, but less than half preferred the televised social studies (50). A very large sample of Southwestern Indiana high school students (82) gave these judgments on four of their televised classes:

	Like TV Class	Think They Learn More From It	N
Government and socio-economics	66.0	60.3	1016
U.S. history	58.8	52.0	1866
Geometry	37.1	24.5	207
Junior high science	72.1	69.3	3805

Norfolk students reported that they liked televised science more, televised geometry less, than regular classes (66, 67).

Two hundred sixty-seven Nebraska high school students gave the following judgments on six of their classes (64, 65):

	Learned More			Enjoyed More		
	From TV	No Difference	Classroom	TV	No Difference	Classroom
Algebra		×				×
Geometry		×				×
English	×				×	
Art	×			×		
Physics	×				×	
Spanish			×			×

It is worthy of note in this table that enjoyment apparently goes along with learning.

Attitudes of college students toward ITV are also specific to subject matter. Students in five Oregon colleges and universities (82) felt that their televised chemistry course was in general better than classroom teaching in stimulating their learning, but that a course in literature was about the same in that respect as classroom teaching, and a course in English composition was if anything less effective than classroom teaching. Students in Chicago (32) expressed themselves as being more willing to take their physical science course by TV than their social science, and more willing to take social science than humanities by TV. At New York University (52) students in two classes were asked during the first and during the second semester whether they preferred the TV section or an ordinary lecture section. These were the responses:

	English		Cultural Heritage	
	1st Sem. (Percent)	2d Sem. (Percent)	1st Sem. (Percent)	2d Sem. (Percent)
Preferred TV section	31	20	51	78
Preferred non-TV	69	80	49	22

Thus the stock of the composition course went down, while that of the cultural history course went up. At San Francisco State (28) both classroom-TV and home-TV students were asked whether they preferred TV or non-TV sections of three courses. Home students were more favorable to TV. Psychology was most favorably rated among the three courses. The responses:

	N	Dislike TV Much (Percent)	Prefer Classroom (Percent)	TV Satisfactory (Percent)	Prefer TV (Percent)	Enthusiastic Over TV (Percent)
Psychology						
Campus TV	37	16	43	32	3	5
At-home TV	50	8	18	34	24	16
Economics						
Campus TV	33	39	36	15	6	3
At-home TV	41	12	46	32	2	2
Basic communication						
Campus TV	24	12	71	17	0	0
At-home TV	29	10	17	52	10	10

In addition to the U-shaped curve of attitudes by age, then, we have a linear trend which might be described as being more favorable to subjects where demonstrations are important (for example, natural science and art), less favorable toward subjects where student-teacher interaction and classroom discussion and drill are important (English composition and social studies). We shall have more to say about these two trends. But even these do not fully describe the pattern of student attitudes toward ITV. Even the location of seats in a large classroom may directly relate to attitudes, as Penn State found (18) when it plotted the seat assignments of students who asked to be transferred out of the TV course. And in a number of colleges and high schools, surprising differences in attitudes have appeared in different sections of the same televised course, differences that appeared only to relate to the classroom teachers. In other words, it appears that a large number of non-TV elements enter into the making of attitudes toward televised instruction.

The continuing measurements of student attitudes at Penn State are especially interesting because the television program there has now been under way for seven years. During the early years of that period, Carpenter and Greenhill report (18, 41) there was "a gradual average change to a somewhat higher level of acceptance." Furthermore, "students appear to be discriminating more clearly than formerly between televised presentations and other more central factors in their instruction. For example, the quality and characteristics of the instructor, the quality of the presentation and the significance of the course material . . ." Television "as such" ceases to be very important; it is merely another instrument, like a telephone or a slide projector; it is a standard way of teaching, and the important questions are who teaches, what does he teach, and how. When the novelty wears off as it has at Penn State, if TV courses gain the reputation that they offer the best instruction a college can provide in a given subject, then there will be no question, the Penn State people believe, about their acceptance by serious students.

3. Teacher Attitudes Toward Instructional Television

Most teachers who teach on television come to like it. Those who do not teach tend to be suspicious and resistant. This opposition usually is short-lived in the case of elementary teachers, most of whom come to like and depend on television as one part of their teaching resource. In Hagerstown, where perhaps the most extensive experiment in closed-circuit ITV has been conducted, teachers were asked whether they would prefer to teach the class they are now teaching with or without the aid of television; 83 percent said they preferred to do it *with* television (42). High school teachers seem to be, on the average, a bit less favorable and more resistant, but among Detroit teachers, 68 percent reported that their attitudes toward television had become more favorable since they have had some experience using it in the classroom (26). And country-wide among elementary and high school teachers and administrators there has been a generally favorable evaluation of ITV, as the following tabulation indicates. In six school systems teachers and administrators were asked whether they believed students learned more, the same, or less from televised instruction as compared to ordinary classroom instruction:

	Teachers:					Principals:		
	West Florida	Wich-ita	Mil-waukee	Miami	Ana-heim	Mil-waukee	North Carolina	Ana-heim
N =	(45)	(33)	(51)	(82)	(93)	(9)	(163)	(101)
	(Per-cent	(Per-cent)	(Per-cent)	(Per-cent)	(Per-cent)	(Per-cent)	(Per-cent)	(Per-cent)
Believe Students Learn MORE	56	48	40	45	54	33	59	87
SAME	33	16	47	48	37	56	37	13
LESS	11	36	13	7	9	14	4	0

The real center of teacher resistance to instructional television is in the colleges. Researchers studying the Oregon System of Higher Education (83) found "considerable resistance by individual professors." The Dean of the College of Liberal Arts at the State University of Iowa reported, after a survey, that his faculty was unfavorable to any extensive use of TV in teaching (84). The events at Compton College show that when television is introduced without adequate preparation and faculty support, this resistance may become explosive.

But if the following figures from Penn State are representative, then college faculties also tend to become more favorable toward ITV. These are responses to a question asked Penn State teachers on the quality of TV instruction as compared to regular classroom teaching (17):

	1955–56	1956–57
	N = (48)	(55)
	(Percent)	(Percent)
TV better	10	22
TV same	33	38
TV worse	52	38
No answer	3	0
Don't know	2	2

And even in the Oregon system where "considerable resistance" was found, faculty attitudes were more favorable than unfavorable:

	Oregon College of Education	Oregon State College	University of Oregon	Willamette University
	N = (28)	(171)	(123)	(26)
	(Percent)	(Percent)	(Percent)	(Percent)
Excellent approach to teaching; should have extensive use	7	17	14	0
Pretty good approach; should have some use	68	45	44	42
Haven't made up my mind	11	16	19	15
Rather poor approach; should be used in limited situations	14	18	19	31
Should not be used for instruction	0	2	2	12
No answer	0	2	2	0

Teachers discriminate sharply among TV courses. Asked to compare the progress their TV classes were making as compared to the previous non-TV classes, a sample of Dade County, Florida, elementary school teachers answered as follows (23, 24):

	More Progress	Same	Less	N
	(Percent)	(Percent)	(Percent)	
Science	67	25	8	52
Music	23	52	25	48
Art	25	44	31	52
Physical education	52	43	5	48
Spanish	26	53	21	47
Health and safety	50	43	7	48

Asked which telecasts were most valuable to them, a large group of Anaheim, California, teachers and principals voted the science and social studies classes most helpful, the Spanish class only slightly less helpful, and the arithmetic telecast of comparatively little help (1). A sample of 1,191

Milwaukee elementary teachers and principals (62) gave the following judgments as to which telecasts they wanted as resources:

	Primary Teachers (Percent)	Intermediate (Percent)	Upper (Percent)	Principals (Percent)
Art	71	62	69	59
Science	67	74	53	80
Arithmetic	18	9	10	27
Reading	18	12	18	24
Language arts	16	15	17	21
Social studies	32	33	26	49
Music	50	33	38	47
Physical education	54	43	22	53
Foreign language	12	23	16	34
Handwriting	12	13	6	30
Spelling	6	4	2	16

The most favored courses seem to be the ones that can bring useful demonstrations (science) or in which the teacher needs special help (physical education, music, art); the least favored courses are those that are built around classroom drill (reading, writing, spelling, arithmetic).

There is no comparable report of college teachers' preferences over a broad range of televised courses.

THE CHIEF QUESTIONS

Beyond the basic problems of learning and attitudes, several questions are asked oftener than others about instructional television. Among these are:

1. IS THERE ANY KIND OF STUDENT WHO PROFITS MORE THAN OTHER KINDS FROM INSTRUCTIONAL TELEVISION?

A bright student learns more than a slow student, a motivated student more than an unmotivated one, in almost any learning situation. But given equally bright, or equally motivated students, is there any level of ability or motivation at which learning by television is markedly superior or inferior?

On these problems the data are muddy. Here, for example, is at least a partial tabulation of the studies of mental ability as related to instructional television:

Fritz, 1952. Military subjects at Fort Monmouth. Divided radio electronics students into high and low aptitude groups. Some of each group were taught by TV. Found no significant difference in scores of TV and non-TV groups when equated for ability (37).

Kanner, et al., 1954. Split both TV and non-TV groups of basic trainees at Camp Gordon into high and low aptitude groups. N.s.d. in high group, but 10 of 17 tests in low group favored TV; other 7 tests n.s.d. (48).

Williams, 1954. Taught four groups of students at University of Toronto by TV, radio, lecture and reading assignments, respectively. TV higher than lecture in high and low ability groups, but equal in average group (97).

Kumata, 1958. Michigan State University students. Unable to reproduce Kanner's finding of superiority of TV instruction for low ability students (54).

Seibert, 1958. Purdue University students in English composition. Found that low ability TV students compared less favorably with control group than did high ability TV students (79).

Seibert, 1958. Purdue University students in freshman mathematics. No important interactions between mental ability and method of instruction (80).

Macomber and Siegel, 1960. Miami University students in educational psychology, economics, physiology, zoology, and government. Breaking both TV and control groups by quartiles on mental ability, they found 1 significant difference out of 4 in top quartile—this in favor of TV group. In bottom quartile, found 2 significant differences out of 4 in favor of TV, 1 in favor of control. Breaking the groups by halves on mental ability, they found no significant differences out of 10 in the upper, 2 significant differences out of 10 in the lower half. Both these were in favor of the control group (59).

When the research evidence is as unclear as this, observations by experienced teachers may be as valuable as a research study. But these observations, too, are far from unanimous. Milwaukee teachers voted nearly five to one that TV was better for the fast than the slow learners. Anaheim teachers and principals, asked which ability group benefits most from televised instruction, responded as follows:

	Teachers	Principals
	(Percent)	(Percent)
Fast learners	17	0
Average learners	28	38
Slow learners	31	25
No difference	24	38

A group of 226 North Carolina teachers were asked whether ITV or classroom instruction was better for the different ability groups, and responded thus:

	TV Better	No Difference	Non-TV Better
	(Percent)	(Percent)	(Percent)
Superior students	93	2	5
Average students	79	8	13
Slow learners	73	9	18

It may well be, as some recent and unpublished research suggests, that both the brightest and the slowest students may derive some differential benefit from televised teaching—the former, because they learn rapidly anyway, and television can theoretically offer them a great number and variety of responses to learn; the latter, because television concentrates their attention as the classroom often does not. But it must be admitted that we do not yet understand the relation of mental ability to differential learning from television.

It is the general feeling of most persons who have taught or done research in connection with instructional television that motivation is closely related to the results they have obtained. Erickson and Chausow, for example, thought lack of motivation probably explained the lower results of students who were assigned to television sections, just as high motivation explained the very good results obtained in teaching home students by television (32). But the results have been equivocal in cases where the motivation has been measured and controlled. For example, when Mullin motivated some eleventh-graders (not others) by offering a monetary reward for a high examination score, he found that the motivated students learned more than the others from a televised program on education, and concluded that the classroom was probably a better place than the TV room for unmotivated students. This seems to make sense, in that the classroom teacher may well be better able to take care of individual problems and thus raise motivation. But when Dreher and Beatty (28) measured need-achievement in their TV and classroom students, they could find no significant difference in the amount of learning by television or classroom groups among the high or the low achievers.

No significant results have yet turned up in the literature to suggest that any other common personality traits make for greater or less learning from televised instruction as compared to classroom teaching.

2. DOES SIZE OF CLASS MAKE ANY DIFFERENCE IN LEARNING FROM INSTRUCTIONAL TELEVISION?

Students generally prefer to be in small rather than in large classes, but no differential effect of class size on learning from ITV has been reported in cases where viewing conditions were equally satisfactory. Penn State (16) varied the size of television classes between 19 and 120 students without producing differential results in learning.

3. DOES TELEVISED TEACHING MAKE ANY DIFFERENCE IN RETENTION OF SUBJECT MATTER OVER A LONG PERIOD?

One study of military training (48) found that television students remembered more of the subject matter one month later. Another military study (13) and five civilian studies (11, 17, 55, 72, 80) found no significant differences.

4. IS THERE A NOVELTY EFFECT IN THE REPORTED RESULTS?

It may be taken for granted that there is. In some cases, it can be isolated. For example, an early military study (1952) found that trainees preferred to study from, and learned more from, lessons which they thought were kinescopes (television recordings) than from films—even though the "films" were identical to, or poorer in quality than, the kinescopes. Several years later (1955), the finding could not be repeated (76). It was assumed, therefore, that the novelty effect of television teaching had worn off.

A number of the studies in school systems and colleges, however, have records of three or more years of experimentation with instructional television, during which time their students have in many cases taken a number of courses by television. Yet there seems to be no downward curve of achievement in these studies. Many observers feel that the growth in skill at using television counterbalances the loss of novelty effect.

It must be remembered, also, that the novelty effect is not always favorable. Many college students have not welcomed the opportunity to study by television when they have first been offered it. Many students have been made self-conscious and resistant, rather than achievement-minded, when researchers have paid more attention to them.

Although we cannot rule out the novelty or the Hawthorne effect, still there is little evidence to indicate that these might be giving us, over-all, spuriously high scores from ITV classes.

5. ARE WE MEASURING THE "INTANGIBLES"?

The more "intangible" they are, the less likely it is that they are being measured. Yet the question is important, and must be faced seriously.

The intangible qualities which people most often talk about in connection with supposed lacks in televised teaching are those related to social interaction. It is contended that instructional television substitutes for direct personal contacts, for the give and take of discussion and recital, a passive relationship of the student to a televised image. Students of television now tend to believe that the viewer is much less passive than formerly thought, but the rest of the statement is manifestly true: television cuts down on interaction within the classroom. What effect does it have? In the San Francisco study (28) there is evidence that students in television classes knew fewer of their classmates than students in nontelevised classes. In the lower grades, where pupils are together all day, and television absorbs only a minor part of the time, this result would not be expected. There is no evidence to indicate that reduced interaction in the classroom has any harmful effect on children's personalities, or on their social skills, although this is conceivable. Milwaukee teachers rejected overwhelmingly the suggestion that the TV classroom is "cold, or lacking in human warmth" (62).

The other set of "intangibles" most often mentioned are those related to individual differences. It is contended that one of the functions of education is to help a child solve some of his own problems. These may be solved either by personal counseling by the teacher or another official, or by skills and insights derived from the classroom. The skills may be measured, but the outcomes are not. Therefore, an important set of outcomes may not be represented in ordinary measurements of learning. These contentions are manifestly true, and to the extent that television makes it harder for the student to get individual counseling or to assemble his learning around his personal needs, then there may indeed be some intangible loss. The question is whether, in a well-planned learning experience, of which television is a part, there need be any less opportunity for a student to solve his personal problems.

The research has so far been unable to locate any other intangible losses resulting from instruction by television. There has been some attempt to find out whether televised teaching—because it presents an "authority" rather than inviting democratic discussion—might develop authoritarian personalities in students. Carpenter and Greenhill (18) found no evidence to confirm this. The same researchers, however, found that a group of students taught by the discussion group method scored higher on a test of problem-solving than did a comparable group taught by television. In general, however, television students have held their own in tests of critical thinking, problem-solving, and other non-rote aspects of learning.

6. WHAT DO WE KNOW ABOUT THE RELATION OF FORMS OF TELEVISED
TEACHING TO LEARNING?

There is a great deal of research on the forms of effective teaching from film,* and much of this is undoubtedly applicable. The amount of such research concerning television is growing. However, the net result so far is to reinforce the belief that good teaching is much the same on television or films or the lecture platform.

A student who wants to learn can learn from a great variety of experiences. Williams (97) assigned parallel groups to television, radio, and classroom teaching, and still another group to read in the library and attend no classes at all. All these groups learned, although the television group learned a little more. Stuit and others (85) compared a variety of ways of studying political science: TV lecture, TV discussion, small and large group discussion, and lecture. There was little difference in learning. Brandon (14) compared the same individuals communicating the same

---

* For example, see May, M. A., and Lumsdaine, A. A. *Learning from Film.* New Haven: Yale University, 1958. Also, Hoban, C. A., and Van Ormer, *Instructional Film Research, 1918–1950,* Report SDC 269-7-19, Port Washington, N.Y.: Special Devices Center, 1950.

material in the form of a lecture, an interview, and a panel discussion, and found no significant differences.

One trend in the literature is toward simplicity of treatment. Although Klapper (52) found that students liked TV-teaching better with a number of visuals than when it was straight lecture, Carpenter and Greenhill (18) found that lecture and blackboard alone made for more learning than lecture plus charts, plus models, plus training films, plus visiting speakers, plus dramatizations, and so forth. A replication of this experiment in another class, however, resulted in no significant difference, which is itself a useful finding. The implication is that complexity of presentation, and a great variety of visual cues, may distract a student from the main principles of the presentation. This was tested by Kumata (74) who presented two advertisements, one with visuals in color projected on a large screen, the other with black and white visuals projected on a television-size screen. He found that subjects remembered more details from the colored version, but remembered *principles* better from the black and white version.

One of the rules held to by television professionals seems not to apply to teaching by television. This is "eye-contact," meaning that the speaker looks the viewer directly in the eye. Westley and Mobius (93) found this made no difference in learning.

WHAT WE KNOW AND MOST NEED TO KNOW ABOUT LEARNING FROM INSTRUCTIONAL TELEVISION

On the basis of this information, what can we say about the process of learning from instructional television?

We can say confidently that students learn from it, and that they learn fast and efficiently. But of that we have been fairly certain for some time. The further step we have now taken has put us in position to say something about the conditions under which a student learns *more* from television, and something about *what* he learns from television.

But before turning to those matters, let us consider for a moment the central fact that apparently about as much learning takes place in a television class as in a nontelevision class. In a sense, this is a remarkable discovery. As Hoban says (43), there is every reason to expect that there should be *less* learning in a television class. There is an absence of the intellectual give and take believed to characterize some of the most effective teaching. There is little opportunity to adjust to individual differences, rates, and needs. The student can't so readily feed back his responses, or signal his lack of understanding, or clear things up with a question. There is indeed good reason to expect that conditions would make for a less favorable outcome and a less well-informed student.

However, we have seen that 86 percent of 393 experimental comparisons in life situations have resulted in as much or more learning in a television, as compared to a conventional, classroom. Why should this be? Is it something in the quality of the teaching, or something in the nature of the process?

One of the significant things about the literature of instructional television is the repeated observation that teachers who are going on television feel the need to put many additional hours into preparation. Some of these teachers are given an entire term free of teaching, or put on special appointment for the summer term, in order to get ready for teaching a television class. Ordinarily, when one teaches a television class, he teaches nothing else: one class. And when a teacher is putting one of his courses on television, a great effort is made with lesson plans, student guide, workbook, visuals, and so forth.

Remember that these teachers are not teaching their television courses for the first time. In many cases, they have taught the subject for years, in the classroom. They have taught it along with half a dozen other subjects. They have never before insisted on a free term to prepare, or trial films to see themselves teach, or a schedule reduced to one course; nor have they made such efforts with outlines and materials. Indeed, they have never had the opportunity to indulge in such relative luxuries.

Regardless of whether the class is televised on open circuit or closed circuit, it puts the teacher's classroom on *open* circuit. The teaching is on the screen for all the teacher's colleagues to watch. The sanctum of the classroom is opened to critical eyes. And therefore, we are getting better prepared and more skillful teaching on television, and this is doubtless overcoming some of the disadvantages which result from lack of classroom interaction.

But let us look further at those disadvantages. What are the great weaknesses of television? It doesn't stop to answer questions. It doesn't readily permit class discussion. It can't very efficiently conduct drill. It doesn't adjust very well to individual differences. It tends to encourage a passive form of learning rather than an active seeking.

It also has great strengths. It is very good at bringing demonstrations to the classroom: it lets everyone look through a microscope at the same time, gives all the medical students a good view of surgery, handles films and other changes from straight classroom presentation with a minimum of transitional difficulty. It lets a school or a college share its *best* teachers, rather than rationing them. It provides a change of pace, often a lift, for the classroom. It brings a sense of timeliness to classes where that helps. It concentrates attention.

These advantages are not small. They help to explain why television has not done so badly in the classroom as many observers expected it would.

More important, they help us to understand why certain subject-matter areas have been taught more effectively than others. We could predict, for example, that courses which gain from great demonstrations (as science does) would gain from television. One would expect science to gain more from television treatment than, for example, philosophy, which depends largely on clear verbalization. One could predict that subjects like reading, writing, and spelling would not gain much from being televised, because mastery of those skills depends so largely on individual practice. We could predict that social studies, which gain from timely demonstration, would gain more from television than a course in history. This is approximately the pattern we find in the table on page 54.

Clearly there is an interaction between characteristics of subject matter and characteristics of the student and the school at a given grade level.

In grade school, television is still fresh and interesting to children. As a teaching device, it is accepted as simply another instrument from which they can learn—like the textbook, the film projector, the language laboratory, and the blackboard. They have never gotten used to any kind of instruction that does not include television. They take to it naturally, and seldom think about alternative ways they might be learning.

Things are different when television comes to high school or college students. In general, they are less favorable to education anyway. Education has lost its edge. Many of them are unwilling learners. Furthermore, they have become accustomed to a different kind of teaching. They are used to asking a question when they feel the need to ask one. They have learned to enjoy, many of them, the classroom interaction. In college, many of the students are extremely serious about career goals, and personal contact with a professor is something they feel they are paying for. They tend to regard a television screen as a place to look for entertainment, not a place to study with a professor.

In addition to this, students at the higher levels typically are aware of unfavorable faculty attitudes toward television. The college teacher, in particular, is threatened by the idea of having his classroom opened up to critical eyes. He sometimes regards colleagues who are successful on television as showmen, rather than scholars. These attitudes are communicated to students, and it is not surprising that motivation at the higher levels has sometimes been less than in the early grades or in the case of home students.

There is a difference that is still more important between the meaning of television to the lower grades and to the higher ones and college.

In grade school, television is typically thought of as only a part of the learning experience, and efforts are taken to integrate it, just as the textbook, the film, the blackboard, the class drill, are integrated. The teacher is with the child five hours a day, and only half an hour or so of that is given over to television teaching. Therefore, the lesson is carefully built around the television experience. Care is taken to motivate the children to want to learn from television, and to ask the teacher the questions they cannot ask television directly. The program is thus prepared for, and followed up, and is accompanied by other learning experiences (such as drill and discussion) which television cannot so readily accomplish.

In other words, it is usually the classroom teacher, rather than the television teacher, who is in command of the situation. The TV teacher is a valued ally and helper. But a teaching team is in operation, the different roles are meshed, and the student still has a teacher of his own to give him personal attention and help him progress in his own best way.

Colleges are much less likely to integrate a television course into a broader course. Whereas in grade school television is usually thought of as a resource, and the classroom teacher is still in command, in college television takes over, and the television teacher is in command. In both high school and college, the administrations are more likely to put a good teacher on the screen and let him give a lecture course.

It is interesting to us that no college has yet used this concept in what seems to be one of its most exciting applications. Recall the pattern of an English university like Oxford or Cambridge. These universities typically offer a limited series of lectures each year, voluntary to students, and supposedly given by the greatest authorities who care to expose their ideas in this way. Some of the students go to a number of lecture series; some go to almost none. The chief activity of the student is to prepare for a continuing series of intensive tutorial sessions with teachers, to work in laboratories, and to read for a challenging set of examinations. This pattern is one to which television seems almost ideally suited. Why not put the best lectures on television, on a voluntary basis? This would require fewer lectures, and better ones. It would leave more time for individual study and guidance. It would put the emphasis where it seems it ought to be: on active learning by the student.

So far as we know, television has never been employed in that way by an American university, and in many ways it seems an opportunity lost. If the colleges are not going to integrate their television teaching into such a learning plan as the grade schools use, then this voluntary lecture plan seems one of the most promising ways to use it.

One of the keys to understanding the pattern which we have been describing in this paper is the extent to which instructional television is perceived as different and as a threat. It was much more often so perceived when it was very new, and it is more often so perceived now in college than in the grades. The schools which have used it for a few years now tend to take it in stride. They realize that it can do certain things very well and other things not well at all. The attitude studies referred to in the preceding pages are full of teachers' criticisms of the way they themselves were using television. The chief mistake they admit to is the same one, from school to school: not enough "follow-up time." Not enough time to answer the questions, to add the necessary drill and relate the television material to other material, and otherwise integrate it into the package. When there is a "team" in charge of the teaching, when the classroom teacher is centrally concerned with the total learning experience, then this kind of problem usually gets solved. Television comes to seem no more different than other aids to good learning. Television is not in command as it typically is in college-televised teaching. It can be much used or little used, as works best. It can be leaned on heavily for science, and hardly at all for spelling or arithmetic. It is not threatening; it is a friend and aider.

The concept of a teaching team and an arsenal of resources is about to be strengthened by the availability of self-teaching programs and devices. These will aid the teacher in drill and practice, as television aids him by contributing expert lecturing and skillful demonstrations. They will complement television where it is weakest, and leave the teacher freer to take care of individual learning problems, and to help the student combine the various resources open to him.

Neither these self-teaching devices nor television will put the classroom teacher out of business. Indeed, our observation is that the classroom teacher, who wondered if she might be obsolescent when the television teacher appeared, is now really more important than ever. We are encouraged in this belief by reading this statement in the report of the Philadelphia Public Schools:

> "The classroom teacher has emerged as a key entity of the 'teacher team.' Excellent TV lessons are enhanced by skillful handling of pupil questions, lesson extension and application. Pupil learnings and attitudes are determined by the skill, enthusiasm and attitudes of the classroom teacher. TV will not supplant teachers: rather it creates the need for more good teachers." (74)

To the researcher, as well as the educator, this has an implication: that he would do well to shift his sights from the uniqueness of television to the totality of the learning behavior and process. We have no intention of giving advice to educational administrators, but perhaps may be permitted to say a few words to researchers.

It is still of great importance to clear up, if we can, the interaction of television learning with different levels of ability. It is also clearly of importance to find out more about the "intangibles" which may be differentially learned or not learned from television and which are not measured by the usual end-of-term test. And there are a number of questions of what goes on the screen or on the sound track which need to be cleared up.

But the most important research on instructional television, now, it seems to us, is research on the total process of which television is a part. When Carpenter talks about television research as system research (19), he is, in effect, asking how television fits into the learning experience. How can it be used best, and for what? How can it best be combined with other experiences, to make learning a given subject most efficient? In other words, we are really asking how children most efficiently learn to read, or to spell, or to compute, or to understand the Second Law of Thermodynamics, or to speak French, or to discriminate good literature from bad, or to internalize the goals and values of their nation and their culture. We are not suggesting that nothing is known about those things, merely that much more needs to be known. One of the great things about instructional television, as about self-teaching devices, is that they necessarily focus our attention on the larger process if we are to understand the part they play in it.

REFERENCES

1. Anaheim School District. *Preliminary Report of ITV Project for School Year 1959–60.* Anaheim, California, October 1960. (Mimeo.)

2. Anderson, G. R., and VanderMeer, A. W. "A Comparative Study of the Effectiveness of Lessons on the Slide Rule Presented via Television and in Person." *The Mathematics Teacher,* 47: 323–27; 1954.

3. Baldwin, N. W., Jr. "Subjective Measurements in Television." *Amer. Psychologist,* 9: 231–34; 1954.

4. Barrow, L. C., Jr., and Westley, B. H. " 'Exploring the News': An Experiment on the Relative Effectiveness of Radio and TV Versions of a Children's News Program." *Audio-Visual Comm. Rev.,* 1959, 7, 14–23. (Also in Schramm, see 77 below.)

5. Becker, S. L., and Dallinger, C. A. "The Effect of Instructional Methods upon Achievement and Attitudes in Communication Skills." *Speech Monogr.,* 27: 70–76; 1960.

6. Becker, S. L., Dunlap, R., and Gerber, J. C. *A Comparison of Three Methods of Teaching Modern Literature.* Iowa City: State University of Iowa, June 1957. (Mimeo.)

7. Becker, S. L., Murray, J. N., Jr., and Bechtoldt, H. P. *Teaching by the Discussion Method.* Iowa City: State University of Iowa, 1958. (Mimeo.)

8. Belson, W. A. "Learning and Attitude Changes Resulting from Viewing a Television Series 'Bon Voyage.' " *Brit. Journ. Ed. Psychol.,* 26: 31–38; 1959.

9. Bennett, J. J. *Accounting I on Closed Circuit Television.* University, Alabama: University of Alabama, 1958. (Mimeo.)

10. Bennett, J. J. *Trigonometry by Means of Closed Circuit Television.* University, Alabama: University of Alabama, 1958. (Mimeo.)

11. Benschoter, R. P., and Charles, D. C. "Retention of Classroom and Television Learning." *Journ. Appl. Psychol.,* 41: 253–56; 1957.

12. Bobren, Howard M. "Student Attitudes Toward Instructional Television: Additional Evidence." *Audio-Visual Comm. Rev.,* 8: 281–83; 1960.

13. Boone, W. F. *Evaluation of the U.S. Naval Academy Educational Television as a Teaching Aid.* Report 7010. Annapolis, Maryland: U.S. Naval Academy, 1956.

14. Brandon, J. R. "The Relative Effectiveness of Lecture, Interview, and Discussion Methods of Presenting Factual Information by Television." *Speech Monogr.*, 23: 118; 1956.

15. Bundy, Wayne. *An Experimental Study of the Relative Effectiveness of Television Presentational Techniques and Conventional Classroom Procedures in Promoting Initial Comprehension of Basic Verb Form Concepts in Elementary Spanish.* Detroit, Michigan: University of Detroit, Department of Communication Arts, 1959. (Mimeo.—Abstracted version in Schramm, see 77 below.)

16. Capraro, T. C. "A Study of the Effects of Class Size, Supervisory Status, and Two-Way Communication upon Learning and Attitudes of AF-ROTC Cadets in a Closed-Circuit Instructional Television Program." *Dissertation Abstr.*, 17: 20; 1957.

17. Carpenter, C. R., and Greenhill, L. P. *An Investigation of Closed Circuit Television for Teaching University Courses.* Instructional Television Project Report Number I. University Park, Pennsylvania: Pennsylvania State University, 1955.

18. Same. Report Number II. 1958.

19. Carpenter, C. R. "Approaches to Promising Areas of Research in the Field of Instructional Television." *New Teaching Aids for the American Classroom,* Stanford, California: Institute for Communication Research, 1960, pp. 73–94.

20. Cincinnati Public Schools. *Report of Three Experiments in the Use of Television in Instruction.* Cincinnati, Ohio, 1959. (Mimeo.)

21. Coleman, W. H., Jr., Dutton, E., and Bookout, J. C. *Learning Aural-Oral Spanish Skills by Television.* University, Alabama: University of Alabama, 1960.

22. Columbus Public Schools. *Greater Columbus Area ETV Project, 1959–1960.* Interim Report. Columbus, Ohio, 1960. (Mimeo.)

23. Dade County Public Schools. *Educational Television Experiment, 1957–1958.* Miami, Florida, 1958. (Mimeo.)

24. Same. Report of the Project in the Third Year, 1959–1960. Miami, Florida, 1960. (Mimeo.)

25. Davies, V., Gross, E., and Short, J. F., Jr. *Experiments in Teaching Effectiveness Applied to Introductory Sociology.* Pullman, Washington: State College of Washington, 1958. (Mimeo.)

26. Detroit Public Schools. *The Television Teaching Project.* Report for the Year 1958–1959. Detroit, Michigan, 1959. (Mimeo.)

27. Same. Report for the year 1959–60. (Mimeo.)

28. Dreher, R. E., and Beatty, W. H. *An Experimental Study of College Instruction Using Broadcast Television.* Instructional Television Research, Project Number One. San Francisco, California: San Francisco State College, 1958.

29. Dyer-Bennet, J., Fuller, W. R., Seibert, W. F., and Shanks, M. E. "Teaching Calculus by Closed Circuit Television." *Amer. Math. Monthly*, 65: 430–39; 1958.

30. Ellery, J. B. *A Pilot Study of the Nature of Aesthetic Experiences Associated with Television and Its Place in Education.* Detroit, Michigan: Wayne State University, 1959.

31. Englehart, M. D., Schwachtgen, and Nee, N. M. "Summary Report on the Instructional Experiment in High School Physics in the Chicago Public Schools." *Audio-Visual Comm. Rev.*, 6: 157; 1958.

32. Erickson, C. G., and Chausow, H. M. *Chicago's TV College—Final Report*

of a Three-Year Experiment. Chicago, Illinois: Chicago City Junior College, 1960. (Multilithed.)

33. Evans, R. I. "An Examination of Students' Attitudes Toward Television as a Medium of Instruction in a Psychology Course." *Journ. Appl. Psychol.*, 40: 32–34; 1956.

34. Evans, R. I., Roney, H. B., and McAdams, W. J. "An Evaluation of the Effectiveness of Instruction and Audience Reaction to Programming in an Educational Television Station." *Journ. Appl. Psychol.*, 39: 277–79; 1955.

35. Finn, J. D. "Television and Education: A Review of Research." *Audio-Visual Comm. Rev.*, 1: 106–26; 1953.

36. Florida West Coast Project for the Utilization of Television in Large-Class Teaching. First Year Report and Evaluation, 1959–1960. Tampa and St. Petersburg, Florida, 1960. (Mimeo.)

37. Frank, J. H. "An Evaluation of Closed Circuit Television for Interceptor Pilot Training." *Dissertation Abstracts*, 15: 2060–61; 1955.

38. Fritz, M. F., Humphrey, J. E., Greenlee, J. A., and Madison, R. L. *Survey of Television Utilization in Army Training.* Report SDC 530-01-1, Port Washington, Long Island, N.Y.: Special Devices Center, 1952.

39. Gordon, O. J., Nordquist, E. C., and Engar, K. M. *Teaching the Use of the Slide Rule via Television.* Salt Lake City, Utah: University of Utah, 1959. (Mimeo.)

40. Grasslight, J. H. "Learning via Television Instructor." In Adams, J. C., Carpenter, C. R., and Smith, D. R., eds., *College Teaching by Television.* Washington, D.C.: American Council on Education, 1958, p. 46.

41. Greenhill, L. P., Carpenter, C. R., and Ray, W. S. "Further Studies of the Use of Television for University Teaching." *Audio-Visual Comm. Rev.*, 4: 200–215; 1956.

42. Hagerstown Board of Education. *Closed Circuit Television Teaching in Washington County, 1958–59.* Hagerstown, Maryland: Board of Education, 1959.

43. Hoban, C. F. "Hope and Fulfillment in Educational Television Research," *Audio-Visual Comm. Rev.*, 6: 165–71; 1958.

44. Husband, R. W. "Television vs. Classroom for Learning General Psychology." *Amer. Psychologist*, 9: 181–83; 1954.

45. Irwin, J. V., and Aronson, A. E. *Television Teaching, Conventional Lecture vs. Highly Visualized Film Presentation.* Research Bulletin 11. Madison, Wis.: University of Wisconsin Television Laboratory, 1958. (Mimeo.)

46. Kanner, J. H., and Rosenstein, A. J. "Television in Army Training: Color vs. Black and White." *Audio-Visual Comm. Rev.*, 8: 243–52, and 9: 44–49, 1960.

47. Kanner, J. H., Runyon, R. P., and Desiderato, O. *Television in Army Training: Evaluation of Television in Army Basic Training.* Washington, D.C.: Human Resources Research Office, 1954.

48. Kanner, J. H., Katz, S., and Goldsmith, P. B. *Television in Army Training: Evaluation of Intensive Television for Teaching Basic Electricity.* New York: Army Pictorial Center, 1958.

49. Kasten, D. F., and Seibert, W. F. *A Study of Televised Military Science Instruction.* Television Project Report 9, West Lafayette, Indiana: Purdue University, 1959. (Mimeo.)

50. Jefferson County Schools. Project Report: *Television in the Elementary Schools.* Louisville, 1960. (Mimeo.)

51. Kansas City Schools. *Report of the Second Year: Educational Television Project in the Kansas City Public Schools.* Kansas City, Missouri, 1960. (Mimeo.)

52. Klapper, H. L. *Closed Circuit Television as a Medium of Instruction at New York University, 1956–1957.* New York: New York University, 1958.

53. Kumata, H. *An Inventory of Instructional Television Research.* Ann Arbor, Michigan: Educational Television and Radio Center, 1958.

54. Kumata, H. *Teaching Advertising by Television.* East Lansing, Michigan: Michigan State University, 1958. (Mimeo.) (Also in Schramm; see 77 below.)

55. Kumata, H. *Attitude Change and Learning as a Function of Prestige of Instructor and Mode of Presentation.* East Lansing, Michigan: Michigan State University, 1958. (Mimeo.) (Also in Schramm: see 77 below.)

56. Kumata, H. "A Decade of Teaching by Television." In Schramm, W., ed., *The Impact of Educational Television.* Urbana, Illinois: University of Illinois Press, 1960, pp. 176–92.

57. Lepore, A. R., and Wilson, J. D. *An Experimental Study of College Instruction Using Broadcast Television: Project Number Two.* San Francisco: San Francisco State College, 1958.

58. Los Angeles City School District. *An Evaluation of Closed Circuit Instructional Television in Los Angeles City College and Los Angeles Valley College.* Los Angeles, 1959. (Mimeo.)

59. Macomber, F. G., and Siegel, L. *Final Report of the Experimental Study in Instructional Procedures.* Oxford, Ohio: Miami University, 1960.

60. Milwaukee Public Schools. *The Milwaukee Experiment in Instructional Television.* Milwaukee, 1958. (Mimeo.)

61. Same. *Evaluation Report for the 1958–1959 School Year.* Milwaukee, 1959. (Mimeo.)

62. Same. *Evaluation Report, 1959–1960.* Milwaukee, 1960. (Mimeo.)

63. Mullin, D. W. "An Experimental Study of Retention in Educational Television." *Speech Monogr.*, 24: 31–38; 1957.

64. *The Nebraska In-School Television-Correspondence Study Program.* Progress Report for 1957–1958. Lincoln, Nebraska, 1958. (Mimeo.)

65. Same. *Report for 1959–1960.* Lincoln, Nebraska, 1960. (Mimeo.)

66. Norfolk City Schools. *End of First Year National Educational Television Report.* Norfolk, Virginia, 1958. (Mimeo.)

67. Same. *Educational Television Evaluation Report.* Norfolk, Virginia, 1960. (Mimeo.)

68. Norfolk Suburban Park School. *The First Year of Educational Television.* Norfolk, Virginia, 1959. (Mimeo.)

69. *The North Carolina In-School Television Experiment, 1958–59.* Greensboro, North Carolina: University of North Carolina, 1959. (Mimeo.)

70. Parsons, T. S. *A Comparative Analysis of Some Outcomes of Instruction by Kinescope, Correspondence Study, and Classroom Procedure.* Ann Arbor, Michigan: School of Education, University of Michigan, 1955.

71. Pasewark, W. R. *The Effectiveness of Television as a Medium of Learning Typewriting.* Doctoral Dissertation, New York University, 1956. (Typewritten.)

72. Paul, J., and Ogilvie, J. C. "Mass Media and Retention." *Explorations*, 4: 120–23; 1955.

73. Pennsylvania State University, Division of Academic Research and Service. *Research on the Communication Process: A Report Covering the Period September 1958–September 1960.* University Park, Pa., 1960. (Mimeo.)

74. Philadelphia Public Schools. *Report of the National Experiment in Television Teaching of Large Classes.* Philadelphia, Pa., 1960. (Mimeo.)

75. Rock, R. T., Jr., Duva, J. S., and Murray, J. E. *Training by Television: The Comparative Effectiveness of Instruction by Television, Television Recordings, and Conventional Classroom Procedures.* Report 476-02-2. Port Washington, N.Y.: Special Devices Center, no date.

76. Rock, R. T., Duva, J. S., and Murray, J. E. *Training by Television: A Study in Learning and Retention.* Report 476-02-3. Port Washington, N.Y.: Special Devices Center, no date.

77. Schramm, W. *The Impact of Educational Television.* Urbana, Illinois: University of Illinois Press, 1960.

78. Seibert, W. F. *Cost Estimates for Televised and Conventional Instruction.* Television Project Report 7. West Lafayette, Indiana: Purdue University, 1958. (Mimeo.)

79. Seibert, W. F. *An Evaluation of Televised Instruction in College English Composition.* Television Project Report 5. West Lafayette, Indiana: Purdue University, 1958. (Mimeo.)

80. Seibert, W. F. *An Evaluation of Televised Instruction in College Freshman Mathematics.* Television Project Report 6. West Lafayette, Indiana: Purdue University, 1958. (Mimeo.)

81. Shimberg, B. "Effectiveness of Television in Teaching Home Making." *Educ. Testing Service Res. Bull.*, RB-54-19, 1954.

82. Southwestern Indiana Educational Television Council. *Second Year Report, 1959–1960.* Evansville, Indiana, 1960.

83. Starlin, G., and Lollas, J. E. *Inter-Institutional Teaching by Television in the Oregon State System of Higher Education.* Eugene, Oregon: Oregon State System of Higher Education, 1960.

84. Stuit, D. B. "Some Faculty Reactions to Teaching on Closed-Circuit Television." *Journ. Higher Educ.*, 18: 339–43; 1957.

85. Stuit, D. B., Harshbarger, H. C., Becker, S. L., Bechtoldt, H. P., and Hall, A. E. *An Experiment in Teaching.* Iowa City, Iowa: State University of Iowa, 1956. (Mimeo.)

86. Tamminen, A. W. "An Evaluation of Changes in Parents' Attitudes Toward Parent-Child Relationships Occurring During a Televised Program of Parent Panel Discussions." *Dissertation Abstracts*, 17: 1268–69; 1957.

87. Tannenbaum, P. H. *Instruction Through Television: A Comparative Study.* Urbana, Illinois: University of Illinois, 1956. (Mimeo.)

88. Tannenbaum, P. H. *Instruction Through Television: An Experimental Study.* Urbana, Illinois: University of Illinois, 1956. (Mimeo.)

89. Throop, J. F., Assini, L. T., and Boguslavsky, G. W. *The Effectiveness of Laboratory Instruction in Strength of Materials by Closed Circuit Television.* Troy, N.Y.: Rensselaer Polytechnic Institute, 1958.

90. Tucker, H., Lewis, R. B., Martin, G. L., and Over, C. H. "Television Therapy, Effectiveness of Closed Circuit Television as a Medium for Therapy in Treatment of the Mentally Ill." *AMA Arch. Neurol. and Psychiatry*, 70: 57–69; 1957.

91. Ulrich, J. H. "An Experimental Study of the Acquisition of Information from Three Types of Recorded Television Presentations." *Dissertation Abstracts*, 15: 2346; 1955.

92. United States Naval Training Device Center. *Instructional Television Research Reports.* Port Washington, N.Y.: U.S. Naval Training Device, Technical Report, NTC 20-TV-4, 1956. (Mimeo. and multilith.)

93. Westley, B. H., and Mobius, J. B. *The Effects of "Eye-Contact" in Televised Instruction.* Madison, Wisconsin: University of Wisconsin Television Laboratory, 1960. (Mimeo.)

94. Wichita Public Schools. *The Wichita Experiment: A Summation and Evaluation of the First Year, 1957–1958.* Wichita, Kansas, 1958. (Mimeo.)

95. Same. *Report of the Second Year, 1958–1959.* Wichita, Kansas, 1959. (Mimeo.)

96. Same. *Concluding Report, 1959–1960.* Wichita, Kansas, 1960.

97. Williams, D. C. "Mass Media and Learning—An Experiment." *Explorations,* 3: 75–82; 1954.

98. Willis, B. C. *Evaluation Report of the Two-Week Experiment of Direct Teaching on Television.* Chicago: Chicago Public Schools, 1956. (Mimeo.)

99. Zorbaugh, H. "Appraising the Gains of Televised Instruction." In Adams, J. C., Carpenter, C. R., and Smith, D. R., eds., *College Teaching by Television,* Washington, D.C.: American Council on Education, pp. 24–25, 1958.

TESTIMONY BY WILLIAM BRISH

Before the Television Advisory Panel, U.S. Office of Education

Mr. Brish is Superintendent of Schools in Hagerstown, Maryland, where a very large trial of instructional television has been made.

W E HAVE HAD a very interesting experience in our school system working with television. To us it has been more than just an opportunity to work with the media, because it has been a focal point that has let us concentrate on many of the things we wanted to do anyway, such as working on curriculum, teaching procedures and other problems of education. I have had no personal experience with broadcast ETV, except occasionally to see programs and make supplemental use of some of the things that the ETV stations and NETRC are doing. We have, however, been attempting to secure an ETV station for our community, and we view this as the capstone of our effort. We want to have both closed and open circuit and to be able to work in the community with the type of things which we are denied by closed circuit.

It's a little difficult to ask the question—what educational jobs can television do—and expect to get a simple, direct answer. However, I am sure that as we continue to work with television, it will become easier to work with the medium. We are finding, of course, that TV is greatly misunderstood. It is misunderstood both by educators and by the public. TV really is a resource; it is not something that you can explain as a specific job done by a piece of equipment. Now I am sure you are aware that television is one of the most promising of the mass media. I think it offers us in education more than the aspects of most mass media because viewers react to it as individuals. They don't react to it as members of a large group or a mob. Many people emphasize that with television you can put 500 pupils in a room, and one person can teach them all. That is just the mass idea, whereas the characteristic of television which intrigues us is that even though it involves a group situation, the reactions of the viewers are really individual reactions, and you can take advantage of this fact. It could be a great mistake to say that here is a medium which we must think of only in terms of everybody doing the same thing in the same way. Television might be one of the very things that can help us work with individual differences more than we ever have before. I can't substantiate this, and yet it is one of the important ideas that our group is thinking about in working with television. I would like to mention a few ideas such as this rather than discuss other uses of television in education that are obvious. It's easy to see how community leaders can be brought to the television studio and made available to all pupils in the system, or how community happenings can be made a part of the social studies program, or how commercial programs can be made available for school use. We expect to use the Inauguration next week as part of the instructional program because of our closed-circuit system.

One of the first things that were apparent to us in thinking about television was that we were making a mistake if we didn't think of it as an additional kind of learning experience rather than one which takes the place of some of the things that are already being done. It is an additional kind of learning experience, and I think that we can make a strong case for its use on such a basis. This does not mean that schools stop doing the important things they have been doing. Neither does it mean that a teacher in a face-to-face relationship group with pupils is not important. Face-to-face relationships are important, and ought to occupy, I would say, most of the school day. But I don't believe it is the only way that pupils learn. Schools are really not living up to their responsibility in our day and age if they do not help pupils to establish skills in self-learning. And in the ways we have organized our schools we do not give pupils much opportunity for this kind of self-direction.

We in Hagerstown have tried to use TV to provide in some cases even smaller groups than we have had before during the school day. We have felt that there ought to be a small part of the school day when you have a well-planned experience in which a pupil is to a certain extent put on his own responsibility. We know that learning is something that goes on all during our lives. When pupils leave school, they will not have a teacher organizing things for them, or asking questions and telling them to do this and that. And so, we are saying that the television experience is going to be different and is going to give the pupil the opportunity to develop skills that are important. I think that this is one of the most important potentials of TV. I believe that it eliminates the criticism that we run into all the time when somebody says, "Yes, but pupils need to be with people who understand them." True, they need to have that kind of a situation, and they do have it. But I don't believe that pupils need that same situation every minute of the school day. And I think that when we use television as I have described we provide many kinds of possibilities that didn't exist before.

Another thing that we have felt to be important is the idea that when a part of a lesson is carried by television and goes to every pupil taking a particular course, we have a unity that we never had before. This unity is an advantage to teachers and pupils. In the first place, it has been the result of much planning; but it also means that all pupils, no matter who the teacher is, have had a short, common experience. For a part of this course there is thus a thread that runs through and connects it. I don't think that this takes the place of the teacher and the need for the personal contact, but I think that this thread adds something valuable that we have never had before.

One of the questions in the next five years that we are planning to investigate is whether or not the small amount of uniformity in fourth-grade arithmetic, for example, the thing which was not there before, is what makes the difference in reaching a higher pupil achievement. By the way, everybody knows that you can't teach arithmetic by television. I hear this statement often. You can teach music and science, but anybody knows that you can't teach arithmetic. And it does seem that it is so, because you need practice and personal direction. Well, of course, we *have* been teaching arithmetic by TV, and what people may not realize is that television provides in a visual way carefully planned-out explanations of the basic ideas on which the number system rests. And when you have that in addition to the other things, you have something that is very worthwhile. In our system, we now have in some schools pupils who have had part of their arithmetic experiences in the fourth, fifth, and sixth grades by television. Last June in testing with the Iowa Achievement Test, we found that 42 percent of all the pupils in the sixth grade in the schools which have had TV for three years scored over an eighth-grade achievement level. We have never had anything like this before. To us, that represents a substantial growth, because our general pattern at the end of the sixth grade is to have about 18 percent scoring above an eighth grade level in arithmetic. So we are thinking here in terms of television as a resource and what we should do because we are getting these results.

You might be thinking that pupils differ in their ability, and hence it isn't right to have them participate in the same lesson. We are trying to develop lessons that challenge the bright pupils and enrich their learning experiences; and help other pupils to understand a bit better because of the visuals and the careful organization. For example, here is a fifth-grade pupil who has never learned the addition of numbers or the multiplication tables, and you say, "Well, he certainly ought to learn these before he does anything else in arithmetic." Until he has learned them, if he can't even add and subtract, why take up fractions? We feel that we can present fractions in such a way that even if the pupil can't add there are some ideas about fractions that he can get that will make the number system a little plainer. He will need to know some things about fractions whether he can add or whether he can't add. So it isn't quite as bad as it sounds, and the thread that we run through a situation like this is one of the points that we really want to continue exploring.

This leads up to another point—that in any particular situation all the pupils who are viewing the television presentation are having, in a sense, a common experience. I believe that in our thinking about individual differences we have lost sight of the fact that there are some benefits that come from having a common experience—not only the sense of belonging, but also the ability to make sure that people have the opportunity to see a thing in the same perspective. We, therefore, are now saying that here is an opportunity to use this common experience as a basis for working with individuals more than we have ever done before. It is just like reading: reading isn't having a youngster memorize some sounds and associate them with symbols. You have to have some experience to interpret, and our good teachers of reading in the elementary school are those who are developing experiences and talking about those experiences so that the children understand what it is that they are talking about. Then they write it down and it becomes a basis for reading. I think that this common TV experience gives us the same opportunity. I have often used the illustration of a youngster coming to school in the morning, finding a little turtle, bringing it to school and everybody getting excited about it. The teacher puts the turtle up on the front desk and gets the youngsters to talk about it, write something about it, then read what they write. The television common experience can be something along that line, and it can be very well planned in advance.

I think that many of the advantages of TV are self-explanatory. We have tried to enrich and broaden our program, and we have added courses. We have devoted a great deal of attention to courses for gifted students. In some cases, some of these courses would be appropriate, maybe, for only three or four pupils in a small school. In the past, we would have said, "We just can't offer the course in this school; the faculty is not large enough to make possible such small classes." But now we put such courses for gifted pupils on television, and even if there is only one interested person in a school, that person can take the course. Since we are talking about gifted pupils, I might also mention that we feel one of the most important things we can do for them is to put them on their own and make them accept responsibility.

Television has been very effective in in-service education and as an in-service training device. We believe in academic freedom and regard the classroom as the castle of the teacher. What the teacher does in his classroom is the result of his planning. As a result, in education we have tended to build up insulation and isolation; and in a way this is good and in a way it is bad. Businessmen wouldn't work in this way. Now this situation is not entirely comparable; because the teacher is working in a very subjective area with human beings and not with inanimate materials. Here is a problem that could be very intolerable for teachers and yet pupils need the continuity of a well-planned program. They have a right to expect, for example, if they take a course in American history that the teacher will not spend five or six months on the Civil War and then take whatever time is left for the important happenings since the end of that conflict. I think pupils have a right to see the sweep of American history, and with television it is possible to pace the course to accomplish this. We didn't realize before just how few times a teacher has had the opportunity to see other teachers teach. We have had a program whereby we send teachers to watch other teachers teach, and yet when we raised some of these questions we found that many of our teachers have seen another teacher only three or four times in 30 to 35 years. They know what the teachers were like when they were in college, but they really haven't seen teaching since then. I believe that it is good for them to see teaching and that even the best can profit from such an experience because it provides a basis for discussion especially about new ideas. I heard a teacher say, "Well, I don't like the way that's being done, but seeing it gives me a better idea of how I would do it." Another teacher said, "I have heard this idea talked about and I have always said I've never understood it. But if that's what you mean by it, I see what to do." One of the most important results, however, is the motivation it provides for curriculum work. When teachers got together in the past to talk about the science programs in the seventh, eighth, and ninth grades, they relied mainly on the experiences that happened in their own classrooms. Now they have the common experience of the telecast as a basis for working on the curriculum.

We have been very conscious of financial problems. We have closed circuit in a county system with 462 square miles and 51 schools. Most of our schools are in the Hagerstown area and with less than 50 miles of cable we can reach more than three-fourths of our pupils. It will take another 125 miles of cable to reach the last quarter of our pupils. Thus, when we get out into the rural areas we are going to more than double the cost just to reach a very few pupils. Our cable cost for the present 80 miles, which reaches 17,000 pupils, is $115,000 a year, and it will cost us with the extensions about another $40,000. We are making some consolidation so that we will end up with a cost of about $150,000 a year for the cable.

Now when I said that our major concern was not saving teachers I didn't mean that we would not take advantage of the fact that we are doing things in a different way. We do not employ teachers just to employ a certain number. We employ what we need and redeploy the savings resulting from using a few less teachers to pay the cost of the cable and for production work in television. We set up our television instruction on the basis of bringing pupils together in large groups for a part of their lesson experience and in small groups—smaller than we have had before—in face-to-face situations for the other part of their work. The combination of large and small groups uses fewer teachers than would be used if classes were organized in the normal way. I think we need to justify the fact that pupils can profit from this experience and that they are not short-changed. In television experiences in which the pupils are reacting to the instruction as individuals, I think they are getting opportunities that they didn't get before. We have had opportunities for planning that we have never had before. I was talking to a group of seniors in one of the Hagerstown high schools last week where they get three hours of television a week. The only lessons that they receive by television are in senior English. They have a combination of three hours of television in large groups and two hours in small groups in a face-to-face situation. They said, "This is the best English course we have ever had."

By spending money we would have been spending otherwise we are able to provide services which we would not have been able to provide if we had not used television. Actually, we are effecting some savings; we are using about 30 fewer teachers than we otherwise would have used. In some of our high schools we are saving just one teacher, but, you see, it adds up when you put all the high schools together. We have saved 30 out of roughly four hundred teachers. We are also reducing the number of classes that some of our teachers meet. This is a saving, too, enabling them to devote more time than before to the individual differences and problems of students.

We use our junior college students for the operation of the equipment and production. We set up a course in the junior college with a trained engineer who works with boys who are interested in the technical aspects of television. As a part of their course in electronics they are studying repair and maintenance of the equipment. We have two staff members who have college degrees in television production. They train the junior college students who are interested in courses in production for handling the operation of the studios. This means that our costs are partly covered by laboratory work. Students are paid for the rest of the time they work. Our total cost of operation, including power and salaries and so forth, runs somewhere around $30,000 per year.

Of the greatest importance, however, is the fact that television has been the motivating force for doing curriculum work. During part of the day students are in a situation which is not dominated by a teacher-answer situation in which the teacher asks the question and the pupils respond.

In the television experience we can teach some things about paying attention, about listening, about concentrating, about taking notes, about withholding judgment. We feel that television is resulting in more independent study. We are keeping notes to find out whether pupils are going to the library on their own more now and looking up things and reading more books.

Our assumption has been that students ought to have some experiences in which they are in large groups part of the day, in small groups part of the day, and engaged in individual study part of the day. Television helps us with the large groups in a very effective way. What we have tried to do with television is to concentrate on the aspects of the presentation that can be handled very effectively in television. We decide what these common learnings are so that a teacher who will teach small groups through the day will not have to do them over for each lesson period. We do them once on TV and then let the teacher have other time for the kind of activities that are profitable in the face-to-face situation.

There is also an opportunity in television to coordinate various kinds of audio-visual aids and to put them under fingertip control so that the small segment of a movie that is needed fits into the lesson exactly. The television screen gives the teacher an effective means of directing and controlling the attention of the pupil. It provides a special, central point of concentration for group instruction. The pupil can see on television just what it is the teacher is talking about, and nothing else. This cannot be done in any other kind of a situation. You can't look at me as I stand here without seeing the ash tray and cigarettes and all this material; but if you put your eyes on the television set you are seeing just the thing that I want you to see. The television camera can greatly magnify a small part of the area to be shown. During the dissection of the eye of a calf during a biology class, the enlargement was so great that students could actually see the little lens in the eye pop out—the teacher said that the students gasped at seeing this. In a conventional class only two or three would have seen it, but even then it would not have been as dramatic as this.

I don't know the real importance of the eye-to-eye contact that you get with television. It is a fact that when the teacher looks at the camera, she is looking straight into the eye of each pupil. I think there is a bit of psychology here that we know very little about.

I think that the TV opportunity to present the right kind of visuals sometimes leads people to go to extremes. I don't think that you should have visuals in a television lesson just to have visuals.

I do believe that there is a place in education for television. I sincerely believe it, but that doesn't mean that TV takes over and monopolizes the school program. It is just as important to have television as a part of a school program as it is to have textbooks. Now, textbooks are of extreme importance and can become even more so as we move on in education. I think there are all sorts of resources that we ought to put in proper perspective. One of our big problems is how we are going to coordinate television with other important resources so that it makes a contribution and isn't just something that provides the opportunity for putting on a show. We are using team teaching, and that is a very difficult thing to work out. Pupils have to develop skills in using television as a resource and using it intelligently. Finally, I think we must make television more than just a passive experience in which people sit quietly looking.

TESTIMONY BY FRED HECHINGER

Before the Television Advisory Panel

Mr. Hechinger is Education Editor of "The New York Times."

THE PLACE OF TV in education should be the same as that of books. Bad books are of no help in education. There is a thin line between learning and entertainment in TV because of the place which TV has in the home. Its appeal is very much to the relaxed. Television in the home very rarely becomes purely educational unless it makes some specific demands on the viewer. The amount of education and learning it provides is strictly in the mind of the viewer. This is true of all media. You have to make some direct demand on the viewer. That demand can be implied or it could be a compulsion of assignments, such as where commercial TV is used by the local university for credit courses.

TV, to be really of value, has to be thoroughly integrated into the educational program. Because of the feelings about the new medium it is customary to talk about ETV as enrichment only, a supplement only. In the strictest sense, we could say that books are only a supplement to education; but we don't believe that. Books are as much a part of education as the teacher. That is why there must be thorough integration of the medium into the educational process.

There are some things that can't be shown in education except through TV. It can place you on the scene when an event is happening.

Not many of us realize at the present time that not one State in the Union requires of its language teachers that they be able to speak the language that they teach, although there are some cities which have this requirement. There is no teacher who could get away with this on TV.

In the field of medical television, many students now get a better view of an operation by watching it on TV.

Bad teaching is magnified many times over on TV. By the same token, good teaching is not only magnified by TV, but becomes contagious. In spite of the difficulties and problems faced in the Washington County, Maryland, TV system, there is a beneficial effect of TV, not only on the carefully trained TV teachers, but through the effect of these teachers on the other teachers. This doesn't merely mean that the TV teachers are the superior teachers, but it means that we have broken the confinement that has forced teachers to become locked up in their classrooms (after they finish their practice teaching) with no criticism of their work. This criticism is something TV is offering us now by opening an avenue of comparison.

Another problem is the timing of TV on commercial stations. Educational programming has not been on at times when the general, or even interested public, has the opportunity to take part in it. The timing of really educational programs has to be solved if they are to be more than a bone thrown in the direction of public service.

There is another problem: the amount of material which TV involves. Even if we had enough money, we do not have enough talent to keep TV stocked with superior performance, educational or otherwise. TV should be cut up into smaller segments so that an expensive production would not be a one-time show. This would be one way out of the cost dilemma of ETV. In terms of in-school TV, one of the greatest hopes of the future is the prospect of relatively inexpensive video-tape equipment so that schools could shoot and bank some of their own better TV performances. This could lead to an exchange of talent. There is greater potential in that sort of thing than in the Airborne experiment.

In looking at TV and ETV particularly, we want to study very carefully the lesson of the BBC. The British have used school radio for a long time before we "discovered" it, and used it with great effectiveness. They might be watched in what they are doing in TV for exactly the same reason.

In whatever we do, in TV, we have to expect opposition from some of the more conservative people in the schools. The only way we can overcome this is by demonstrating what has been done. There are two motivating forces in teaching: insecurity and ham. Our job is to play down the insecurity and play up the ham.

In the main, we have failed miserably in integrating into education all of the other media, other than the book. They are extras. The teacher usually couldn't get what teaching aids she wants when she wants them. It sometimes takes over a year to get science films into the classroom and by that time the teacher no longer needs them. Some classrooms are not equipped for blackout. A good many teachers are not very mechanically minded. TV has to be part of the classroom. You would have movies, for instance, only on days when you have nothing else to do. You have either a poor kind of integration or none at all.

What was wrong with some of the books I examined, essentially, was that they assumed that history could be taught by stringing along a series of inoffensive facts, that history could be taught without opinions and without interpretation. This just cannot be done. The other group of textbooks (early readers) were prefabricated committee jobs rather than written books. TV has an answer to this. On the social studies side, TV is an obvious answer: for instance, the Omnibus show "They Shall Have Power." This has tremendous potential in teaching. It is great teaching. In the other area, that of the early reader, TV applies indirectly. If TV can teach foreign languages, it can be used to teach English and reading, too. At that point, good books become even more important. Comic books provide action, whereas school readers often go on for 30 pages or more and nothing happens.

If television has the same weaknesses that textbooks have, it will result in the same weaknesses in learning. In a school system, there is no medium which can effect these changes more potently and directly than TV. There is nothing that is as communicable a disease as TV.

Is there any precedent in the land-grant college act and the problem of financing ETV? Obviously, the land-grant matter is a precedent on all matters of federal aid to education. There might be another parallel to look into, since the land-grant Act dealt with the disposition of government-owned land.

How do I feel about the issue of control that is implicit in federal money for ETV operations? It is always wrong to say from the outset that federal money brings or does not bring controls. Whenever you accept money, there is always the danger of some control. In the NDEA (for good or bad reasons), there is some measure of control through the pinpointing of science, math, and foreign languages. None of this is necessarily bad, but it is a measure of control. There is no danger in federal grants per se. But there is danger in any legislation if the grants are given in a way that attaches strings to them.

Is there evidence in any way that the American people are against federal aid? A great many might say that they were against federal aid, but they would say so because a label has been used to create an impression of something that isn't really so. Even the most ardent supporters of federal aid imply the danger of controls.

How do I feel about sources of money to train people for ETV? Should we continue to depend on the foundations or should we be more active with the taxpayers' money? The financing cannot be done in any other way than by the use of public funds on all levels.

TESTIMONY BY ROGER REVELLE

Before the Television Advisory Panel

Dr. Revelle is Director of the Scripps Institute of Oceanography, and Dean of Research, University of California.

MY JUSTIFICATION for taking a somewhat pessimistic view of commercial television is basically a Christian one. Man is not only partly divine; he is also partly an animal. The Christian doctrine that he is born to sin and suffer has a great deal of validity. People have potentiality for both good and evil. If we put this in biological terms I think that it is quite proper to say that the animal most analogous to a man is a rat. Both men and rats are infinitely adaptable. Commercial television in general, it seems to me, brings out the very worst in people. There is some fundamental sinfulness about the medium.

We need diversity, but commercial television is tending to bring a very low level of conformity. Newspapers offer something for everybody—various columnists, editorials, news. But in television there is lack of diversity and lack of controversy.

The second sin of commercial television is superficiality. I've been on many television programs, and the thing I am always struck by is the lack of time. You never have time to get below the surface. A half-hour program always turns out to be twenty-four minutes, and it attempts to cover such a tremendous field that you can't say anything about anything. This results in appalling superficiality.

There is also lack of competition, particularly lack of competition for quality. This is coupled with high unit cost of the productions. One commercial TV program costs as much as one book.

Changing the subject now to educational television, I agree with Mr. McGill that there has been a tremendous decrease in the hostility of educators to this during the past few years. This is because they are beginning to realize what educational television can and cannot do. It is not a substitute for the free give and take between teacher and student, but it is a supplement to textbooks and formal lectures. I'm not sure that one should look for great actors among professors as lecturers on educational television. It's quite true that great professors usually are great hams, and they could use a much wider audience than they usually enjoy. But if you look at "Continental Classroom" and consider the character of Harvey

White you will see that he is not a great dramatic personality. What he is good at is the clear presentation of facts. Nobody is ever going to get inspired by a lecture of Harvey White's, but they are going to learn some physics. The same is true of Baxter in chemistry. Nobody would ever think of going to Florida because Baxter is teaching there, but many people do nevertheless learn some chemistry from his television lectures. Television is a good medium for the presentation of facts, and this means that what it can do will very much change the character of American education—I think very much for the better, because it will reduce the need for formal lectures. The requirement that professors should have a teaching load of at least nine hours could conceivably disappear. The formal lectures could very well be carried by television, and what you could substitute would be the British system of smoking at one student in a tutorial conversation or at small groups of students in a preceptorial discussion. I doubt that educational television will actually lead to much economy, but it is possible that it could lead to a very great improvement in American higher education, by freeing many professors from formal lecture and thereby increasing the personal, conversational, and really intellectual and spiritual contact between the teacher and the student. Educational television should also make it possible to increase the student-to-faculty ratio. This is essential in our desperate educational situation.

ETV can be used very successfully in many of the sciences for laboratory demonstrations which, ordinarily, large classes can barely see.

For the above reasons I would express myself as wholeheartedly in favor of educational television as a revolutionary teaching aid. I would feel that much larger amounts of money could well be spent for it at all levels, from the local school system to the federal government. I am not particularly concerned about who does it. We have sufficient safeguards against the federal government's controlling education. It really doesn't matter where the money comes from.

In regard to the need for channels, I would say that for research purposes as well as for communications our need for channels is essentially limitless. It would be foolish for a panel such as this to try to say how many channels will be needed ten years from now, because no matter how many you have you haven't got enough. What's really needed is technical change in the use of the electromagnetic spectrum, and I think that this will happen within the next few years.

I feel that the idea of taxing commercial interests for their use of TV channels is a good one. Not only is there precedent for this in our national forests and grazing lands but also in the gas tax for building of our public roads. (In reply to a question, Dr. Revelle indicated that he regards the present public service requirement in commercial TV as a weak substitute for a tax.)

III. EDUCATIONAL TELEVISION'S COMMUNITY JOB

What is the distinctive responsibility of noncommercial as opposed to commercial television in representing the public affairs interests and needs of the community? What are its distinctive responsibilities in art and culture? What can we reasonably expect of educational television in these areas? Such questions as these are taken up in the following pages.

THE FUTURE OF PUBLIC AFFAIRS PROGRAMS

By Harold D. Lasswell

Dr. Lasswell is Professor of Law at Yale, and a long-time student of mass media and public affairs

How is it possible to harmonize the public affairs programs on TV with the goals of American society as a whole and with policies toward general media of communication?

Note first of all that we speak of American society rather than government since our ideology emphasizes the primacy of the people, the whole of the commonwealth, over government, law, and politics. The latter are specialized social institutions which are viewed with reserve, even with suspicion, as a result of national unease in all that touches upon power. Power—so the tradition says—is "corrupt" or rather, it is corrupting. Therefore, even though it is impossible to live in a divided world without perpetual preparation against the eventuality of war, it is of the first importance to circumscribe public power, the power of government, by precautionary measures. Hence the division of authority between federal government and individual states, the separation of authority among the legislative, executive, and judicial branches of government, and the limitations sought to be imposed upon officials of any kind on behalf of private rights, among which rights in communication are among the most obvious. In addition to these arrangements, of course, is the basic commitment to popular government, and to an electorate that is organized to express the majority opinion by ballot. Whatever variations there may be among Americans in regard to their institutions, they are well aware of the negative aura that surrounds the fact of power.

In no domain of policy are the ideological subtleties and complexities of American life more visible than in regard to television. These nuances are obvious on several grounds. Television is new; yet it is already subject to a complicated set of controls which are believed to be justified in the light of past experience and precedent in dealing with previous instruments of communication, notably the news press and the motion picture.

Television is not only news; it is, in a sense, the final advance in network communication. It is final in that it combines the versimilitude of film with the simultaneity of radio. It is network communication because it interposes between the audience member and an event an organized network that selects what is available for an act of communication to be completed. The network limitation would disappear if each individual possessed a "super-eyeglass" that he could focus at will upon Washington, D.C., or the Kremlin, and participate without intermediaries in whatever proved of interest. At the moment the technical prospect of perfecting the "super-eye" is not believed to be good. Hence our present discussion of communication policy proceeds upon the assumption that a network of intermediate agencies will continue to select what the citizen may see at any moment and as a necessary correlation of selection to exclude him from other alternatives.

Properly managed TV public affairs programs can provide members of the body politic, wherever they live, with direct participation in current happenings of crucial significance; and, in addition, employ the sensory richness of the medium to make the context—past and future— come alive. If we exclude "spot news" coverage from the realm of public affairs broadcasting the peculiar contribution that TV can make to civic enlightenment is cast into high relief. Public affairs programming—to use the expressive cliché—aims at giving "the facts behind the facts," that is, a view in depth historically and prospectively of the present moment in man's destiny.

It is not necessary to labor the point that human beings differ enormously from one another in capacity for receiving a message communicated in print or by means of the unaided voice. Enlightenment means context: it includes the *clarification of goal* at every level—local, regional, national, international, universal; it includes the presentation of yesterday's relevant event—*trends to date*; it embraces the *analytic examination of factors that condition* the past—comparable case histories in national development, for instance; it covers the *projection of future potentialities*, and the presentation and evaluation of *alternative policies*. TV is inclusive and vivid by its technical character; it lends itself to the contextual approach to the understanding of our place in the passing stream of local and cosmic events.

Up to the present no one can responsibly claim that TV has been employed to a degree that approximates its potential. One way to emphasize the situation while at the same time providing an indication of ideological factors is to imagine a simple design for the handling of TV.

An imaginary design

Imagine a multichanneled TV network that gives everyone an opportunity to stabilize his viewing habits according to an ample and established minimum schedule of programs presenting news, public affairs, and education. In such a plan, license to profit from TV stations depends upon keeping certain prime viewing hours, at least, available for such programs. Today, of course, commercial TV sells the most desirable time, which relegates public affairs programs, for instance, to less advantageous hours. Such programs may also be "bumped" when their time is sold, which is a huge roadblock in the path of audience building. If access to channel time is guaranteed, it becomes possible to conduct audience-building campaigns.

The procedure originally developed by advertising agencies in relation to radio is adaptable to the purpose of raising the money required to do a good job. Imagine that 15 percent of the gross income for advertising on commercial TV is made available to a national fund administered by an American Public Affairs Foundation, and that the Council is authorized to prepare programs directly or by contracting with services which compete with one another for excellence in this field.

Since a multichannel system requires the use of frequencies throughout the entire range, listening equipment must be capable of receiving all frequencies. Hence equipment manufacturers are appropriately required to include all capabilities in all sets.

Because of the close connection between public affairs programming and educational broadcasting, the public affairs plan is closely linked with national policy toward specialized educational stations. Comprehensive coverage for educational purposes requires reserve frequencies for educational TV in every community where TV stations of any kind may exist. Capital grants are made available to educational TV channels when the locality is willing to assume certain minimum obligations.

Public affairs programs are not properly limited to audiences resident in the United States since Americans travel and live abroad, and the peoples of other countries deserve access to our agencies of enlightenment even as ideally we might have access to theirs.

Our tripartite system

The present pattern of national TV is far from exhibiting the simple design outlined in the preceding paragraphs. In harmony with our ideological concern for pluralistic rather than monopolistic control, the system exhibits three control schemes: private profit; private civic (nonprofit); governmental.

Our system of public order allows—indeed obligates—private businesses to seek profitability. But this is *not* done because our social order wants to encourage selfishness. We do this in the expectation that the pursuit of private profit can serve the common good. Our policy is based upon the expectation that American productivity will be enhanced; and further that non-monopolistic private business safeguards popular government since it is relatively independent of the favor of public officials.

At the same time, we have learned not to put all our eggs in one basket. We supplement, and sometimes supplant, the private profits channel by the government channel or by the civic (nonprofit) channel. It was long ago recognized that the channel of private profit was not well adapted to education and enlightenment. Hence for the most part public policy relies upon the government channel for the huge network of tax-supported schools, colleges and universities that we have today. Policy also looks benevolently upon the civic channel in these matters; we have a supplementary educational network supported by private gifts and administered for nonprofit purposes. To some extent, of course, the civic channel is in fact tax supported, since exemptions are given for gifts. It is true that profit-making schools do exist; as a rule, however, in fields such as dancing, music, and mechanics.

There is nothing novel about the use of a three-channel system in connection with TV news, public affairs, and instruction. The tripartite system of control is well established in many areas. Consider health, comfort, and safety, for instance: Hospitals are supported by taxes, gifts and, payments; they are governmental, civic, or profit-making. In some matters, we note, it is believed to be most inappropriate to rely upon the private profit-seeking channel at all. For many people it is shocking to think of a profit-seeking church or of a family organized for profit.

A tripartite arrangement presupposes public regulation as a means of correlating channels with the common interest. Although commercial interests are licensed to conduct business with an obligation to serve the public interest directly, they have not been held strictly accountable. It is true that the Commission may refuse to renew licenses. However, the Commission is actually handicapped by the enormity of this sanction. As matters stand, the FCC has few sanctions between a slap on the wrist and annihilation. The FCC does not have at its disposal, and has not insisted upon having, the diversity of means required for a complex regulatory task. Moreover, the Commission has not been as helpful as it might be in clarifying the program obligation. Such timidity is characteristic of American officials—administrative, legislative, or judicial—in dealing with the media of general information, since our history has made us fearful of the cry of censorship; and the Supreme Court has been slow in stabilizing policy expectations regarding the vague criteria in the Bill of Rights.

The responsibility for public affairs broadcasting is confused and diffused. Censorship—that is, the actual exclusion of potential news and comment—depends upon network officials who are obligated to reconcile their profit-making possibilities, which are relatively definite, with relatively ambiguous criteria of civic enlightenment. American experience with educational and civic affairs suggests that a different control mechanism is more suitable to the service of the common good. Hence the recommended use of a national foundation composed of devoted and outstanding educators and independent men of affairs.

The importance of TV for national objectives

Today we are increasingly aware of the significance of the media of general communication for the survival and growth of the American people. It is not to be forgotten that the American republic began as a revolutionary commonwealth. An aspiration that held it together was the challenge of providing a model of free government so impressive to all men everywhere that the people of the world would take public affairs in their own hands and eliminate monarchial rule from the face of the earth.

There was a time, not many years ago, when it seemed certain that the battle for free government was won. More recently, however, the future of freedom appears far from sure. As a slogan, yes; as a practical reality, no. The slogan of free government is part of the public vocabulary of nearly every significant government and political party. In many parts of the world men are denied freedom in the name of freedom. If Americans are to be informed of the facts of life we must see rhetoric in the context of effective, rather than formal, participation in decision.

The first applies as pungently to the internal affairs of the United States as to the domestic politics of the new states of Africa or the communist lands of Asia. During the coming decade, for instance, the arms race with the Soviet world may or may not be settled by negotiation. If the race is unsettled—and especially if it is left in an ambiguous state— the internal role of the security forces—the military and the police—in the United States will be critically important with the advance of automation and other devices of concentrated and centralized control, and the emergence of coalitions of engineers, scientists, public relations specialists, organization, and personnel managers. Current transformations will be greatly accelerated. If leisure increases (and income remains stable or rises) the question will be whether most Americans join a laughing crowd, divested of responsible concern for the community, or accept membership in a public.

Every autocratic regime pays tribute to the potency of film, radio, and TV by subjecting these media to public monopoly. The policies of the monopoly are highly illuminating. First of all, the power to monopolize is the power to exclude, the power to deny to the mind of man the challenge of personal responsibility that inheres in the task of choosing among diverse versions of "fact" and varied recommendations of policy. In the public order of autocracy or of totalitarian states the focus of public attention is captured for the purposes of the ruling few. Rival versions of the past, competing estimates of the future, diverse specifications of ideological goal, alternative policies for the future: this richness is denied the totalitarian subject, who is held in a state of tutelage by self-appointed superiors. Monopoly control makes it possible to whip up a twenty-four-hour rage at the latest alleged atrocity by the American enemies of the Soviet. Under conditions of the kind it is easy to see why Soviet authorities think of the "mass" media as instruments of "crowd" psychology; that is, instruments for conditioning the emotions of uncritical masses. From the point of view of totalitarian rulers, television is a regrettable innovation; despite the obvious impact, they find it, after all, redundant. But for the circumstance that TV is a sign of technological eminence, Soviet authorities would be willing to overlook it entirely.

In theory the situation is very different in a democratic commonwealth. We have said that TV has not been employed to a degree that approximates its potential. No conspiracy is involved; the situation is the blind result of poor balance in the adjustment of American ideology and American institutions to the changing facts of life.

The gravity of the discrepancies between the desirable and the actual is not to be ignored. Suppose you were an enemy of the United States and were hired to demoralize the American nation. What strategy would you use? In all probability you would do what you could to keep the present situation as unchanged as possible. You would know that the essential point is to blind the eye of the American people, which is largely a matter of distracting public attention from responsible understanding of the facts of life. This is accomplished not by the tactic of the Big Lie—as in Nazi Germany or the Soviet world—but by the tactic of the Big Laugh. Not that laughs are demoralizing in their proper place, which is in balance with genuinely informative and gripping presentations of the life and death facts of life.

The standing alibi of commercial TV is that Americans want to laugh; "the audience," not we, want to laugh ourselves out of history. But this is not necessarily true. In a nonrecreational frame of reference Americans are quite capable of acting responsibly. The new expansion of public affairs programs on educational TV is an indication of this.

Educational TV and public affairs

Public affairs programming has benefited from noncommercial educational sponsorship because it has been allowed to develop in a different context from the commercial market. In the national market advertisers typically think of success in terms of the potential national audience. The press for universal coverage has a disastrous effect upon informative broadcasting. When the target is the largest possible viewing audience the safest programs are recreational. They aim at common denominators which, since they are common, are least differentiated. When the theoretical national audience is the goal, there can be little cumulation from one program to the next, or little introduction of material that is adapted to higher levels of education and experience. Cumulation takes the form of stressing the personality of a performer, and acquaintance with his style of speech and gesture. In this sense each program series that is aimed at the "mass" audience becomes a special subculture within the whole of popular culture. It lives by appealing to the unconscious predispositions of the audience; and these are most safely aroused by allusive rather than explicit, direct statement. Humor establishes a mood of irresponsibility, of unreality which, since the program is not to be taken seriously, widens the area of permissible allusion. However, as every entertainer knows, there are limits which, when exceeded, evoke a storm.

The requirements of public affairs programs are quite different. Here the emphasis is upon direct statement—upon realism, judgment, responsibility. At their best public affairs programs are cumulative, building upon a common audience framework of knowledge to which it is possible to add informative and interpretative detail. Effective programs do not aim at a universal audience; they are directed at the stratified components of the potential audience. Audience building means that a given stratum of the community is trained to view programs at definite times, and to stay out of the audience when little of interest is going on.

It is not too much to say that educational TV begins at the opposite pole from commercial broadcasting, although both necessarily overlap. In educational programming it is taken for granted that, for the most part, the potentially universal audience is to be serviced piecemeal through time. The commercial approach, on the other hand, is to aim at universality every time. Phrased in this extreme form it is obvious that commercial broadcasters have long since reconciled themselves to half a loaf. They do, in fact, often aim at selected audiences, not at the hypothetically universal audience. In practice, the housewifely audience is assumed to have an insatiable hunger for new ways of preparing spaghetti; kids love horror and suspense; and the old man is supposed to dote on balls—basket, foot, and base. The commercial approach, however, is never reconciled to the limited audience; all kinds of devices are used to get parents into the audience for child shows, and to trap more women for sporting events.

Educational broadcasters, in turn, begin by aiming at selected target audiences, often in the classroom. But they know very well that community support will be stronger if they diversify their appeal and multiply the components of the community who dial educational stations. They figure out ways to bring parents and children together to learn languages; they angle science programs to catch inquisitive adults as well as school children. And there are subtle pulls to get a bigger at-the-moment audience by shading educational standards—on some musical programs, for instance. It is to be noted that public affairs programs often widen the audience coverage of educational stations by appealing to educated adults, and especially to professional and managerial groups. At the same time the core audience may continue to be classes in contemporary history, civics, or social problems.

According to the stereotype the commercial broadcaster is a man who would sell his mother for an ad; the stereotyped educational broadcaster is a man who bores his audience to death for their own good. Now these stereotypes have kernels of truth—otherwise they would have no vitality. The supreme value outcome sought by the commercial broadcaster is, and must be, profits for the station owner. The supreme value outcome of the educational broadcaster is professional respect for skill in education and enlightment. The institutional structure of the commercial industry is such that if it does not strive to earn profits for the stockholder it actually violates a legal obligation. The institutional structure of educational broadcasting, by contrast, is nonprofit and professional: it is legally and morally obligated to serve the common good directly.

Wherever educational TV stations have taken hold they have begun to make a genuine difference in the public affairs programs available to local communities. The fact is that educational stations got under way slowly, though recently they have begun to multiply with some speed. In part the slow start is to be attributed to the decentralized structure of education in the United States; in part to the reluctance of educators to adopt new methods without a trial period. Fortunately, a large private foundation stepped into the breach and made enough capital funds available to permit a few stations to operate pioneer stations. The pioneers had a complex job. It was necessary to re-train talent originally recruited for other purposes, and to attract and train talent for the new instrument. They also experimented in local communities and regions in order to mobilize educational and civic support. They have been increasingly successful in obtaining gifts and in sharing school appropriations. They have developed a backlog of indispensable program material and joined hands with foreign educational networks in furthering common aims. The pioneers devised new techniques of coordinating station programs with school needs. Specifically, too, they have moved steadily into the news and public affairs area, especially the latter.

In this connection it is informative to contrast New York City, for instance, which has no educational outlet, and San Francisco, which now has a vigorous educational station. A study of the programs available during the week of January eighth shows that in New York City about 4 percent of TV time was devoted to news during a recent test week; 3½ percent additionally dealt with public affairs. San Francisco commercial stations gave slightly more play to news (4.21 percent) than New York City. The educational TV station had a higher figure (6.84 percent); but the most significant contrast was in public affairs programs. The commercial stations averaged 2.25 percent of program time; the figure of the educational station was 16.73 percent. The San Francisco and New York commercial stations performed at about the same combined news and public affairs level (6.47 and 7.47). For the San Francisco educational station the combined record was 23.57.

The practice of the San Francisco TV station accurately expresses the willingness of educational TV managers to move vigorously into the public affairs field, since they recognize the obligation to supply context in order to supplement spot news. Presumably the percentage of its total program time would diminish somewhat if the station were active more hours per day. But it would undoubtedly continue to run higher than commercial stations.

The art of public affairs programming is in a primitive stage of development. Fortunately it has been enriched by initiatives from many sources, not the least of which are other democratic commonwealths. Notable examples of technique are some of the documentaries prepared by the British postal authorities and by the Canadian Film Board. In this country the dreary round of newsreel horse races, disasters, fashion shows, and sports was briefly punctuated by "The March of Time," prepared under the auspices of a news magazine. Private foundations subsidized the preparation of experimental TV shows that were screened on Sundays over commercial networks and established important prototypes for the use of the medium. Commercial TV networks, despite all pressures, have often shown what might be done by courageous leadership. Occasionally private commercial sponsors have taken a chance on controversy. But the advice of hard-headed market advisers is to shun the controversial for fear of audience reaction against cigars whose virtues are plugged by debatable masters of ceremonies, or cars whose compactness can only be fully appreciated by buyers who associate it with love of mother instead of debates over national security.

At times general attention is sufficiently focused upon public affairs to render it commercially advantageous for profit-seeking channels to present background information and interpretative comment, besides giving spot news coverage. A protracted electoral campaign, or a prolonged crisis in domestic policy or international affairs provides such an occasion.

Crisis coverage, however, leaves much to be desired from the point of view of informed public judgment. If the community is taken by surprise, sudden mass coverage can endanger public order by encouraging the formation of a "crowd mind." In local communities this happens when sentiment is highly unified against other communities, which may give rise to sectional conflicts imperiling national unity, or foreign relations are made more complex. Crises are not to be avoided; but the chances of destructive results, domestically or internationally, can be reduced by wise anticipation of the critical challenge and proper preparation. This is the true challenge of all media of public information in a democratic society. It is the true test of adequacy.

In the Soviet world audience tutelage is a matter of public policy; in the United States audience tutelage in irresponsibility is a by-product of market strategy. We have, however, underscored the point that it is well within the pluralistic tradition of our country to supplement the market, when the market transgresses public interest, by nonmarket channels of action—preferably by civic rather than governmental channels.

During the next few years when the independence, even the existence, of America is at stake, it is not unreasonable to propose that existing initiatives for the responsible consideration of public affairs shall be encouraged. Educational TV has demonstrated the steady growth that is possible even within rather primitive limits of technique, and in the absence of key stations in New York City, Washington, D.C., and Los Angeles.

Policy program

The national interest requires the expansion of public affairs programs throughout the nation; and in view of the history to date this points to the importance of national coverage by educational TV networks. Educational TV has the continuity of dedication that is required to build a steadily enlarging core of viewing audiences in every community composed of responsible opinion leaders willing to devote themselves to the consideration of fundamental issues and to the interpretation of these matters for the benefit of their neighbors—neighbors who may themselves be drawn progressively into audience participation. In this way the American people can retain and build public opinion. They step out of the "mass," the "crowd," and function as citizens—as members of the "public" with "opinions" to supplement their "sentiments."

To the extent that public affairs broadcasting is linked with the destiny of educational TV the following policy measures are obviously necessary: (a) require all receiving sets that are manufactured to include facilities for the reception of ultra-high frequencies, in addition to high and standard frequencies; (b) reserve frequencies for educational TV in every community where TV stations of any kind may exist; (c) provide capital grants for educational TV channels for all communities—preferably on a matched basis that invites local initiative.

To the extent that responsibility for public affairs programming remains in private commercial hands, some steps at least can be taken to guarantee *minimum* adequacy of performance: (a) provision for prime time to be made available for news, educational, and public affairs programs; (b) diversification of the sanctions available to the FCC for the proper performance of its functions; (c) clarification by the FCC of standards of public service.

We have drawn attention to another solution to the problems presented by public affairs broadcasting: establish an American Public Affairs Foundation responsible for appropriate program services, financed by 15 percent of the gross receipts of commercial TV for equivalent time. This would mean, obviously, that of every billion dollars spent for prime TV advertising one hundred and fifty million dollars would be available for public affairs—plus news—broadcasting purposes during prime viewing hours specified for all stations. Private TV interests might conceivably make arrangements of the kind, especially in the early stages of a new technical innovation like "pay as you see" TV. More entrenched commercial interests may find it less congenial, though it can reduce their great vulnerability to attack. It may be necessary to make the new arrangement by statute.

As a means of keeping informed of the levels of performance on TV it is important to provide adequate current surveys of TV programs. To some extent this auditing task is a proper function of the Federal Communications Commission. Official appraisals, however, are somewhat negative since they are very conscious of official standards and look to the discovery of violations. A more positive approach is also needed. Such an appraisal program would be under the control of *an independent civic board* since it is designed to operate informally. The board would take responsibility for clarifying its own working standards of public service, and for reporting on current trends toward excellent or inadequate TV achievement.

To say that time is running out is not the same as prophesying that all is lost because many golden years of opportunity for America are lost through private cupidity and public negligence. There may be a time to supplement frivolity by responsibility in all that concerns civic enlightenment.

TELEVISION'S PLACE IN ART AND CULTURE

By Gilbert Seldes

Dr. Seldes is Director of the Annenberg School of Communications, University of Pennsylvania, and author of numerous books on television and other public arts.

I

THIS REPORT OF MY own thoughts and, I suspect, of the ideas of other people, is bound to be colored by a certain prejudice.

Except as an arm of in-school instruction, separate channels for ETV seemed to me undesirable. I felt (ten years ago) that the creation of such channels would widen the already dangerous gap between the reasonably well educated and the deplorably ill educated. Also that (no matter what the law or the FCC said) the arrival of an ETV station would tend to relieve the commercial broadcaster of some of his cultural obligations and might also tend to encourage educational broadcasters in their dislike or fear of all the processes by which TV *attracts*—before it begins to entertain or sell or educate.

My hope was for a desirable cultural programming imbedded into the commercial programs so that the same people who were attracted to the latter might catch and perhaps come to care for the other.

It became clear to me that commercial TV either would not or could not accomplish such an exposure.

I am, consequently, a "reluctant convert" to the idea of separate channels. By now, I have found much to admire in the functioning of ETV.

But it will be clear that my whole drive is still toward some form of integration.* (When UHF becomes the single system, the first step will have been taken. If not on the same station, two kinds of programs will at least be in the same *air*.)

II

This prejudice is associated with my own formulation (for propaganda purposes) of the generally accepted idea that education exists outside of the school system.

In order to justify the demand I make for a constantly increasing ex-

---

* One of the prime functions of ETV is to contribute to making commercial TV more useful to the community. ETV can do this by forming more critical, more intelligent, and more demanding audiences for commercial TV.

amination of all TV, I put it that we have a pluralistic system of education in which pre-kindergarten to postgraduate is only a segment. The others include advertising, magazines, the pulpit, our political campaigns, and many others. And, of course, broadcasting. The propaganda is that no part of this pluralistic system can be permitted to function without constant examination by a "major minority." In a sense, all my professional work is intended to increase the number of and the awareness of that minority group.

III

I am not qualified to discuss ETV as a means of instruction. If we do not already know, we soon must discover what subjects are useful and into what areas ETV is merely an intruder.

But direct instruction cannot be dismissed from a total view of ETV in relation to our arts and culture. In particular, we will face in the next decade a variety of machines for teaching. It may well be that ETV, now considered a mechanistic process tending to displace the human element, will become the mediator between the new machines and the older kind of teaching, that ETV will be much more on the "human side" by contrast with these machines.

The guiding principle would again be for ETV not to attempt what can be better done in other ways. Such subjects as can be best acquired by use of the teaching machines should be left to them—as such subjects which cannot be taught without the teacher, such subjects with which ETV interferes, should not be attempted.

Since the attitudes and the capacities of adults are formed or influenced in childhood, the bearing of in-school ETV on the general culture is significant. At the moment, I believe that the principles governing this side of ETV will closely resemble those governing the general activity of ETV in adult education or cultural broadcasting. But I am not sure.

Granted that instructional programs must be created with the needs of a special audience in mind, that nothing which can diminish their effect must be added (or omitted), it is still possible that programs addressed to high school and college students may be useful to a nonschool audience. The rule here would be that such programs should be available, but that no great effort to attract the outside audience should be made.

Except where specifically noted, the rest of this memorandum is concerned with that side of ETV which can be called cultural, the area of adult education being included in that term.

IV

A simple way to block out the functions of ETV is to assume that it need not duplicate the work of C (for commercial) TV and to discover what CTV cannot or will not or perhaps should not do.

On the positive side, the overlap is extensive: both C and E TV can and should arouse interest in a variety of subjects, for instance. But it may be impossible for CTV to satisfy all the interests it arouses and it may, therefore, be one function of ETV to capitalize on this arousal-function of CTV.

I have put CTV in my list of elements in a pluralistic educational system. It is clear from the other elements listed that being a segment of the system does not imply the use of the same methods in pursuit of a single aim. One of the methods of education which is *not* often used by broadcasters (in prime listening time at least) is teaching. It is my conviction that this is proper and that in such fields as economics, for instance, CTV should be discouraged (if it cannot be forbidden to teach) and in certain others, such as abnormal psychology, it should work under the strictest outside supervision.

(By teaching economics, I mean something approaching indoctrination. It seems to me improper that doctrine affecting the relations of employer and employee should be promulgated under the sponsorship of a corporation or of a labor union.)

It should not be difficult to make a list of the relatively few areas from which CTV should absent itself.

If ETV can be effectively used in these (excluded) areas, it should be used. However controversial the subject may be in itself, the pursuit of knowledge must be untrammeled. The unique and invaluable quality of ETV is that it is disinterested. It was unrealistic of me to suppose, when I was against separate channels, that this quality could exist in the atmosphere of commercial broadcasting, even on sustaining programs on CTV.

We can set aside such programs as Sunrise Seminar and Continental Classroom which are in many ways precisely what ETV has done or should do and constitute, in a way, a votive offering of CTV, an expression of gratitude for possessing channels largely closed to ETV.

In addition, CTV has produced more and more programs recently which are of pronounced cultural interest. They depart from the intentions of ETV because they are not presented in a planned order—an order, that is, in which the complete apprehension of the fifth in a series depends on familiarity (at least) with the preceding four. (A few exceptions exist.) And as they are not cumulative, they are not and do not pretend to be inclusive. That they are taken to be complete, rendering further attention to the subject treated unnecessary, is a grave fault. In part it stems from the atmosphere: even the most tightly woven of CTV's dramatic or comedy series is presented as complete in itself.

Some presentations, with the most pretentious auspices, not only depart from, but go against the grain, of all education. The series on science sponsored by Bell Labs with the names of learned societies at the end is the most flagrant offender.

Anticipating a point I shall develop later, I would say that one of the functions of ETV is the correction of such distortions.

The egregious vulgarity of the Bell Labs program is important to us because that program brings into high relief some of the elements which far better cultural programs on CTV feel obliged to incorporate.

The function of these elements is first to diminish all demands on the audience and then to eliminate any sense that learning of any kind requires *work*. Even such programs as Bernstein and the Philharmonic are to an extent constructed so as to dissipate attention—or to make sure that attention attaches itself to a rapid succession of different objects.

We must keep in mind the possibility that CTV cannot put on programs calling for attention concentrated over a relatively long period and that it can only indirectly encourage its audiences to seek further knowledge involving study and the unaccustomed activity of thinking.

And this, in turn, lands us in a difficult situation: we must decide whether we are to have two totally different kinds of broadcasting—different in tone, in presentation, in the demands they make.

If we reject this—and I think we must because separate kinds of broadcasting multiplies the disasters which I feared in separate channels—we must find the ways in which the two systems can each use the other. In the case of ETV, how it can use certain elements of CTV without sacrificing its primary purpose.

V

Before making assumptions about the process of assimilation—which on the bad side means that ETV incorporates some of the more attractive faults of CTV—we must observe the fundamental merit of our commercial system of broadcasting: that it can and does *change*. (Even if it changes for the worse at times, it is a non-rigid system which means that the direction in which it changes can be influenced from outside itself.)

If CTV changes in certain aspects, the borrowings and adaptations ETV will make need not be at all injurious.

This returns me to my footnote on page 103. I put it then on the grounds of usefulness to the community that ETV should take part in altering the nature of CTV. I put it now on the second ground, that the two systems should be able to live together and this will be easier to accomplish, will involve less sacrifice of essentials, if CTV, to an extent, changes in such ways as to share more common ground with ETV.

The most effective way—the one, also, which requires the most tact and discretion—is this: ETV should be a direct and open critic of CTV.

Considering how hostile many people, totally outside the field of education, are in their reactions to CTV, it may seem excessive to ask educators to insist that criticism is an act of judgment involving appreciation and correction. This is the area of tact. We must make it clear that we understand what CTV is doing, are aware of its efforts and successes.

This critical appreciation I want should exist in both spheres of ETV— it should reach into the schools and to the adult community.

In the schools, ETV might accomplish what otherwise seems to me— after five years of trying—impossible. That is the introduction of the materials of the mass media into the curriculum of grade and high schools (with the consequent appearances of courses in communication as regular events in the colleges).

This is not the same thing as using special TV programs (a production of Hamlet, e.g., or a special on geophysics). It means courses on the Western in American Entertainment from the Dime Novel to the TV Serial— the incorporation of the usual materials as objects of study. If ETV took the lead, place might be found for such study in high schools at the latest. The development of a critical attitude toward TV (and the other mass media) would be a natural result.

In a different atmosphere, the subject can form a constant part of the service rendered within its own community by individual ETV stations apart from what is done by NETwork ETV. As in the schools, television is studied in the way the English romantic poets or Roman history is studied, so in the home, television is discussed and analyzed as economics and music may be.

(One such program is now being planned by Station WHYY. It would at times be a review of what had occurred on the air within a recent period, would bring representative citizens into discussion with representatives of the producing stations and networks.)

The wished-for result is the enlargement of the critical public. Ideally such a program as that planned by WHYY should appear on the commercial stations, but (again after some five years of trying) I find it impossible to persuade stations to undertake such self-criticism.

In attempting a judicious and critical report on CTV, in which ample opportunity is given to stations to present their view of their own accomplishments, ETV lays the groundwork for another form of cooperation.

VI

In broad terms, ETV can invite CTV to make the public aware of what ETV is doing. As an institution profoundly "affected with the public interest" ETV should be subject to public criticism and this can properly occur both in the daily press and on CTV stations.

It is unlikely that the programs of ETV will be regularly viewed on commercial stations—the parallel reverse situation will not persuade CTV operators to devote that much time to the subject.

But it is possible to get local CTV stations to publicize what ETV is doing. Without pressure or argument, Station KING in Seattle gave an hour's preview of the ETV schedule at the beginning of a season—as a result of a casual suggestion.

VII

Reciprocal programming, an extension of the above, is possible on a considerable scale.

The difficulties are obvious. I take a sample case: a CTV station is to present an hour program on space-flight. In all probability, the station does not know when its network will schedule this program. Nor will it want the ETV station to cut into the potential audience by doing a background study—even if this study specifically stops short of the ground covered by the CTV program.

But if the ETV station knows far enough in advance, it can schedule a program or programs after the CTV presentation to capitalize on the interest aroused. And the CTV station will publicize this further attention to the subject—since it is, in effect, a testimony to the significance of what CTV has done.

In some instances the CTV station may invite ETV to attack the subject in advance. Again the publicity value is high to both sides and skillful editing can dovetail the two kinds of program so that each leads into or out of the other.

However these reciprocal actions are scheduled, they serve a basic purpose: through them, ETV undermines the conviction which, as I have implied, CTV must transmit to its audiences—the conviction that in a single program or a single series the entire subject has been covered, that nothing of interest or concern has been omitted, that the viewer has nothing more to *do*. It is a prime function of ETV to persuade viewers that neither knowledge nor understanding is ever finished.

VIII

This function ETV performs quite apart from any stimulus provided by CTV. If we define this function in the simplest terms it is to perpetuate the sense of the continuity of our culture. ETV does this (again in simple terms) when it makes people aware of the nature of the arts and the satisfactions to be drawn from them.

And, of course, one of the arts which it must deal with is the art of education.

IX

We have here a special case because ETV is itself a part of the educational system. But I believe the general principles, the approach and in great part the methods, will conform to the same elements in dealing with this art as in the others.

Perhaps the chief difference is that here we can say with considerable confidence that we want people to *know about*—without pretending we will bring them to *know*—the subject. It is possible that in all the out-of-school work it does, ETV will function best at the *know-about* level, and its value will lie in that *knowing-about* is a necessary—an essential—step beyond *hearing-about*, which CTV accomplishes.

Knowing about in ETV is knowing the truth about, the essence of, the relations of, the significance of.

In the special case of education, ETV must add perhaps a stronger element of correction. Just as the popular image of the teacher, the one presented in popular iconography, is a caricature, the concepts of education, what it is and does, what it is useful for, its part in a complete life—all these are distorted. ETV has already suffered from this. It is "tuned out" before it is ever tuned in because of the associations with its name.

The alteration I am considering, a change in the atmosphere in which education has its being, will be brought about by everything ETV does, particularly by its presentation of the arts and sciences. Possibly this indirection is a better way than an immediate effort to deal with education itself. Inevitably if a direct effort is made it will be part of the total cultural function of ETV; it will not stand alone. The question is whether it should be brought in at all—or can we trust to the indirect effect of everything else we do.

My own inclination is toward using the direct attack also. At every point the prejudice against school and schooling (which is as old as Shakespeare at least) is "noise" between ETV and its receivers. The concept of the educator as the enemy of society is somewhat more recent. One of the most powerful of accepted ideas is associated with a series of pictures: teacher's pet—the weakling boy prodigy—the grind at college—the pedant at the end of the process. While it proceeds with other matters, ETV can accelerate its effect if it undermines and demolishes this series of images.

And part of the undermining process is, of course, to reduce to a minimum the elements which at any time give validity to the ancient prejudices.

It is hardly self-serving to include education in the arts which ETV makes known to the public. The need for interpreting what is current in educational practice, of providing some comprehension of the changes taking place, puts on ETV the compulsion to interpret its own function to its public which involves self-criticism.

The over-all purpose is as it would be in relation to music or architecture or mathematics. What satisfactions does the mature human being get from having had—and continuing—an education? What greater satisfactions from knowing more and thinking more clearly about these things?

I do not, at the moment, know how an ETV station would set about giving a series of programs on education. I am sure that what is done should be related to the status of the school system in the community served.

X

It is useful to accept a recent division between the performing arts and the others (the graphic and plastic arts in particular, although the arts of fiction and poetry would also belong here since they can be apprehended without being performed).

Here as elsewhere we have to pass our own statute of limitations. In one of its aspects all television is a form of the total dramatic art and, ideally, can project from the screen all that is projected from the stage. Quite apart from technical difficulties, it can hardly do as much for painting or architecture, among others.

Where the medium does not go beyond the scope of the illustrated lecture, its highest potential may be only to foster the growth of a body of amateurs whose perceptions are constantly enlivened and whose sensibilities are constantly becoming more acute.

I do not prejudge the case when I say that if this is all ETV (or any TV) can do, the methods used can legitimately be shaded toward the familiar techniques of attracting and, with discretion, diverting, the attention. The general rule is that whatever attracts without interference, whatever seduces without corruption, should be used. The caveat is that no program can safely arouse expectations without fulfilling them—the mode of attraction must be correct for the mode or tone of the subject.

ETV programs have in the past erred in both ways: some seemed based on the presumption that whatever persuades an audience to stay with a program is of necessity a corruption of the program's essence; others have imitated, none too well, the techniques of CTV, even to suggesting the tones of the commercials, and have proceeded from that point to sedate instruction.

XI

It is impossible to put down rules suitable to the various arts. One enterprise ETV can undertake, in cooperation with public and art schools, is keeping alive the capacity for simple creation which, it is now understood, tends to decline and even disappear long before grade school is over.

This would again be an encouragement to amateurism—a risk ETV can easily afford to take in this field. (As I have been discussing chiefly programs for adults at home, I note that this function may be most effectively carried out during school hours. Its usefulness at other times may become marked in another generation when the fruits of in-school direct lessons in drawing, painting, and sculpture are evident.)

If we accept the probability that a person sitting in front of a TV set is not properly placed for getting as much out of a picture as he would be with a portfolio of reproductions or certain issues of *Life* and *Look* in his hands, we can also say that an art program can inspire a visit to a museum or a gallery at least as effectively as the other media.

The late Henry Francis Taylor (who once said that "for the graphic arts, the invention of television is as important as the invention of movable type was for literature") hoped for more from TV. The Metropolitan Museum of Art, of which he was then director, was already overcrowded. He thought television could bring the arts into the home. On the other hand, the programs planned by the Art Institute of Chicago had as their goal an increased attendance—the Institute at that time could welcome 25 percent more people.

In contemporary popular graphics, ETV can move more easily. Line drawings, advertisements, and posters lend themselves better to observation. Associating these familiar forms with their relatives in the fine arts and subjecting the popular arts to understanding criticism can well be done by ETV.

All of this put together amounts to a meagre function for ETV in the graphic arts. To an extent ETV is reduced to the arousal-of-interest factor of CTV with the difference that ETV never makes a closed circle of arousal and satisfaction—it still sends its audiences ahead, elsewhere, to further discoveries.

We recognize this with less prejudice in the field of architecture. In many ways the most public of the public arts, architecture has endless facets of human interest. But the TV screen is not the best place to observe even its aesthetic factors.

But from the TV screen can come something to make the book or the museum or any direct observation of works of art incomparably more valuable: a sense of the relation of one art to another and of all the arts to a well-developed life. Since the TV screen can, within the same limitations, do as much for science, it can also relate the arts and the sciences, not pretending to be a prime or final source of knowledge, but being what it must be, a guide to understanding.

XII

The place of ETV in those arts which it can *render*, as contrasted with those it can chiefly discuss, and its relation to CTV in this field, are not complicated.

We note a steady movement in CTV toward using more drama of a very high order and toward productions closer to the intention of the original. The more significant the play, the less likely any serious falsification. We can anticipate productions of the established repertory of theater equal to those of the professional stage.

Given the economic factor which prevents ETV from engaging the expensive (and often the best) talent, it would seem reasonable not to duplicate what CTV is doing. It is also reasonable and desirable to rebroadcast the CTV productions whenever they are made available. (Here and in several other fields, the importation of tapes and kines from Britain and Canada is desirable.)

In contemporary drama, when a single independent station produces 40 to 50 plays a year, it is natural for ETV to transmit rather than to produce. (The Play of the Week was bought by an ETV station and attracted so large an audience that the following season, a CTV station in the community took over. The ETV station management was saddened—but the whole process was beneficial to all concerned.)

In the adjacent field—the dramatization of stories and novels—the history of CTV is mixed.

In general, the process of adaptation combines two purposes: exploitation of the qualities for which the original is famous and assimilation of these same qualities to the familiar ones of contemporary television. A novel by Henry James becomes a story of intrigue and *Vanity Fair* begins to resemble a daytime serial. The process antedates popular entertainment—the translations of Homer have also been made in the light of contemporary taste.

And with the enthusiastic approval of some of our most famous writers, CTV producers have totally altered the content and significance of the works they have bought.

Here the corrective function of ETV is evident. In the direct criticism of CTV which I have proposed, the significance of these debasements can be stressed. Whenever possible, faithful presentations should be made. And (as always) the raising of the general level of taste will eventually provide so large an audience for the good work that the second-rate will fall into a low second place.

XIII

These two examples from the graphic arts and from the dramatic, present, I believe, the typical problems of ETV in relation to CTV and, by extension, to other media (mass or limited) which use the cultural materials available to us.

At the beginning I spoke of the division between the things television does well and those done better in other media. I have watched TV and other media long enough to know that confinement to what is done best is impractical. Certain limitations impose themselves—one doesn't use radio as the preferred medium for acrobatics. But we must recognize such circumstances as make television, today, a proper if not ideal, medium for transmitting music. It has become better suited to the ballet than it was 15 years ago. And so on. Each separate art brings its own problems of technique. All of them, together, bring the same problems: what we want to do, why, and are the materials at hand suitable?

I recognize the boundaries of this paper: it reflects not only my experience of the mass media, but also what I think about education as an art and as a function of our society. In what follows, certain other assumptions are made. I think they will be self-evident. In any case, the suggestions I make can be considered without definitions of culture and several other concepts. My definitions are, as I say, implicit in my proposals.

XIV

We shall probably be discussing the sciences and science as a whole in several other papers. I bring it into relation to ETV's position toward other institutions of our general culture because I think ETV can do something here which cannot be done elsewhere.

Again I must omit the more strictly educational use of ETV in the sciences. It seems accepted that the laboratory sciences in particular are in the most favorable field for television in general and naturally for ETV —the apparatus and the action are both instantly appealing.

There are some aspects of special importance. That ETV is itself bound to bring "the two cultures," science and the humanities, closer together is, I should say, self-evident. For the next few years it may be one of the duties of ETV to make sure that in the process of reconciliation, the humanities do not surrender too much. The placing of the different sciences in relation to one another and to the national culture, is one of the things that ETV can do—by the proportion of significance it gives to various elements, by the way it constantly brings their mutual relationship into the open.

The other function is to make science known. To make its nature and its accomplishments and its potential effects more and more widely known —this it seems to me is urgent.

And I have to note here that even within the past few years I have been aware of a reluctance on the part of scientists to accept the obligation of making their work known.

What I look forward to is the formation of a joint effort in which television (preferably both C and E TV) and organized science will each provide a group capable of understanding the other.

It is easier for me to describe the group provided by television: a pool of talent (writers, directors, analysts, and technicians) who know enough to understand what the scientists are saying, with sufficient talent and devotion to make this knowledge understandable by constantly increasing numbers of people, using the capacities of the television system.

(I should like a similar pool available for service to economists and urban developers and poets as well, but I feel that the problems of science are the most urgent now.)

In my mind, this pool of talent should be voluntary and should organize itself, crossing the line between C and E TV in a common effort.

It would be the work of ETV, given its closer contact with certain scientific bodies, to discover what, at any moment, needs to be said. And, at times, to urge upon men of science, their duty to communicate.

My maxim here comes not from a communicator, but from a Nobel laureate in physics: "If, in the long run, you cannot let everyone know what you are doing, what you are doing is worthless." This was said by Erwin Schroedinger. I proposed it to J. Robert Oppenheimer whose only variation was: ". . . if you cannot, in the long run, hope to let everyone know . . ."

XV

And this brings me to the last of the specific subjects I will mention: communications.

In addition to acting as a critic of—and collaborator with—CTV, we have the necessary work of analyzing the nature of the process we are using, of discovering what the powers of communication are, and of making people aware of them.

The proposals made in Sec. V are beginnings only. I think that all of us, no matter how long we have been concerned with the subject, still hold that we have only made a start in our discoveries in communications.

XVI

Since the subject is to be treated in another paper, I have omitted reference to ETV in relation to public affairs and to government. To sum up, I must consider its relation to our society in general terms.

I see little more than a surface ambiguity in the character of ETV—an institution pledged to preserve the basic ideas of education which involve work under disciplined conditions while using technical means most often devoted to entertainment, sometimes devoted, perhaps unconsciously, to undermining the whole process of education.

The difficulties exist. We have to be aware of them even in routine operations and the moment we begin to plan new subjects or new techniques we could be overwhelmed by them.

We can overcome them if we think not of how TV is used for one purpose or another, for one seemingly in opposition to another, but as a method, like reading, which can also be used for the most trivial and the most austere purposes. If we think of people paying attention to it in a process which continues as the process of reading continues, not only from early childhood on, but in our daily lives when we in the course of an hour may read a comic strip and road signs and symbols and a book of philosophy—then I believe we need not be too troubled by the dual nature of our instrument.

I believe we can be clear as to our aims, and devoted to them, without being either afraid or contemptuous of the means which television has put into our hands.

No matter what our declared intent may be, every use to which we put ETV is going to have an effect on our society. This effect may be only a reinforcement of the effect of other institutions (of learning or otherwise). It may—and I think it must—correct and counteract some of these other effects, for one reason because we are all committed to a various, not to a monolithic, society.

Part of the education we shall get as we use ETV is going to be discovery: we will discover more and more precisely what we want our society to be. Fortunately, other people will discover what they want and these wants will not always coincide with ours. If they are more skillful in the use of the same instruments we use, as at this moment they are, we will have to learn skill.

But education has always been a patient process. Patience is too expensive a virtue for me to cultivate—and it is easy for me to recommend it to others. But chiefly I recommend action. It seems to me that we are making action possible by what we are doing: we are taking thought.

Notes by the Author

1. In Section I, the implication is that ETV is preponderantly on UHF channels. This is, of course, not the case. I am the victim of a local situation—in New York there is no ETV station and in Philadelphia it is on UHF. My phrasing reflects my experience.

It is, however, important to note that the number of UHF channels for ETV will increase and it is my guess that the proposed action by which the FCC will look into the possibility of changing a VHF station from commercial to educational use in NYC and Los Angeles, will not proceed very far.

It is still in the interest of ETV to look toward a single (which has to be UHF) system.

2. One of the cultural institutions omitted from consideration in my paper is the home.

In two aspects, ETV enters the home: programs of instruction supplementing those broadcast during school hours and programs which are either intended as adult education or generally cultural.

In the first, we can assume that one parent (or other adult) is at home and may be curious or interested—the turned-on set attracts attention to itself. To an extent the adult may watch what the child watches. Given the primary purpose of these broadcasts, they cannot be essentially modified in order to attract adults—but the chances are that above a certain school grade the subject will have several points of attraction. It would, for instance, be proper to refer back to what was known in a given area twenty years ago compared with what is now known (as in certain sciences) and this back-reference will be of interest to the adult. And there is evidence that adults are fascinated by the method of teaching itself.

We have an opportunity to develop shared-education. One desirable consequence is the greater participation of parents in the management of the public schools in their communities.

Through the schools, parents can be informed of the home curriculum and local newspapers can be influenced to carry the ETV schedule so that it becomes a natural part of TV viewing. Just as teachers now often let parents know that the children should be allowed (or encouraged) to see certain CTV programs for later use in the schoolroom, parents can also be told what programs the children are to observe on ETV which will be of special interest to adults.

3. The situation is reversed, with further opportunities of shared education, when evening programs are transmitted primarily for adults.

Again a certain amount of casual attention can be counted on—the situation differing chiefly because CTV is in competition for the child's time.

It should be possible, at a minimum, to let parents know that certain ETV programs relate to specific subjects in the school curriculum, whether these are or are not televised.

The interrelation of in-school, after-school, and general cultural programs needs to be emphasized, so that each arouses interest in the others.

4. I have assumed that other papers will discuss the changes in methods of teaching demanded by ETV. It is not a subject on which I can speak with experience. One aspect of it is, however, related to my general theme.

Among the institutions of learning with which ETV should have the closest relations is the school or college in which teachers learn how to teach. It should be a specific purpose of ETV to make sure that the use of television in schools and colleges is studied as part of teacher-training and that a steadily increasing number of teachers learn how to use television—not only as the teacher in the room who watches a program with her students, but as teacher on television and, if at all possible, as producer of programs.

Without special knowledge, I make the guess that teachers who will not themselves be on the screen, but will work with ETV programs in the schoolroom, have also a need of special training—in cooperative effort with the TV teacher, in knowing how and why certain TV techniques are used, etc.

5. My paper is concerned chiefly with education through high school.

I do not know enough about the situation in college to speculate usefully. An experiment I am now starting is based on some dissatisfaction I experienced at college where big courses were either lectures (without small seminars) or sections without meeting the authority on the subject, only instructors. Obviously a combination can be made if the course is divided between a speaker on the air and seminars following with instructors who have watched or otherwise become acquainted with the televised program.

I have a favorable impression of closed-circuit TV at Dartmouth, but it is rather vague. I do not know the Chicago Junior College plan—but will try to find out immediately.

6. That ETV must constantly be self-critical has been implied. An inflexible set of standards is not required, but when principles of good conduct in ETV have been discussed and accepted, those concerned with its future need to be constantly alert.

In the past few weeks I have been told that many producers of series for ETV are trying to make each single program within a series self-contained. Without observation I do not know how far this will tend to destroy the orderliness and cumulative effect of a series.

Perhaps here, as in many other areas, we need inventiveness in techniques. There is, I would hope, a way of incorporating a review of past programs into new ones or a way of placing a review program at intervals, which would preserve the educational validity of a series and still achieve some of the effect of completeness.

7. I emphasize a point made in Section IV of my paper: that identifying CTV as part of our pluralistic educational system is intended as recognition of an existing situation. It does not imply identity of purpose. Nor does it imply any judgment of the quality of the education which CTV provides.

It appears to me that CTV in its programs and commercials sets up standards of excellence, that it tells us what is a good life, that it establishes norms of behavior for possible imitation. It does this largely through its entertainments. (We have from Plato through T. S. Eliot to Himmelweit testimony to the educational effect of even the lightest entertainments.)

The standards and norms of CTV are often hostile to those of education in the classic sense—as they are often hostile to those of the pulpit or of the aesthete. It is necessary for ETV not only to correct the excesses of CTV, but also to make itself the center of all the countervailing powers which can give some balance to the total process of education we go through.

I have suggested that the work of ETV will be more effective if it can modify and accept some of the methods of CTV. I am not too afraid of ETV becoming "easy to take" because I feel that at this moment, in dealing with grownups, we are dealing with people far more hostile to education than children ever are. We must lead them gently at first into areas which the mass media, among other things, have taught them to dislike or to fear.

But moving gradually does not mean moving off the road.

TESTIMONY BY MAX LERNER

Before the Television Advisory Panel

Dr. Lerner is a news columnist, and Professor at Brandeis University.

IF I WERE ASKED to sum up very quickly the things that I am anxious about in television as a whole I would use three words: depersonalization, manipulation, and homogenization.

—*depersonalization*, because the audience is regarded as a mass audience and not as individuals in any sense.

—*manipulation*, because the aim is to use them rather than to stretch them, to influence them toward purchasing goods. Such manipulation depends also upon the depersonalization in which the audience is regarded as replaceable parts. In my book the crucial point that I try to make concerning television in relation to the other arts is that in the other arts you sell a product to the audience whereas in television you sell the audience. In an art which is geared to selling the audience it is almost inevitable that the qualities of mind which are developed in the people who are involved with this do not make for an educational outlook.

—*homogenization*, because in order to make the greatest sales possible there is always a tendency to water down.

The thing that interests me most now is trying to sharpen the differences between these two enterprises, the one that sells the audience to a sponsor and the one that tries to reach particular youngsters—or particular adults, for that matter—with education.

What I am suggesting now is the need to have somewhere a group of people—wherever their subsidy will come from it will not come from the sponsorship of advertising—doing the total job, perhaps the job of entertaining as well as educating. I don't know whether this would be a third force, in addition to commercial and educational, or not. But they would do the total job from the standpoint of trying to set standards. I believe we need in America not only a competition of ideas but also a competition of standards. Recently my colleague, Walter Lippmann, has taken up basically the same idea and has advanced it with the kind of lucidity and eloquence which only he is capable of. I would like to approach the whole thing from the standpoint of national purpose. That is, if national purpose is important, what are the channels through which you achieve it? National purpose is something integral to whatever goes on in the minds of the people. Thus, the shaping and rediscovery of the national purpose is integral to the shaping of the minds of youngsters. This is really a Periclean conception: Pericles used to define the state as simply the training and education of the character of the young. Figures which I have seen at NETRC on the number of hours per day which our children spend with television have left me both dismayed and excited—dismayed because of what it is that they are spending their hours with, and excited because of what it could be.

Let me approach this from another point of view by asking a few questions. For instance, what is happening to our population distribution? The city is becoming a shell of what it used to be. The point about the second enterprise is that you do care about the individuals, you do care about their minds, you do care about their personalities. You care very much. In fact, that's your principal objective. Educational television is the kind of television which is aimed at the minds of particular people, not in order to manipulate or persuade or help sell products, but in order to help shape and develop those minds. Educational television has to be concerned with both training and education: training being the transmission of skills, and education being the development of the capacity for meeting problems. One of the characteristics of educational television, in my experience, is that the people in charge are craftsmen, people who care about this purpose of reaching minds. I don't get the same feeling from working with commercial television, even in its public service aspects. I go along with the great necessity of maximizing as far as possible the amount of public service that the commercial people are going to do, but the great difficulty about it in my mind is that it is the same people who apply themselves to it. So that the fact that they label it "public service" does not, for me, render the product terribly different in quality. You cannot have educational television unless you have people who are not conditioned in these ways but are conditioned as craftsmen, as artists, as thinkers, as scientists. I hope that the American people begin to understand the difference. It's a question of "Who's running the show?"

On the Educational Policies Commission which I just joined this year we listened to a report from the superintendent of schools in one of our giant cities, and it was a hair-raising experience to hear what education in that city really is these days. Thomas Jefferson wouldn't recognize it. Much of education there is just policing delinquency, much of it is social work among rather ignorant and uneducated groups, much of it is just language training, and so on. I think that we have to approach the problem of ETV partly from this angle. What do you do in the cities? What this superintendent is trying to do is to use his small group of good teachers on television so that other teachers can watch them in a form of teacher training, as well as a form of student education in the classroom. Another thing that ETV can do in such places is to reach the mothers and fathers in the housing projects with the same education that their children are getting. To me this is thrilling. It couldn't have been done without television. In other words, this is no longer a luxury. It has become a prime necessity, a central mechanism that we have to use.

Now what about the people who have left the cities and gone off to the suburbs? You get in the suburbs more of a feeling of community-centeredness than you do in the city. People who had never gathered together before in the city do gather together in the suburbs. I can see the possibility of ETV being used here in combination watching and study sessions, in which reading material associated with the programs is also distributed. I have a feeling that more and more ETV can be watched in discussion groups in this way.

What about the small towns? They are shells, too, in a way, with so many people leaving them to go to the big cities. This makes it all the more imperative that they be reached in some way—and reached not just by what goes by the name of entertainment but reached in more meaningful ways as well.

Take one other approach, and that is from the standpoint of the life cycle of Americans. It is interesting to note the points of convergence of culture and personality. This happens in a series of stages in our life history. There are certain vulnerable and very decisive stages, particularly in the growing-up years. This is where I am most deeply concerned now. I think that most of us who have studied it at all are agreed that there has been a decline in community in American life and a failure of norms among young people. Perhaps it is because of this that television has made such an impact on the young. My hunch is that youngsters don't want to be entertained; they want to learn, and I think that what they are learning is values. If there is this vacuum of values for many reasons—and there are many, many reasons for this—what the youngsters get from TV is likely to move into that vacuum. Again, we're very anxious about the nature of those values. What happens afterward is equally important, not only those years but other life stages of Americans—for instance, the middle years, particularly now when the children grow up and the mother is still relatively young and when the life span of both sexes is increasing. There is an opportunity for a kind of recapture of the excitement of life in those years for both mother and father. This has never been true in American life before.

I've been taking a number of approaches, you see, and I'm going to take one more. There is great preoccupation with the mass quality of our society, but we are more than a mass society. Within the mass there is also a minority culture, creative America. I am more interested in that minority culture right now than I am even in the mass culture. In the present crisis of our national life the whole problem of education has shifted. We have had one long revolution in education ever since the beginning of the nineteenth century, giving a minimum of education to the children of all of our ethnic groups. We have succeeded in that largely, and we should be proud of it. But the problem now has become a sharper one. The problem now is that we have a relatively short time in which to achieve certain stated goals in diplomacy, in political leadership, in economics, in education, churches, art, etc. These goals can be achieved only by a relatively small number of people, by a minority rather than the mass. Our second educational revolution lies in the task of developing this minority culture rather quickly. We have very few teachers trained, for instance, in the difficult discussion method of teaching, and the only way that you can train teachers in this is by having them watch it in action. ETV seems the best hope for doing this quickly. There are many technical difficulties in all of this, but overcoming technical difficulties is what we are good at.

Incidentally, if we ever are subjected to thermonuclear destruction we may discover in ETV a very real potential which no one had thought of before, the potential of helping with the tragic but necessary task of rebuilding.

I associate myself completely with Mr. Frederich Ford on the necessity of stirring up the educational profession to asking for more, and for allocating to them as much as we can—and I may say that even if they are not able to use it terribly well at the beginning they will learn how to use it well. They will learn because if the job is urgent enough there are a number of them who are dedicated enough to do it.

(In reply to a Panel question concerning the goals of the minority culture:) Lenin used to say that in Communist societies the question was "Who whom?"—meaning, "Who does what to whom?" "Who liquidates whom?" "Who rules whom?" I suspect that our question so far among many of our youngsters has been "Who gets what?" "What's in it for me?" I would say that part of the process that we are dealing with here is to change the question. . . . It is difficult to pinpoint the 10 to 15 percent of our students who are mentally gifted. Some of the flashy ones turn out to be not terribly good after a while. They were just flashy, that's all. Some of the bright ones are bright only in the sense that they give back your answers to you. Sometimes the very best of them are the ones who have a fire burning in their bellies, as Carlyle used to say. They may not be terribly fast, but they've got the fire, and the fire comes out eventually.

Educating this group is really a very egalitarian idea. Thomas Jefferson used to say that what counts in a democracy is the aristocracy of virtue and talent—not the aristocracy of blood, of heredity, of power, of money, of color, of religion, but of virtue and talent. That is true egalitarianism. Get at the youngsters with character and ability and get at them no matter what their skin is like or their name is like or anything else. And pay as much as needs to be paid to develop this. If your purpose is national, then your means needs to be national. If this is our treasure, then we had better use it properly. To me, this is a completely democratic idea.

Let me illustrate it by telling you what happened to me in Warsaw a couple of years ago, after my book was published. A group of Communist journalists and professors said to me, "We've heard about your book, but we haven't read it. It's a long book. . . . Tell us in one word what is the essence of American civilization! That was a tough job, to condense a thousand pages into one word. I thought very hard, "What is it? Freedom? Authority? Democracy? Tolerance?" Then I finally heard myself saying "Access."

They said, "We've heard of American success, but we've never heard of American access." I said that we have a Declaration of Independence which says that all men are created free and equal. I hope that we are created free, but I know that we are not created equal. As a parent I know it; as a teacher I know it. Every businessman knows it. We have very unequal potential. But I said that we have a very curious idea in our democracy and that is that there ought to be equal access to equal opportunity for each of these people with very unequal potential to develop this unequal potential to the fullest.

IV. THE PROBLEM OF IMPROVING PROGRAMS

How do educational television programs look to a friendly critic? To a commercial program producer? To a noncommercial station manager? To the national program center? To a distinguished adult educator? And how do these different observers think that programs may be improved?

A FRIENDLY CRITIC ON ETV PROGRAMS

By Sydney W. Head

Dr. Head is Director of Broadcasting and Film Services at the University of Miami.

PART I OF THIS MEMORANDUM attempts to clarify some questions of principle and practice concerning the function of noncommercial television broadcasting in relation to commercial television broadcasting. Part II attempts part of a working definition of ETV. Part III consists of a series of recommendations based on the implications of the definition, and Part IV adds some further recommendations.

I

When television criticism follows the model of traditional literary and dramatic criticism it is likely to go wide of the mark, for television is experienced by most viewers not as a series of isolated events, like so many separate books or stage plays or theatrical films or concerts, but as a concatenation of related events. Any given program is likely to be viewed in a setting provided not only by adjacent programs, but also by an established viewer-orientation toward the service as a whole. Current theories concerning the effects of mass media emphasize the importance of non-content influences which modify the perception of media content, the intervening variables other than content which affect the meanings of messages for audiences. One of the recognized intervening variables is the medium itself, more precisely the particular representative of a medium to which an audience is attending at the moment.

This notion has almost from the beginning of broadcasting been an important factor in the strategy of commercial broadcast station management; more recently it has been articulated in the concept of "station image" and subjected to considerable analysis. The attitudes audiences form which go into making up a station image are the product of many influences other than the specific content of programs. For example, the "personalities" heard and seen on a station and with whom the audience identifies the station have a powerful influence; so do publicity and promotion, network affiliation, visual impressions, the pacing and "sound" of continuity, the status of sponsors using the station (they have their own images which can enhance or detract from the station image).

It follows from the experience of commercial broadcasting that a critical evaluation of ETV programs necessarily leads one to consider non-content factors, which really means evaluation of general management policies as a whole. These policies in commercial broadcasting revolve around the unitary motive of commercial profit, which provides a relatively clear-cut, mensurable goal so that the relations of policy to programs and programs to audiences are relatively easy to define. Legal regulation in the public interest modifies this goal but does not actually obscure it. Educational broadcasting, however, appears not to have such a clear-cut goal, as can be seen by the wide divergence of policies among the existing stations, most strikingly the differences between community-sponsored stations and state-sponsored networks of stations.

Yet much as one ETV station may differ from another in its objectives and program policies, there is at least one thing all have in common: ETV stations, by definition, are expected somehow to differ crucially from commercial stations. This difference is their justification for existence. Measurable differences certainly exist in practice. Schramm has enumerated a number of them: ETV stations are on the air, on the average, less than half as long as commercial stations; they use only about half as much national network programming (and even this is not network programming in the technical sense), they produce about three times as much live programming proportionate to their total programming, over three times as much informational programming but less than half as much news, their audiences are minuscule compared to audiences of commercial stations, and so on.

None of these differences, however, helps us in definitively classifying a given, single program. We cannot, in practice, look at each individual program in isolation and always say "This is uniquely a commercial station program" or "This is uniquely an educational station program." Commercial television has its "Continental Classroom" and ETV has its dramas and quizzes. The practical distinction between the two services lies, apparently, in unspecified differences of degree and differences in program organization: commercial television is not likely to devote more than a small fraction of its total air-time to "Continental Classrooms," nor is it likely to schedule even one "Continental Classroom" at 8:30 in the evening.

Since the crucial difference in the services appears not to lie in the content of particular programs but in the more abstract realm of relative quantities and temporal relationships, let us look for a definition in the area of those principles which are needed to form judgments about these relativities. In other words, what in principle differentiates ETV from commercial television, and what does this in turn imply about practice?

In terms of public policy, the reasoning underlying the decision to withhold a minority of available television channels from commercial service appears to be the belief that commercial motivation necessarily imposes limitations upon the scope of the service it produces. This is not necessarily a value judgment, in the sense that it is immaterial whether the limitations are "good" or "bad" as long as limitations exist. We regard it as axiomatic in our society that public communication should be as free from restraints as possible, leaving it to the free play of the competition among ideas to produce the maximum variety and leaving it to the individual to make his choices among the options provided.

Experience as well as *a priori* assumptions leads us to believe that the commercial motivation does in fact impose limitations on broadcast programs. We expect, for example, a certain imbalance in content due to the reluctance of advertisers to take chances—either on new ideas or on controversial or unpopular ideas. We expect that, most of the time, when there is a choice between two programs, one of which will be more popular than the other, the more popular program will be chosen, irrespective of the intrinsic merits of the two programs. I suppose no one was so naïve as to imagine that setting up a class of noncommercial broadcasting stations would automatically compensate for all the limitations presumed to be inherent in commercial programming. Nevertheless, we felt justified in expecting that the noncommercial service would be demonstrably different from the commercial service—different, moreover, in the direction of providing some of the aspects of service which commercial programming, by its very nature, seems likely to lack altogether, or at least to lack in appropriate quantity.

Before pursuing the implications of this position regarding the *raison d'être* of noncommercial channel reservations, I must digress briefly to dispose of a somewhat different position. This is the cynical argument that it makes little difference what kind of service ETV provides because its real function is not so much to provide a service itself as to pose a continuing threat to the commercial service. In this view, ETV's function is that of a whip, poised to lash the commercial stations into line when they get too greedy. This view may be more widely held than we would like to think. It surprised me to hear it voiced at the conference of the panel which is writing these memoranda. It hardly requires adding that there are surely more direct and efficient and suitable means of controlling commercial broadcasting than this one.

One other digression before returning to the main theme. In this memorandum I am looking at ETV programming from the point of view of *broadcasting* as such, with all the implications this concept has with regard to public policy and the essential nature of the services involved. When an ETV station is used simply as a relay device to feed in-school programs it is not fulfilling the broadcasting function. The same purpose could be accomplished by other methods without occupying a broadcasting channel. In so far as ETV stations are used for this purpose there is no point in attempting to evaluate their programming from the broadcasting point of view.

This, I realize, is a rather radical statement from the standpoint of those concerned with the viability of the ETV service. In my own community, for example, we might well have no ETV station at all were it not for the fact that most of the time the station is used for precisely the relay purpose I have described. Pragmatically, if asked "What would you rather have—non-broadcast use of the channel during the day so that the school system can save money and improve teaching, with the dividend of a broadcast service in the evening—or no ETV station at all?" I would have to choose the first alternative. But this does not make it a desirable situation, nor does it justify the situation in principle.

It is unfortunate, I think, that a dichotomous point of view has been allowed to develop within the field of ETV—though perhaps it was inevitable. There seems to be a distinct trend toward a pulling apart of ETV interests into separate camps—in-school teaching on the one hand and noncommercial *broadcasting*, as such, on the other. We see this in the sharp contrast between community-sponsored and school-sponsored stations; we see it in the tendency to erect a *mystique* of television teaching as a form of communication by television with unique characteristics setting it apart from other forms of television production; we see it in the rivalries between broadcast-oriented personnel and education-oriented personnel. The widespread use of closed-circuit television has, of course, greatly encouraged this trend toward divided viewpoints.

Returning now to the main theme, I proceed from the proposition that the justification for noncommercial channels is the need to insure that the country's television broadcasting service will not be constricted by commercial television's supposedly inherent programming limitations. Let us examine some of these presumed limitations and the extent to which ETV appears to fulfill the role of ameliorator.

One of the most essential ingredients of the public communications media from the viewpoint of public policy is the exposition of conflicting opinions on subjects of general significance—in short, controversy. It is generally believed—and evidence is not lacking—that the commercial service has a natural tendency at best to avoid controversy, at worst to suppress it. It is understandable that advertisers do not wish to give offense, even to small minorities; it is understandable that, when the object is to reach majority (or at least very large minority) audiences, unpopular opinions are likely to be neglected; it is understandable that a medium which is itself a private commercial enterprise is likely to reflect the pre- vailing commercial philosophy. Nevertheless, under the pressure of regu- latory standards, commercial broadcasting does give us at least a smatter- ing of controversial material in its programming. Whether it covers as wide a range of subjects as it should and whether it occupies as large and prominent a place as it should relative to other types of program content in the commercial service is the debatable point.

When we turn to the practice of noncommercial stations, a surprisingly parallel set of statements might be made. ETV, too, has its reason for avoiding controversy; ETV, too, does nevertheless program some contro- versial material. And again, it remains debatable whether this material is as prominent or as frequent in the noncommercial service as it should be. We find in noncommercial stations a more varied set of inhibiting con- siderations, perhaps, but nevertheless they are there. If the station depends upon community support it has to be very careful not to get into contro- versial areas that might alienate its chief supporters—who, ironically, may well be representatives of those same business interests which influence commercial television. If the station depends upon tax sources, it has to be very careful not to embarrass elected officials or representatives whose constituents might question the use of public funds to further points of view with which they are not in sympathy. In the absence of comprehensive objective quantitative comparisons between the two services (meaningful data would be exceedingly difficult to assemble) one can do no more than make an informed guess. My guess is that, at the very least, commercial television does as good a job in handling controversy as noncommercial television—possibly a good deal better job. At the worst it can certainly be said that ETV does not represent any dramatic improvement over com- mercial TV in this area.

From this pessimistic conclusion flow several possible further deduc- tions: (1) ETV is, to this extent, a failure and an unjustified burden on the frequency spectrum; (2) ETV has not succeeded in this area so far but must and can do so in the future as it matures; (3) the neglect of controversial program material is not exclusively the by-product of com- mercialism in the television service, but is in fact due to factors more intrinsic to the nature of television itself.

My opinion leans toward the last of these deductions. I think that the critics of broadcasting, over the years, have tended to start with historical antecedents in mind and have not made sufficient allowance for the unique characteristics of broadcasting as a public medium as compared to the older public media. I have discussed this viewpoint at length elsewhere and will merely reiterate here the conclusion that John Stuart Mill's single dissident among the whole of mankind "might talk on a street corner, cir- culate pamphlets, make a documentary film, or use many other private avenues of expression; but he could not reasonably assert a right to use the public facilities of broadcasting." In other words, no matter what the sponsorship of a broadcasting station—advertisers, taxes, or donations— that sponsorship is bound to have some restrictive influence on the station's programming, directly or indirectly. Timidity about causing trouble, reluctance to offend, fear of economic or other reprisal—these are inevitable in any undertaking as large, as expensive, as complex, and as replete with public ramifications as a broadcasting station must be. If a program is suppressed or a subject avoided it makes no essential difference whether the reason was fear of not getting elected again or fear of having an advertising account canceled.

This conclusion does not imply that ETV should be relieved of the obligation to program controversial, or potentially controversial, material, any more than commercial broadcasting should be relieved of that obligation. It simply means that it was a mistake to assume that ETV was destined to compensate fully for this particular weakness of commercial broadcasting.

Moving on to a second program area where it is generally held that commercial broadcasting is limited because of its commercialism, let us consider the area of inventiveness and novelty in programming. This can be variously expressed—the need for experimentation on the one hand, or the fact of stereotyping and slavish imitation on the other. To what extent has ETV lived up to expectations in this area? Again, objective data of a comprehensive sort would be hard to come by, but my impression is that ETV has created precious little that is genuinely new and exciting, while commercial television has done a good deal in this direction. I am sure the ETV program people who have worked so hard and devotedly to do much with little will challenge this conclusion, but I believe it is broadly true. Moreover, it is perfectly understandable and forgivable; for it is literally not possible to be creatively original very often or very consistently, and if you haven't the money for the exploration of many dead-ends and for jettisoning many aborted efforts it's all the harder. So I do not mean to underestimate or to dispose lightly of the real achievements of ETV in this area but merely to point out that, once again, if we thought that imitativeness, lack of originality, and conservatism in programs was exclusively the product of commercialism in broadcasting we were overlooking the much more fundamental cause in the nature of the medium itself.

I turn now to a third program area where ETV was expected to make up for the deficiencies of commercial broadcasting—the frequent production of programs of high cultural value. During the years of the initial promotion of the idea of implementing the reserved channels, a favorite selling point was that opera and ballet would at last find a home in broadcasting. Evaluation of the performance of ETV in this area in particular (but certainly in the two previously discussed areas as well) requires consideration of the size of the audiences of the two services. For example, how long would it take all the ETV stations together to reach the audience of a single NBC Opera production, and how many comparable productions has ETV had to offer? The comparison, I realize, is unfair, but it should be made if only to lay to rest the unrealistic and illusory promises that have been put forward in the name of ETV in the past.

Let us consider a little further the question of the ETV audience—its size and its composition. The published data on ETV circulation, while understandably put in the most optimistic statistical form possible, if coldly appraised indicate an extremely small audience. Generally the audience for any single program is so small as not to be quantifiable by conventional audience-size measurement methods used in commercial broadcasting. This limited reach cannot, of course, be ascribed alone to failure of ETV programs to attract audiences. Hypothetically, 50 stations could blanket the country, reaching over 90 percent of the population, but ETV stations are neither so powerful nor so strategically located as to have this physical reach. But even within the larger metropolitan areas, the audience for the individual ETV program is generally so small as to raise a question about the justification of the expense of reaching it.

However, ETV does not, like commercial television, regard viewers in purely quantitative terms. It appears that, small though the ETV audiences may be, they are qualitatively significant in that they tend to include that stratum of the population in which the opinion leaders are found. Again referring to current theories on mass media effects, it is recognized now that the mass media do not replace personal influence, that the audience of the media should not be regarded atomistically. Nevertheless, television *is* a mass medium. Any television station has the potentiality of reaching from 70 percent to over 90 percent of the population within its signal area; with this potentiality, it would seem exceedingly inefficient and wasteful of resources for a station to settle for an audience of only 1 or 2 percent.

II

In order to get sharp focus on issues, I have deliberately put the foregoing generalizations in the most pessimistic forms possible. I feel this kind of negative emphasis is a necessary corrective for this reason: the whole history of ETV has been one of a constant struggle to sell and promote an idea, and I have nothing but respect and admiration for the idealism, enthusiasm, and perseverance of those who have led in this struggle. But, as we look forward to future growth and progress in ETV, it is important that we don't let this promotional aura obscure our own judgment.

The previous section was intended to lay the groundwork for a realistic definition of the function of ETV because it seems essential for its future development to arrive at some kind of consensus about what ETV is in relation to commercial television. I think first of all it should be obvious now that ETV is not the cure-all for the deficiencies of commercial television. It cannot, by virtue of being noncommercial, automatically rise above the limitations inherent in the medium of television itself. And even if it could, no purpose would be served if it did not reach audiences of significant size, a size appropriate to the costs of erecting and operating the ETV stations.

Two requisites are necessary to the realization of ETV's potential as a valid, full-scale alternative service: first, a suitable definition of goal in terms of service, second, sufficient freedom of action to pursue that goal with minimum restraints from the forces which always threaten programming freedom.

The goal of ETV, to put it axiomatically, is (or should be) to provide first of all a *service*—not just a conglomeration of programs, but a *sequence* of events which relate directly to the needs of its audience as they emerge throughout the day, the week, the year. To this extent, ETV's function is no different from that of commercial television. The difference lies in the identity of the audience and the kinds of needs served.

A second axiom is that it's the function of ETV to serve a *specific* audience, representing perhaps the upper quartile in terms of education and social awareness. ETV cannot be all things to all men—this is the problem of commercial television. But having identified that minority ETV seeks to serve, ETV must really serve it—not only *provide* the service, but build the audience *for* the service. It's a matter of defining a limited objective but also of reaching that objective fully.

The audience-objective must necessarily be a matter of local option. Obviously Boston has a different potentiality than Chapel Hill in terms of audience. But in each service area an appropriate audience-goal needs to be set up, both quantitative and qualitative. Each station should aim at a minimum number of viewers on the average per program, representing a defined segment of the total population in its area.

Freedom to develop these goals requires that station management be as independent of irrelevant pressures as possible. This means managerial personnel with a highly developed sense of professionalism—*broadcasters*, not school administrators or political appointees or fund raisers. The station management should act as a buffer between the inevitable pressures from special interests and the integrity of the service. The loyalty of management should be first to the audience sought to be served. Management should not have a divided responsibility such as occurs when, for example, the same man has to cultivate the favor of a donor as has to make a program decision which will affect that donor. There should be an arm's length relationship between the two functions.

Without something approaching this degree of programming freedom it is hard to see how ETV can justify its existence, in the long run, as a valid complement to the commercial service. The alternative is the degeneration of ETV into a relay facility for in-school systematic teaching—a perfectly legitimate and desirable use of television, of course, but a non-broadcast use and a radical retreat from the admirable ideal of ETV which animated its pioneer proponents.

III

Applying the notion of service, as developed above, to one's impressions of current ETV practices, some specific suggestions for future development can be deduced. I realize that the flat generalizations on which these suggestions are based need to be softened and qualified by the recognition of many exceptions in the actual practice of some stations, but again I think it healthy at this juncture to face criticism in its most challenging form.

For one thing, the ETV service has been too *intermittent*. In order to serve ideally it should *always* be there with something appropriate to the needs of each part of the day, the week, the year. Most ETV stations program sporadically—they close down entirely on the weekends (just when their service might be most useful), they go on and off the air erratically. It is fundamental to the nature of broadcasting to be consistently available and ETV simply does not meet this criterion.

Second, the ETV service has been too *unpredictable*. This comment covers a multitude of practices which in general amount to the point that a viewer cannot count on receiving a logically and aesthetically satisfying sequential service. For example, he may settle down to a stimulating discussion program only to find himself thereafter faced by a course of formal instruction in some subject of extremely specific and limited interest. If he is not one of the limited few, the service has, for him, been interrupted and he may well abandon it for the rest of the day, if not the rest of the week. Or he may adjust himself to a program in one style or at one level of production only to be brought up with a disconcerting jerk by a program in a totally different style or at an entirely different level of production. Variety is essential, of course, but not variety which is arbitrary, meaningless, unplanned, unpleasant.

Third, the ETV service has been too *inflexible*. In adopting the conventional program lengths, ETV has submitted to an inflexible program structure which it might well have escaped. Not having to worry about the multitude of commercial commitments which necessarily rigidify commercial television, ETV could have come up with a more flexible program structure allowing for more responsive service.

Fourth, the ETV service has been too *pompous*. This term is intended to cover a multitude of practices, errors of both commission and omission. For example, not infrequently you see a program introduced with a ceremoniousness appropriate to the launching of an aircraft carrier, only to find that the ship being launched is a simple little rowboat. More important, however, is the omission of elementary everyday services which could help a great deal to build the habit of ETV watching. These could be merely such routine information as time and weather checks, or could get into more elaborate services such as authoritative current market information for the housewife, news reports, consumer guidance, and so on. Another important area is the choice and build-up of the on-camera and off-camera spokesmen for the station, who more than any other non-content factor are crucial in establishing station image. They are the humanizing influence, the basis for establishing direct personal rapport with the station. I have the impression that the personnel assigned to this crucially important role are often far too conscious of their educational responsibilities and not at all conscious of the realities of television communication.

Fifth, the ETV service has lacked appropriate *style*. All of the previously mentioned topics as well as many more might be subsumed under this heading. Certainly a pompous style would be undesirable, certainly unpredictability involves a lack of consistency in style. ETV stations should be style-conscious and should seek to impress their service with a unique style, recognizably different from the style of all competing stations; whatever its particular genre, it should at least be a style which dramatizes the idea of *service*.

Sixth, the ETV service has not been sufficiently *competitive*. I mean by this that it has not sufficiently recognized that television's competition is every possible other form of human activity. Obviously watching other TV stations is one of the most damaging forms of competition because watchers are by definition television-prone. Thus it behooves the ETV station to program competitively as against its commercial colleagues—in general to devise a service which will be either different or better than that which is available from commercial television for the ETV target audience. But all the other forms of competition have to be considered, too; here station promotion becomes important, and station promotion should be considered as much a part of the television service as the label is a part of the package, the cover a part of the book, the stop-sign a part of the traffic artery. I realize that all ETV station managers are aware of the importance of promotion and a good deal has already been done to help improve it, but I question whether this aspect of the service has been anywhere near fully developed.

Seventh, the ETV service has not found its proper role in the area of *news and current affairs*. This, I confess, is a most difficult problem because news is a major ingredient of both local and network commercial programming and ETV cannot conceivably afford to compete directly with these expensive operations. Yet ETV can never acquire the status as a service that it needs if it neglects the news and current affairs function. Somehow it needs to find its own special brand of service in this area— one which will not be merely repetitive of the commercial service and one which will be especially suited to ETV's target audience.

IV

Finally here are a few concluding recommendations on other points that have been alluded to, or at least implied by, the observations in this memorandum.

In-school broadcasts. It should be a matter of policy that broadcast television stations should be eventually relieved of the responsibility of acting as relay stations for in-school programs. All formal instruction on broadcast television stations should be at a level and in a style suited to general adult consumption, even if the primary purpose is to serve in-school audiences.

Network programs. It is fundamentally unhealthy for ETV to depend upon a single network source of programming. Competition is needed, yet how to obtain it in a noncommercial setting is a difficult problem which requires study.

Live programs. Stations are attempting entirely too much live programming for their resources, even granting that a large proportion of live programs are no more than lectures in televised courses. More syndicated material is needed from more sources.

Station image. Studies should be undertaken of station management policies in relation to station image looking toward greatly expanded regular audiences.

Personnel. ETV should (just as commercial television should) be a great deal more concerned than it is about the fundamental training of future station personnel, looking toward a high degree of professionalism.

Remotes. Direct pickups from the scene-of-action of real events is the purest form of television. ETV should do more of this kind of television. Some stations have been notable for achievements in this area. ETV has an opportunity here for a distinctive service because commercial television is too inflexible to exploit these possibilities fully. In the same connection, a true national network (i.e., interconnected) is badly needed to give the ETV a chance to reach its full potentialities in this area. We should be getting daily live programs from Washington, for example. The network could feed blocks of live remote programming which local stations could cut in and out of at will. Skillful use of edited tape can add greatly to the flexibility and impact of actuality programming.

A COMMERCIAL BROADCASTER ON ETV PROGRAMS

By Irving Gitlin

Mr. Gitlin is an outstanding television producer, now on the staff of the National Broadcasting Company.

THIS PAPER REFLECTS some of the things that a commercial broadcaster of public service programs has observed about educational television station broadcasting. It offers a few suggestions for consideration as we look ahead for ten years. Such a procedure is neither presumptuous nor fantastic for a number of reasons. In the first place, educational television, by overcoming tremendous obstacles, has earned the amazed admiration of many commercial broadcasters. Also it should be remembered that many public service programs are not sponsored, and when they are, the broadcaster, not the sponsor, controls program content. In other words, the job of a public service department is not so radically different from that of an ETV station manager in regard to programming.

There are differences, of course—many and vast ones—between the operations of a commercial public service department and an ETV station, but it might be useful to look at the similarities as well. The programs of a commercial public service department manager are only a part of the total schedule of the station or network. An ETV station manager is responsible for the total schedule. You don't have the cushion of an over-all schedule to fall back on. But this very fact is an advantage to the ETV manager. He can arrange his program schedule to suit the time of the audience he wants to reach—and once he determines what that time pattern is, he can keep it consistent.

Nevertheless, no matter where we are in television programming, we must face certain of the same decisions. We have to know what our audience is—to know to whom we are talking; we must have producers and writers; we have to meet basic costs of production and tailor the format and quality of production to fit the amount of money we have available. The way we meet these problems may be similar or quite different, depending upon our goals and our special interpretation of audience needs.

A number of research studies have demonstrated that the audience for educational television is about one-third of the total potential audience in a community. And some researchers appear to be of the opinion that is almost as big an audience as the ETV stations can get at the present time. Commercial public service broadcasters (both in radio and television) have accepted this figure gladly for years. This is the elite—the doers—the "influentials" in the community. I question the wisdom of this decision. In the first place, it seems doubtful that educational broadcasters are meeting the needs of the community if they reach only this elite group, because it seems to me that these active segments of the various communities can and are getting the information they want in other ways—from discriminating reading, lectures, courses, and even from conversations with like-minded friends. If ETV can reach only this group of adults, perhaps it should concentrate on the young where the need for education is the greatest. Also this concept of serving only one-third of the potential audience seems to pull the rug out from under the hope that educational television can ever be properly supported. And I am not implying, as someone has suggested, that the people ETV is reaching do not need any more education, nor indeed that there are any people who do not need more education. I am merely wondering whether or not this one-third elite may not be getting the continuing education it needs from other sources—"Harper's Magazine," "The Atlantic," and the other things I mentioned. Perhaps they do not need educational television as much as other parts of the general potential audience.

Moreover, isn't there a danger that even this audience, which is discriminating by definition, eventually will be lost to ETV stations which are forced to limit the quality of their production because they lack sufficient income? I am simply saying that we must find a way to put an economic floor under the support for educational television, and that we will not do it if we are content to reach only one-third of the potential audience.

My network and others have discovered recently that we are beginning to go into another stage of public service audience size. With some programs in prime time we can reach a much larger percentage of the total potential audience. I admit it isn't only a matter of dollars. We must have writers and producers with talent, imagination, and courage. The CBS Hong Kong program—produced when I was still with CBS—is an illustration. William Holden told the story of Hong Kong and that made the program. A large audience watched it because they wanted to see him. Nor was using Holden just a gimmick because he had lived in Hong Kong. He still has some financial interests there and cares about the place. Here is an example of how educational broadcasters can convert a natural interest in the glamour of a subject—in this case Hong Kong and William Holden —into an educational experience. I am sure that the people who watched that program learned more about Hong Kong than any tourist spending two weeks there. We got into the heart of the city, its real problems, its real people, and showed actually what happened from day to day, from week to week.

In my opinion the educational television stations will have to decide whether they want merely to be repositories for the high points of culture in our society and always live under a deficit, or whether they will give themselves a broader base. Some people have asked me if I mean by this that the ETV stations must appeal to the largest possible audience. My answer is that this is one answer, although not the only one. Shouldn't we perhaps tax ourselves to educate for the future and use television for more in-school programming, for programs for the handicapped, and many other groups? The point is there is a basic economic problem which must be solved if educational television is to survive. I am convinced that educational television requires a sufficient fall of dollars to pay for all kinds of excellent programming, whether from tax support or broad-base audience support.

There are plenty of bright young men and women who could produce such quality programs, but it takes money to hire them. The money must come from somewhere. What are we going to do to get it? I agree that the basic, interested audience for public service is the elite one-third of the potential. If the programs are great, if enough dollars are spent to get truly creative producers and writers, educational television can reach into the other two-thirds. The problem of television is showmanship—in the best sense of that word. We have set too narrow goals. We have limited our audiences. When we start fighting for audience not for its own sake, but because we have a worthwhile program produced artistically and because we have found some way to get motivated audiences, then we will begin to get somewhere.

I don't mean that the whole educational television schedule should consist of big, expensive productions. There are some very good things being done around the country—on local commercial stations—which are produced for little money. A group of people who know the subject sit around and indulge in good loose talk. But have they checked what is going on in local communities? Sometimes it seems as if the ETV stations are afraid of experimentation, afraid of a broad base of production.

Is it because the ETV stations lack independence? Are they subjected to their own kinds of pressures and, therefore, feel they must conform to rigidly set patterns? Possibly this problem of independence can be solved in part by the National Educational Television and Radio Center, because it is true that commercial television has much greater freedom in news and public affairs than do governmental or quasi-governmental broadcasting operations. The Center can do things, perhaps, which the local stations would have difficulty with. I believe that in both commercial and educational television there will always be issues which a community cannot handle locally but will accept from the national level. For example, we at NBC did a study of sit-in strikes in Nashville. The program was shown in Nashville and Atlanta, which were experiencing sit-in demonstrations at that time. I doubt very much whether the local stations could have produced this program at the time.

I have heard some ETV broadcasters say that pressures would be lessened if the stations all had a broad base of financial support—more money from more sources. That might be. Certainly a program manager for a station not entirely dependent on the state legislature or the public school system is not in the same position to be dictated to as the man whose station can be closed down because a state governor or school superintendent is offended by a program and can cut off funds—or threaten to.

Yet I have heard also that even community stations, where financial support comes from many sources have pressure problems at times. Money alone, even if it were a great amount, could not guarantee independence at the local stations. Individuals do not develop in a vacuum. Neither do social structures. The American civilization is by principle composed of varied patterns. Communities, even within nearby regions, often differ radically. And of course these differences are reflected in the character of the educational television stations. Each community has its inherent pressures which affect all the social structures within the community to some extent. And, as there are differences between communities, there are great differences within communities, especially in these times of great mobility of population. This is what makes it even more important for educational television stations to reach out and interest the other two-thirds of their potential audience. If a wide and deep base of financial support is necessary, and I believe firmly it is, loyal, stalwart, and far-reaching moral support from their communities is even more important to the educational television stations. However, as we learned from the song, like "Love and Marriage," you can't have one without the other. Unless educational television stations can find some way to produce on a regular basis, dramatic, artistic program series which will become a habit for most of the television set owners in their communities, they will not get either the money or the loyalty they need.

I urge you not to put all your eggs in one basket. Don't appeal consciously and exclusively to your one-third elite basic and ongoing audience. They will stay with you. You understand how their minds work— up to a point. However, I sometimes wonder whether those of us in public service programming do not sometimes stand in awe too much of this intelligentsia. Don't we get a little precious about them? After all, educational broadcasters, for the most part, are from the same stratum, and we are not likely to turn off exciting, well-done, even humorous programs, if they are solidly based in fact, philosophy, and art.

We broadcasters are communicators. If we do not have something of importance to say to everybody, we should not be in the broadcasting business, because the FCC ruled that all TV stations, especially the educational, noncommercial stations must serve the needs of the total community. It seems to me that educational broadcasters have an obligation sometimes to talk to everyone in language everyone understands. Such conversations are bound to pay off in both moral and financial support.

Nor am I saying that ETV stations should do more of the same things the commercial stations do. You have your creativity—your own reasons for existence—your own ideals. Don't be afraid of them. Examine them with your listeners. Build their understanding and develop your own image in the community. I would suggest that you do not—perhaps should not—always deal with the most controversial issues in the community. Look at all the issues in the area. Get close to the people who must support you and learn what their most urgent concerns are. Edge into the local issues and build confidence in your station by taking a balanced position on them so your audience can learn to clarify its own thinking.

On this point of getting to know your community, Lyman Bryson used to say that all broadcasters—as well as scientists—are too inclined to talk for themselves—and to themselves. Perhaps educational broadcasters are even worse offenders because they even do not talk very often with commercial broadcasters. The local commercial stations have many of the same problems as the educational stations, especially the same budget problems. You may not like the ways they try to solve them, but I believe if all of the television managers in a community—commercial and educational—would examine their problems together on a periodic basis, all would learn things of value.

Meetings of this kind would be of no value if false pride entered in. Yet, I feel that either in single sessions or on a more or less regular basis, if the ETV stations would take the initiative in getting together the top television professionals in their communities, both sides could serve as useful mirrors for each other. These sessions would have to be on a no-holds-barred basis, however, to do any good. They could well result in developing very useful complementary television services for each community.

One surprising thing I learned in a recent trip to Moscow is that Moscow Television uses a similar technique. How effective this is is open to question—but at least once a month the Moscow broadcasters meet with selected representatives from factories, stores, and all sorts of places to pull apart Moscow Television's programming. In this way, the television producers have audience contact which is most valuable. Whether they pay attention to the criticisms or not, these meetings are a very useful community relations gambit.

Implicit in all I have said is my conviction that television is more than a vehicle of dissemination. It's an independent medium, a creative force. Television makes news, for instance, as well as conveys it. Educational television has, therefore, a special responsibility to summon to its ranks the best of all the intellectual talent it can, the finest creative talents with the greatest moral integrity possible, in order to meet the challenges of these times. Educational television has a responsibility to recognize creative ability and the individual who has it and uses it because the creative individual puts his impress on each program he is associated with. This responsibility transcends the medium itself and, indeed, transcends the mechanics of the educational system. The challenge increases with the complications and growth of our educational needs. To meet it will take courage, dynamic leadership, and money. The problem of where to find these jewels belongs to the educational television managers themselves. And I am sure they can.

A STATION MANAGER'S VIEW OF THE PROBLEMS OF PROGRAMMING

By Hartford N. Gunn, Jr.

Mr. Gunn is Director of educational television station WGBH, in Boston.

THE DIFFICULTIES OF WRITING about educational television programming are considerable. It seems appropriate, therefore, to review some of these difficulties because they directly affect the viewpoint of the writer as well as all those who seek to comment upon or evaluate the program efforts of ETV.

We are agreed generally that the primary "business" of ETV is programming and the effect this programming has on the audience in terms of the amount and value of the information supplied, attitudes modified, and action precipitated. We are agreed, one would hope, that ETV is concerned with the general improvement of the society in which we live through the education and instruction of the individual. However, when we leave this broad plateau of comfortable generalities to confront the local ETV station, its policies and philosophies, we find substantial disagreement on what ETV programming should be and how best to accomplish it.

Some stations see their role as exclusively programming to school and college classrooms via direct instruction. Within this group there arises the question of whether this is best accomplished by total instruction (substitution for the classroom teacher) or by supplementary instruction and enrichment. The shades of meaning and the differing philosophies are many in this field, and more than one ETV broadcaster has found himself snarled in a battle of semantics and learning theory.

Other stations see their role as that of programming primarily for adults at home. Here, too, there are questions of how this should be accomplished. Some stations place the emphasis on credit courses; other stations on noncredit and more informal presentations.

Many, if not the majority, of ETV stations at this time program their station with a combination of all of the above plans. The result is an extremely complex program arrangement which defies useful generalizations to a considerable extent and complicates any evaluation of ETV.

There are other complicating factors; particularly the fact that the means of producing ETV programming are not equally distributed and, further, that these means (or lack of means) may not be within the power of the local station management to control. This point is quite often overlooked by the critics of ETV programming. ETV stations differ widely, for example, in size and quality of staff, equipment and studio facilities, educational talent and resources, money, FCC allocations (VHF vs. UHF and high- vs. low-band channels), effective policy-making boards, and station experience. These problems are further compounded by the lack of good current research, both qualitative and quantitative, on ETV programming and station operations.

It is against these many program philosophies and the varying means to carry them out that the writer will attempt his commentary and criticism. Necessarily, they must be viewed in this context and be recognized as one manager's opinions.

Looking at ETV programming in 1961, one can see that considerable progress has been made—against some major obstacles. It is not as much progress as the enthusiasts and critics would like to see, nor is it as much as might have been accomplished had we in ETV and those who have supported us been more farsighted and perceptive. Nevertheless, there is evidence of something worthwhile being done and at a reasonable cost.

As of May 1, 1961, there were 56 ETV stations on the air, programming approximately two thousand hours per week to a potential audience in and out of school, adult and child, of approximately 26 millions* of people. If we can project Professor Pool's recent audience study (4) at M.I.T. of the audience for WGBH-TV in Boston, approximately a third of the 26 million are regular viewers of ETV programs. Exactly what this ETV audience receives and the impact upon their attitudes and actions are not known, but information from the remaining sections of the Pool audience study that are as yet unpublished indicates that something more than passive viewing is taking place. The complete data will be available shortly.

We do know, however, that the regular adult audience for ETV is a special and most important one. "They . . . seem to be characterized by a trait which might be called involvement, activity or alertness" (4). They are the doers, the influential, the controlling group of the community. ETV viewing by this group is selective and purposive rather than continuous and passive. ETV does not make good background noise for other activities. If it is tuned in at all, it requires a high degree of concentration.

These findings taken together would lead one to believe that a substantial number of people who determine the activities in many fields are receiving and concentrating upon programming of some substance.

The writer does not have the equivalent figures for the in-school usage of ETV programs, but believes it to be substantial. For example, the in-

---

* From NETRC data, 1960.

school television programs of the "21" Classroom school broadcasting service in Massachusetts reaches 160 separate school systems in parts of four states. Some 50,000 or more elementary school children receive their instruction in French by television—just one subject in one school TV project. Considerable research has been and is now being prepared on the impact of ETV on the school audience, a substantial proportion of which already indicates a favorable response to ETV, if not an enthusiastic one, in many instances.

There are other measures of accomplishment in ETV programming— the larger number of national program awards, greatly increased attention from other media (particularly newspapers) and substantial community support. Each ETV station can also point with not unwarranted pride to certain programs that have measurably and importantly affected their communities; for example, the programs in the South on literacy.

While programming in one sense must be judged by what it is and what it does, it is necessary (as the author has noted) for constructive critics and commentators to put the accomplishments (or lack of them) in the proper framework.

Eight years ago when the first ETV station went on the air nobody knew very much about it. Everybody had his own idea or dream of what it could or should be and some even had had experience with ETV's electronic relative, educational radio, but everybody eventually was to find at least a part of his dreams impractical or disappointing in practice.

ETV had (and has) other problems besides its newness and the enthusiasts' great expectations. ETV programming was and is still severely limited in funds relative both to its educational resources and the need of the audience for these resources. The only advantage that it has had financially since its inception has been that it lacked sufficient money to grow too fast and become too fat, as has been largely the case in commercial television. On the other hand, it too often has had not enough money to do the job it was asked to do. This has led to much bitter criticism of ETV programming which many stations were helpless to correct.

Money has a lot to do with many of the other problems that face ETV, but it is not by any means the cause of all of our difficulties.

Money, for example, would have helped to get better ETV station personnel but would not have solved the problem completely. ETV was a new medium and there was no trained group of people waiting to propel it forward with the required taste, imagination, intelligence, and dynamism. This training took a great deal of time—compare the kinescopes of programs made for NETRC by stations in 1955 with those of 1960–61. The programs show the hard work of five years or more.

ETV is still short of first-rate personnel, particularly in the positions of producers, directors, program, production, and general managers. These are the people who, along with the talent, largely determine the success or failure of ETV programming. We still find it more profitable to raid one another's stations for personnel. We still find, also, that most college courses in television omit training for ETV or do it poorly.

Program resources and talent have always been a problem, for they are not evenly distributed. Some stations have an embarrassment of educational resources and talent to draw upon. Others are woefully lacking. In some instances these latter stations have excellent staffs and more than adequate facilities and yet suffer this lack of sufficient top educators who have something to say and who can (or can learn to) say it effectively. The effects of this situation can be seen dramatically in the national ETV programs where there was—and possibly still is—the assumption that because all ETV stations had video-tape and/or kinescope recording equipment, they all can produce with local talent substantial and consistent programming of national and international significance. The impact of this philosophy on the quality of national ETV programming in the author's opinion sometimes has been somewhat less than even our most ardent enthusiasts might have accepted.

The problem of personnel is not confined to the station alone, for ETV still must fight to attract major educators to participate in its programs. The academic groves are still ruled by such institutions as "publish (a book) or perish," television's low status symbol, the faculty committee on permanent appointments with its concern for the dangers of "popularity" and interest in the research-oriented person as opposed to the teacher. All of these things make it difficult to get the right man to do the right job. Fortunately for ETV and its audience, this situation is improving, and many great teachers are speaking out over ETV more frequently and on more significant topics.

The technical facilities such as studios, cameras, recorders, etc. are gradually improving and becoming less of a problem. Early program efforts for the national ETV network were severely limited—in fact, many were virtually invisible as a result of poor kinescope recording, equipment maintenance, and operation. Video-tape recording equipment and NETRC's drive for improved engineering performance have helped improve the over-all technical level considerably. It is not unusual, however, to find stations with good educational resources and good staffs working with inadequate facilities and vice versa. Today ETV programming demands (particularly on the national level) have outrun the facilities available for their production.

There are two other areas that have helped to determine the framework within which ETV was programmed. First, the channel allocation situation which has just come into some prominence and, second, the policy-making groups such as boards of trustees, school boards, and administrators who have been largely ignored and are deserving of more attention.

To the extent that UHF channels have been assigned to education in VHF areas, ETV programming has been greatly handicapped. Many of the largest and most important cities such as New York, Washington, D.C., Philadelphia, Los Angeles, Detroit, and Cleveland, have UHF reserved channels. The result has been that only Philadelphia, Atlanta, Cincinnati, and Detroit have been courageous enough to put in ETV stations for which there were virtually no receivers and, therefore, little—if any—audience. While these stations have managed to build some audience, they find it difficult to do extensive adult programming without greater support, which is impossible under such an arrangement.

Under the circumstances it is not surprising that there are no ETV stations in the other cities such as New York and Washington. This has been a critical blow to ETV and its programming, for it denies ETV stations and their network an effective outlet for their national programs where they can be seen, judged, and have the opportunity to inform and persuade key financial decision-makers in business, foundations, and government. An example of the strange hardship that the New York and Washington ETV desert works is the fact that NETRC's major public affairs program *Prospects of Mankind* could not get important government and business leaders to appear *unless* the program could be seen by their families and their peers in these two cities. Special arrangements had to be made to show the program on commercial stations before they would come on. The other problem associated with the lack of stations in New York and Washington is that there are no ETV production facilities from which to originate major programs that require the unique resources of these cities.

The question of the role and operation of boards of trustees and similar school policy-makers who own ETV stations is another factor in ETV program problems and has not been explored adequately. However, the writer can do little more to raise the point; namely, to what extent does a board influence programming for good or for bad and to what extent does it support ETV management in their attempt to supply the various resources necessary to produce a top program schedule. Boards in general are not always known for their courage, their imagination and leadership. Operating an ETV station is a major responsibility to society. It requires great attention, guidance, and support. One wonders to what extent these boards have influenced ETV programming—either positively or negatively.

When we review the problems that have faced ETV, it is the more surprising what progress has been made and how significantly and important ETV programming has become.

We need a context within which to judge present program offerings and to point up the need for new ones. Certainly such a context should include major problems that face the citizen and his society at all levels—local, national, and international. One can do no more than suggest some of these: the need for education of the citizen in international affairs to match the new role of the United States as leader of the free world, the need for the greater understanding of science with emphasis on the new areas of nuclear energy and space research which are completely beyond the educational background of the average adult, the moral and policy problems raised by such scientific advances, the urban sprawl, and the problems of the city.

These and other major problems whose scope and rate of growth continually increase require our immediate attention and yet they must be funneled through an American communications system that, despite its technological advances, seems relatively less and less able to cope with them. We need more and better information and more and better analysis and interpretation. The number of newspapers in many cities is shrinking with the resulting concentration bringing too often a smaller range of opinion and less interpretation. The changing economic and program structure of both commercial radio and television seems poorly adapted to our growing needs in these areas. While the trend has been reversed somewhat in commercial television, nevertheless the pressure grows to treat stations as an ordinary investment to be judged by the balance sheet rather than by its programming. Discussing the problem of setting and maintaining standards of programming in commercial television, Jack Gould notes, ". . . all of TV lives in a house without a floor," (2) and in an earlier article, the ". . . commercial incentive to try to be all things to all viewers imposes a serious cultural limitation." (3)

If we include education itself as a part of our communications system, we see that it, too, is beset by the problem of greater information to impart to more people, and it has relatively fewer teachers, facilities, and dollars to do it with.

It is in the context of needs of the magnitude outlined above that we must design ETV programming for the future. Some of the major program issues raised by this review are: *balance* in terms of school vs. adult and formal vs. informal program presentations; *quantity; scope and depth* of programming; and *quality* of presentation. These issues cannot be dealt with at length here, but some comments may be useful.

It seems to the writer, where a community has only a single ETV station (and especially if it is a wide-area VHF station), there is an obligation to do an equally comprehensive and respectable job for *both* adults and children, both in and out of school. The need of education for adults (the decision-makers of *today*) is particularly acute. Their formal education has stopped, and they are poorly prepared to deal with the major problems that face them.

A station should strive also to program its channel to the fullest extent possible. Serious consideration should be given to reserving and using additional ETV channels so that programming can be expanded for all groups and interests within the community.

The most important program issue is the scope and depth of ETV programs. John Gardner states in his recent book:

> Leadership in the United States is not a matter of scores of key individuals, nor even of hundreds, nor even of thousands—it is a matter of literally tens of thousands, even hundreds of thousands of influential men and women. These individuals, in their own organizations and communities, shape public opinion, create the climate in which public opinion is formed and determine the course of our national life. (1)

If we accept this statement and recall the special ability of ETV to reach these individuals, then it would seem that ETV should make a more conscious attempt to program for their needs. A service for these leaders calls for *daily* national and international news *and* interpretation. It means ETV must establish national and overseas contacts to provide the necessary news and commentary. It means also greater international program exchange with possible cooperative program planning and production between U.S. ETV and foreign broadcasting systems.

Community problems must be examined and discussed to keep the local issues in focus along with those of national and international importance. Unfortunately, ETV programs on community issues are not as numerous as they should be, primarily because of the more controversial nature of such programs—controversial in the sense that issues are closer to home and produce a greater emotional reaction in the audience. Incidentally, here is where a strong board, good station management, and sufficient funds to insure a complete and accurate reporting job can make a major contribution to the improvement of their community.

Admittedly, this is defining educational television in a broader sense than many stations would care to. While a case can be made for staying with a very formal and narrow interpretation of the role of ETV, one wonders how often boards and administrators find it convenient to define themselves out of an area such as community issues that poses real problems and that demands considerable judgment and skill.

The greatest stumbling block to the programming of community issues is financial pressure. Most ETV stations get their funds from political or semi-political bodies such as legislatures and school boards or from the general public which normally includes a number of major business and individual contributors who make the difference between financial success or failure. The problem presented to the ETV station in the presentation of such programs is obvious. As the key political leader of one state put it:

> The price of my support (for your ETV bill) is no programs on controversial issues. By controversial issues I don't mean the national and international junk. I mean the *local* stuff.

This may not be a common occurrence, but the very possibility of such an occurrence is enough to impose a considerable degree of self-censorship in this program area.

The writer is not suggesting that ETV stations necessarily (indeed, it may not be legally possible) crusade and editorialize directly on community issues, but rather provide a forum for informed citizens and leaders to discuss such issues on a regular basis and in depth. Documentary reporting, which is another approach to community-issue programming, is usually beyond local ETV station budgets. It is more difficult and places even greater responsibility on the station in regard to fairness and accuracy. However, whether it is a commentator, a forum, or a documentary, one must recognize that even to mention some issues—let alone discuss them— is "controversial" to some powerful interests.

There is no easy answer to the problem of community-issue programming. It is deserving, however, of greater attention by all organization boards, and managements concerned with the growth of ETV. The problem becomes more critical when one observes the disappearance of local newspapers as discussed earlier. How is the community of the future to be informed of its problems and aroused to its duty? This is a major question for all responsible citizens.

Other program areas that require attention are the American heritage and the advancement of our American culture through commissioning and performing American drama, music, dance, and opera. One continues to be embarrassed when foreigners visit the world's richest country only to find that even its educational television system is devoid of the American performing arts and artists. In fact, ETV relies upon foreign broadcasting systems for much, if not most, of its great drama.

ETV programming should be given the support and encouragement to work with experimental techniques and formats. Attention should be given, too, to more and better programs for children out-of-school and the women at home during the day. In general, ETV has made only pitiful efforts for these two audiences. The possibilities of a major service here are enormous, as the present radio and television offerings for these groups are among the most limited and shabby.

Much more could be written on the scope and depth of ETV programming, also. The writer closes this part of his paper with a suggestion that the reader review the obstacles and problems in programming an ETV station mentioned earlier. It will be apparent that these limitations and strictures on program production are still with us and that they affect directly the programming areas just discussed. These restrictions must be tackled if ETV is to fulfill a significant role in America's communications system.

What can be done specifically about ETV programming? Here, for the sake of starting the discussion, are some suggestions:

1. A continuing review and discussion through research, through seminars and forums, through journals, through every device we can think of, of the major issues of ETV programming, including audience balance, scope and depth, quantity and quality of programs. This must be done not just by the professionals in ETV but by the leaders in academic, political, business, labor, and similar fields. Emphasis should be placed on local programming with a constant exchange of ideas and policies among all stations. School programs should be reviewed and evaluated by educational authorities from colleges and universities as well as the elementary and secondary schools.

2. Regional networking, preferably on a live basis, should be encouraged. Regional networks offer substantial possibilities for the improvement of ETV programs by spreading the cost, relieving overburdened and limited facilities and by utilizing more fully individual talents and resources within a region. The regional network is a means to supplement the national program offerings so that more hours of better programs can be made available to a greater number of people. Further, it encourages the development of new stations and the eventual live interconnection of all ETV stations on a national basis.

3. The National Educational Television and Radio Center must be strengthened in every way if it is to provide the leadership and program service that only a first-rate national network can. NETRC can set the ETV local program style, tempo, and level through its own example and in its program acquisition and underwriting. Technical advances as well as program and audience needs combine to make a review of live or limited live program distribution mandatory. International exchange which has been started by NETRC must be augmented. Cooperative planning and program production on an international scale hold much promise.

NETRC already is reviewing its role in acquiring and producing programs for in-school use. A materials resource library (including research, film and tape clips, visuals, and supplementary materials) would be helpful to local school producers as would the availability of cooperatively planned and produced series of a larger dimension than is possible at the average local station. A re-examination of the means of national ETV program production is required, also, in order to tap more adequately the existing educational resources and talent.

To accomplish this and the many other activities will require a new and expanded financial base. The Center operates on a budget which is the equivalent of a dozen episodes for commercial television of *The Untouchables*, suggesting that there might be a slight imbalance in our scale values. The support for the Center must be constant, reasonably substantial, have built into it provision for growth and freedom from the pressures and restrictions that chasing dollars from powerful organizations can bring. This suggests an endowment of considerable size. It is to be hoped that one can be found.

4. To improve ETV programming requires more and better personnel as well as recognition and appreciation for their work. A management apprenticeship program is already being worked on by the National Association of Educational Broadcasters and is an essential undertaking. Management seminars along the lines of the successful National Association of Broadcaster's classes and case study program at the Harvard Business School would be useful. Awards might be employed to spotlight the work of talented directors, artists, designers, and technicians. Only the motion picture industry has seen fit to recognize the efforts of the *people* behind the productions. There is, at this time, no national recognition of the *individual's* contribution to ETV programming.

5. As noted earlier, there are urgent program reasons for securing VHF channels for ETV in New York, Washington, D.C., Philadelphia, and Los Angeles. As this is being written, New York is negotiating for the purchase of a major VHF channel, and Philadelphia is in an FCC hearing to acquire one. This leaves Washington and Los Angeles to be attended to.

6. Several problems suggest a new but somewhat controversial solution. There seems to be a need for a number of stations to act as leaders by providing the test cases and laboratory for new ideas and methods, by setting the pattern for independence and "academic freedom," and by setting program and production standards. Further, there are major centers of population as well as educational and cultural resources which require more than average facilities and staff. These are the areas of major national influence as well as the areas of major national program resource. These areas are expected to lead, to bear the brunt of the national program production load, and to influence key people favorably in behalf of ETV. For the most part, these cities are ill-equipped to perform these functions. In fact, some of these key cities don't even have an ETV station. It is the writer's opinion that this is a national problem and that consideration might be given to the establishment of "bellwether" stations with national production capabilities. Again, for reasons similar to the situation with NETRC, this should be done by endowment; if possible, the amount of money available to determine the number of stations, and the specific cities to be selected by a national panel of distinguished citizens with attention to the available educational resources, the size and influence of the popu-

lation, and the suitability and character of the board of trustees or administrators.

7. A review of the financial structure of ETV and recommendations for its change and improvement are in order. The writer has mentioned financing in connection with the NETRC and the possible "bellwether" stations. All present and potential ETV stations, however, need greater support. There must be a realization on the part of business, government, and foundations that all ETV requires their support and that it can't be left to the Ford Foundation, individual citizens, and small local foundations to do the whole job. It is particularly unfortunate that some people most directly responsible for the growth and improvement of education have either ignored the medium or have opposed it. One might feel that in view of what ETV has accomplished that this situation reflects on the nature of their organization more than on the nature of ETV. ETV touches nearly all areas of local, national, and international concern. Technically, ETV is part of one of the most powerful and far-reaching communications systems that man has invented and, in content, ETV is a part of the great tradition and inheritance of public and private education. It deserves more attention and better support from those interested in and those responsible for these fields.

The general ETV program picture is most encouraging, primarily because it shows steady improvement. The only question concerns increasing this rate of growth to keep pace with the need for effective communications in the United States. This requires new ideas, new methods, constant re-evaluation, and increasing concern and support.

One perceptive observer of American life has said:

> At just this moment in history when we need all of our vitality and drive and capacity for sustained effort, we are in danger of losing our bearings, in danger of surrendering to a 'cult of easiness' . . . . Virtually everyone agrees that we need a re-affirmation of our shared purposes and a re-dedication to their accomplishment (1).

Is there a place in our society for a major communications system, local in control and execution, national in scope and influence, dedicated solely to our cultural and intellectual growth, and supported by private philanthropy and public funds and programmed by our great educational community?

REFERENCES

1. Gardner, John, *Excellence.* New York: Harper, 1961.
2. *New York Times,* April 23, 1961, p. X17.
3. *New York Times,* January 22, 1961, p. X11.
4. Pool, Ithiel de Sola, and Barbara Adler. *Educational TV: Is Anybody Watching?* Center for International Studies, MIT, Cambridge, Mass., November 1960.

HOW THE NATIONAL PROGRAM CENTER
SEES THE OUTLOOK

By Robert B. Hudson

Mr. Hudson is Vice-President in charge of programs, National Educational Television and Radio Center.

Rᴇcᴇɴᴛʟʏ, ɪɴ ʀᴇᴠɪᴇᴡɪɴɢ NET programs for 1960, I was able to observe that "Educational television programs are better than ever." This paraphrased slogan of the motion picture industry was applied for comparative purposes, obviously, rather than as an indication of superlative accomplishment. It was applied as a trend indicator to show that the program quality curve is up. I took occasion to cite two factors that support this view:

First of all, the production staffs of the educational stations—our principal producers—appear to be stronger across the board. The increased strength and skill is especially evident in the half dozen stations that have supplied the larger number of programs to the national program service. With these latter stations it is not just a matter of their having another year of experience behind them (that has helped, too); rather it is a willingness to separate production for the Center from the ongoing business of the station and the assigning to it of highly qualified persons from within or outside of their staffs.

A second factor bearing on improved program quality is the increase in the number of independent television and film producers now contributing to the NET program service. Part of their involvement may be attributed to an increase during the year of program support grants that frequently called for program series to be produced on film, but equally important there is a growing number of new producing organizations that know how to create programs that capture the spirit and serve the ends of educational television.

Add to the above trends the wealth of foreign television films and video tapes of an educational nature that are showing up on NET stations in an ever increasing flow—from England, France, Germany, Italy, Canada, Australia, Japan; from all of the members of the European Broadcasting Union; from some of the Iron Curtain countries—it is evident that the quality of the national program service is richer and more diverse than at any time in the past.

The increased strength across the board of the program and production staffs of educational television stations is most telling at the local level. They are gaining in experience and confidence and for the most part exhibit professional attainments. All of this shows up in the daily schedule (at least in that part of it that the limited staff can concentrate on; nearly all stations are under-manned).

All of the above suggest that the viewer has reasonable grounds for expecting more from his educational television station. He does indeed. His growth stock is growing, but the "growth stock" of educational television is so flagrantly undercapitalized in people, facilities, dollars and, in some instances, commitment on the part of educators of small vision and ritualistic traditions that its true potential may not even be sighted for years to come. In short, the program outlook for educational television is a gradual "bootstraps" improvement until there is a dramatic breakthrough.

The breakthrough which is needed involves: 1) trained staff personnel in adequate supply; 2) a faculty and performing artists assigned on a rotating basis and observers of the contemporary cultural and political scene; 3) studio and transmission and reception facilities and money with which to operate them in all major localities; 4) a nation-wide interconnected educational television network; and 5) a commitment by educators to use the television instrument as a tool of education, and by citizens to look to it and accept it as a window to the world of ideas, to the arts and joys of mankind, and to both the humane and the harsh aspects of reality.

All of the papers compiled under these covers are concerned with the breakthrough imperatives in greater or lesser degree. All of them, ultimately, have a bearing on program quality: it takes perceptive and skilled personnel to produce quality programs; it takes the very best local and national technical facilities to deliver to the viewer a quality product; it takes imagination and courage on the part of school administrators and teachers to plan and enrich the instructional program through the use of materials from remote sources, but the rewards are great. All of these factors work singly and in combination to affect program quality. But assuming their presence, the critical factor is the availability of a faculty and of performing artists on a rotating basis, and a corps of observers of the contemporary cultural and political scene.

Buildings do not make a university. The faculty is the university. The faculty employed by educational television will give validity and substance to programs. It will be the best faculty in the world today, coming from many disciplines and from many parts of the world. Faculty members will spend a tour of teaching and recording duty for a term or an academic year in a production center and return to their permanent posts. Obviously, this plan holds for persons preparing instructional programs for use in classrooms. Already Mme. Anne Slack has spent three full years in Boston preparing and recording *Parlons Français* for elementary schools; and Prof. Harvey White spent a year in Pittsburgh broadcasting and recording a high school course in physics and another year in New York presenting a television physics course as graduate training for teachers.

Nor does the "faculty" idea confine itself to instructional television. John Dodds took a year off from the Humanities Program at Stanford to work on *American Memoir*; Huston Smith and Ralph Patrick, philosopher and anthropologist respectively at Washington University, required a semester each in the preparation of *Search for America*; Martha Myers was given a year's leave of absence by Smith College to play and produce the *A Time to Dance* series; Roy and Johana Harris accepted as part of their teaching assignment at Chatham College a full year's music appreciation course on WQED; and Prof. Zechariah Chafee Jr., literally gave the last year of his life to broadcasting and recording his Harvard course on constitutional law.

The educational television faculty idea has been tested. It has proved sound and needs only to be implemented on a carefully planned, long-term basis. Consistent excellence in the presentation of substantive material is an achievable goal for educational television.

Television is a superb medium for the arts—all of the arts, but especially for the performing arts. Any national program of excellence must cater to and draw upon these lively arts. The proximity and the potential relationship of the NETRC to the Lincoln Center for the Performing Arts— the Metropolitan Opera, the Philharmonic, a Repertory Company, the Juilliard School, and others augurs well for the wedding of educational television and the arts. The plastic arts too are welcome in television but better ways of presenting them can and must be found.

Just as educational television must have its own drama repertory companies, so it must seek out and televise the great orchestras from coast to coast and serve as patron to its own chamber and combo groups. Recent NET program series with the Fine Arts Quartet rehearsing and performing Beethoven and Bartok, and with Max Morath on the *Ragtime Era* are cases in point. The great music festivals of the world must be brought to educational television—Salzburg, Vienna, Prague, Zurich, Edinburgh, Strasbourg, Spoleto; and opera from La Scala and Vienna, Bayreuth, Glyndebourne, Covent Garden, Paris. More than this, the great performing artists of the world must be seen and heard through educational television— Casals, Heifetz, Rubinstein, Sviatoslav Richter, David Oistrakh, Birgit Nilsson, and countless others—their performances preserved for enjoyment tomorrow as well as today. The younger artists in this country and abroad—winners of the Brussels, Leventritt, and other international contest awards—can find in educational television a natural, ready medium for conveying their gifts to a wide public.

Observers of the contemporary scene should have high priority as educational television hitches its star to individual need and national significance. Keeping informed, understanding events, holding perspective, and maintaining values in the whirlpool of the twentieth century tries many of us beyond our available time and capacities and we need help. Television in general has failed us though there are bright spots. Educational television has made some fresh approaches, but it has scarcely entered this field.

There is some evidence around us that the individual suffers because modern society tends to relate to the individual through group orientations. He is bombarded daily with messages which seek to stimulate his action in behalf of this or that worthy (and often unworthy) enterprise. Yet, his individualism often having been minimized, he is hesitant to act. Often he simply cannot, for he does not know how. He is not sure in whose name he is called upon to act. As we in this country support our national effort through democratic action, it is fundamental to our way of life that each of us as citizens is capable of making immediate evaluations in the context of a swift and vital moment. These decisions, however, must flow from our confidence in our own personal system of values. Thus, the very meaning of this culture and its people is sustained by the individual who knows and respects himself, and who is capable of determined and selective self-action. By seeking always to discover the needs of the various publics within the broad public which is America, educational television must help the individual to hold his perspective and to maintain his values in this marvelous but dangerous moment which characterizes the time of our planet in this mid-twentieth century.

More and more those who populate the world of educational television must seek to discover ways of enlarging the vision and enriching the scope of the individual. As those of skill and insight become more familiar with the television instrument, they will devise ways of entering the American home as welcome agents charged with the joyful task of identifying and sustaining human dignity.

For quality programs, educational television stations must be interconnected. In the area of public affairs, this will enable a timely and a national impact. There must be a corps of observers (model: American Universities Field Staff; Christian Science Monitor regional bureaus) and documentary teams reporting regularly, not only on political and special events but on people and the things that are important to them.

The federal government must be covered, not just for hard news but as an institution that both reflects and shapes our lives. The process of decision-making must be examined and illuminated. The moral code and behavior patterns, and issues of private and public morality require the attention of educational television, as, indeed, do most public policy questions before the Congress and before the people.

Public affairs programming has the unique opportunity of serving in formulating thought and opinion, providing a basis for the *making up of minds*, a fix on which successful public policy must rest. But it takes more than "in depth" news reports and "slice of life" programs to guide us through these turbulent times when the human mind is prepared to wrap the whole planet in a shroud. Thus far all of our best efforts and ingenuity have produced no assurance whatever that it will be deterred from that end. The prolonged failure of traditional means of getting through to people on our great problems does not prove useless our communications devices. It does suggest their sterility in conception and ineffectiveness in application. Some new creative approach is indicated. Substantive and psychological research must be undertaken. Models must be created and tested. Perhaps a swing away from the "event" orientation toward the "chain of events" perspective, toward the careful study of trends and of their predictive aspects would help. But whatever the new creative approaches to be developed, they must be rooted ultimately in a tradition of private, public, and international morality. Quality programming in this direction is a clear and present goal of educational television's corps of observers and, indeed, of education itself.

TESTIMONY BY C. SCOTT FLETCHER

Before the Television Advisory Panel

Mr. Fletcher was President of the Fund for Adult Education, until that enterprise was terminated in 1960. He also served as chairman of a task force which produced the four preceding papers.

As to the question of a climate of constructive relationships between educational and commercial stations, the more there is a sharing of ideas among the people who are connected with this type of medium, the more the public will benefit. We are dealing with a medium which is in its infancy. It depends on the people behind the camera. The relationship between educational and commercial stations is developing every day and in a healthy fashion. At one time, people in commercial TV said that ETV would not work since there would be no sponsors to pay the bill. Few people really understand the medium and how best to use it.

On the question of public affairs I would say that certain media do a good job in the field of national and international affairs, especially certain newspapers. A few good programs have resulted from collaboration between local newspapers and the local TV and radio stations. The commercial stations are operated for profit and they cannot do more than a certain amount in the area of public affairs, but they are doing more in this area and are finding it profitable. In some instances no public affairs program can go on the air unless it is the product of the members of the staff of the network. CBS, for example, will not put any public affairs program on the air unless it is produced by the staff of CBS. More and more public affairs programs are being paid for by sponsors. It is part of the whole idea of ETV that ETV stations will, in the future, bring such public affairs programs to the public, and at a prime time. There has been some lack in ETV in this area. If you use education in the true sense of the word, you cannot say that information programs are education. ETV, because of the way it was established, can provide real educational TV programs during prime time which the commercial stations cannot do. The ETV potentialities are hard to predict because they are so great and so varied.

When you ask what educational jobs TV can do best, it seems to me that one advantage of TV over movies is that you can see things as they happen and that one studio TV camera or motion picture projector can serve millions at one time. Everything depends on what the people who have the means in their hands do with it. A TV set can be counted upon to do many jobs, except take an interest in the audience that it serves.

In reply to your question on the organization and support of ETV, I would say that, to date, the initiative, with some exceptions, has developed locally, with some national implementation, such as that provided by the NETRC, JCET, and NAEB. The money came from many local sources for the support of ETV stations. Financing was not sufficient to begin with and has not been sufficient since then. ETV was brought into being to serve the community as the library serves the community. One aspect of financing is that there should be a national headquarters to plan an annual drive to get funds, community by community, for the financing of local stations. The future financing of ETV has not been thoroughly discussed. It should involve a national drive for a national concept and movement. The potentialities of ETV, as we now know them, should no more go out of existence in a community than a library should. These are such valuable assets that we have to get it into the minds of the public that here is an asset which must be financed in various ways. We should never be placed in a position where the policy control of what goes on a station would be affected by funds. The control would remain local.

Concerning provisions for highest quality programs, I feel that talented young people should be given an opportunity to show their creative abilities without being hindered. The finances should be in such a shape that we can attract these talents and hold them. Research indicates that, given the same teacher and provided that teacher is a good teacher, the youngsters or adults in the TV classroom will do as well and sometimes better than the students in the regular classroom. Teachers have to be good teachers in the first instance and should be able to use TV when they want to use it. They should have the right to decide how and when they will use TV. TV should be placed in the hands of skilled teachers, for use as the teachers deem advisable. We have to be everlastingly at work to show the teachers of our youth and our adults how they can use TV more effectively.

In general, I would say that, with some notable exceptions, ETV, on the whole, has not measured up to its great promise. The tendency is to turn off something which is not interesting and to forget the educational channel unless something notable appears. When there is an organized effort, the audience can be held and the invitation to learning can become an invitation to organized participation.

We cannot predict how long the present situation in the public affairs field will go on. Consider the three major networks and the time slots where their good public affairs programs usually appear. There is no reason why arrangements cannot be made to make these programs available to ETV stations at prime time but without the commercial. The commercial stations cannot afford to give prime time free. But ways can be found so that those who want them can get these kinds of public affairs programs and others which are basically educational.

At the present time, no local educational station could afford to put on the kind of costly public affairs program of which I have been speaking, nor could the NETRC afford to produce this type of program. How then do we secure funds to develop more quality programs for ETV? In Ohio, all motion picture theaters were taxed and the money was made available to the State Department of Education which used the money to buy films to be made available to the schools. ETV stations should not be supported as a result of a tax imposed on commercial stations. Any funds provided to support ETV would be welcomed provided the control remained in the hands of local authorities. This is the way we handle our schools and libraries. In California, the money from gasoline taxes can, by law, be used only for the improvement of highways in the State of California. Provided an equitable means is found to make private and public funds available for this vital instrumentality of ETV, it should be done with the above proviso.

(Mr. Hechinger gave the example of the tax on radio and television sets in England which is then used to support the BBC. Mr. Fletcher pointed out that the main difference is that everyone in England who has a TV or radio set can receive BBC programs, whereas not everyone in the United States who has a receiver can receive ETV stations. He added:)

If you want to have quality programs, you need three things: a climate which will entice the talented to give the best possible vent to their talents; a willingness to pay; and a determination to produce programs that will be great.

V. THE PROBLEM OF FINANCING

What does it now cost to support educational television? What future costs may be anticipated for capital expenditures and for station operation? What further increase in expenditures will be necessary if educational stations are to operate at an "adequate" rather than a "minimum" level? And what are the possible sources of such support?

THE ORGANIZATION AND FINANCING OF ETV IN THE NEXT TEN YEARS

By John F. White

Mr. White is President of the National Educational Television and Radio Center

WHEN ONE ATTEMPTS TO PROJECT the development of ETV over the next ten-year period, he cannot confine himself to a discussion of programming and instructional services but must, in fact, first determine the probable organizational and financial development.

Each of these aspects, the organizational and the financial, must be considered on both the local, or regional, and national levels. And at both levels we will see the strengthening of present units and the creation of new ones. In the 1959–61 period the operating budgets of ETV stations on the air were increased on the average by approximately 30 percent; a similar figure applies to their capital investments. At the national level, the National Educational Television and Radio Center has in that same period shown budget growth of about one-third. In my opinion, there is nothing either magical or surprising about this. The older stations have matured to the point where they now set higher standards for newer stations, while all stations are overcoming institutional fears or prejudices and are rendering community services that earn for them increasing support—and bring demands for still greater service.

Local and regional

What will happen in the next ten years? There will continue to be a growth in station activation—to the point where, in that period, all sections of this country will receive ETV service. Specifically, I anticipate the following developments:

1. Solution by the FCC of the UHF-VHF conflict, so that by 1971 ETV channels will be competitive wherever they exist. We will see the activation of ETV stations in such metropolitan areas as those of New York, Los Angeles, Cleveland, Baltimore, and Washington. These stations will be supported at least in part through voluntary contributions.

2. Because most of the blank spots on the ETV map represent regions that are sparsely populated and, therefore, are without financial resources for activation, we will see grants of federal and state funds for this purpose.

3. Because in these same regions there is also a shortage of cultural and in-

structural resources, we will observe the creation of a number of state and
regional networks. These will consist of the principal producing stations
and booster stations in places where production resources are limited.
4. The creation of state and regional networks will also serve to cut down the
operating costs of the individual stations. These operating dollars will be
derived from a variety of sources in return for services rendered, i.e.—

   a. from school systems and colleges in return for instructional services
   (including adult education, to which I believe there will be a growing commitment).

   b. from state sources, probably on a matching basis, for the above
   services and through direct appropriation for state-wide and interstate services.

   c. from local foundations, business, and industry for the production
   of programs in specific areas. (There also will be some general
   support from foundations, business, and industry.) In addition,
   individuals and groups will make voluntary contributions.

This diversity in financial support is not only likely; it is to be fos-
tered. Through such diversity we can best maintain the freedom that is
so essential to the production of significant programs. Moreover, if the
stations perform well the services open to them (and they will), this diversity of financial support is their best guarantee against economic crises.
It is also the best guarantee of quality, for station managements will be
forced to "earn" support and will be less likely to be "comfortable" and
accept mediocrity as a means to "security."

The same diversity will be found in station controls. In 1961 approximately 65 percent of the stations are controlled by universities, public
school systems, state ETV commissions, or other tax-supported bodies,
while 35 percent are independent, nonprofit corporations. No matter
what form of control exists, however, individual stations will in the next
ten years seek operating funds from the diversified sources discussed
earlier. It is apparent even in 1961 that independent stations must depend
upon tax dollars for the operation of their instructional services; on the
other hand, publicly owned stations have come to recognize that they
require foundation, corporate, and individual grants to underwrite certain
local program costs.

In the matter of station controls, it needs also to be stated that in the
next ten-year period the addition of stations will stem largely from public
(that is, governmental) and institutional sponsorship. At the same time
a battle must be waged to retain the independently controlled stations and,
wherever possible, to add to their numbers. There will be those who view
tax support as the easy way out, but they must be resisted, for—just as
with the state-supported and private universities and colleges in this nation—the coexistence of public and independent stations provides an essential climate in which these stations work together, but challenge one

another; lead one another, but follow one another; compete with but protect one another. And all of this adds up to a stronger, freer, healthier, and more effective total service.

It should also be noted that in many (but not all) areas one channel will not meet the total demand and that, therefore, we will see the activation and operation of multiple channels. (Oklahoma City and Pittsburgh already have two ETV stations each.) Such additions will not cost excessive amounts to operate when "built into" existing facilities.

National

All of these facilities will depend upon a national source for important program material of two types—instructional and cultural. Now, in 1961, there are a variety of such program sources and these will continue to grow, but in the years ahead—as now—there will be one principal source whose purpose it is to respond to station requirements, whose function it is to provide national leadership for this ETV movement. In other words, I believe that the next ten years will see the development of a larger, stronger, better-financed NETRC.

In that period a nation-wide interconnection of ETV stations will become operative. General programming and certain instructional material, when local demand justifies it, will be distributed by this device. The local station will record the material it desires from these lines and telecast it in accordance with its own program schedule requirements. There also will be a library service of instructional materials, and each spring the local school authorities, in cooperation with local ETV authorities, will select from catalogues the offerings they wish to screen and, if these are found acceptable, have delivered at specified times during the following school year.

Obviously, it will require many more dollars than are available at the moment to meet the demands for quality and provide increased service. This money too will come from many different sources. An emerging pattern of industrial and foundation support for program projects will continue to develop and expand. At first there will be a strong, and to some extent justified, suspicion among educators of instructional materials developed through support from these sources. But the quality of these materials—the result of careful planning by competent professional educators—will do much to erode the last of the many fears that have plagued the development of this new teaching instrument—television.

One will also see federal dollars available at the national level for the development of televised instructional material. It is perhaps only at the national level that federal money can be obtained for ETV programming. With dollars secured by contract from specific governmental agencies for program projects, one can predict with confidence that government will play an important role in the development of educational television in the next decade.

Provision of a strong and professionally qualified national agency to attract these funds and supply the leadership and service necessary is almost sine qua non. The NETRC is at present fulfilling many of the functions of that agency, but it will require major basic financing for research, program development, and proper staffing if it is to do the job that should be done—if it is to exert national leadership of the ETV movement itself.

What leadership will be necessary? Station activation and stimulation, legislation, experimentation, and fund raising—these are just a few of the areas that will cry for attention. Over the years this will involve expenditures of millions of dollars. And these dollars must be earned through performance; they cannot be obtained because ETV is a nice idea or "good thing." But they will be earned. The money will come. And it will come from a variety of sources, thus insuring the future of noncommercial, educational television as a free public-service asset of all the American people.

THE FINANCING OF EDUCATIONAL TELEVISION

By Lyle M. Nelson

When Mr. Nelson wrote this, he was Vice-President of the University of Michigan. He is now Director of University Relations, Stanford University

No ONE WILL BE SURPRISED with the statement that financial support remains educational television's greatest single problem. From community ETV stations to closed-circuit installations, the story is the same. Inadequate financing has made it necessary to cut corners in operation, to eliminate everything except bare essentials and even to compromise with program quality.

Yet the record is an impressive one. Even to those accustomed to measuring success by the balance sheet, the evidence is daily mounting that educational television is a national asset of considerable value. A dollar and cents tag can be placed on it, and this value is increasing with every inventory.

As of the moment of this writing, there are 55 educational television broadcasting stations on the air. By the time this report is printed, the number undoubtedly will be larger because such is the growth of the medium. What is even more significant, however, *only one station (KTHE, Los Angeles UHF) has failed since the first station, KUHT of Houston, went on the air in 1953.* A record of 55 successes and one failure is a fairly good one by most standards.

ETV BROADCASTING STATIONS

While complete figures are almost impossible to obtain, there are at least some raw data on the total value of educational television stations presently operating. The National Educational Television and Radio Center as recently as March 1961 surveyed its member stations in an attempt to obtain a reliable inventory of the nation's ETV assets.

From this survey, and from cross checks made by the author, a conservative estimate would place the capital value of the 55 ETV stations then operating at approximately $29,400,000. On a similar basis, the annual operating budget for running these stations for the 1960 calendar year was about $14,800,000.

Although averages are mostly meaningless, they sometimes help to make total figures more easily comprehensible. It is interesting, but perhaps not significant, that the total figures given above represent an average capital investment of approximately $530,000 and an average annual operating budget of approximately $270,000.

NETRC study gives ranges

Much more revealing is a cost breakdown of the 1961 survey by the NETRC covering the 53 stations affiliated with that organization. It reveals the following:

1. Seventeen of the stations were community-operated.
   a. Their 1961 total capital investments ranged from $153,000 to $1,358,000 with the median at about $497,000.
   b. Their 1960 operating budgets ranged from $76,000 to $1,010,000 with the median at $275,000.
2. Nineteen of the group were college or university-owned stations.*
   a. The capital investment of this group ranged from $268,500 to $980,000 with the median at $250,000.
   b. Their 1960 operating budgets ranged from $50,000 to $569,000 with the median at approximately $175,000.
3. Eight of this group were operated by school systems.
   a. The total capital investment of these stations ranged from $153,000 to $800,000 with the median at about $553,000.
   b. Their 1960 operating budgets ranged from $122,000 to $455,000 with a median at about $293,800.
4. Nine stations were licensed to a state authority.
   a. *Capital Investment*
      Their 1961 total capital investments ranged from $529,000 to $900,000, with the median at $697,000.
   b. *Operating Budgets*
      Their 1960 operating budgets ranged from $80,000 to $842,900.
      A median here would be misleading because of the wide variations in operating costs and multiple-unit operations.

It must be emphasized, however, that figures vary greatly from station to station. Obtaining some basis of comparability has been almost an impossibility. Direct comparisons are therefore only partially accurate and can lead to unwarranted conclusions if not carefully made. Especially is this true of operating budgets. Whereas some stations—particularly community stations which are independently budgeted—include generally all administrative and maintenance charges, in university or school-system-operated stations, such charges are sometimes absorbed by the parent institution.

Ranges on the other hand do provide some guide to communities and

---

* One station is dually licensed to both a university and a public school system.

educational groups contemplating establishment of similar operations. In this connection it is perhaps significant to note the lowest and the highest budget figures for each of the three groups of stations, both for capital expenditure and for operations.

Type of Station		Capital Investment		Operating Budget	
		Low	High	Low	High
Community-operated	(17)	$153,000	$1,358,000	$ 76,000	$1,010,000
College-university operated	(19)	268,500	980,000	50,000	569,000
School-system operated	(8)	153,000	800,000	122,000	553,000
State authority operated	(9)	529,000	900,000	80,000	842,900

It should be added that the extremes at either end of the ETV station price range have not necessarily been reached. The proposal to buy out an existing commercial TV station to provide a VHF educational outlet for New York City, for example, runs into considerable money. An offer of $6.2 million reportedly has been made. Jack Gould, television writer for *The New York Times,* has estimated the annual operating cost of such a station at "conceivably more than $1,000,000 a year" (1).

At the other extreme, the possibility of a low-cost UHF station which would operate with much less power than any presently on the air has been advanced by the National Educational Television and Radio Center. In a book, *ETV and the Schools* (6), NETRC points out that capital outlays of $50,000 are within the realm of possibility and that two current applicants estimate their over-all operating budgets at $30,000 and $35,000.

Suggested budgets for ETV stations

Tables A through F attempt to translate some of the operating data on present ETV stations into guides for those planning similar installations. The first set of tables (A through C) sets forth what is considered a realistic budget for a minimum-limited operation. The second set of tables (D through F) is based upon professional standards and operations and a wider geographical service area.

To prepare these tables certain assumptions had to be made. These are noted on each table and documented where necessary. It should be of special interest, however, that estimates are based upon a VHF station with, in one case, 18 kilowatts of effective radiated power and, in the other, 316 kw ERP.

It also should be pointed out that salary figures, and to a certain extent personnel requirements, will vary considerably from community to community. In addition, there also will be a difference depending upon whether the station operates under a union or a non-union contract.

CLOSED-CIRCUIT SYSTEMS

If cost figures vary among ETV broadcasting stations, the spread is even wider in the field of closed-circuit television. To bring about any measure of comparability in the reports available would require an expert cost accountant about ten years. By then, of course, he would have to begin all over again with an entirely new situation.

There are no reliable figures on the number of closed-circuit systems now in operation. Estimates range from 135 to 350 in use for formal educational purposes. Most of these estimates do not include industrial closed-circuit installations, even when they are used for training purposes. They do, however, include installations operated by the armed forces.

The most reliable data on closed-circuit systems in educational institutions is contained in a report by the Joint Council on Educational Broadcasting. Entitled *Current Developments in Educational Television* and issued in February 1961, the Joint Council report (8) lists the following closed-circuit systems:

Year	Inst. having CCTV systems	No. of CCTV systems in these inst.	No. of military CCTV systems used for training purposes
1956	64	70	7
1958	119	133	21
1960 (July)	185	200	24

Figures for 1956 and 1958 are based on questionnaires returned in surveys. Those for 1960 are based upon a count of additional CCTV installations reported in newspapers and magazines and in direct correspondence with the Joint Council. None of these figures include CCTV systems currently in use for medical diagnosis, scientific research, and other purposes not strictly instructional in nature.

Based upon these data, a conservative estimate would place the total number of CCTV installations in use for educational purposes at between 250 and 300 as of April 1961. These systems, it should be added, vary from a single camera connected to a few receivers to well-equipped studios with cable links to elementary and secondary schools in different parts of a county.

Value of CCTV installations

On the basis of these data, and a careful study of the equipment listed for the 133 CCTV systems included in the 1958 study of the Joint Council, a total capital value of approximately $10,750,000 can be placed on the 250 (using the low estimate) CCTV systems now in operation in educational institutions. The annual operating costs probably run in the neighborhood of $4,250,000.

Again, however, ranges are more important than totals or averages. Some of the systems list capital costs at under $8,000, whereas others, such as Hagerstown and the University of Texas, run to as high as $250,000. Annual operating budgets likewise vary from $6,000 to $215,000.

At the risk of oversimplification, there appears in tables G and H the author's estimate of the minimum capital and operating budgets for professional quality closed-circuit television systems. It will immediately be claimed, especially by manufacturers of certain lines of inexpensive equipment, that these figures are on the high side and that excellent, efficient systems can be installed and operated for much less than the figures given.[*]

Perhaps so. On the other hand, the selection of CCTV equipment depends entirely upon the function it is to serve. Low-cost equipment to serve simple demonstration-type functions only can be purchased for around $4,000 to $5,000. This equipment, however, is extremely limited in application and offers virtually no possibility of recording, supplementing demonstrations by use of film, etc.

In consequence, the author believes that the estimates given are realistic ones. They are based upon the recommendation of competent engineers and the experience of CCTV systems currently operating. It will be noted, too, that the costs are presented in such a way that some items can be omitted and added later if desirable. The question-and-answer system is one of these. These estimates also are based primarily on individual catalog prices. Discounts on specific purchases may apply and can best be determined by negotiating directly with manufacturers.

In summary, to install a closed-circuit system for general instructional purpose (as against simple demonstration-type functions) and to insure reasonable professional results and minimum maintenance over a period of years, an expenditure of around $40,000 is required for equipment. Likewise, a realistic operating budget, including all relevant costs, will run somewhere in the neighborhood of $25,000 annually.[†]

Others will claim less, but the school board or university seriously interested in closed-circuit television as a long-range investment and concerned with achieving some measure of professional quality in the final results would be wise to budget a little more at the outset instead of running the risk of disappointment in result and a more expensive investment later. Furthermore, it should be noted that while the estimates of cost of closed-circuit systems are based upon the use of videcon cameras, a number of institutions and school systems have felt it imperative to have image

---

[*] One manufacturer now advertises "less than $1,260 buys you a complete CCTV system."

[†] One of the best studies of equipment needs, facilities, operation, etc. is *Design for ETV*, published by the Educational Facilities Laboratories, 477 Madison Avenue, New York 22, N.Y., 1960.

orthicon equipment instead. This equipment, which in general provides as good picture quality as received from a broadcast station, would add from $20,000 to $40,000 to the cost of equipment. Those who favor image orthicon equipment point out, however, that the investment is a wise one in terms of long-run economy and operation.

NETWORKING COSTS AND PROBLEMS

Aside from the production of educational materials for closed-circuit use and the broadcasting of programs from an ETV station, there arises the question of how to get the greatest value from a program by recording it in some fashion and making the film (or tape) available for other purposes. Obviously it would be economical, as well as desirable from a quality point of view, if programs could be used in more than one geographical area.

The NETRC service

To meet this need, the National Educational Television and Radio Center was organized in 1953. Today it provides a minimum of ten hours a week of program material to the nation's ETV stations. On a national scale it is the only organization which furnishes such a service.

The Center's budget is a matter of public record. The cost of this service, therefore, is readily available (7). For the year ending December 31, 1960, the Center spent $3,632,235 for national program production and distribution.

At present, the Center's program distribution is by means of video tape and film. A "live" network would greatly increase distribution costs, but would provide many advantages not possible under the present distributive system.

As an intermediate step, the use of telephone company facilities in the early morning hours to distribute programs to all ETV stations simultaneously has been suggested. This proposal, which would require FCC approval, would seem to have a great deal of merit because it would permit the same day transmission of programs which could be tape recorded and used by the individual stations. At the same time, rates should be lower than regular charges for live distribution.

It should be noted, too, that the Center's budget is a modest one, especially when compared with commercial network productions. So-called commercial "spectaculars" have run as high as one million dollars, which is almost one-third of the Center's yearly budget for 1,500 programs.

Finally, it is important to considerations of long-range financing to note that of the Center's total budget for 1960, only about 10 percent, or $362,442, came from station affiliation fees. The remainder came from Foundation grants, special production contracts, and related sources.

Midwest Airborne experiment

Most adventurous in the way of regional network plans is the Midwest Program on Airborne Television Instruction (MPATI). The consolidated budget for this project, approved by the Midwest Council on Airborne Television Instruction at a meeting on April 13, 1961, totals $8,260,000 to cover the period through May 31, 1962.

There are some indications, however, that the budget is low and that actual operations will exceed the amounts listed below. In addition, the capital costs do not include the purchase of two DC-6 planes from which Airborne's programs will be beamed. These two planes cost approximately $2,000,000, a part of which will be recovered when and if they are sold following conclusion of the project.

The budget for Airborne is broken down as follows:

Aircraft operations	$4,368,706
Educational services (including program of professional assistance to teachers and administrators) and staff service to area committees	566,384
Production of educational materials (taped lessons and printed guidance material)	2,158,189
Program service and distribution to participating schools	276,827
General administration including fund raising	526,258
Research and evaluation	84,105
Public information	135,909
Development of permanent organization	25,996
Contingency	117,626
TOTAL	$8,260,000

It might also be mentioned here that the rationale behind the MPATI project is based upon the assumption that using the aircraft is less expensive than covering the same territory with ground-based facilities. It has been estimated that it would take fourteen ground-based transmitters to cover the same geographical area. Comparative estimates of the two systems have been given as follows:

	Airborne Facility	Equivalent Ground-Based Facilities
Capital costs	$3,463,000	$10,229,000
Annual costs with 5-year amortization period		
Operating	$ 776,000	$ 809,000
Amortization		
Principal and interest	806,200	2,381,300
	$1,582,200	$ 3,190,300

As for future plans, Dr. John E. Ivey, President of MPATI, recently discussed three levels of operation in a speech on this subject (3). The first level would be a rock-bottom minimum operation costing approximately two million dollars a year. The second level would require about five million dollars. To achieve maximum usefulness would require about ten million dollars annually.

Other regional networks

In recent months, considerable interest has been shown in state-wide or regional networks of educational television stations. If federal support of some kind is provided for the expansion of educational television broadcasting facilities, it is almost certain that regional networks will take on even greater importance.

In terms of program potential and possible economies of operation, this development is beginning to emerge as one of the most significant since the early days of ETV. There are at the present time at least a dozen local networks in operation or in planning stages (5).

Many of these "networks" consist of little more than relay stations between existing and proposed broadcasting units. Nevertheless they involve a considerable investment of money and hold real promise for providing an effective pooling of educational resources of a state or group of states.

From the standpoint of effective program utilization at minimum cost, perhaps the most interesting experiment now being conducted is the Texas State ETV network. Serving 11 institutions of higher education, it is expected to provide 40 hours of programs in the first year.

The Texas system is being built at a total capital outlay for microwave towers and facilities of $285,000. This, of course, is exclusive of broadcasting and production facilities. The system will have four points of origination and will operate on an annual budget of approximately $20,000, again exclusive of programming.

One of the objectives of the Texas project is to study cost factors and possible savings to be accomplished by a cooperative effort of this kind. It is an experiment which is well worth watching by all who are interested in education by television.

On a more limited scale, the experience of the Oregon State System of Higher Education with a two-station, two-studio network demonstrates the economies to be gained from operations of this kind. The initial station (KOAC-TV), microwave units, two studios on the campuses of Oregon State University and the University of Oregon, and related equipment cost in the neighborhood of $200,000. The annual operating budget for 26 hours a week is approximately $120,000 exclusive of the costs of NETRC service (9).

Since this system went on the air, a second transmitter (KOAP-TV) has been added in Portland. Capital costs for this station are not available, but are expected to run around $200,000.

A typical day's schedule for the two Oregon stations includes three hours of telecourses produced in studios at the University of Oregon and Oregon State University plus four hours of adult education programs, most of them from NETRC. The inexpensive operation of the Oregon stations, together with the high quality of programming, indicates that efforts of this kind can play a significant part in educational broadcasting.

THE NEXT TEN YEARS

But what of the future? Will educational television continue to grow? Will ETV stations now existing on marginal budgets find a more substantial financial basis? Will closed-circuit operations prove to be economically sound in meeting some of education's forthcoming pressures? Will a national "live" network, providing instantaneously anywhere in the country the finest in cultural and educational programs, be financially feasible?

It is easy to be pessimistic. The amount of financial support necessary is staggering by most standards. So far there has been no great national ground swell demanding support for educational television. The only definitive report on closed-circuit costs suggests it is necessary to average more than 200 students in a TV class before television begins to become more economical than normal teaching methods (2).

Yet the future requires that the nation plan ahead in education more so than in any other phase of national life. Improvements in teaching methods are a necessity if the nation's schools are to preserve standards of quality in the face of on-coming numbers. The nation's cultural and educational development, receiving precious little nourishment from commercial mass media, also would seem to require a "fourth network."

From a practical point of view it is clearly reasonable to expect at least another 75 ETV stations on the air within the next ten years.* These stations undoubtedly will be underfinanced and the growing pains will be such as to convince the skeptic that they will never live to maturity.

A few won't. But the vast majority will go forward. The idea of ETV

---

* Some authoritative sources estimate that this number will be reached in five years. Certainly the number is a minimum figure for the ten-year period. If current legislation before Congress is passed, it is also possible that the number will be higher.

is new and, like so many innovations of this kind, it suffers from comparisons with established concepts of education and from failure to grasp what it can do *beyond* the boundaries of present methods of instruction and education. Progress will be difficult. There will be a long period of little movement followed by a substantial breakthrough, then another slow period of growth. The invention of the printing press did not immediately insure books in every home.

As to the cost, there can be only the roughest of estimates. Depending upon the number of stations, the availability of federal matching funds, and the degree of improvement of technical equipment, these estimates range as follows:

	No. of Stations	Capital Costs	Annual Operating Budgets
Low	50	$24,000,000	$14,000,000
Medium	75	36,500,000	18,500,000
High	125	55,000,000	31,000,000

In all probability, barring the possibility of substantial federal and state support, the actual figures will be somewhere close to the mediums given above. This would mean that an additional 75 new stations with a capital outlay of close to $36,500,000 and an annual operating budget of approximately $18,500,000 will be on the air by 1970.

An important national asset

Combining these figures with the value of ETV stations already on the air, the nation's total investment in this medium for education is likely to be in the neighborhood of $66,000,000 by 1971. Annual operating budgets should be somewhere around $34,000,000.

How will all of this be financed? The temptation is to answer "somehow" and let it go at that. Certainly such an answer would avoid chances of disagreement on specific methods. It also would be a safer position against the criticisms of hindsight.

But there is need for practical thinking as well as for vision. It is impossible to plan for the future without analyzing as objectively as possible the problem as it exists today, making realistic projections of what it will be tomorrow, and then weighing alternative courses of action.

Educational television is in financial difficulty. Any realistic approach to the future must begin with that admission. The degree ranges from critically serious to mildly inadequate. Only about ten stations out of 55 now broadcasting have what could be considered an adequate, sustained source of income. This is no basis upon which to start.

Sources of income for ETV

Furthermore, an examination of the sources of income for most ETV stations currently operating lends little encouragement. Reduced to essentials, these sources turn out to be five of major importance. The table following shows how these were distributed for 51 stations in 1961.

Sources of Income
Presently Operating ETV Stations*
1961

1. Public schools and boards of education	31%	⎫	57% total tax
2. State, county or city appropriation	26%	⎭	sources
3. Private colleges and universities	8%	⎫	
4. Business and industry	5%	⎬ 20% total "private"	
5. Civic groups, local foundations and individuals	7%	⎭	sources
6. Fund projects	6%	⎫	23% total special
7. Special projects	17%	⎭	sources
Total	100%	100%	

* Includes 51 stations reporting in 1961 NETRC Survey. Source: National Educational Television and Radio Center.

First, there are payments from school systems, universities, and colleges, and other public and private educational agencies. These are the main undergirding of most stations, but in general they have two disadvantages: (1) They are based, primarily at least, upon services received for in-school broadcasting, leaving precious little for the broad adult educational program where ETV can make at least as great a contribution and (2) This does not represent an assured source of income which will weather depressions and the vicissitudes of changing educational boards of control.

This source of support will remain, the author believes, the "bread and butter" account of most local ETV operations. Recent studies by NETRC indicate that from 30 to 40 percent of the financing of local ETV stations comes from this source. Perhaps some increase can be expected, but it is likely to be directly related to expanded services for in-school programming.

Second, contributions from business, industry, and interested civic groups. Nothing should be said to minimize the farsighted, pioneering efforts of this group of supporters. Year after year they have shouldered a major burden of ETV's cost. They have, in the author's judgment, made ETV possible, whereas otherwise it would have failed. The nation owes a great deal to the leadership and generosity of this farsighted group of businessmen.

But can such support be expected to continue? Probably not on a scale to match the challenges ahead. It will continue to be important ten years from now, and it will be a significant factor in the progress of ETV, perhaps the most significant in terms of "free" money available for those extra features which spell the difference between good and great. Nevertheless, these supporters cannot be expected indefinitely to carry such a heavy burden.

Third, membership contributions from the public. Theoretically this should be the major basis of support for ETV at least on the local level. Practically it just isn't so. Only one station today achieves any measure of financial help from this source and only during the past year has it grown to a significant item in the operating budget.*

The story is an old one. Why pay for something you can get free? How long would public libraries exist on such a basis? How many community cultural centers and programs would long continue if they were forced to rely on public subscription?

The answer is clear. This source of income will not long support ETV in the style to which it should be accustomed.

Fourth, foundation grants. A major factor on the national level, foundation grants so far have supported most of the activities of the National Educational Television and Radio Center. They also have served to stimulate the development of local stations and to sustain them in time of need. In this field, the most significant contribution by far has been made by the Ford Foundation, whose wisdom, generosity, and foresight have advanced ETV by many years.

Even so, it seems logical to expect foundations to make their continuing contribution, if any, at the national level and not to local ETV operations. Again, the source of support does not seem to have sound long-run possibilities for financing the day-to-day operations of ETV stations.

Fifth, and finally, production contracts. These are generally contracts for programs produced locally for national distribution. The national agency, almost always the National Educational Television and Radio

---

* KQED, San Francisco, which now has 12,000 member subscribers who contribute from $10 to $100 yearly. The income from this source now represents about 40 percent of that station's budget.

Center, pays not only the cost of production, but some slight overhead against a station's administration and operations.

Continuation of such a source of station support assumes, however, that the money will be available from somewhere for national program needs. The same dollar cannot be spent twice. Either it must go for national networking services or for local station support. Such help also is sporadic and raises a problem of the loss of local control.

Furthermore, to depend upon such a means of support also assumes that the rewards will be passed around among stations almost without regard to program-producing abilities and without regard to the quality of the product. The Mutual Broadcasting System idea foundered on such a rock. There is no reason to assume that ETV would fare better.

This review of income sources was not intended to be all-inclusive. There are many others: cooperating educational institutions, KQED's auction which annually nets somewhere around $40,000, private sponsorship of individual programs, and even the possibility of endowments. The list can be extended almost indefinitely.

It is clear, however, that if ETV is to reach its full potential, a combination of these and other sources of income will be required. Both private and public support are necessary and desirable—necessary in terms of preserving and extending the network of ETV stations and desirable in terms of broadening the financial base so as to minimize the danger of control from any one source.

A realistic look at the future suggests that some form of public support is essential to the future of ETV. At the risk of stirring up a major national controversy, the author would like to state his firm conviction that the future of educational broadcasting—a public asset of incalculable value to all citizens—hinges upon a combination of local and national tax support.

On the local level, public support of one kind or another is needed to provide the operating base to which private sources are added to strengthen and extend program resources. It would seem desirable, both from the standpoint of the geographical area covered and also to disperse control, that this base be cooperating school districts, a combination of several communities, or a state council. An ETV station has been compared to a community library in terms of its relationship to the public well-being. This is an appropriate comparison except that an ETV station is much more likely to have a wider service area both geographically and in numbers of citizens reached.

Establishing such a base of support will not be an easy task. There are many arguments against it and many pitfalls to be avoided in putting such a program into operation. Yet it probably is inevitable.

Support on the national level

On the national level, three possible sources of support deserve serious consideration. Two of these are related in that they would involve federal government participation of some kind.

The first possibility involves private financing only and assumes that a number of the nation's major educational foundations would join together to take on this commitment as a long-range continuing obligation. A strong case could be made that no more substantial contribution to the nation's cultural and educational welfare could be made in any field of foundation endeavors. Such support, providing it is sufficiently long term in nature, also could serve as the base to attract other private gifts for specific purposes and programs.

However, continuing obligations of this kind generally are not looked upon with favor by the foundations. The commitment involved also would be a substantial one in terms of the resources even of a considerable number of these foundations.

An estimate of ten million dollars annually has been placed by one authoritative source on the cost of a national program service extending to an additional 75 stations the same service now being provided to the 53 stations affiliated with NETRC. Such an estimate is undoubtedly low if the service is to be strengthened and expanded.

Based upon extending this service to an additional 75 stations, doubling the number of hours from ten to 20 a week, providing instantaneous "networking" transmission of programs (probably via telephone company lines as previously noted) and improving the quality of programs, a realistic estimate of cost would be somewhere in the neighborhood of $34 million. A rough budget is attached as table K. It should be noted, too, that this estimate is well below the cost of any of the existing commercial networks.

Barring a cooperative national foundation effort, the only other answer would seem to be some type of federal government support with all the implications which it raises. One high-ranking government official has suggested this come in the form of an assessment against commercial broadcasters for the privilege of using a public resource. The idea won't be popular, but it deserves consideration as one of several possibilities to meet the needs of national ETV.

The other alternative is a direct allocation of federal funds, preferably to an independent agency set up to minimize the problems of federal control. There will be many voices raised against this thought. The specter of federal control of communications media still is very real and frightening for most Americans.

To those who say it is impossible, there is the record of federal support of the Smithsonian Institution. The BBC in Great Britain and the CBC in Canada have avoided this problem reasonably well over the years. And the universities of Michigan and California, both among the world's greatest, are more free than some of their "private" counterparts, thanks to the wisdom of their founders in providing protection against political domination. The counterbalancing influence of strong private networks and stations, which it would be necessary to preserve and strengthen, also should be an important factor.

In terms of the nation's general welfare, the sum is not large. In terms of maintaining for all the people a significant and valuable addition to the nation's cultural and educational resources, it represents a small investment. In terms of political overtones and consequences, however, the problem is a perplexing and difficult one which deserves the serious study and attention of our most enlightened leadership.

Closed-circuit TV's future financing

The foregoing discussion has dealt primarily with broadcast educational television, locally and nationally. What of closed-circuit uses of the medium for instructional purposes?

It seems almost a certainty that closed-circuit television instruction will have an increasingly important role to play in the nation's educational system. If for no other reason, the numbers to be educated will demand it.

Estimates of the number of closed-circuit installations by 1970 vary greatly. Some enthusiastic supporters have predicted that every school system and institution of higher education will have such an installation in limited use at least by 1970. Since there are some 40,000 school districts and 1,016 accredited colleges and universities, this estimate would place the number at around 41,000.

More realistic estimates, however, based upon closed-circuit installations now in use and the statements of school administrators would reduce this number considerably. Again, three levels of possible development are suggested based upon what assumptions are made concerning the amount of support available and how rapidly technical breakthroughs will be achieved.

	Number of Installations	Capital Cost	Annual Operating Cost
High	9,000	$265,000,000	$180,000,000
Medium	4,000	125,000,000	67,000,000
Low	1,000	35,000,000	17,500,000

It should be pointed out that the cost estimates listed above are less than they would be if the recommendations included in tables G and H were followed. This is based upon current experience of closed-circuit television in which some of the costs are written off to regular ongoing budgets. If a larger number of installations is reached, it also is assumed that there will be more low-cost units included.

All of the figures above may seem staggering at first glance. They are quite believable, however, when held against the nation's total budget for education.

Before any substantial movement in closed-circuit TV can come about, however, it will be necessary for this means of instruction to prove itself more convincingly than it has today. To do so will require creative uses beyond the framework of conventional teaching. The tendency to compare CCTV in costs with present methods of education also will have to be overcome.

If the advantages of CCTV are compared with conventional teaching strictly on a cost basis as methods exist today, it will be difficult to convince the practical, economy-minded school board member and college administrator. Cost analyses are difficult to find in CCTV literature and are not sufficiently convincing to overcome skepticism and the natural reluctance to change.

Studies done by Pennsylvania State and the Hagerstown Public School System still provide about the only systematic answers to the cost question (8, 10). They don't, at the present anyway, suggest any substantial saving over present instructional methods until large numbers have been reached.

Moreover, there is cause for concern that closed-circuit TV, strictly local in nature, will work to the detriment of the very thing it seeks to enhance—quality standards of instruction. In the hands of overzealous promoters, in the face of attempts to look upon it as a panacea for all of education's problems, and in the selection of inexpensive equipment and poorly qualified personnel who have rushed in from other fields, there is real danger that closed-circuit television instruction of a purely local nature will be weighed and found wanting.

Against this, however, must be placed the far more important factor of a national exchange of really high-quality programs bringing to all communities the finest teachers in every subject field. Existing and proposed regional and national networks, together with other national exchange arrangements, offer real promise of success toward fulfilling the high goals set for education by television.

In summary, the financing of educational television, closed-circuit or broadcast, will remain even at best a difficult problem. In practical terms there is no easy, simple, inexpensive answer. Let no one be misled: the costs will be great and the returns sometimes will not seem worth the candle. In the next ten years the disappointments may almost equal the successes.

Slowly, however, acceptance of this new means of communication and education will inch forward, significant and unforeseen breakthroughs will occur, financial support will be found, excesses curbed, and an appropriate niche found for a significant contribution to the nation's welfare. In periods of doubt, of which there will be many, the words of Alfred North Whitehead still ring true:

"In the conditions of modern life, the rule is absolute: The race which does not value trained intelligence is doomed.

"Not all your heroism, not all your social charm, not all your wit. . . .

"Not all your victories on land or at sea can move back the finger of fate. Today we maintain ourselves. . . .

"Tomorrow science will have moved forward yet one more step, and there will be no appeal from the judgment which will then be pronounced on the uneducated."

To see that such a judgment is never pronounced upon the American people has been, and always will be, the primary object of education. It is an object to which education by television, given intelligent planning, clear-eyed responsibility and some measure of daring can yet add its little bit.

REFERENCES

1. Gould, Jack. "Big Opportunity." *The New York Times*, Feb. 26, 1961.

2. Greenhill, L. P. *The Potentialities of Closed-Circuit Television for Teaching in Colleges and Universities.* University Park, Pa.: Pennsylvania State University, May 1959.

3. Ivey, John E. Address at Lafayette, Indiana, March 10, 1961.

4. Joint Council on Educational Television. *Current Developments in Educational Television.* Washington, 1961.

5. National Association of Educational Broadcasters. *The Feasibility and Role of State and Regional Networks in Educational Broadcasting.* Washington, 1960.

6. National Educational Television and Radio Center. *ETV and the Schools.* New York, 1958.

7. Same. Financial statements for the year ending December 31, 1960.

8. Pennsylvania State University. *An Investigation of Closed-Circuit Television for Teaching University Courses.* Report No. 2. University Park, 1958.

9. Starlin, Glenn D. Personal communication, April 1961.

10. Washington County Board of Education. *Closed-Circuit Television Teaching in Washington County, 1958–59.* Hagerstown, Maryland, 1959.

TABLE A
Capital Costs—Minimum Operation
VHF ETV Station

Estimated coverage for station with 18 kw ERP
10-mile radius, Class A
18-mile radius, Class B

Equipment *excluding* land, utilities, or grounds improvement:

Transmitter (1 kw) and allied equipment	$ 50,000
Tower (300 ft.)	15,000
Antenna and transmission lines	23,000
Transmitter and studio building (partially air-conditioned), $35 per sq. ft.	100,000

Studio equipment:

2 cameras, 3-in. RCA image-orthicon $32,000	
Switcher 6,000	
Film chain, projectors, and 1 slide projector. 20,000	
Audio 4,500	
Master control and test 10,000	72,500

Lighting and studio draperies	7,000
Equipment for film, staging, graphics, engineering workshops	6,000
Office furniture for six offices, typewriters, and duplicating machine	4,000
	$277,500

Note:

Camera: 3 lens only.
No film production or program recording equipment.
No manufacturer's discount.
Pedestals and mike booms not included.

TABLE B
Operating Costs—Minimum Operation
VHF ETV Station

NET affiliation (population below 200,000) ....$ 7,200
Program services — music and sound effects, records, pictures,
graphic supplies, staging supplies, properties, trucking, lamps
for lighting, etc.   4,500
Engineering supplies, minor parts, audio tapes, replacement parts,
tubes, tower maintenance, etc.   9,000
Power   3,000
Telephone, telegraph, and postage   2,000
Administrative costs, office supplies, travel, books, professional
memberships in broadcasting associations, etc.   3,000
                                                             _____
                                                             $28,700

Notes:

a) Does not include stipends for teachers or other talent appearing as part of
   regular assignment.
b) Does not include following:
   Building maintenance or heat.
   Rent.
   Depreciation on equipment.
   Legal or engineering consultative services.
c) An additional saving can be made if administrative costs can be assumed as
   part of a regular on-going program.

TABLE C
Personnel Requirements—Minimum Operation
VHF ETV Station

Manager–program director ....$ 9,000
Chief engineer   8,500
1 Producer-director-switcher   5,500
1 Part-time director   2,000
1 In-school coordinator-producer-writer   6,500
3 Engineers-technicians   15,000
3 Part-time technicians   7,000
1 Office manager–bookkeeper   4,500
2 Part-time office clerks and receptionist   3,000
1 Traffic-continuity writer   4,800
2 Cameramen (also help in programming such as music librarian,
   announcer, artist, etc.)   8,000
1 Floor manager–staging assistant   3,600
1 Staging and lighting–director–cameraman   5,200
1 Film traffic, editor, librarian   4,500
3 Production assistants   5,500
                                                             _____
                                                             $92,600

TABLE D
Capital Costs—Professional Standards of Operation
VHF ETV Station

Estimated coverage for station with 316 kw ERP:
35-mile radius, Class A
52-mile radius, Class B

Equipment *excluding* land, utilities, or grounds improvement:

Transmitter (50 kw) and allied equipment .... $	250,000	
Tower (500 ft.)	30,000	
Antenna and transmission lines	54,000	
Microwave link, studio-transmitter	12,000	
Transmitter building	30,000	
Studio building	500,000	

Studio equipment:

Three 4½-in. image orthicon cameras............$60,000		
Two 3-in. image orthicon cameras (also used for remote)	32,000	
Remote truck	8,000	
Switcher, studio and field	11,000	
Film (2 chains, 3 motion picture projectors, 2 slide projectors)	34,000	
Master control and test (including video and audio terminal equipment	20,000	
Audio	12,000	
Special effects amplifier	12,000	
Four house monitors plus related equipment......	2,500	191,500

Lighting (2 studios and remote-studio draperies)	30,000
Kinescope recorder (double system sound)	35,000*
Three video-tape recorders	110,000
Remote microwave gear	10,000
Film unit (motion picture cameras, still cameras, tripods, lenses, magnetic tape recorder)	8,000
Film unit furnishings (splicers, projectors, editing tables, etc.)	2,500
Office equipment and furnishings (10 offices)	6,000
Graphics equipment	2,000
Staging equipment	3,500
Engineering workshop equipment and VTR storage........	3,500
	$1,278,000

* Optional.

TABLE E

Operating Costs—Professional Operations
VHF ETV Station

Net affiliation (population 500,000–1,500,000) ....$	10,700
Program services: music and sound effects, film rental, royalties, pictures, graphics, staging and production supplies, properties, costumes, lumber, trucking, lamps, etc.	12,500
Engineering supplies, minor parts, remote truck upkeep, replacement parts, tubes, tower maintenance, etc.	15,000
Image orthicon tube replacement	15,000
Power	8,000
Film: raw stock, chemicals, printing materials, still processing, travel of film crew, etc.	4,000
Video-tape supply	20,000
Magnetic audio tapes	400
News wire service	1,300
Telephone, telegraph, postage	6,000
Remote lines	1,500
Administrative and office expense, travel, membership in professional associations, books, etc.	8,000
Promotional—program schedules, printing, mailing	4,000
	$106,400

Notes:

a) Does not include stipends for teachers or other talent.
b) Does not include the following:
   Building maintenance or heat.
   Rent.
   Depreciation.
   Legal or engineering consultative services.
c) Administrative expenses variable depending upon charges against other activities.

TABLE F

Personnel Requirements—Professional Operations
VHF ETV Station

1 Station manager ....$	15,000
1 Program director	12,000
1 Special projects manager	10,000
1 Production manager	10,000
1 Chief engineer	12,000
2 Writer-producers	16,000
1 Director-producer	7,500
3 Directors	18,000
1 Continuity writer	5,200

```
 7 Engineers .........................................   39,375
 1 In-school coordinator ................................    8,000
 4 Cameramen at $4,500 .................................   18,000
 2 Floor managers .......................................    8,500
 2 Staging and lighting ..................................   12,000
 1 Graphic artist ........................................    7,000
 1 Research assistant and music librarian ....................    4,250
 1 Promotion—community school relations ..................    7,200
 4 Production crew at $3,600 .............................   14,400
 1 Announcer-newscaster .................................    6,000
 1 Business manager–bookkeeper ..........................    8,000
 4 Secretaries—traffic at $3,500 ...........................   21,000
10 Part-time help: crew, projectionist, film, staging, art, engineers,
    office ..............................................   18,000
 1 Film supervisor–photographer ..........................    8,500
 1 Film editor ..........................................    8,000
 1 Film librarian .......................................    5,000
                                                        ─────────
                                                         $298,925
```

TABLE G
Estimated Equipment Costs
Closed-Circuit Television System

```
2 Vidicon cameras, professional type .......................$20,000
1 Camera switcher ......................................    4,000
1 Film chain (1 16-mm projector, 1 2x2 projector)—B and H pro-
    jector and Dage chain...............................   12,000
1 Sync generator and test ................................    4,000
Audio-control room (mike boom, $600) .....................    2,500
Lighting ..............................................    1,500
Staging equipment, draperies, easels ........................    1,000
Film equipment—viewers, editing, storage rack ...............      500
Audition 16-mm projector ................................      700
Distribution system within one building feeding 10 classrooms:
    20 Receivers at $175 .................................    3,500
    20 Stands at $25 ....................................      500
    Cable and amplifiers .................................    2,000
    Question-and-answer system ..........................    2,000
    Off-the-air receiver and antenna .......................      500
                                                        ─────────
                                                          $54,700
```

Notes:

a) Difficult to estimate without specific study are costs for studio remodeling and air conditioning, conduit installation from control room to viewing rooms, remodeling of viewing rooms, and draperies.

b) Less expensive vidicon cameras and film chain could reduce cost by $10,000.

TABLE H
Estimated Operational Costs
Closed-Circuit Television System

Tubes and parts ....$	3,000
Office supplies, postage, telephone	500
Operations staff for six hours a day:	
1 Producer-director-coordinator	7,000
1 Engineer	6,000
Part-time operator and set maintenance	2,000
4 Part-time camera operators	2,000
Part-time art help	1,000
Part-time staging help	1,000
1 Secretary-traffic-bookkeeper-director-librarian	3,800
Office furniture	500
	$26,800

Notes:

a) These estimates do not include:
    Salaries of teachers and administration.
    Special visual aids and film rental.
    Depreciation.
    Maintenance.

b) Office furniture perhaps can be eliminated if already available or available from other sources.

c) Student and other part-time help can be substituted for secretary and for producer-director if necessary.

TABLE I
1961 Operating Budgets
NETRC Affiliated Stations

Stations Licensed to a Community Group	Stations Licensed to a University	
78,000	50,000 (1959)	211,000 (1960 figure)
110,000	76,100	232,000
154,500	89,300	235,700
223,000 (1960 figure)	102,200	259,000
225,000	102,400	320,100
260,000 (1960 figure)	124,000	346,900
275,000 (1960 figure)	124,000	362,500
275,000	167,100	519,000
324,000	181,000	569,000
327,000	197,900	
337,800		
370,600		
424,500		
450,000 (1960 figure)		
750,000		
1,010,000		
1,038,400		

Stations Licensed to a School System		Stations Licensed to a State Authority
122,000	293,800	80,000 (estimate)
131,000	300,000	104,000
234,000	380,000	110,600
293,800	455,000	388,000
		842,900

1. Most of the figures were gained directly from stations in 1961. For those not reporting in 1961 the 1960 figures were used or, in the few cases where figures were unavailable, estimates based on other sources were made.
2. Figures for WQED and WQEX, Pittsburgh, are combined.
3. Figures for KETA-TV, Oklahoma City, and KOED-TV, Tulsa, are combined.

TABLE J
1961 Capital Investment
NETRC-Affiliated Stations

Stations Licensed to a Community Group	Stations Licensed to a University	Stations Licensed to a School System
309,000	268,500	153,000
389,100	308,000 (estimate)	220,000 (estimate)
411,000	333,000 (1959 figure)	368,500
416,700	333,000	439,700
425,500	360,000	536,200
439,700	370,000	553,000
453,000 (1960 figure)	404,000	617,700
465,000	412,000	800,000
529,800	414,900	
550,000	434,500	Stations Licensed to a State Authority*
560,100	455,000	529,000
607,300 (1960 figure)	513,300	529,000
660,000 (1960 figure)	527,500	697,000
668,000	578,000	697,000
720,000	624,000	697,000
955,700	669,400	900,000
	959,600	
	979,200	
	1,184,400 (1960 figure)	

1. Most of the figures were gained directly from station reports in 1961. For those not reporting in 1961 the 1960 figures were used or, in the few cases where figures were unavailable, estimates based on other sources were made.
2. Figures include $53,000 NETRC video-tape recorders.
3. Figures for WQED and WQEX, Pittsburgh, are combined.
4. Figures for many additional production centers, a state microwave installation, etc., are not shown above. Hence the total of these figures would not represent the total capital investment in ETV broadcast-related facilities.

* Where separate stations exist with separate studios and locations licensed to one authority submitting a single investment figure, this figure is broken into equal parts to represent *each* such separate station.

TABLE K

Suggested Budget—National ETV Program Service

I. *Program acquisition and development*
   A. Includes increasing number of hours from 10 to 20 per week, strengthening and expanding programs offered in music, drama, public affairs, children's interests, foreign exchanges, humanities, social sciences, fine arts $15,750,000
   B. *Program promotion and utilization*   750,000
   C. *Program research, testing, and experimentation* 2,500,000
II. *Engineering and distribution*
   A. Extension of services to additional 75 stations and increasing distribution to 20 hours per week 2,000,000
   B. "Long Line" program network (estimated cost of using telephone wires for daily service, off-hours, special, etc.) 2,500,000
III. *Instructional materials budget*
   A. Production of five full courses per year for in-school use plus research and promotion 3,500,000
   B. Utilization and production of related materials 1,000,000
IV. *Administration*
   A. General administration, scheduling, station relations and development, legal, etc. 6,000,000

TOTAL NATIONAL BUDGET......................$34,000,000

Acknowledgments

I am indebted to a great many persons for the information contained in this report and for critical reading of early drafts of the manuscript. In particular, I would like to express my appreciation to my colleagues at The University of Michigan—Garnet Garrison, Fred Remley, Hazen Schumacher, Donald Wood, and Edward Stasheff—to Robert Hudson, Kenneth Yourd, James Robertson, Cyril Braum, Paul Owen, and Lee Franks of the National Educational Television and Radio Center, Jon Rice and Robert Nissen of KQED, Glenn Starlin of the University of Oregon, and Robert Schenkkan of the University of Texas. They helped to clear the crystal ball through which I viewed the next ten years.

VI. THE PROBLEMS OF RESOURCES AND FACILITIES

What will be the manpower needs of educational television over the next ten years? On the basis of our best estimate of how much use educational institutions are likely to make of ETV, how many channels will be needed in the next decade? What needs can be projected for the exchange of instructional television materials, and how can these best be met? What should educational institutions know about developments in ETV facilities so that they can plan adequately and without being quickly outmoded.

PERSONNEL AND TRAINING NEEDS IN EDUCATIONAL TELEVISION, 1961–1971

By Martin J. Maloney and Stanley T. Donner

Dr. Maloney is Professor of Speech and Broadcasting at Northwestern University. Dr. Donner is Professor of Broadcasting and Director of the annual Radio and Television Institute, Stanford University.

EDUCATIONAL TELEVISION BEGAN, in the United States, with the decision of the Federal Communications Commission, in 1952, to reserve 242 channels for nonprofit, educational broadcasting. In the intervening years, about one-fifth of these channels have been applied for, and used, with varying degrees of success. In 1961, nearly ten years later, ETV has emerged from its experimental stage; it is not merely a gadget, or a luxury; it is, in potential at least, an exceedingly useful instrument for improving American education and for meeting increasing demands on the educational system in a reasonably economical way. But neither in 1952 nor in 1961 has anyone produced an optimum plan for the use of ETV, which at present includes not only the VHF stations now operating, but a number of closed-circuit and some UHF broadcasting systems.

This paper is a part of a study to provide such a plan, certainly for the second, and possibly for subsequent decades of American ETV.

Projections of student population indicate that college enrollments will nearly double between 1959 and 1970, and that grade and high school populations will increase by 60 percent in roughly the same period. If we juxtapose these statistics with the fact that there was a shortage of 195,000 teachers in the United States in 1959–60, we reach the evident conclusion that these promised increases mean a tremendous strain on the educational system, in terms of staff, physical facilities, and money (1). Two other factors add to the complexity of the problem. One is the enormous increase in knowledge, particularly scientific knowledge, which students now need to know (2). "It is estimated that the body of scientific information to be taught in the junior and senior high schools of the nation will double in the next ten years" (3). The other is that money alone cannot solve our difficulties, for several reasons. Time is needed, as well as money, to develop able teachers; the mere doubling or tripling of facilities does not necessarily imply high educational standards; competition in all fields for educated manpower means that we cannot divert our best graduates into any one profession (4). We should be much at fault if we did not study the capability of television in improving education, in extending the effectiveness of our available teachers, and in easing the demands for great increases in plant and equipment. And if we find that ETV can serve any of these ends, we must also determine what provision we should make for its future.

I. THE PROBLEM: THE METHOD

This paper, which has to do with personnel and training needs for ETV during the coming decade, addresses itself specifically to the following questions:

(a) What is the order of manpower need which may be anticipated during the next ten years as community educational stations become more numerous, and as educational television comes to be used more widely and often in schools?

(b) How can educational television recruit the high-quality personnel it will need if the medium is to be exploited to the full?

(c) How can classroom teachers be trained most effectively to use television in teaching?

(d) What new types of teachers, users, and supervisors must be trained if television is to be used effectively in the schools?

We may summarize our answers to these questions, roughly, thus:

(a) A numerical answer to this question, however carefully derived and phrased, would be inadequate and misleading. The personnel problems of ETV are not to be met by training thousands of persons in techniques which are already well known, by means of courses and training programs which already exist; they will rather be solved if we can determine what skills and attitudes will permit the full exploitation of ETV, and then devise training courses appropriate to these findings. Thus, we shall probably need to produce two or three thousand television engineers; from five hundred to a thousand production personnel; twenty-five hundred to three thousand teacher-performers; two or three hundred communication experts—yet not only do the courses necessary to educate these people remain to be devised, but in some cases the very knowledge they will need remains to be discovered. Our basic problems are research and planning, and not the mass production of personnel.

(b) While it is true that salaries for ETV personnel need to be increased, the main problem in personnel recruitment is to develop ETV into a profession with its own peculiar skills, its own values and satisfactions. We sorely need more people who are committed to ETV as a lifework; they must be assured that it is not simply a gadget, to be replaced in a few years by another gadget; they must be made sure that the use of ETV requires skills, understanding, and abilities as valuable and honorific as those involved in any other profession. The problem is not merely to create a "good image" of ETV; the image must be true to fact, based on careful research and planning by educators, and on distinguished performance by professionals in the field.

(c) In contrast to the foregoing problems, the training of classroom teachers to use ETV *is* a mass production enterprise, which must be undertaken by schools of education, probably in collaboration with departments of speech, communication, and psychology. Our recommendation is that every prospective teacher in the United States be given proper training in his or her role and skills vis-à-vis ETV; and that practicing teachers, by means of workshops, refresher courses, and the like, receive the same training. While some workshops have been set up for this purpose, we shall obviously need many more.

(d) This final question as to what new types of teachers, users, and supervisors must be trained is answered in our conclusions stated above. While there is available apparatus for training ETV personnel in our universities and colleges, we need to consider new roles, new kinds of performance, and new courses of instruction wherever we turn in this important area. Our conclusion here is that no one to date has done what really needs to be done to make ETV a maximally effective instrument.

Our method of preparing this study has been, in part, conventional: We examined the voluminous literature of research, comment, and speculation on ETV, to discover that relatively little has been put in print on our subject. We refer to such literature as we found pertinent in the pages following.

On the assumption that the future of ETV would be determined by population trends in the United States, we examined various projections of the general population for this period, of school populations, estimates of primary, secondary, and college and university expansion (5).

In the main, however, we proceeded by what might be called "census research"; we assumed from the start that the best predictions of the future of American ETV during its second decade would be made by those who had studied it and been active in it during its first. These people, we thought, would include programmers and managers of ETV stations; enginers involved in electronic research; persons concerned with the production of ETV programs, as with NETRC; specialists in education and communication; and teachers concerned with training television personnel. We conducted lengthy interviews with 20 such persons, and have received extensive written comments and analyses from 40 more. Of the persons from whom we requested written statements and analyses, we had response from about 65 percent (6). We have collated the information thus acquired and, in the paper which follows, attempt, among other things, to report the preponderance of fact and opinion, indicating divergences either in the text or in footnotes.

II. DEFINITIONS AND FUNCTIONS

Our first effort at defining educational television rests on a distinction between the *intent* to inform and the *intent* to entertain. Obviously, a soap opera may be regarded by its devotees as instructive, and it is even possible that a television course in shorthand might be regarded by some as amusing. But such observations serve only to blur a useful distinction (7). We therefore regard those programs which are contrived to convey information, or to teach skills and techniques, as educational; and those programs which have other purposes—as to amuse, excite, narcotize, and so on—as noneducational (8). We reserve a great and important third area from these categories—what one of our respondents has called "the shadow area of the arts," being prepared to recognize a program of chamber music or a Shakespearean production as neither educational nor entertaining in the strictest sense of these terms, though certainly sharing in both characteristics.

Educational television, so defined, would of course include many of the public service and informational offerings of commercial stations and networks, including such outstanding programs as "Continental Classroom." However, we do not regard commercial programming as important to the purposes of this paper. Presumably, so long as the legal controls on American broadcasting remain substantially unchanged, commercial broadcasters will offer public-service educational programs, to one degree or another. But there is no indication at the moment that this service will require much more staff or effort in 1971 than it has in 1961.

Our interest here is in the continuance and possible expansion of ETV stations and networks, and of closed-circuit operations; and in the possibilities of using ETV as another in the battery of audio-visual devices through improvements in video tape (9).

Educational television will undoubtedly serve many purposes in the next decade. For example: formal courses for in-school use; "enrichment" programs for extra-school viewing; credit and noncredit courses for continuing education; programs for preschool children; music, drama, and the like, for general viewing; classroom observation in teacher-training programs, and similar arrangements for the teaching of surgery in schools of medicine, typing in secretarial schools, and so on; transmission of significant lectures to larger audiences within schools and universities; remote observation of scientific experiments. The list might be greatly extended.

To simplify our discussion, we would first make a somewhat loose distinction between "systematic" and "nonsystematic" uses of television in education (10). In the category of "nonsystematic" uses of ETV we would include programs intended to satisfy the cultural, aesthetic, and general informational interests of audiences at whatever age. The "systematic" uses would include programs for in-school viewing, enrichment programs for in-school viewing, enrichment programs when they are designed to supplement a school curriculum, high school or college courses whether offered for credit or not, and so on. The nonsystematic services of television seem most likely to be offered by ETV stations, as a more or less important aspect of their normal programming, and by public-service programs on commercial stations and networks. The systematic function of

ETV is most likely to be served by ETV stations and networks, closed-circuit systems, and the use of ETV programs as audio-visual aids (11).

III. NONSYSTEMATIC USES OF ETV

In part, this aspect of programming in educational television is a kind of measure of the failure of commercial broadcasters to provide adequate service to at least some segments of the available audience. A case in point: educational stations have done relatively little with news, or even with news commentary, presumably because they cannot and do not need to compete with the services of commercial stations; on the other hand, educational broadcasters have done a great deal with children's programming, a field in which the efforts of commercial broadcasters have been subject to rigorous criticism. Similarly, we suggest that programs of serious music have appeared successfully on ETV, as they have on FM radio, simply because commercial broadcasters on radio and television have not satisfied the public demand for them.

It is our strong impression, however, that the majority of nonsystematic uses of ETV has grown out of a parallel in growth between this medium and the adult education movement in the United States. Educational offerings reasonably describable as adult education have, of course, long existed in this country; but it seems fair to suggest that adult education as a large-scale, popular movement really emerged from the depression of the thirties. Using to some extent the earlier Scandinavian systems as their models, but sparked largely by university extension- and farm-education programs, and by the free evening schools set up by the federal government during the depression, these programs grew enormously, usually on a fee-supported basis, in the years following World War II. ETV came in at the very crest of the wave, circa 1950–55; and as a result, most community- and college-operated stations were, in their early years, largely devoted to nonsystematic programming designed to satisfy the somewhat miscellaneous needs of their audiences for stimulation, aesthetic pleasure, and practical knowledge (12). Of the educational stations licensed between 1950 and 1955, most were operated either by tax-supported institutions (such as WHA-TV, the University of Wisconsin) or by quasi-public organizations (such as KQED, San Francisco, Bay Area Educational Television) which had pressing and immediate public needs to consider, before the longer-range goals of systematic education could be worked out (13).

Also, it seems clear that an economic factor has played, and will continue to play, a considerable part in determining ETV programming; and that financial support for ETV, after all, only reflects a complex of attitudes and biases common in our culture, and of political, military, and other pressures on the nation as a whole. We reconstruct our major findings thus:

Adult education, as represented on ETV by what we have here called "nonsystematic" programming, is socially marginal in the United States; that is to say, it is regarded at best as a desirable service, but with overtones of luxury—not as a necessity to survival; and even as a luxury, it is valued by only a segment of the population (14). Although ETV stations early in their history put a considerable stress on nonsystematic education, they have since tended to favor in-school broadcasting, credit courses, and the like, because there has proved to be more specific demand and consequently more reliable financial support for the ETV station from the latter effort than from the former.

Indeed, we suspect that the entire adult education has had cause, since 1955, to realize its marginal nature. In the Sputnik era, grants by government and private foundations have tended to flow into projects for systematic rather than nonsystematic education; institutions offering adult programs have succeeded best where they could contrive attractive student-oriented courses at very low cost to the student (15); community ETV stations have discovered that their operating budgets can be only fractionally covered by memberships, subscriptions, and other forms of public contribution (16).

Nonsystematic programming, we believe, will probably not *increase* greatly on ETV within the next ten years; with this conclusion our respondents seem ultimately to agree. We do not argue that such programs are dying for lack of support—on the contrary, we observe that many recent examples have been conceived and produced with real distinction, and have consequently gained and deserved wide public attention. But we believe that such programming will continue to be marginal, though important; and we believe that where any major increase in stations or other ETV facilities takes place, it will be justified by its services to formal programs in schools and colleges, rather than by its contributions to nonsystematic education.

IV. SYSTEMATIC USES OF ETV

The history of ETV as an aspect of formal education is part of the story of the radio/audio-visual complex in education—a part, however, sharply to be distinguished from the whole. Films, tapes, recordings, and other AV devices have of course been used for many years as teaching *aids*, with more or less success; they have also been employed as single teaching devices, without the aid of "live" instructors (17). But ETV, when it came into being in the early fifties, was quite different from, though obviously related to film, radio, and the rest. Perhaps the main initial difference was quantitative; the decision of the FCC, in 1952, to allot television channels for educational use in 242 communities promised to create an instrument for teaching unprecedented in scope and power; and the appearance, within nine years (18), of even 55 stations seemed to make this promise a reality. Another difference was more subtle; the twin facts that ETV works by broadcasting, and that therefore control over program content and style cannot be wholly in the hands of teachers and school administrators, has proved important (19). This situation has perhaps created some resistance by teachers and local administrators to the use of broadcast ETV; on the other hand, it obviously offers a saving in personnel and an improvement in the quality of programming, and it makes available more expert service in teaching and production, as compared with either conventional classroom teaching or school-controlled, closed-circuit operations.

During the fifties, the cold war—especially after the launching of Sputnik I—came to seem almost as much an educational as a diplomatic-military struggle, with much discussion of the technological and scientific gap between East and West, the existence of which was attributed in large part to a difference in trained manpower. This was, as well, a period of great concern over the defection of American military personnel in Korea to the Chinese—a phenomenon which became much exaggerated in the discussing, and which was, at last, partially traced to a failure of education, or indoctrination, in this country.

The American tendency in this century has been, as a rule, to find machine solutions to human problems; and of course, these solutions have not always proved unsuccessful. Consequently, when toward the end of the fifties video tape and other technical devices appeared—the possibility of broadcasting from planes and later satellites, for example—they seemed, perhaps correctly, to offer a mid-century solution to American educational problems.

These several factors seem to have combined to create a variety of uses and projected uses for ETV and similar devices.

1. *Television: the machine as instructor*

Here we have to examine two closely related questions: whether television can or should be used as a sole instrument in teaching; and whether, if the medium is so used or not, any savings in money, personnel, or facilities can be expected. We shall treat these questions in reverse order.

First, we judge that there is considerable semantic confusion involved in the various discussions of whether or not ETV is "economical." It makes considerable difference, in speaking to the problem of economy, whether one thinks of television as the *sole* teaching device, or television supplemented by the efforts of the classroom teacher; or whether one thinks of "economy" as involving an absolute decrease in costs, or a smaller increase in proportion to student population than might otherwise be expected, or a relatively modest increase as educational programs are expanded; or whether one thinks of "economy" as meaning more effective education at higher price (20).

Precisely because of this confusion, which will surely persist in general discussions of the subject, we think that ETV ought not to be *defended* on the argument that it will mean less expensive education. As long as ETV means the purchase of a video-tape recorder at a price of $20,000 or a closed-circuit system which could cost several thousand dollars a month, or a UHF broadcasting arrangement which may involve an initial cost of from $100,000 to $300,000, one can hardly pretend to be talking in bargain-basement terms. On the other hand, anyone who supposes that the costs of education in the United States can be cut, or even maintained at the present level, is simply naïve; we have too many people to educate, and too much knowledge to impart to them. The most that we can expect from ETV is that it will help to accomplish the enormous tasks set to our educational system, efficiently, and at a not-impossible price. But perhaps we should examine some of the variations on this theme.

The first problem, obviously, is whether television can or should substitute for the classroom teacher or situation. If it could do so infallibly, the related problems of educational costs, supply of teaching personnel, and classroom space would be much eased (21).

Even a cursory examination of the history of education reveals that conventional methods of teaching derive from the pre-Gutenberg era. These methods assume that the classroom is the natural and inevitable context of education; the teacher is the source of information; books and other materials are used as supplements, literally as audio-visual aids to learning. These assumptions have, with many, the force of natural law, both because of their antiquity and because they support the educational system as it presently exists. But what if we assume instead that learning may take place in other contexts, and that the teacher need not be the repository of information? Let us suggest instead the following: that learning may occur in the living room, or anywhere else, if information is provided through a book, an audio tape, a video tape, or a television broadcast; and that we do not necessarily need a trained teacher to convey such information effectively (22).

The dozen years of ETV research have produced a considerable amount of evidence to indicate that these suggestions are true. Sherburne, in a recent article, summarizes a sizable part of ETV research with wit and accuracy:

A perusal of the AVCR Research Abstracts, the NAEB Fact Sheets, or any other research summaries, shows the enormous repetition of this question. (Does television teach as well as conventional methods?) And as a result we now know that television can be used to teach high school students, elementary pupils, the Army, the Navy, college students, housewives, student teachers, and IBM salesmen. It can act as a conveyor of learning for subjects including home nursing, physics, algebra, dressmaking, college composition, typewriting, psychology, and maintenance of military telephones. It can do this, amazingly enough, in Florida, Alabama, Pennsylvania, Illinois, and even Canada, England, and France. And apparently students can learn at 6:30 a.m., noon, late afternoon, the early evening, or late at night (23).

In the face of these findings, the argument has been advanced that the instructor's skill and experience are the crucial factors in the learning situation: a good teacher can teach either by television or in the classroom. But even this reservation seems questionable, at least for some kinds of instruction (24).

It is not our purpose here to argue that education should be divorced from the classroom, the live teacher, the experienced teacher, and instead be automated. We do not think that any such change either will or should take place. We wish simply to indicate that television can be used, alone, as an effective teaching device; that it can, for some purposes, be turned into a kind of teaching machine at no discoverable loss to the learning process. And since we are obviously forced to use our resources in teachers, material, and money with the greatest economy if we are to accomplish the massive tasks set to the educational system, these facts are of great importance and should determine much of the future of ETV.

Some additional evidence on these issues is offered by the experience of those institutions which have offered courses for college credit via television. ETV courses, offered for credit to home viewers, have generated a certain amount of enthusiasm in recent years. Pennsylvania State University, San Francisco State College, the University of North Carolina, and Iowa State Teachers College all have experimented with this expedient, and apparently with some degree of success. Perhaps the most elaborate attempt at college education by ETV has been made by the Chicago Junior College system, in offering a full junior college program over station WTTW, Chicago.

Evaluation of these programs indicate that it is possible for students to learn college subjects as effectively in their living rooms as on campus. The Chicago experiment, to cite only the one case, seems to show that the ETV college program can mean a considerable saving in classroom space and teaching personnel. Thus far, however, serious interest in this sort of offering seems to have been confined to a few colleges and universities; and we can find little if any evidence that the interest will spread (25).

Our judgment is that these courses are seen as "adult education," and consequently are not really of central importance in the educational picture. If this estimate is correct, we incline to believe that credit courses will continue to be offered on ETV, but that they will probably not increase greatly over their present levels.

We should perhaps add here that, although some ETV broadcasters may believe or hope that their broadcasts will supplant the live teacher and the conventional classroom situation, neither the belief nor the hope is shared by many teachers. We see many indications that there is strong and frequent teacher resistance to ETV in almost any form (especially, of course, when teachers see the medium as a kind of mechanical substitute for their abilities and skills). How effective this resistance may be is difficult to determine, even in a specific situation; but there can be no doubt that it exists, and must be regarded as a conservative factor in the entire ETV situation. In particular, this factor will have much to do with the extent to which ETV is used in seemingly unconventional ways.

2. Television as supplement

One of our respondents remarks wisely that television is a flexible tool, which can be used in many ways. Where there is a teacher shortage, or an outright lack of teachers, he says, television can and should be used to supply the lack; where there is a need to improve instruction by supplementing the efforts of classroom teachers, or to serve overloaded instructors by reducing the amount of repetitive work they do, it may be used for these purposes. We quite agree; but would add that we believe that the principal use of ETV in the immediate future will be to supplement and reinforce conventional classroom teaching.

Conventional ways of teaching, like conventional ways of doing anything else, tend to persist as long as they produce the desired results—and sometimes, of course, long after they have ceased to produce the desired results. On the one hand, the great problems which American educators must solve in this decade press for a change in educational methods and instruments; on the other, the innate conservatism of the system forces a continuation of old methods as long as they can be used at all. We should be greatly surprised to see genuinely revolutionary changes in education by 1971; we think that there will be a gradual modification of educational methods, in which television will play an important part; but we think also that television will be used to supplement and extend where the old methods cannot quite reach.

Our main task, then, is to look at the present and potential uses of ETV as a part of the formal educational system, from preschool to the university and its professional schools.

It is clearly impossible to predict, in flat arithmetical terms, the number of people whose services will be required by ETV within the next ten years. The problems of the *kinds* of people, and/or their training, are more open to prediction. However, with reference to the problem of simple numbers, we may suggest a set of factors which could be influential:

Population. Clearly one of the main pressures on school administrators at the present time is the increasing student population in the United States. School populations have shown sharp and regular increases for some years—a tendency which seems destined to continue. For example, Office of Education statistics and projections show a recorded enrollment in American grade and high schools of nearly 39 million as of 1957–58. This figure was expected to increase to well over 44 million by 1960–61, and to 54 million by 1969–70. A similar pattern appears in college enrollments. From 3,364,861 in 1959, they are expected to mount to more than 6 million by 1970 (26). These figures would indicate that an increase in staff and instructional facilities of the order of 60 percent must be planned for this period. But this is by no means all: Administrators have to face the problem of providing more effective education for this vast horde of students, and probably in a greatly increased range of subjects—for example, by 1971 more different languages will probably be taught in American schools than ever before, and taught more efficiently and at an earlier stage of the student's career.

It is, of course, possible to conceive that these problems will be met without the aid of ETV; but the idea seems most unlikely. At the very least, there will be situations in which teachers, equipment, and classroom facilities are simply not available to meet educational needs (there are many such situations at present); ETV will certainly supply these needs, *faute de mieux*. And at most, and best, as ETV continues to prove itself as an effective educational tool, it may become more and more important to the administrator's strategy in coping with his considerable problems.

War. Any deepening of the cold war, any threat from relatively minor conflicts, even an obviously dangerous series of setbacks in "peaceful competition" with the East, would probably increase, and would certainly maintain, demands on education generally, and on the engineering of education in particular. Response to these demands would, we assume, come initially from the federal government (at present, much of the federal tax money which is being poured into educational projects is spent in the name of defense), but ultimately, of course, from state and local governments.

On the other hand, a successful effort to ease world tensions might well result in decreasing demands on educational facilities, decreasing financial support, and less demand for personnel. However, we would point out, first, that the likelihood that American problems on the international scene will ease is remote and, second, that the effects of such a change, if it occurred, would not be short-term ones. If, miraculously, the problems of Latin America, Southeast Asia, the Far East, the Middle East, etc., could be solved at once, demands on the educational system would probably not be much changed by 1962–63, and programs designed to satisfy these demands would probably not be modified much before 1964–65. Pressures and programs, once they exist, tend to perpetuate themselves.

Depression. Anything from a mild recession to a serious depression would tend in one way to increase demands on educational facilities; as jobs become scarcer, some people will inevitably resort to further education as a way to equip themselves to compete in a limited job market.

We hardly suppose that a recession, even a fairly serious and prolonged one, would make much difference in the deployment of educational facilities; the effect of a really disastrous economic setback, even, is questionable. On the one hand, we note the tendency of government in the thirties to create jobs, which would mean a stress on human rather than machine effort; why develop ETV further when we have unemployed teachers? On the other hand, as one of our respondents points out, there might be more reliance on machines than men in a depression, if the machines were already in.

In short, though severe depression *might* mean less use of ETV, our belief is that this factor will prove negligible during the period 1961–71.

Shift to UHF. Opening of the Ultra High Frequency range for television would mean that many new channels would be made available for educational television. The problem is that most present television sets, which are capable of receiving only VHF signals, would have to employ converters in order to receive UHF and that manufacturers would have to agree, in the future, to produce receivers capable of both. This means that the shift to UHF cannot occur overnight as far as general broadcasting and reception are concerned. Widespread purchase of converters seems improbable, and the procedure of the FCC in dealing with set manufacturers would allow several years before the new UHF-VHF receivers came on the market. At best, then, ETV broadcasters can expect to use UHF channels to reach general audiences only in the late sixties, if then.

Low-power UHF broadcasts directed to specific audiences for viewing within a limited area—for example, on a university campus—is another matter. The University of Utah has already successfully installed such a system, and other such systems are now in the planning stage. This kind of installation would be, in effect, closed circuit, since the signal would be receivable only within short range, and then only on UHF receivers.

In short, many more ETV channels are technically available than are now in use—and still more may be opened up by the possibility of broadcasting on three megacycles rather than six. Many obstacles, technical and economic, hinder the full exploitation of these possibilities; but if, as we anticipate, the need for ETV becomes more acute and obvious, these difficulties will be overcome. The fact is that television is technically ready to meet many of the educational needs which we have outlined above.

New technology. We began by assuming that this factor would be of prime importance in determining personnel needs in ETV; and so, indeed, it may turn out to be. However, the data which we have been able to uncover force us now to a somewhat conservative view; we do not suppose that the shape of ETV will be radically altered by new inventions and technical developments, although they will undoubtedly occur. We have already discussed the implications of UHF; other than this, the most interesting recent technological developments related to ETV are as follows:

(a) *ETV networks.* The term "networks" may be used, though loosely, to cover several situations which presently exist in ETV. Educational stations have for some time enjoyed the benefits of a national program service through NET (National Educational Television) established by the Educational Television and Radio Center. Networks, more appropriate to the term, have been in existence for some time. The first of these was in Alabama, whose network reaches 80 percent of the population of the state and where more than 250 schools are receiving programs. Florida has a network of several stations connecting by microwave relay the state-supported universities and colleges. North Carolina and Oklahoma are operating networks. Georgia, Kansas, Ohio, Oregon, Maine, and South Carolina are developing state-wide networks. A New England network, a Mid-West network, as well as a thirteen-state Southern regional network, are in the planning stages (27). It is certain that other states will follow these examples. Such systems are, of course, decidedly economical in that they greatly extend the services of ETV at a modest increase in costs. The principal objection to them seems to be that they centralize the control on educational materials too much—an objection which has, of course, also been made in educational radio, educational films, and state-selected textbooks.

The interesting possibility here is the prospective appearance of a "fourth network" which would, one assumes, unite all of these services into a national ETV system. Again, we hardly suppose that any such development will take place by 1971, though considerable progress may be made toward it. But such progress will not mean greatly increased personnel needs; existing ETV stations and program services could, by using relay transmitters, provide much of what is necessary.

(b) *Airborne television.* Broadcasting on a multiple-channel system from a plane will be a reality in 1961; the center for the experiment is Purdue University. In theory, airborne television is to provide the equivalent of a regional network service to a fairly large area in the Middle West which could not otherwise properly be served by ETV.

Airborne—and eventually, satellite—television will have its fair trial. At the moment, airborne television seems likely to prove an interim device, since it is obviously less reliable than conventional broadcast or closed-circuit TV. Broadcasting from satellites, if such a system develops, will certainly come after 1971.

(c) *Video tape.* The widespread use of video tape in schools waits on the development of small and relatively inexpensive tape machines. At present, the cost of video-tape equipment has been cut, on American models, from about $40,000 to about $20,000; a Japanese competitor promises to cost about $8,500. There is obviously some distance between this situation and the availability and cheapness of the audio-tape recorder, a distance which will probably not be made up, at least for many years.

Video tape, together with small school closed-circuit set-ups, *could* render obsolete the actual broadcasting of educational materials, except for two general classes of factors. First is the matter of cost. Video-tape equipment is expensive, and closed-circuit set-ups, both in initial expense and maintenance, even more so. The cost per student would be high indeed. Only school systems and universities with large financial resources—and inevitably with very large enrollments—could afford them. Second, the use of video tape and small closed-circuit systems would put ETV in the general category of audio-visual devices; and, while films, audio tapes, and the like have been useful in education in the past, they have hardly revolutionized the educational process. The reason: Audio-visual devices have been, by definition of their nature, in the hands of teachers and administrators to use as they wished; and the fact is that they have been used as a supplement of minor importance to conventional techniques in teaching. There is no reason to suppose that the use of video tape would be much different.

Followed to its conclusion, this use of small school closed-circuit television, or video tape used in this fashion, would defeat the basic purpose of broadcast educational television: to provide quality education to large numbers of students at a relatively low cost per pupil.

In general, we estimate that the main services of ETV in the immediate future will be provided through broadcasting: networks serving increasingly large areas, stations reaching general audiences, low-power UHF stations serving special local needs. Closed-circuit ETV will probably continue to be used within colleges or universities or in large school systems where the buildings are so grouped as to permit the economies and other advantages of that system to exist. Video tape, in all likelihood, will continue to service broadcast and closed-circuit ETV, permitting delayed broadcast, repeated use, and program exchange. Video tape will come into much wider use as its cost decreases, but it will not supplant broadcasting. Airborne and/or satellite television will, for the most part, either provide a supplementary service to education, or will be used as an interim device, to provide coverage to otherwise unreachable areas.

To return to the problem of numbers: educational facilities will have to be increased by about 60 percent by 1971, to continue educational efficiency at the present level; to improve the educational effort, a considerable additional investment in facilities and teacher training and the like will be required. ETV, at the present time, is coming to the end of its "experimental" stage; that is to say, it has been tried out in various ways, as a sole teaching instrument, as a supplement to classroom teaching, and so on, and its effectiveness has been studied and demonstrated, but it has not been recognized universally or used as a "normal" weapon in the educational armory. The various pressures which we have described, as well as the ordinary tendency to use more extensively a new and useful instrument, should force at least a doubling of American ETV services by 1971.

V. PERSONNEL

The foregoing projections of ETV functions and size indicate that the following kinds of personnel will be needed:

a. *Engineers*

Obviously, the training of broadcasting engineers is fairly well standardized, and needs no discussion here; the sources of supply are fairly well set. The principal problem is one of sheer quantity; how do we get *enough* competent technical personnel? One of our respondents, an ETV station manager, says in effect, "I can have my pick of directors and producers, but where do you find a good engineer?" This question is likely to grow more pointed as time passes; the need for engineers in ETV will probably increase out of proportion to the need for most other kinds of personnel, since the most probable technical developments in ETV (a network operating with relay transmitters, for example) tend to be economical of production personnel and performers, but prodigal of equipment and, inevitably, engineers.

We recommend that a special survey be made of professional organizations and schools for electronic engineers, to ascertain their numbers, professional motivations, potential income, and so forth. It seems evident that ETV will have to engage in some recruiting activities in this area, preferably through one or another of the national organizations concerned with ETV; the place to begin would be the engineering, trade schools, and junior colleges that specialize in training broadcast engineers, video and audio technicians, and cameramen. Student help under some technical supervisor often will serve a closed-circuit operation, but professional technicians are needed for broadcast television. The recruiting campaign would have to be based on a fairly reliable knowledge of the profession.

b. *Production personnel*

This term is intended to include directors and producers, writers, lighting and design personnel. During the first years of ETV (and, for that matter, of commercial television), these people came from a great variety of sources: some had experience in radio, some in films, some in theater; some were graduates of the various colleges and universities which offer work in radio, television, and film; some came in with no especially pertinent training or experience, and learned on the job.

As we look forward to the second decade of educational television, this picture has changed considerably. There would now seem to be two main sources of supply for ETV production personnel.

One is commercial television. The demand for new personnel in this field seems most unlikely to increase in the next few years; indeed, it is more likely to decrease. The use of packaged programs on commercial television, the practice of re-running programs, and the likelihood of automated stations, suggest that fewer careers will be available in commercial broadcasting, rather than more. At the present time, for example, outside the two main commercial centers of production—New York and Hollywood—it is probable that the ETV stations do nearly all of the original production work that is done. There is some tendency, in spite of the generally lower salaries on ETV, for commercial personnel to shift to education (28).

A second source is the college or university which offers professional training in television. The supply of graduates of radio-television-film sections and departments seems fairly well balanced with demand at the moment; the great burst of student interest in the field which was noticeable in the period 1945–55, and was reflected in heavy enrollments in broadcasting courses, has now leveled off, and may well not greatly increase in the future without some effort at recruiting. Also, we should note that most radio-television-film departments are lamentably weak in the attention they pay to educational television; students are, in almost all cases, directed toward commercial broadcasting and trained for it.

Of course, if ETV stations increased by 1971 to 100, or even to 200, this would create a demand for only a few hundred more directors, producers, writers, and so on; we do not feel that this numerical increase is the crux of the problem. What will undoubtedly be important is the fact that, before 1970, it will be possible for a young man or woman to think of making a lifetime *career* of educational television, where at present he is likely to see a job in ETV as a more or less interesting but decidedly interim assignment. Educational television, we think, will by 1971 have become an institution; the positions connected with it will have been clearly defined, along with their economic and professional potential. Students whose motivations, interests, and talents suit them to ETV will be drawn to it, as others will be drawn to other professions.

The creation of this image of ETV as an institution is mainly the responsibility of practitioners of the profession now in the field, and we do not question that they will be successful. But departments of radio-television-film and schools of education can do much to aid in this process. They have a genuine responsibility to allot a fair proportion of, first, their research time and, second, their teaching time to educational television, its techniques and uses. By and large, this allotment of time even at present is shamefully scanty.

As for the training of ETV production personnel, though we freely admit that there may be no difference between the camera trained on an announcer during a cigarette commercial and one trained on a professor explaining about French irregular verbs, we feel that the ETV production man must have a certain background which his commercial counterpart need not share; for example, he should know something about educational methods, about the process of communicating information, about the learning process; and above all, he should know enough about the history, philosophy, and research findings pertinent to his medium to have a deep commitment to it and to its use as an educational instrument. It is this commitment which will make a profession of educational television while the practice of commercial television remains simply a business; the groundwork for it should be laid in the course of the student's education.

c. *Teacher-performers*

We have already noted that schools and departments of education have, for the most part, failed to provide adequate instruction in ETV. Although some instructors in such schools have, to their great credit, recognized the importance of television, they have generally been concerned with the effect of commercial television on children rather than with the positive potential of ETV. The training of the teacher-performer offers an example of what is now required. Although a large number of these people will hardly be needed—a few thousand, at most, over the next ten years—their training and recruitment offer serious problems. We suggest, in the first place, that prospective teachers who show particular talent for and interest in lecturing and demonstration work be given special training in courses jointly sponsored and taught by speech and communication experts and educators. Obviously, standards of scholarship in subject-matter areas must be set high for such persons; simple teaching techniques are not enough (29). Finally, the student teacher-performer should have a sound basic grounding in the skills of radio-television-film performance and production, and he should be familiar with the main concepts developed in mass communication research. We do not suppose that, in most situations, the teacher will be called upon to serve as his own writer-director-producer; but he should know what is involved in these activities, at least sufficiently to permit him to collaborate well with the professionals.

d. *Classroom teachers*

Classroom teachers who work in any situation in which ETV is used must inevitably develop new skills and find for themselves new roles. They will no longer be in the position of serving as sole information sources, yet they must be informed to even a higher degree than before, because they must stand as resource persons able to amplify and to go beyond the content presented on ETV. They must concentrate their efforts on making the taped or broadcast material maximally effective. The communication of the television teacher to the students is only one step in the learning process. The classroom teachers must lead their students to reflect, to analyze, generalize, foresee, and imagine; to select among alternatives; and in these ways to develop their capacities to the fullest. As Clarence H. Faust put it: "There will always be the need for the teacher who serves, to use Socrates' phrase, the function of the midwife bringing knowledge to birth in individual minds." (30) If we view education and the teacher's function in this way, we may find that ETV—like teaching machines—will reduce the burden of teachers and restore them to their earlier, more useful, and more appropriate roles. At any rate, teachers will develop what will probably prove much subtler and more complex teaching techniques. Obviously, they must be familiar with whatever theory and research is available on aspects of the communication and learning processes which are pertinent to their situation, and they must be prepared to reduce this theory to workable classroom routines. This probably means that schools of education must not only offer the appropriate work in psychology, communication, and speech, but that intensive research programs must be instituted to augment present knowledge.

Here the training effort will be a great one; it seems obvious that the sort of education outlined above should be part of every new teacher's background; and that, as appropriate courses are developed, they should be offered to practicing teachers as refresher and professional improvement work. The effort to bring together and collate the appropriate information, institute new research, and develop courses will be considerable, since—to our knowledge—this program will represent a completely novel aspect of teacher-training.

e. Television consultants

Finally, some highly specialized persons will be needed in nearly all phases of ETV as media advisers. These will be of two kinds. The first might be called the "television consultant," and his function will be to advise and assist in both the development and the use of ETV programs. Therefore, he must be expert in the operation of the mass communication media: he must be well grounded in learning theory, and educational practices and curricula; he must be a liberally educated man. Perhaps his special studies of communication and education should be all on the graduate level. Because one of the most serious handicaps to the development and proper use of ETV has been the absence of trained personnel to provide leadership, the "television consultant" may be in demand in every school district involved in the use of television. Several hundreds of these specialists will be needed.

f. Communication experts

The second kind of specialist is the "communication expert." He would need to have the same kind of education as the consultant but extended to the doctoral level. He would be thoroughly versed in television and the other mass media, able in communications research, and knowledgeable in one or more of the behavioral sciences. He would, in consequence, know a great deal about the mass communication media and instruments, and he would be familiar with a variety of forms of research and their findings.

Our judgment is that few communication experts will be needed in ETV by 1971, perhaps only 50 or so; but their importance to the medium is not to be calculated in terms of numbers. Their decisions may influence for the better the expenditure of millions of dollars, and the success of educational efforts involving hundreds of thousands of people. And the unhappy fact remains that, at the present time, we do not have even a dozen of them.

CONCLUSIONS

Of the various conclusions which we have reached *en route* to the end of this report, we would emphasize these:

(a) In general, the personnel needs of ETV in the next decade are not to be reckoned in great numbers, and we are not—with one exception—

concerned to set up large-scale training programs. We shall need, at most, a relatively small number of extremely well-trained and educated key personnel, a few thousand in all. But we cannot stress too heavily that the numerical size of this group is unimportant; their caliber, professional standards, and commitment to their work will be all important. Fifty thousand average teachers, directors, writers, performers would not insure that ETV will have its maximum usefulness within the decade; five thousand first-rate professionals could exploit the medium to the fullest.

One exception to this statement is that of the classroom teachers. We repeat, we believe that every teacher in the United States, present or prospective, should have a sound, basic familiarity with television as an educational instrument.

(b) While some of the courses necessary to the educational effort we foresee are in existence, many have yet to be devised. And before some of these courses of training can be devised, we believe that considerable new research and a great effort at collating and evaluating past research need to be undertaken. Indeed, we do not hesitate to say that the whole problem of educating for the profession of ETV needs to be thought through from its first assumptions to the last course assignment.

(c) The problem of recruiting wears many faces. Thus, we are obliged to consider how we can interest educators in various fields—speech, education, and communications most notably—in undertaking the programs we believe are necessary; how we can overcome the frequent resistance to television as an educational tool; how we can bring to the attention of able students the concept of educational television as an attractive and rewarding career. We do not propose, in this paper, to attempt to work out answers to these problems. We believe, however, that ultimately their solutions will be expressed in these terms: more knowledge of what educational television is and can do, through continued research in the field; more diffusion of the best available knowledge concerning ETV; a vigorous and concerted effort to improve our training programs and to devise new ones, both for the benefit of new students and professionals. We do not believe very heartily in the possibility of creating a "new image" of ETV through persuasion or argument; we think that educational television will create its own image, but that those of us concerned with the medium can, by the means outlined above, help make that image appear as significant as is in fact the reality to which it points.

NOTES

1. For an excellent summary of the situation and the problem, see *Design For ETV: Planning for Schools with Television* (New York: Dave Chapman, Inc., Industrial Design for Educational Facilities Laboratories, 1960), pp. 7–16.

2. *Teaching by Television* (New York: Ford Foundation, Office of Reports, 1959), p. 2.

3. *Educational Development Program* (Volume II: Report to the Local Education Commission of Atlanta and Fulton County, Georgia, by its Education Council, 1960), p. 10.

4. Eurich, Alvin C., "Shibboleths in Higher Education," *Quality and Opportunity in Higher Education* (Boulder, Colorado, Proceedings of the Second Regional Workshop on Higher Education, Western Interstate Commission for Higher Education, 1959), p. 10.

5. Unpublished projections of primary and secondary schools populations, issued August 1960, by the U.S. Department of Health, Education, and Welfare; also W. Robert Bokelman and John B. Rork, *College and University Facilities Survey, Part 2*, Washington: U.S. Government Printing Office, 1960.

6. We wish here to express our appreciation to our respondents, who were more than generous with their time and knowledge. The elaborate and carefully reasoned analyses which they made on an early summary of this paper have contributed greatly to the final draft.

7. We offer this distinction for purposes of study, and not necessarily as a guide to programming practice. One of our respondents suggests that the distinction should not be, and indeed is not observed in practice; however, we note the anecdote, passed on to us by another respondent, of the ETV program director who argued bitterly against scheduling the NET "Ragtime Era" programs, an excellent series dealing with preferences in popular music, because they were "too entertaining."

8. In the main, our "noneducational" category would include what has sometimes been called "popular art" or "mass art."

9. The mass production of inexpensive video-tape recorders and players might well, we suspect, create a revolution in the use of ETV materials in the classroom and elsewhere. One of our respondents goes far beyond our own speculations by suggesting that we contemplate the notion of a sort of home juke box with video screen, on which one could punch up the desired program: a college education in one's living room. This possibility, oddly enough, was envisaged by a Chief Engineer of the BBC, P. P. Eckersley, in a book written in the 1920's. But we hardly suppose that even 1970 will see the device in general use.

10. These are terms of our own devising, since there appear to be no other satisfactory categories to make the distinction we wish to indicate. In a summary of this paper, which was submitted to many of our respondents, we used the terms "adult education" (instead of "nonsystematic") as opposed to "formal" education. Several of our respondents pointed out that "adult education," while the term usually suggests some degree of informality, hardly should be used to cover such items as symphony concerts or dramatic productions, and is further disqualified by the fact that audiences for these programs may range in age anywhere from preschool to octogenarian. One respondent argued, in considerable heat, that since viewers could respond to and use programs in a variety of ways, no such distinction can or should be made. We believe, on the contrary, that a distinction based on the manifest purpose, content, and style of the programs is reasonable and can be useful.

11. We judge, from various responses made to our questions and comments, that the status of ETV as an "audio-visual" device is a matter of controversy. Although educators writing about ETV often link the two terms, educational broadcasters emphatically do not. We were reminded, by station managers, for example, and correctly enough, that ETV did not develop "out of" educational film or even radio, and that its most distinguished practitioners were not trained or experienced as audio-visual personnel.

We would agree that the present status of ETV owes much to the fact that it has not been treated as simply one more in the battery of audio-visual devices; but we would also note our conviction that the future uses and status of ETV depend less on history than on technology: does the future lie with broadcasting or closed-circuit or video-tape playback?

12. This is not to forget or underrate the efforts of these stations in other directions. Donald G. Tarbet, in his *Television and Our Schools* (New York: Ronald Press, 1961), reminds us of the early attempts, 1952–55, at systematic teaching via television carried on at the University of Iowa, Purdue, and Kansas State, as well as of later efforts at formal education via TV, such as the Chicago Junior College system's successful attempt at offering a full two-year college course for credit on WTTW. (pp. 6–9)

13. *Ibid.*, p. 5, *et seq.*

14. This observation is most true in areas where educational standards have been high, the illiteracy rate low, and the adult population fairly sophisticated. Indeed, Geiger and Sokol, in a study done in Boston, suggest an additional complexity when "adult education" is offered by TV: If one regards television, as perhaps most prosperous and reasonably well-educated Americans do, as a medium of entertainment, then *educational* television is a kind of contradiction in terms, since "Education and entertainment just don't mix." See Kent Geiger and Robert Sokol, "Educational Television in Boston: Memorandum No. 3" in Wilbur Schramm (ed.), *The Impact of Educational Television* (Urbana, Illinois: University of Illinois Press, 1960), p. 44 *et seq.* Our Puritan heritage thus appears to limit ETV in some of its operations; for a similar attitude, see note 7 above. However, in districts where educational opportunities have been lacking, adult education on television may and should become a much more central concern.

15. See, for example, the continuing popularity of such programs as offered by community high schools.

16. There was considerable difference of opinion among our respondents concerning the present status and possible future of nonsystematic programs. Some report that the stations with which they are affiliated, or know about, do not derive profit from ETV courses, or from their services to schools; others say that they do receive financial and/or moral support as a result of their nonsystematic offerings; one respondent writes that, in his experience, "adult" programs have usually been amateurishly done and scarcely worth continuing; one or two others ask what ETV stations will broadcast in the evening hours if not programs for general viewing. The range of opinion and prediction appears to follow this pattern: from such negative comments as "Adult programs are declining because they never had much real form or content" and "Yes, but should we permit them to go?" through such middle ground as "They are so far strongly supported here" to the argument that, as schools move to closed-circuit efforts, ETV stations will be forced to fall back on nonsystematic programming.

17. For example, many of the uses of film and recordings by the U.S. Armed Forces.

18. By March 1961.

19. Many of our respondents—broadcasters in all cases—tend to stress the difference between themselves and the *utilizers* of ETV.

20. Most of our respondents do not suggest educational television as an economy measure, and the Hagerstown experiment seems to bear this out. What savings in staff time were realized were used to reduce the student-teacher ratio and to add music and art to the curriculum (*Teaching by Television, op. cit.*, p. 45). In Dade

County, Florida, there was a saving of 27 teaching positions and 29 classrooms, (*Ibid.*, p. 56). Penn State during the years 1956–57 found television less costly than conventional teaching. The "break-even" point was 200 or more students, (*Ibid.*, p. 25). The same "break-even" point has been reported in other studies. The Army has found that where large groups of trainees are involved television is far more economical than conventional methods. (Carpenter, Hall, and others, *New Teaching Aids for the American Classroom*, Stanford: The Institute for Communication Research, 1960, p. 127.)

21. Our respondents seem curiously divided on this score, in spite of the weight of experimental evidence. Only one seems at all convinced that teaching can be accomplished by television alone in other than special situations; the others appear to feel that ETV programs are, in the main, most effective when they are reinforced by good classroom teaching, although they point out that college courses have been successfully taught by television alone, as in the case of the Chicago Junior College offerings, and those of San Francisco State College. One or two offer the hopeful suggestion that ETV might might be useful as a solo device in other situations.

22. Thomas Clark Pollock points out that really good thinking about education from now on must begin with the recognition that oral transmission in the classroom is not necessarily the only setting for education. ("New Patterns and New Media for Education," in *The North Central Association Quarterly*, Vol. XXXV, No. 4, April 1961, p. 299.) Roy M. Hall in "The Shadow of New Media on the Classroom," speaks of the schools in the immediate future of having a more widely dispersed classroom and educational program than in the future. (*New Teaching Aids, op. cit.*, p. 10.)

23. E. G. Sherburne, Jr., "ETV Research in the Decade Ahead," in *Audio-Visual Communication Review*, Vol. 8, No. 4 (July–August 1960), p. 194.

24. Kanner, experimenting with television as a means of training Army personnel, reports: "It is also generally agreed that a good knowledge of the subject matter is a prerequisite of television teaching as it is for all teaching. Some years ago, while conducting a television research study, an occasion presented itself for testing some of these conceptions. We had previously prepared and tested the use of television for presenting electronics instruction, using experienced instructors. The scripts for these presentations had been prepared on a prompting device, and tests had been developed and used for the major aspects of the study which was concerned with using television to reduce teaching time. I suggested that we find someone who had never taught before and was not familiar with the specific contents of the hours we were teaching. An enlisted man was found with these qualifications and we gave him two hours of rehearsal for each two hours of instruction we planned for him to teach. He read from a prompter until the director felt his delivery was adequate. We had him teach these two hours of electronic instruction to a number of classes and then gave the students the tests developed for these subject matters. The tests indicated that these students learned at least as well from this 'naïve' instructor as others had learned from instructors teaching a year or more." Joseph H. Kanner, "Future Trends in Television Teaching and Research," in *Audio-Visual Communication Review*, Vol. 5, No. 4, Fall 1957, p. 515.

25. Our respondents seem to share this view; aside from pointing to the success of the Chicago experiment, they offer little in the way of evidence or argument to indicate that these offerings will expand greatly, and some are rather skeptical of the concept of credit courses on television, and of the nature of public interest in them.

26. See U.S. Office of Education Projections, previously cited.

27. John R. Beery and Arnold Perry, "Open-Circuit Educational Television," in *Television in Teacher Education* (Washington, D.C., 1960), pp. 14–15. Also see Richard B. Hull, "ETV History and Status," in *North Central Association Quarterly*, Vol. XXV, No. 4, April 1961, p. 295.

28. This shift can be explained by the diminution of "live" telecasting by commercial stations and the challenge and excitement of ETV. Our respondents differ in their opinions of this source of production personnel. One view is that ETV would be greatly benefited by the wide experience of commercial people. Another view is that commercial people may give ETV production a certain finish, but they may lack both an understanding of educational purposes and lack of rapport with educators.

29. Research is needed to show us what qualities make for a good teacher-performer. Evidence of this kind would be most useful for the selection of teachers and for their appropriate training. Further exploration of the Army researches into the use of inexperienced teachers under certain strictures of time and special content is also called for.

30. Faust, Clarence H., "Educational Philosophy and Television," in *Educational Record*, January 1958, p. 5.

ALLOCATIONS FOR EDUCATIONAL TELEVISION

By George R. Town

Dr. Town is Dean of the College of Engineering, Iowa State University

THE PURPOSE OF THIS REPORT is threefold: first, to present a summary of the factors which make television channels scarce; second, to explain the basic differences between and the relative advantages of different parts of the frequency spectrum (VHF versus UHF) as used for television broadcasting; and third, to make suggestions as to what those interested in educational television should do about the problem of channels for educational television broadcasting.

This report is written for those who are not experts in the engineering aspects of television broadcasting. An attempt will be made to keep the treatment rigorous but at the same time couched in simple terms. The material presented in Section 1 may appear to be obvious and to be so well known as not to merit space in this report. An appreciation of this material is, however, basic to an understanding of the later discussion of the differences between VHF and UHF television; and therefore a number of topics have been presented in more detail than would otherwise have been considered appropriate. Those who already have some background in the general aspects of television allocations may wish to proceed immediately to Section 2, starting on page 221.

1. SCARCITY OF TELEVISION CHANNELS

To transmit any type of intelligence by radio waves, a band of frequencies is required. These radio frequencies, as far as present-day broadcasting is concerned, lie in the general region extending from a few hundred thousand cycles to several hundred million cycles (or, in other words, from a few hundred kilocycles—or kc—to several hundred megacycles—or Mc). The width of the band required to transmit the intelligence depends upon the type of intelligence or signal which it is desired to transmit. As a very rough, and frequently inaccurate, rule, the width of the band often may be said to be approximately twice that of the highest frequency occurring in the basic signal (or intelligence) which is to be transmitted. For example, the highest pitched sounds which can be heard by the average person have a frequency of perhaps 15,000 cycles. Actually, very little of the power and intelligibility of speech and music are lost if the frequencies are limited to 5,000 cycles (5 kilocycles) rather than to 15,000 cycles (15 kilocycles). This is the figure used in the design of the standard, or amplitude modulation (AM), broadcasting system with which all are familiar. Here each channel is 10 kc (10,000 cycles) wide. The standard AM broadcasting band extends from 535 to 1605 kc; and 107 channels, each 10 kc wide, are provided in this space in the radio frequency spectrum. As a specific example, station WOI in Ames, Iowa, is said to broadcast on a frequency of 640 kc, which is a simplified way of saying that its channel extends from 635 to 645 kc. It should be noted that all radio frequencies in this band or channel are quite a number of times as great as the maximum signal frequency (5 kc) which is transmitted. This is a basic requirement in radio systems.

The fundamental difficulty in finding frequencies for television broadcasting is that the maximum signal frequency which is required to represent the intelligence in a picture is very great. This is not surprising in view of the fact that "a picture is worth a thousand words" in conveying intelligence. Actually, to represent a picture well, a maximum frequency of around 4,000,000 cycles (or 4 megacycles or 4 Mc) is required. By means of certain tricks of the trade, a radio frequency channel only 6 Mc wide (rather than twice 4 Mc, or 8 Mc) can be employed; and there actually is room to tuck in a sound channel also in this 6 Mc band so that the television picture may be a talking picture rather than a silent picture. Note, however, that one television channel 6 Mc wide is nearly six times as wide as the entire standard AM broadcast band which accommodates 107 radio broadcasting channels. Note also that since all frequencies in the radio frequency region or spectrum used to transmit television must be several times as high as the maximum signal frequency (4 Mc), the channels used for television broadcasting must be at least as high as a few tens of megacycles. As a matter of fact, the lowest television channel (Channel 2) extends from 54 to 60 Mc. A basic factor in the allocation of frequencies for television broadcasting is, then, the necessity of using a wide channel (6 Mc) of rather high frequencies (say in the neighborhood of 50 to 1,000 Mc). It must be recognized immediately that all of this space cannot be used for television broadcasting, as many other services also need space in this part of the radio frequency spectrum.

A second basic consideration is that of the range of a television broadcasting station. This is a matter of obvious importance as it determines the spacing of stations operating on the same channel. If the range were unlimited, only one station could use any one channel. Since, however, the range is actually limited, it is possible to assign the same channel to several television stations, provided they are sufficiently far apart. It is now necessary to examine the factors which determine how far stations using the same channel must be separated.

First, let us assume that there is only one television broadcasting station in existence. Its range, or the distance over which it provides service, depends upon a large number of factors. Among these are the power of the transmitter, the efficiency of the transmission line or coaxial cable or wave guide connecting the transmitter and the transmitting antenna, the height of the transmitting antenna above the surrounding terrain, the electrical characteristics (and especially the "gain" or the practical over-all efficiency) of the transmitting antenna, the nature of the surrounding terrain (flat or hilly, urban or rural, wooded or open), the type and magnitude of electrical interferences present, the electrical characteristics (and especially the "gain") of the receiving antenna, the height of the receiving antenna, the efficiency of the receiving transmission line or "lead-in," the electrical characteristics of the television receiver and, last but by no means least, the frequencies or the channel used. This last factor, that of the channel used, has an influence on many of the other factors. The nature of this influence forms the subject matter for much of the remainder of this report; but before considering it, other matters must be discussed.

One important factor which has been listed is "the electrical characteristics of the television receiver." It is fairly obvious that as one goes farther and farther from the television transmitter, the signal strength available at a receiving location becomes less and less. One might be tempted to believe that this decrease in signal strength could be compensated by using a more "sensitive" television receiver; that is, one with more amplifying tubes. This is true to a degree, but only to a degree. At some distance, a point will be reached beyond which further amplification is of no use. The reason for this is that the picture quality available from a television signal is not determined by the signal strength alone, but rather by the ratio of the signal strength to the strength of the various types of interference which may be present. In the case of the assumed single television transmitter, there are two principal types of interference which must be considered. The first of these is electrical noise* external to the receiver. Static is negligible on the channels used in television broadcasting but man-made electrical noise can be very troublesome. The sources include such things as automobile ignition systems, neon signs, electric motors, electric razors, etc. Also, radio transmitters of certain types may produce interference. In addition, there is another type of external elec-

---

* The term "noise" is a carry-over from radio broadcasting where interference is manifested by noise at the loudspeaker. In television, interference causes deterioration in the quality of the received picture. Because engineers were too lazy to coin a new, simple term for this deterioration, it is universally known as "noise."

trical noise over which man has no control. It originates in outer space and is known as cosmic noise or galactic noise. It is the type of "signal" that makes radio astronomy possible, but to the television engineer it is only an annoying source of interference. The second, and usually the more important, type of interference is electrical noise generated within the television receiver itself. Electrical currents consist of the flow of electrons through electrical circuit elements, including vacuum tubes and transistors. The number of electrons flowing per second in even a small current is very great; but nevertheless, each electron carries a discrete, separate charge and the number passing a given point in a circuit is not absolutely constant, but fluctuates slightly. These small fluctuations are the source of an electrical noise which is generated internally in every television (or radio) receiver. The magnitude of this noise can be minimized by proper receiver design, but there is a theoretical limit below which it is not possible to go. Even the best receivers fail to achieve this theoretical minimum noise level. The amount by which the internal electrical noise in a receiver exceeds the theoretical minimum is known as the "noise factor" or the "noise figure" of the receiver.

Now, let us assume that to produce a satisfactory picture, the television signal strength must be 50 times as high as the interference. Also, let us assume, for simplicity, that the only interference present is the internal noise of the television receiver. Near the transmitter, the television signal will be many times as great as the interfering noise. As the receiver is taken farther from the transmitter, the television signal strength becomes less until eventually a point is reached at which it is only 50 times as great as the interfering noise. Beyond that distance, the ratio of the television signal strength to the interfering noise, or the "signal-to-noise ratio," will be less than 50 and the picture will not be satisfactory. Moreover, no amount of amplification can make the picture satisfactory, as the television signal and the noise are both amplified to the same extent and the signal-to-noise ratio remains the same. The only thing that can be done to make the picture satisfactory is to use another receiver with a better noise factor; and, as has been indicated, there are practical and theoretical limits beyond which this is not practicable.

To summarize, the range of the assumed single television broadcasting station is limited by, among other factors, the interference present at the television receiver. One of the most troublesome types of interference, and the one which frequently sets the ultimate limit to the range of the station, is the noise produced within the receiver itself.

When more than one television broadcasting station is in operation, the other stations are potential sources of interference. Let it be assumed that two stations are operating on the same frequency and that the distance between them is, say, 100 miles. (Actually the rules of the Federal Communications Commission—FCC—would not permit operation of co-channel stations, or stations using the same channel, at such a small separation.) Near the first station, its signal strength will be high while that of the second station will be low. It will then be possible to receive satisfactory pictures from the first station as the signal-to-interference ratio will be high. As one moves from the first station toward the second station, the signal strength of the first station will become less while that of the second station will become greater. Eventually a point will be reached at which the signal-to-interference ratio is too low to produce a satisfactory picture. This condition of unsatisfactory reception will persist over a considerable distance as one continues to move toward the second transmitter. Finally a point will be reached at which the signal strength of the second station is sufficiently greater than that of the first station that satisfactory pictures can be obtained from the second transmitter. Each station is thus surrounded by an area which it serves satisfactorily. Between these areas is an area in which neither station produces satisfactory pictures because of the interference caused by the signal from the other station. The rules of the FCC relating to the minimum permitted separation of co-channel stations have been established in an effort to provide satisfactory service to the greatest area. The minimum spacing permitted by these rules depends upon the channels which are used.

Another type of interference is that caused by stations operating not on the same channel as the desired station but on adjacent channels. In this case, the spacing between stations may be much less than in the case of co-channel stations. The reason for this lies in the characteristics of television receivers. All receivers include some tuning device or channel selector by means of which the viewer chooses the channel which he wishes to receive. If these channel selectors were perfect, signals could be received at any one time from stations on one channel only. Actually, the receivers are also responsive to some extent to signals from stations on adjacent channels, although such signals are greatly attenuated in comparison with signals on the channel to which the receiver is tuned. This is why the permitted separation of adjacent channels is much less than that of co-channel stations. The signal strength of an undesired adjacent channel station at the receiving antenna may actually be several times as high as the signal strength of the desired station before an unsatisfactory picture is produced at the picture tube.

Because of other characteristics of television receivers, they are also responsive to other undesired signals as well as to those found on adjacent channels. Each television receiver includes as one of its essential parts a local oscillator which generates a signal at a frequency approximately

45.75 Mc higher than that of the station to which the receiver is tuned. Each receiver therefore acts as a miniature transmitter. If the assignment of channels in a given locality is not made properly, there exists the possibility that a receiver tuned to one station will emit a spurious signal which falls in the channel assigned to another local station. The result would be unsatisfactory reception because of interference originating in the receivers of one's neighbors. Still another result of the employment of the types of circuits found most suitable for use in television receivers is the so-called "image response" problem. This means that the receiver is somewhat responsive to stations operating at frequencies about 91.5 Mc above the station to which the receiver is tuned.

All of these interfering effects, which may be produced as a result of the operation of television stations other than the one which the viewer wishes to receive, result in a limitation in the number of channels which can be assigned in any given locality. If satisfactory service is to be provided by a station operating on a given channel, stations operating on the same and on adjacent channels must be kept at considerable distances from that station. Moreover, operation in the same area on certain other channels will not be possible because of the local oscillator and image response characteristics of television receivers. These limitations contribute greatly to the scarcity of television channels available for assignment.

This section on the scarcity of television channels may be summarized as follows. Television broadcasting must compete with other services for space in the frequency spectrum. Because of the inherently great width of each television channel, television broadcasting requires a great amount of space for even a modest number of channels. The area served by a single television station is limited. One of the most important factors in limiting this area is the electrical noise produced in television receiver circuits. Other limiting factors are those resulting from interference caused by the operation of other television stations. To minimize such interference, limitations are imposed on the choice of channels available to other television stations in the area served by a given station. This means that the number of channels (already limited in their total by the demands of other radio services) which may be assigned in any given area is limited still further. The net result is a scarcity of channels.

2. ALLOCATION REGIONS—VHF VERSUS UHF

The radio frequency spectrum extends continuously from a few thousand cycles per second to several tens of billions of cycles per second. Various parts of this continuous spectrum have received rather arbitrary designations. The region from 30 to 300 million cycles (or 30 to 300 megacycles, or 30 to 300 Mc) is known as the very high frequency (VHF) region. That from 300 to 3,000 Mc is known as the ultra high frequency (UHF) region. The channels assigned to television broadcasting are located in these two regions. Their locations in these regions are shown in the following table.

Channel Numbers	Frequency Range	Region
2–4	54–72 Mc	Low-band VHF
5, 6	76–88	Low-band VHF
7–13	174–216	High-band VHF
14–83	470–890	UHF

The 13 channels* originally assigned by the Federal Communications Commission (FCC) to commercial television broadcasting were all in the VHF region. As the demand for channels increased, the number available in the VHF region was found to be inadequate and in 1952 the FCC allocated the space in the UHF region between 470 and 890 Mc to an additional 70 channels. At that time, the FCC believed that these new channels would permit an increase in the number of television stations sufficient to care for all the needs of commercial television, educational television, and the viewing public. For a variety of reasons, both technical and commercial, UHF television broadcasting has not been generally successful. Of the 528 commercial television broadcasting stations now in operation, 453 are VHF stations and only 75 are UHF stations. Of the 56 educational television stations in operation, 40 are VHF stations and 16 are UHF stations.

The propagation of television waves or signals and the characteristics of television equipment are different at different frequencies. There are a number of significant differences between the results which are obtained on the VHF and on the UHF channels. It should be noted, however, that the change as one goes from the low VHF channels to the high VHF channels to the lower UHF channels to the higher UHF channels is not abrupt but rather is gradual. There are significant differences between the high and the low VHF channels and between the higher and the lower UHF channels, just as there are differences between the UHF and the VHF channels. This section of this report is concerned with a rather detailed discussion of these differences.

The crowded condition of the 12 VHF channels and the ready availability of UHF channels puzzle many. It is the purpose of this section to explain the major technical differences between VHF and UHF television. These technical differences are in part responsible for the scarcity of VHF channels and the availability of UHF channels.

---

* Channel 1 once occupied the space between 44 and 50 Mc. This space was transferred to other services in 1946, leaving 12 VHF channels.

Much of this section is based upon material appearing in the *Report of the Television Allocations Study Organization—Engineering Aspects of Television Allocations*, dated March 16, 1959; in the *Supplementary Report of the Television Allocations Study Organization—Engineering Aspects of Television Allocations—II*, dated June 13, 1960; and in a series of papers dealing with the work of the Television Allocations Study Organization which appeared in the June 1960 issue of the *Proceedings of the Institute of Radio Engineers*. Additional detailed source material is found in Report No. 8432-1 prepared by the Airborne Instruments Laboratory for the Federal Communications Commission and entitled *Evaluation of Receiving Techniques Suitable for UHF-TV Reception*; in a privately printed copy of a lecture by Howard T. Head of A. D. Ring and Associates entitled *Wave Propagation and Interference Effects in the Television Broadcast Bands*, which Mr. Head delivered at the Capitol Radio Engineering Institute in Washington, D.C. on February 21, 1961; and in an as yet unpublished paper by William L. Hughes and George R. Town entitled *Some Comments on the Technical Realities Concerning Television Allocations*.

The most significant differences between VHF and UHF television performance are due to propagation effects, to receiving antenna characteristics, to receiver noise factor, and to external noise. Some of these differences (for example, propagation effects) are truly basic in their nature and are likely always to exist. Other differences (for example, receiver noise factor) are due at least in part to the current status of the design of VHF and UHF equipment and may eventually be minimized through engineering research and development.

2.1 *Wave propagation*

Because it is not subject to control by man but rather is a phenomenon of nature, the propagation of signals is of prime and basic importance in any consideration of the differences between VHF and UHF television. It is interesting to note that within line-of-sight distances from a transmitting antenna, theory based on the assumption of a perfectly smooth reflecting earth indicates that the signal strength at a receiving location is directly proportional to frequency. This would indicate that for the same radiated power from a transmitting antenna, a station at the middle of the UHF band would produce ten times as strong a signal as a station at the middle of the low VHF band. The extensive measurements of the signal strengths of VHF and UHF stations made by the Television Allocations Study Organization (TASO) showed that in areas in which the terrain closely approximated the assumed smooth earth conditions (as, for example along the Lake Pontchartrain Bridge at New Orleans and in the San Joaquin Valley south of Fresno, California) these theoretical predictions were fulfilled. It is a fact, however, that these are far from the conditions usually encountered. Most terrain is at least somewhat irregular, and frequently is rough. Many viewers live in shadowed areas not within line of sight of the transmitting antenna. In hilly and mountainous country, most people live in the valleys where the shadowing is worst. In cities and towns, buildings intrude into the line of sight. Even in relatively flat rural regions, wooded areas are common and trees are usually found in the vicinity of houses where they at least partially shield the receiving antennas. Under these normally encountered conditions, the smooth-earth assumptions are no longer valid and UHF signal strength is lower, rather than higher, than VHF signal strength.

The results obtained under practical field conditions are shown clearly by an analysis of the data taken by TASO. Extensive measurements of the signal strengths of comparable VHF and UHF stations were made in eight different geographical areas, including very flat areas (San Joaquin Valley), rough areas (Wilkes-Barre, Pennsylvania) and areas of an intermediate character. In each area, measurements were made along an average of 7½ radials running outward from the transmitters. In the eight areas, there were a total of 1232 "points" at which the VHF and UHF field strengths could be compared directly. Actually, each "point" consisted of a path at least 100 feet in length over which the signal strengths were recorded continuously and the median values of signal strength obtained. The over-all averages of the results obtained show that for equal powers radiated by the transmitters, the UHF signal strength was 6.5 db* below the VHF signal strength. If the UHF signal strength is compared with the signal strength from low-band VHF stations, the UHF field strength is found to be 7.5 db lower. All but one of the eight UHF stations measured were in the lower half of the UHF band. If stations in the upper

---

* The abbreviation db means decibels. This is a commonly used measure of the ratio of two comparable quantities. The number of decibels corresponding to a given ratio of two voltages or two currents or two signal strengths or two field strengths is given by the equation

$$(\text{no. of db}) = 20 \log_{10} (\text{the ratio}).$$

The advantage of using the decibel as a measure of a ratio is that of simplicity since if two ratios are to be multiplied (or divided), the corresponding number of decibels are added (or subtracted). In considering the over-all performance of a communication system, the characteristics of each part of which are known, this leads to ease of computation. In this particular case, the difference of 6.5 db means that the VHF signal strength is 2.11 times as great as the UHF signal strength; or, the latter is 47 percent of the former. (It should be noted in passing that if a ratio of two *powers* is being considered rather than the ratio of two voltages or two signal strengths, the multiplier in the above equation is 10 rather than 20. Thus, 6 db corresponds to a ratio of 2 : 1 in voltage, but to a ratio of 4 : 1 in power.)

half of the UHF band had been used, their signal strengths would have been even lower in comparison with VHF signal strengths.

The TASO results are in general accord with propagation curves published by the FCC from which comparisons can be made between operation at the middle of the UHF band and at the low VHF band.* These curves show that over distances from 10 to 60 miles from the transmitter (or equally for distances from 20 to 50 miles), the VHF signal strength is higher than the UHF field strength by 6 db when the transmitting antenna height is 1,000 feet and 9 db when the transmitting antenna height is 600 feet. The results given by the FCC curves and by the TASO measurements check well within the expected accuracy of such measurements.

It must be emphasized that the figures quoted are over-all averages of data taken under a wide variety of conditions. In specific cases, the results may be quite different. In smooth areas, UHF will not compare as unfavorably with VHF as is here indicated. In rough terrain, however, the differences between VHF and UHF signal strengths will be much greater than those given here. In all types of terrain, the difference between VHF and UHF signal strength increases with increasing distance from the transmitter out to the limits of service.

The differences between low-band VHF and high-band VHF propagation are more difficult to state specifically. No data indicate the average high-band VHF signal strength to be higher. Data taken by TASO, by Head, and from FCC curves indicate that the low-band VHF signal strength is from zero to three db higher than high-band VHF signal strength for equal radiated powers. The actual value may well be one or two db, but this is not a very great difference between low-band and high-band VHF propagation.

These comparisons of median signal strengths do not tell the complete story of VHF versus UHF wave propagation. The TASO data showed that the UHF signals were much more variable than the VHF signals. Recordings of signal strength along the 1232 paths of 100 feet or more in length showed that over these paths, the average variation of low VHF signal strengths was 3.8 db; of high VHF signal strengths, 6.2 db; and of (lower half) UHF signal strengths, 9.4 db.

The shielding effects of trees in the vicinity of receiving antennas has been mentioned. Data taken by Head for TASO show that this effect is severe at UHF. Other data indicate that the effect is less severe but still appreciable at high-band VHF and is of little consequence at low-band VHF.

Still another, and a most important, factor shown by the TASO data

---

* The so-called "Appendix A" curves and the Docket No. 13340 curves, respectively.

is that at the extreme limits, or fringes, of service, the UHF signal strength falls off more rapidly and more completely with increasing distance than does VHF signal strength.

One word of caution needs to be expressed. Radio wave propagation is an extremely variable phenomenon. Scarcely any statement can be made which is not contradicted by measurements made under some particular combination of conditions—terrain, vegetation, climate, atmospheric conditions, obstacles, etc. The best that can be done in describing wave-propagation phenomena is to reach conclusions which are true on the average and which are reasonably significant from the viewpoint of statistical theory. This is the nature of the statements which have been made in this section.

So far the discussion of wave propagation has been confined to conditions which exist within and just beyond the service range of television transmitters. It will be recalled that one of the limiting factors in television reception is the co-channel interference caused by a station (or stations) operating on the same channel as the station which the viewer wishes to receive. Since to produce a satisfactory picture, the desired signal strength must be approximately 20 to 30 times as high as the interfering signal strength, it is obvious that a transmitter can produce damaging interference over a much greater distance than it can serve. This means that the propagation of signals over rather great distances must be considered in studying the interfering capability of a television transmitter. In the interfering range, the propagation of signals is even more variable than in the service range. The most significant fact from the standpoint of television allocations is that the frequency of operation appears to have much less effect at great distances than at the shorter distances in and just beyond the service range. This means that from the viewpoint of propagation, UHF suffers a double disadvantage with respect to VHF: (1) its service range is less and (2) its interfering range is nearly as great.

2.2 Receiving antenna

The receiving antenna is a very important, and in fact a critical, factor in the over-all television system. To see why this is so, it is first necessary to examine the nature of radio-wave transmission a little more quantitatively. In the discussion so far, the term "signal strength" has been used in discussing wave propagation. The technical term which actually should have been used is "field strength," where the word "field" refers to the electromagnetic field set up by a transmitter and propagated through space. The units of field strength, which are very descriptive, are volts per meter. Actually, quite low field strengths are satisfactory for television reception, so another unit, namely millionths of a volt per meter or microvolts per meter, is the unit commonly used. The significance of this unit is that if a uniform field of, say 200 microvolts per meter exists in space, the voltage between two points one meter apart is 200 microvolts or 200/1,000,000 volt. (Again, the decibel is frequently introduced into the specification of field strength. Here the common unit is the dbu which means the number of db above one microvolt per meter. Thus, if a certain field strength is given as, say 46 dbu, the ratio of that field strength to a field strength of one microvolt per meter is 46 db; or, the given field strength is 200 microvolts per meter.)

With this description of field strength in mind, it is possible to determine quickly the effect of frequency on the performance of certain types of receiving antennas. The simplest receiving antenna is what is known as a half-wave dipole. This consists of a metal rod one-half wave length long with a short gap at its center across which the transmission line or lead-in is attached. The wave length is inversely proportional to frequency and is given by the expression

$$(\text{wave length in meters}) = 300 \div (\text{frequency in Mc}).$$

The "effective length" of a half-wave dipole is

$$(\text{effective length in meters}) = (2/\pi) \times (\text{length of dipole in meters})$$
$$= (2/\pi) \times (150 \div \text{frequency in Mc})$$
$$= \text{approximately} \ (95 \div \text{frequency in Mc}).$$

An inherent disadvantage of UHF with respect to VHF is immediately apparent. As has been mentioned previously, the frequency at the middle of the UHF band is approximately ten times as great as the frequency at the middle of the low VHF band. Thus, if half-wave dipoles are used at these two frequencies and if the field strength (or signal strength) is the same, the voltage picked up by the antenna and fed to the lead-in is only one-tenth as great at mid-band UHF as at mid-low-band VHF.

Actually, the practical situation is not quite as bad as this, as far as UHF performance is concerned. Antennas more complex than half-wave dipoles are usually used, especially at UHF. Their over-all size is greater than that of a half-wave dipole and this results in a gain in antenna efficiency. This "gain" of a receiving antenna is numerically equal to the ratio of the voltage derived from that antenna to the voltage which would be derived from a similarly located half-wave dipole.

One might be tempted to jump to the conclusion that UHF antennas can be made equivalent to VHF antennas of the same type and geometrical configuration simply by making them of the same over-all physical size. As a specific instance, consider the example already given of operation at the middle of the UHF band and at the middle of the low VHF band where the ratio of frequencies is ten to one; and where, therefore, the UHF half-wave dipole is one-tenth as long as the VHF half-wave dipole. One might suggest that if a half-wave dipole is used at VHF, ten half-wave dipoles should be used in UHF. Then, if each UHF dipole produces one-tenth the voltage produced by the VHF dipole, the voltages from the ten UHF dipoles could be added to produce the same total voltage as that obtained from the single VHF dipole, with the over-all physical size remaining the same.

Unfortunately, things are not quite this simple. There are factors which limit the gain which can be obtained from practical receiving antennas. One of these is the difficulty of building a high-gain antenna which will perform well over a reasonable range in frequencies. Data gathered by TASO show that the average gain of UHF antennas is only 4 db higher than (or 1.6 times as great as) that of low-band VHF antennas. This by no means compensates for the ten to one (or 20 db) disadvantage due to the shorter wave length at UHF as compared with low-band VHF.

There is still another practical factor which limits the efficiency of high-gain antennas. The rated gain of an antenna is based on the assumption that a uniform field exists in the space occupied by the antenna; or, more exactly, that "the wave front is coherent." Studies reported by Brown, Epstein, and Peterson (RCA Review, Vol. 9, No. 2, p. 177–201, June 1948) show that in open, smooth country, the theoretical antenna gains were approached in practice. In shadowed locations, however, the gain was reduced greatly, and in some instances was actually less than unity. Unfortunately, as was pointed out by Brown, Epstein, and Peterson, it is in these shadowed regions of weak signal that antenna gain is most urgently needed.

The receiving transmission line or lead-in, which connects the receiving antenna with the television receiver, is a piece of equipment whose characteristics are closely associated with those of the antenna itself. The efficiency with which signals are transmitted over the lead-in varies greatly with frequency. Lead-ins of somewhat more expensive type are commonly used at UHF, but even with these, the loss during transmission is much greater at UHF than at VHF. This is true even when new, dry transmission line is used and the increased losses at UHF become even more severe if the line is old and/or wet.

Quantitative data were collected by TASO on the performance of receiving antennas and transmission lines. The following table, which is taken from the TASO Report, summarizes these data.

The conclusions which must be drawn from these data are evident and inescapable. Due to the characteristics of receiving antennas and lead-ins, UHF television operates under a very severe handicap in comparison with VHF television. When operating in regions of equal field strength, the

TV Band	Relative Dipole Efficiency Due to Wave-Length	Gain of Average Antenna	Relative Over-all Antenna Efficiency	Average Loss of 30-ft. Lead-in		Relative Over-all Efficiency, Ant. + Lead-in	
				New, Dry	5 Yr. Old, Wet	New, Dry Line	5 Yr. Old, Wet Line
	(db)	(db)	(db)	(db)	(db)	(db)	(db)
Low VHF	+ 2.9	3.7	+6.6	0.3	1.5	6.3	5.1
High VHF	− 6.1	6.8	0.7	0.5	2.9	0.2	− 2.2
UHF	−16.7	7.7	−9.0	1.1	6.0	−10.1	−15.0

UHF antenna and lead-in deliver only about 10 to 15 percent as high a voltage to the television receiver as do the low-band VHF equipment and only about 25 to 30 percent as high a voltage as do the high-band VHF equipment.

One may well ask if UHF receiving antennas and lead-ins may not be made more efficient. Obviously the question cannot be answered with certainty, but some estimates may be made. Elaborate and expensive antennas can be built to provide higher gains. Some current UHF antennas have gains as high as 13.5 db; but some current VHF antennas also have high gains, as much as 11 and 13 db in the low and high bands respectively. As a result of further engineering research and development, it is probable that the efficiency of UHF receiving antennas will be increased somewhat, but the disadvantageous wave length factor will always exist as it is based on the laws of nature. Because of this, it is not at all probable that UHF receiving antennas will ever closely approach VHF antennas in efficiency. With respect to transmission lines, here again the probability exists that improvements will be made. In particular, the increased losses obtained with old, wet lines may possibly be reduced. Such an improvement would aid both UHF and VHF performance, but it should be of greater importance in UHF operation and would lessen, but not eliminate, the advantage of VHF over UHF lead-ins.

In summary, the efficiency of current UHF television receiving antenna systems (antenna and lead-in) is some 16 to 20 db poorer than that of low-band VHF receiving antenna systems and some 10 to 13 db poorer than that of high-band VHF receiving antenna systems. There appears to be some possibility that these figures may be reduced somewhat, say perhaps to 13 and 7 db disadvantage with respect to low- and high-band VHF respectively, through engineering research and development.

2.3 Receiver

As has already been pointed out, the most significant characteristic of a television receiver, as far as its importance to allocation studies is concerned, is its noise factor. Here again, VHF performance is superior to UHF performance. The table on page 230, which is taken from the

CHANNEL CHARACTERISTICS

Channel Characteristic*	2-6			7-13			14-40			41-65			66-83		
	P	A	B	P	A	B	P	A	B	P	A	B	P	A	B
Noise factor, db	9.7	6.5	4.6	12.2	8.5	6.5	16.7	12.8	10.5	18.2	13.2	10.0	19.0	13.8	9.5
Sensitivity, μv	150	40	4	270	57	6	360	79	10	280	76	8.5	300	81	11
Image ratio, db†	41	73	80	45	68	80	14	32	46	10	29	44	6	26	46
Tuner bandwidth, Mc															
3 db down‡	10.5	7.5	4.0	14.9	9.4	3.5	37	17.5	8.0	34	18.5	9.0	60	25	10
20 db down‡	22	15	6.0	37	23	8.0	125	48	15	178	59	16	247	74	18

* P—poorest; A—average; B——best.
† A high figure is desirable.
‡ A low figure, down to 6 Mc, is desirable.

TASO Report, gives information regarding the noise factor of current television receivers, as well as other characteristics which will be discussed later.

The noise factor is given in commonly used units; that is, in terms of the number of decibels by which the noise of the receiver exceeds the theoretical minimum noise. A high noise factor therefore represents poor performance. It is evident that the noise factor at high-band VHF is about 2 db poorer than at low-band VHF and that the noise factor at UHF is about 5 to 7 db poorer than at low-band VHF. Or, it could be said that on the average, the UHF receiver noise factor is about 5 db poorer than the VHF receiver noise factor.

The limiting element which determines the noise factor of a receiver is almost always the r-f amplifier tube in the tuner section of the receiver; or, if no r-f stage is used, the mixer tube or diode is the limiting factor. The lack of a suitable, low-cost, reliable r-f amplifier tube for use in UHF tuners accounts for the relatively high UHF noise factors. Recently developed devices, such as parametric amplifiers and tunnel diodes, show promise in the laboratory as r-f amplifying devices. As currently used, the necessary auxiliary circuits are complex and expensive. Again, special types of transistors show some laboratory promise as r-f amplifiers with the accompanying advantage of circuits of only normal complexity. All these devices are expensive, and circuitry suitable for commercial use in television receivers is not now available. There is reasonable expectation, however, that if the commercial demand existed, engineering developments might lead to satisfactory and reasonably economical UHF r-f amplifying devices having noise factors of perhaps as low as 3 to 5 db. These improvements would almost certainly result in improved VHF as well as improved UHF performance. The net result might be that eventually there would be no significant difference in the noise factors of VHF and UHF television receivers. It is interesting to note, however, that the Airborne Instruments Laboratory report mentioned previously concludes that for the next several years the best UHF tuners will have noise factors of about 8 db and that this performance will be achieved through the use of improved crystal mixers, other devices being felt to be uneconomical, at least for several years. The possibility of improved vacuum tubes for use as r-f amplifiers must not be overlooked. Very recently developed tubes have been incorporated in laboratory model VHF television tuners with a reported noise factor of 5 db across both VHF television bands. A similar tube has been reported as having a noise factor of 7 db when used in a single-channel television tuner at the lowest end of the UHF band. Other sources indicate that a noise factor of 10 db across the entire UHF television band for a tuner employing such a tube might be reasonable.

In summary, it can be said that the noise factors of current UHF receivers are about 5 db poorer than those of current VHF receivers; that in the next several years, this difference may be reduced to 2 or 3 db; and that eventually the difference may possibly, but not certainly, disappear.

Other characteristics of television receivers are also of significance. The sensitivity is the number of microvolts at the receiver input terminals which is required to produce specified receiver output conditions. From the table, it is seen that the average UHF receiver requires about 50 percent more input voltage than does the average VHF receiver. This is of some importance but until UHF receiver noise factors are improved, it is not of great significance. The data with respect to image response and tuner bandwith are more significant, as they relate to the susceptibility of the receiver to interference originating at the "image frequency" (see page 221 of this report) and to interference originating at stations assigned to the one or two or three channels on either side of the channel of the desired station. It is seen that in all of these respects, UHF receivers have much poorer performance than VHF receivers. The rather high susceptibility of UHF receivers to interference originating on other channels has an adverse effect on the number of UHF channels which can be assigned to television stations in any given locality.

Other characteristics of television receivers are not significantly different at VHF and at UHF. One possible exception is receiver oscillator drift which is on the average two or three times worse at UHF than at VHF. One possible exception is receiver oscillator drift which is on the average two or three times worse at UHF than at VHF. Drift is not, however, a really basic limitation in television receiver operation. A high drift simply requires the viewer to re-tune the receiver slightly after it has warmed up after first being turned on; or, it may limit the applicability of remote tuning devices.

2.4 External noise

A factor which favors UHF television operation is that of greater freedom from some types of interference. Quantitative data are rather scarce, but all available information shows that the effects of noise external to the television receiver are much less at UHF than at VHF. Static and other noise of an impulsive nature (for example, ignition noise) are of negligible importance at UHF. Galactic noise, or cosmic noise, may at least occasionally be of real significance at VHF, especially at the lowest channels, but it is entirely negligible at UHF.

Echoes or ghosts or multi-path effects appear to be less bothersome at UHF than at VHF, although the TASO data indicate that they are not a really serious problem at any frequency except in large cities. In cases where multi-path problems are severe, the smaller size of a highly directive UHF receiving antenna frequently permits the television service man to minimize the effects of multi-path more readily at UHF than at VHF. Airplane flutter is a special type of multi-path interference. It frequently is very troublesome at VHF, especially in the vicinity of large airports. For all practical purposes, airplane flutter is nonexistent at UHF.

In summary, the lack of external noise is an important factor favoring UHF television operation. It is probably the principal reason for the fact that in regions of adequately high signal strength, the best television pictures are seen on UHF, not on VHF.

2.5 Transmitters

In section 2.1 it has been pointed out that, under average conditions, UHF signals are propagated more poorly than VHF signals; or, that the range of UHF transmitters is less than that of VHF transmitters for equal radiated powers. In section 2.2 the poorer performance of UHF receiving antenna systems in comparison with VHF receiving antenna systems was discussed. In section 2.3 it was noted that UHF television receivers now have poorer noise factors than VHF television receivers; and that while this condition may be partially alleviated in the future, UHF will never show to an advantage in this matter in comparison with VHF. In section 2.4 the advantage of UHF operation over VHF operation with respect to external noise was pointed out. With the exception of the last item, all comparisons favor VHF television, and even when making allowance for this last factor, the over-all comparison certainly favors VHF television. One thing which can be done is to provide very high power UHF television transmitters in an effort to compensate for the disadvantages under which UHF television operates. As a matter of fact, the rules of the FCC attempt to accomplish this objective by limiting the maximum effective radiated power of low-band VHF stations to 100 kilowatts (100 kw), of high-band VHF stations to 316 kw, and of UHF stations to 5,000 kw. In terms of decibels, the power of high-band VHF stations can exceed that of low-band VHF stations by 5 db; the power of UHF stations can exceed that of low-band VHF stations by 17 db.

The question as to whether or not it is practicable to compensate for the handicaps under which UHF television operates by using higher power at the transmitter is complicated by one very important factor, namely, the economic factor. There are also technical factors, and these will be considered first.

The principal parts of a transmitting plant are the transmitter itself, the transmitting antenna, and the transmission line connecting the transmitter to the antenna. A high "effective radiated power" is achieved through the use of high transmitter power output, low loss in the transmission line and high gain in the antenna. The usual practice, especially at UHF, is to use a transmitter having a power output of 15 or 25 or perhaps 50 kw and to achieve the high "effective radiated power" through the use of a high-gain antenna (perhaps with a gain of as much as 50 times). At VHF, low-gain antennas are almost always used. The gain used in UHF antennas cannot be increased indefinitely. Gain in a broadcasting transmitting antenna is achieved by concentrating the radiated energy into a narrow vertical angle aimed approximately at the horizon. This is a very advantageous technique as long as it is not carried too far. There certainly is no point in sending energy directly upward from the transmitting antenna. On the other hand, if the radiated energy is concentrated in too narrow a vertical angle, service will not be provided over the entire range between the antenna tower and the horizon. The result is that transmitting antenna gains of more than about 50 are very seldom used. The other method of achieving high effective radiated power is, of course, to increase the actual power output of the transmitter. Again there are practical limitations. In the first place, it is expensive. Commercial UHF transmitters having outputs of as much as 50 kw are available and 100 kw transmitters may be available reasonably soon. The transmitter power output cannot be increased indefinitely, as there are limits to the power which can be transmitted to the antenna over commercially available transmission lines. In order to send greater power up either a coaxial transmission line or a wave guide, its size must be increased. This means a more sturdy tower, not only to support the weight of the heavier line, but also to withstand the greater wind-loading resulting from the larger line.

It is evident that the technical problems involved in achieving high effective radiated power at UHF are not inconsequential, but it appears that they are susceptible to solution through skilled engineering design. It is also evident from the above discussion that the desired results will not be achieved cheaply. Each of the steps involves the expenditure of more money.

TASO collected a large amount of information regarding the costs of transmitting plant (including transmitter, accessories, terminal facilities, installation, building costs, etc.), of antenna installations (including antenna, tower, transmission line, installation, etc.) and of operation (including power, tube replacement, maintenance, etc.). The data were summarized as follows in the TASO Report: On the average, complete maximum power (316 kw) high-band VHF stations were shown to cost about 25 percent more than complete, maximum power 100 kw) low-band VHF stations. Complete UHF stations operating at effective radiated powers up through 300 kw were shown to cost, on the average, about 10 percent less than complete, maximum power (100 kw) low-band VHF stations. Little information was obtained regarding the cost of complete 500 and 1,000 kw UHF stations, as they are few in number; but it appeared that their cost was comparable to that of complete, maximum power (100 kw) low-band

VHF stations. The operating costs of UHF transmitters were found to be significantly higher than the operating costs of VHF transmitters. The increase over VHF operating costs varied from 20 percent for the lowest powers to 100 percent for stations using transmitters with power outputs of 15 kw and higher. Recently developed UHF transmitting tubes are giving substantially greater tube life than older tubes. This will reduce the UHF operating expense somewhat, as tube replacement cost will be less than formerly. This item does not, however, greatly change the comparative operating costs reported by TASO. Looking toward the future, there is no question but that if UHF stations having effective radiated powers of a few thousand kilowatts are built, they will be very substantially more expensive in first cost and in operating cost than maximum power VHF stations.

Before leaving the subject of transmitters, something should be said regarding the types of transmitters included in the general category of repeater transmitters. These are low-power transmitters which receive signals from a main transmitter, amplify them and rebroadcast them. The general term repeater transmitter includes boosters, which rebroadcast on the same channel as that used by the signal received from the main transmitter, and translators, which rebroadcast on another channel. (The term also includes what once were known as satellites, which may originate as well as repeat programs, which may broadcast at high power, and which, from the standpoint of allocations, are the equivalent of regular stations.) Boosters and translators are used to fill in dead areas, or shadowed areas, within the normal range of a main transmitter or to extend the effective range of a main transmitter. Properly designed and installed UHF translators have been proven to be effective, reliable, and economical.

The use of boosters and translators poses problems which are more closely related to those of wave propagation than to those of equipment. Boosters obviously produce interference, in some areas, with the main transmitter whose programs are repeated on the same channel. Unless great care is taken, more service will be subtracted from the area covered by the main transmitter than will be added in the new area covered by the booster. This problem of co-channel interference does not exist when translators are used. The indiscriminate use of translators, however, could lead to a great reduction in the number of channels available to standard television broadcast stations in any given locality, as sufficient channels well might not be available for both standard stations and translators. More will be said regarding this problem later.

2.6 *Field tests*

The most extensive and most carefully conducted field tests designed to determine the differences between VHF and UHF television performance were those conducted by TASO. These field tests were conducted in eleven areas in different parts of the country. In each area, simultaneous observations of television reception in homes and measurements of field strength in the vicinity of homes were made. The 11 areas covered many types of terrain ranging from very flat to very mountainous. In each area, observations were made at a variety of distances from the transmitters, ranging out to the fringes of service. Observations and measurements were made in both rural and urban districts. In 9 of the 11 areas, both VHF and UHF fields were measured and both VHF and UHF pictures were observed. In order to obtain certain special types of needed data, in one of the other areas only VHF stations were used in the test and in the second of the other areas, only UHF stations were used.

The results of these field tests are summarized in the following quotation from the TASO Report.

> Speaking very generally, the field surveys conducted by TASO showed that, near a television transmitter, excellent service was provided by both UHF and VHF stations, but that as one went farther from the transmitter, UHF service deteriorated much more rapidly than did VHF service. In areas of adequately high signal strength, UHF provided both the best and the poorest pictures—the best primarily because of freedom from man-made electrical noise and the poorest primarily because of less satisfactory receiving installations. One significant factor was noted over and over again in all sections of the country. This is that there is no such thing as a "standard" receiving installation. Rather, as one goes farther and farther from a transmitter, one finds the quality of the receiver installations, and particularly the quality of the receiving antennas, improves so that the decrease in signal strength is to a considerable extent compensated. As one goes farther yet, a region is reached in which the signal strength is so low that only relatively poor pictures are obtained; and soon thereafter, it is found that no receivers are purchased. This increase in quality of receiving installations with increasing distance is, of course, to be expected; but it leads to interesting results. The effect produced is that, over a considerable range of distances from a television transmitter, picture quality, as observed in the home, remains at approximately the same satisfactory level; but that when some more or less critical distance is exceeded, the service deteriorates very rapidly. This critical distance depends upon many local factors; but the significant fact is that, in practically all cases, this critical distance is much less for UHF than for VHF. It is even markedly less for high-band VHF than for low-band VHF. Exceptions can, of course, always be found. For example, in the extremely flat and quite treeless San Joaquin Valley, signals from the Fresno UHF transmitters located 3,300 and 4,300 feet above the valley floor spread far down the valley and provide service quite comparable to that provided by the similarly located VHF transmitter. On the other hand, little UHF service is provided in the mountainous region to the east of the Fresno transmitters, although VHF service is quite adequate. In other words, the extent of UHF service is much more dependent upon the terrain than is VHF service.
>
> Returning to the general conclusions, rather than the exceptions, and

speaking in broad terms, the TASO field surveys showed that, under average conditions, with currently used effective radiated powers and transmitting antenna heights, service fell off rapidly beyond about the distances indicated in the following table. In particular areas, and especially with better-than-average receiving installations, good television service was often obtained at greater distances. In other areas, or with inferior installations, poor service was sometimes obtained at lesser distances. In the usual case, service of consistently good quality was maintained out to about the distance indicated. In no case did service cease suddenly as the "critical distance" was exceeded. Rather, at about this distance, the proportion of viewers receiving really satisfactory pictures began to decrease rather rapidly, while those receiving poorer pictures increased correspondingly.

Frequency Range	Channel Range	Critical Distance (miles)
Low VHF	2–6	65
High VHF	7–13	55
Low UHF	14–40	40
Medium and High UHF	41–83	30

The decrease in average service range with increasing operating frequency is plainly evident. Moreover, at the critical distance, UHF service fell off more rapidly and more completely than did VHF service. Within the critical distance, service was more variable at UHF than at VHF and was, on the average, poorer.

Information of a different nature was also provided by the TASO field tests. The simultaneous measurements of field strength and observation of pictures permitted conclusions to be drawn regarding the field strength required to produce pictures of a specified quality under practical conditions encountered in normal operation. In the TASO field tests, pictures in the home were observed and rated by both technically trained observers and by the householder using a six-point scale: 1—Excellent, 2—Good, 3—Passable, 4—Not quite passable, 5—Poor, and 6—Not usable. In the following table, data are given on the median field strength in dbu as measured at a height of 30 feet in a given location and the median picture quality in homes in the same location.

Frequency Range	Channel Range	Median Field Strength in dbu Resulting in Median Picture Quality of	
		2—Good	3—Passable
Low VHF	2–6	50 and above	40 to 45
High VHF	7–13	60 and above	50 to 55
Low UHF	14–40	65 and above	55 to 60
Medium and High UHF	41–83	72 and above	62 to 67

It is interesting to note that the data in the above table and the data given previously regarding wave propagation and regarding receiving antenna installations and receiver noise figures were obtained entirely independently. There are means for checking the consistency of the two sets of data and when such checks are made, the data are shown to be consistent.*

In summary, the TASO field tests showed that several factors, and in particular the fact that receiving installations are not standard but are chosen with a regard for conditions existing at a given receiving location, operate to decrease the difference between VHF and UHF performance which would be predicted from laboratory measurements alone. Nevertheless, substantial differences in VHF and UHF performance do exist out to the limits of service and these differences are in favor of VHF. Also, the service range, or the distance to the limits of service, is far less at UHF than at VHF, as is shown in the table of critical distances. To put these conclusions in other words, the TASO Report states that "current differences in the effective radiated powers used at low VHF, high VHF, and UHF tend to equalize the picture quality obtainable within the service area of a transmitter (except, perhaps, for 'holes' within the service area); but they do not at all equalize the *size* of the service areas obtainable in the three frequency ranges."

2.7 Incomplete information

It might be concluded from the discussions in the preceding sections that complete information is at hand regarding the operation of television systems at VHF and at UHF. This would be an unwarranted and incorrect conclusion. UHF television has not been used to a sufficient extent to permit the collection of certain urgently needed data. In particular, there are wide differences of opinion among competent engineers as to the degree of success which may be achieved by UHF television in large cities, especially in cities of the character of New York with its canyon-like streets. The FCC is currently working actively on the plans for a rather comprehensive test of UHF television in New York City. Funds for this test have been appropriated by Congress. A transmitter operating on Channel 31 will be located in the Empire State Building. Observations of received pictures will be made at some 5,000 locations in and around New York and a series of field strength measurements will be made. This test will not answer all the questions regarding the performance of UHF television in

---

* The data in the above table are also in reasonably close agreement with the definitions of "normal service" recently proposed by the FCC in Docket 13340 for describing the needs in rural service areas. These requirements for "normal service" are: Channels 2–6, 40 dbu; Channels 7–13, 50 dbu; Channels 14–83, 64 dbu.

a large metropolitan area, but it should be very helpful in at least indicating the answers to many questions.

More information is also needed regarding the performance of on-channel boosters. Field experience with UHF boosters has been very meager. It is at UHF that boosters are most needed, especially in rugged terrain and presumably also in large metropolitan areas where deeply shadowed sections fail to receive adequate signal strength. The success of UHF operation in such areas may well depend upon the performance of boosters. It would be most helpful if the FCC UHF tests in New York could be expanded to include tests of boosters.

So far in this report, no mention has been made of airborne television stations. The reason for this is that they were excluded from the purview of this report, it being understood that they would be discussed by others and that this report would be concerned only with conventional types of television systems. It is obvious, however, that tests of airborne systems are urgently needed in order that any discussion of television allocation problems may be complete. Until such tests are actually made, airborne television can be considered only as a proposal, without engineering information upon which to base conclusions. Even if completely successful, airborne television probably would provide only part of the service needed for educational television, a substantial part of which would have to be provided by more conventional means. There is one fallacy which must be guarded against. This is the idea that because of the height of the transmitting antenna above the earth, all airborne transmissions will be along clear lines of sight. This is approximately true in large areas relatively close to the spot above which the plane is flying. At and near the fringes of service, however, the signal comes to the receiving antennas tangential to the earth, encountering obstacles in the form of trees, buildings, hills, etc. In these fringe areas, therefore, signals from the airborne transmitter would be expected to be subject to the same vagaries as those from earth-based UHF transmitters.

Even with respect to such more conventional matters as receiver noise factor, receiving antenna design and transmitter design, no information can ever be expected to be complete, as the art is always changing. Even though wave propagation per se does not change, man's knowledge of the subject is always increasing; and it is always possible that new data or more complete analyses of existing data will change conclusions which now appear to be well founded. The best that can be done is to reflect the present status of the knowledge concerning VHF and UHF television performance and to attempt to make logical extrapolations into the future. This is what has been done in this report.

3. ALLOCATION PROBLEMS AND SUGGESTIONS

The first two sections of this report have been concerned with laying a foundation for a discussion of the allocations problem in its direct relationship to educational television—which is the subject matter of this section. The needs of educational television for channels cannot be considered entirely separately from the needs of commercial television and of other services and therefore reference will also be made to some of the problems of these other users of spectrum space.

The entire discussion in this section will be based on the premise that in the foreseeable future, both commercial television and educational television will wish to have a substantially greater number of television stations in operation than at present. Commercial television and educational television will therefore compete to a greater or less extent for television channels.

3.1 More VHF channels

From what has been said in section 2 of this report, the fact must be evident that from nearly every viewpoint, and especially from the viewpoint of covering the greatest area at the least cost, VHF television has very substantial advantages over UHF television. The question therefore must be raised as to the possibility of obtaining more VHF channels.

It is perhaps worth noting that the Radio Technical Planning Board (which was an organization set up by the electronics industry in 1943 at the request of the FCC), in its studies of the needs of postwar commercial television broadcasting, considered the need for as many as 60 television channels. Its final recommendations to the FCC were that a minimum of 30 channels be set aside in the VHF region for commercial television. Because of the needs of other services for VHF spectrum space, the FCC allocated only 13 channels for commercial television and later re-allocated one of these to other services, leaving 12 for television. It is evident, therefore, that for many years the television industry has been keenly aware of its needs for more channels, and especially of its desires for more VHF channels, and that for an equal length of time the FCC has been unable to grant these desires. In the meantime, other services, including important military services over which the FCC has no control, have been using space in the VHF region and have, indeed, become firmly entrenched therein.

From time to time, proposals of varying degrees of seriousness have been made to attempt to obtain some of the VHF space now used by the military services and to allocate this space to television broadcasting. All such attempts have been fruitless. (Parenthetically, it could be said that in all probability the military services have looked covetously at the VHF television channels, to date equally fruitlessly.) As recently as within the last two years, the FCC engaged in lengthy, serious, and secret discussions with the military services on the problems of the allocation of VHF spectrum space with one object being to make more VHF channels available to television. At least one plan which was considered involved the allocation of some of the present television space to the military services in return for somewhat more space in another part of the VHF spectrum. After a thorough study of the problems involved, the conclusion was reached that the best solution was to maintain the status quo. At least one reason for this decision was the tremendous investment which the military services have in equipment operating in the parts of the VHF spectrum now occupied by these services. Since this investment is certain to increase rather than decrease, and since even present investments make changes impracticable, the prospects of obtaining additional VHF channels for television seem dim indeed; so much so, that this possibility will not be considered further in this report.

3.2 More stations on present VHF channels

Another logical question is that of whether it might not be possible to assign more television stations on the present 12 VHF channels. The answer, of course, is yes—but at what price? The present FCC rules have been set up in an attempt to provide maximum service. Co-channel and adjacent channel minimum spacings have been established in an attempt to minimize interference. In the more populous northeast section of the country (in the so-called Zone I), the co-channel spacings thought to be the minimum practicable have been compromised somewhat in order to permit the operation of a greater number of stations in a greater number of major cities. On the other hand, in a region running generally along the Gulf Coast (Zone III), the minimum spacing of co-channel stations has had to be increased because of better-than-average propagation conditions existing there. Even with the present minimum spacings, co-channel interference does exist; and in some sections of the country it occurs frequently enough and is of enough severity to limit seriously the quality of service provided by some stations. If co-channel spacings were reduced with no changes in methods of operation, interference would increase.

There have been proposals that co-channel spacings be reduced, especially in predominantly urban sections of the country, so that every city could have its own local television station (or stations). If the stations were located in these cities, service in these centers of population might well be improved, but at the expense of a substantial increase in interference and decrease in service in the rural areas between the cities. Such proposals have not been considered to be feasible from a number of points of view.

There are, however, practical possibilities for reducing co-channel spacings *in some instances* without incurring the penalty of increased interference. This could be accomplished by employing certain newly developed techniques. These techniques should be employed judiciously and only after a study of the circumstances existing in individual cases. Few persons would advocate the indiscriminate reduction of station spacings and the resulting deterioration of service which would result.

The first, and most important, technique which could be employed is the use of directional transmitting antennas. Directional antennas are used extensively in standard AM radio broadcasting but have not been used commercially in television broadcasting in this country. The normal television transmitting antenna is designed to radiate energy as uniformly as possible in all (horizontal) directions. A directional antenna is designed to radiate less energy in some particular direction than in others. Its horizontal radiation pattern is thus not circular but is shaped like a cardioid (or is heart-shaped). If a directional transmitting antenna is located properly with respect to the area it is designed to serve and with respect to a nearby co-channel station (with the "null," or direction of minimum energy radiation, pointed toward the latter station), it should be possible to reduce the co-channel spacing appreciably *in some cases* and to permit the establishment of a few additional VHF stations on the present 12 channels.

One of the important accomplishments of TASO was the full-scale field testing of two directional VHF transmitting antennas. TASO also developed and specified the means for checking the performance of such antennas. The TASO tests admittedly did not cover all types of antennas, all channels and all types of terrain, but they did show quite conclusively that under the practical field conditions under which these tests were made, directional antennas with no more than a 15 db null (ratio of radiated energy in the direction of minimum radiation to that in the direction of maximum radiation) performed well and in accord with their predicted performance. The one major unresolved problem is that of the amount of null fill-in, or reflections into the null region from reflecting surfaces in the direction of high radiation, which might be experienced in rugged terrain or in the case of injudiciously located antennas in the neighborhood of large cities. This emphasizes the necessity of a careful study of each proposed directional antenna. There is every reason to believe that the performance of directional television transmitting antennas would be satisfactory in some areas where there are urgent demands for additional stations.

It should be noted that directional antennas can be used to reduce adjacent channel spacing as well as co-channel spacing, again with the same need for a careful study of each case. There is another technique which could be explored in studying adjacent channel spacings. This involves putting adjacent channel transmitting antennas on the same tower* rather than separating them by 55 miles or more, as is now required by the FCC rules. This might be thought to be a radically impracticable idea. A little thought will show, however, that the field strengths of the two stations would be nearly the same. Since an adjacent channel signal can be considerably higher than the desired signal (because of the rejection characteristics or the selectivity of the television receiver) without producing unsatisfactory pictures, this method of operation *might* provide opportunities to add a few VHF stations in special circumstances. At least, it is worth further study.

A third technique which shows some promise is the use of the so-called "very precise carrier frequency offset" method of operation. In this method, the picture carrier frequency of television transmitters is controlled very precisely, say to the order of plus or minus one cycle, at exactly predetermined frequencies. Laboratory tests by TASO showed that this technique led to reduced interference effects between co-channel stations. A logical conclusion would be that the technique could be used in reducing co-channel spacings. Extensive field tests have not been made. Preliminary tests in the VHF band indicate that at standard station spacings, a reduction in interference equivalent to 8 db can be achieved with very precise carrier frequency offset as compared with normal operation. The achievement of the necessary degree of frequency control at VHF appears to be technically possible, although somewhat expensive.

So far, it has been assumed that any additional VHF station would operate at full power. It has been proposed by some that under special conditions, it might be possible to permit the addition of a VHF station in a particular location if its effective radiated power and/or its antenna height were restricted to less than is permitted by present FCC rules. This is a possibility which should not be ignored.

In summary, it can be said that techniques are available to permit a reduction of station spacings *in some instances* without a significant increase in interference. These techniques should not, however, be applied indiscriminately but only after a case-by-case study of the problems which are involved. Neither should it be concluded that the application of these techniques would greatly increase the number of stations which can be accommodated in the present 12 VHF channels. There would be some increase in the number of stations, but it is believed that the increase would be quite modest. Even a preliminary estimate of the number of additional VHF stations which could be established could be made only after a very careful and extensive study.

---

* This proposal was made recently by Dr. William L. Hughes of Oklahoma State University.

3.3 All-UHF operation

A number of proposals have been made to abandon the VHF television channels and use only the UHF channels for television broadcasting. This is not believed to be a practical solution from at least two points of view.

In the first place, commercial VHF television is well established. The viewing public in this country has purchased some 77,500,000 television receivers, 56,500,000 of which are currently in service. These 56,500,000 receivers represent an investment of approximately 13.3 billion dollars. Most of these are equipped to receive VHF channels only. Television viewing has become a major avocation of a high percentage of Americans. As has been pointed out before, the VHF region is on the whole more satisfactory than the UHF region for television broadcasting. Now, does it seem probable that any group elected by the public or any regulating agency dependent upon such elected groups for its support would tell the public that after such-and-such a date (even though the date were five or ten years in the future) all their present television receivers would be useless, that the new receivers which they purchased would cost more and that, in most instances, poorer television service would be obtained?

In the second place, it is not at all certain that the 70 UHF channels, even if fully utilized, would produce a great increase in service in comparison with that now provided by the 12 VHF channels. At first glance it seems that the ratio of service should be 70 to 12 or approximately six to one. But this is not so. The following quotation from the cited paper by Hughes and Town relates to this problem.

One of the great differences between UHF and VHF is the factor of propagation, which is directly reflected in station coverage. The TASO data showed that with existing stations, the range of a UHF station is significantly less than the range of a VHF station. If the VHF range is R times the UHF range, the area covered by the VHF station is R^2 times as great as that covered by the UHF station. Therefore, if the same total area is to be served by UHF and by VHF, and if the spacing between co-channel stations were the same at UHF and at VHF, the effective ratio of UHF to VHF channels would not be 70:12 but rather would be $70:12R^2$. Actually, the necessary co-channel spacing is somewhat less at UHF than at VHF, as the undesired interfering field, like the desired service field, is not propagated as well at UHF as at VHF. In the absence of better information, it is not unreasonable to accept the figures set forth in the FCC rules for minimum co-channel spacings, although further experience with UHF may (hopefully) prove that the required spacings at UHF may be reduced. The ratios of the FCC-specified minimum co-channel spacings at UHF to those at VHF vary between 0.91 and 0.93 in Zones I, II, and III. Taking an average ratio of 0.92, the effective ratio of the number of UHF channels to the number of VHF channels becomes

$$\frac{70}{12 \times 0.92^2 R^2} \quad \text{or} \quad \frac{70}{12 \times 0.85 R^2}.$$

Again, the "taboos" set by the FCC further limit the number of UHF channels that can be assigned in any given locality. Some of these taboos are doubtless too strict. Nevertheless, such factors as receiver local oscillator radiation and receiver image response are basic in nature and do decrease the effective number of UHF channels available for assignment, say by a factor of T. This again reduces the effective ratio of UHF to VHF channels to

$$\frac{70}{12 \times 0.85\, R^2\, T}.$$

The values of R and T do not have to be very great to reduce this ratio to unity or less. If the ratio were unity, this would mean that the 70 UHF channels would serve the same total area as the 12 VHF channels at, incidentally, a cost for transmitters of approximately R^2 times as great.

Stripped of the mathematical formulation, this quotation says that more stations are required at UHF than at VHF to cover the same area or to produce the same service; that the spacing between UHF stations cannot be reduced in the same proportion as the service range and that therefore more channels are required to serve a given area; and that because of local oscillator radiation and image response problems which are present at UHF (but not at VHF because of the manner in which the VHF channels are grouped and spaced), the number of channels available for assignment in any given area is reduced. In terms of total available service provided by the 70 UHF channels, there effectively are not 70/12 times as many available UHF as VHF channels, but some much smaller number; perhaps there are effectively not more than twice as many or, as an extreme upper limit, three times as many UHF channels as VHF channels.* In view of the ever increasing demand for television channels by both commercial and educational interests, it is therefore not technically sound to abandon the VHF region. Both the VHF *and* the UHF regions should be retained, as both will be needed.

---

* As a rough check of the validity of these figures, note that the maximum number of VHF channels which can be accommodated in a given area is seven. Studies made by the National Association of Educational Broadcasters indicate that under the present FCC rules, no more than 13 UHF channels, or about twice the number of VHF channels, can be assigned in a given area. This conclusion was reached without detailed consideration of the needs of adjoining areas. These needs might restrict the number of available channels still further. On the other hand, if the FCC rules were relaxed, by liberalization of some of the present taboos, additional channels in a given area might be made available; but it is not probable that the number of UHF channels in an area could be increased by more than 50 percent by this means. It seems reasonable to conclude, therefore, that the 70 UHF channels can provide no more than from two to, at the most, three times the service provided by the twelve VHF channels; and it is probable that this ratio is much nearer the lower figure (two) than the higher.

3.4 Continued VHF and UHF operation—random mixed

The present intermixed assignments of commercial VHF and UHF television stations (in the same geographical area) are not satisfactory. Experience in commercial television broadcasting over the past nine years has shown that while in an all-UHF area, commercial UHF television is a success, in an intermixed area, the UHF station (or stations) operates at a great disadvantage; in fact, in an area with two VHF stations and one UHF station, the UHF station is almost certain not to survive. To quote Dr. Thomas T. Goldsmith of the Allan B. Du Mont Laboratories (whose company in 1950 submitted a well-thought-out, nonintermixed allocations plan to the FCC, which was rejected), "Intermixture is the kiss of death to UHF television."

It seems inevitable that any successful, long-term allocations plan for commercial television must eliminate the intermixture of VHF and UHF stations in the same service area.

3.5 Allocation of channels for educational television

The first question which must be answered in connection with any study of the allocation of channels for educational television is that of how many channels are needed. In answering that question, it is necessary to look toward the future and not be restricted to thinking in terms of the number of educational television stations which have been established since 1952. It is necessary, rather, to think in terms of what has happened in Pittsburgh and Oklahoma City and what is happening in Milwaukee and Miami where after an educational television station was established, it was found that a second station was required to provide the needed educational services. It is also necessary to think in terms of the increasing school population and the inability or the unwillingness of many communities and states to make provision for conventional educational facilities for caring for the needs of these young people. It is probably necessary to think also in terms of an expanded program of adult education or continuing education, although the needs of the young people in schools probably will be more urgent. Moreover, if sufficient educational television facilities are made available for the use of the schools, they may also be sufficient for adult educational programs for some time.

It is the responsibility of others, and particularly of those working in the fields of primary and secondary education, to develop the specific needs for channels for educational television. However, for the purposes of this report, something must be assumed as a basis upon which to build. This does not have to be an accurate determination, but it is essential that the order of magnitude of the channel requirements be estimated. It certainly does not seem unreasonable that if some cities already see the need for two educational television stations, many areas will eventually need at least the equivalent of three VHF stations. Already some cities visualize the eventual need of six UHF channels and in some of the largest cities, studies indicate that educational television may well need 12 or more UHF channels. On the basis of this assumption, it is not unreasonable to expect that within the next decade or so, educational television will become as large a service as is commercial television broadcasting today.* Commercial television broadcasting now occupies space equivalent to more than the entire VHF television bands. Where can educational television find an equivalent amount of space in the frequency spectrum?

The answer seems obvious. The only place is in the UHF portion of the spectrum. As has been pointed out, additional VHF channels are not in prospect. Some, but relatively few, additional stations can be put on the present VHF channels by the use of new techniques. It is not at all reasonable to expect commercial television broadcasting to vacate their present VHF space, either for the military services or for educational television. What choice is there which will permit educational television to expand except that of using the UHF region?

In section 3.3, it was pointed out that the expectation of almost unlimited service from the 70 UHF channels may very well prove to be a mirage and that these 70 channels may well provide no more real service than, say, twice that provided by the present 12 VHF channels. This emphasizes the necessity of reserving a very large portion of the UHF channels for educational television if this service is to be comparable in size and scope to present-day commercial television broadcasting. A minimum of half of the UHF television channels should now be reserved permanently for education. And these channels should be in the lower part of the UHF television region.

One point needs to be emphasized. The technical requirements for a large number of channels (say 30 to 40) for educational television are set not by the average needs across the entire country, but by the much greater needs in large metropolitan localities which have high population densities throughout relatively extensive geographical areas. Los Angeles and New

---

* As a check, assume that in the first 12 grades of school, each grade receives an average of two one-half hour periods of instruction via television daily. This would necessitate 12 hours of educational broadcasting during the school day to care for the needs of the primary and secondary schools. Additional service during these same hours to local institutions of higher learning and to special groups would easily bring the total requirements to the equivalent of the three VHF channels needed to bring the programs of the three networks to viewers of commercial television broadcasting. Thus, it is not out of line to suggest that educational television should have the equivalent of the space in the spectrum now allocated to commercial television broadcasting.

York City probably represent the most extreme examples. If such areas are to be served, an adequate number of channels to satisfy their needs must be reserved.

One may well say that in view of the many superiorities of VHF channels over UHF channels for television broadcasting, educational television would be penalized unfairly by operating exclusively, or at least largely, in the UHF region. The situation is not, however, quite as bad it may seem. In the first place, it will be remembered that in areas where the signal strength is adequate, UHF television, not VHF television, produces the best pictures. High quality pictures are needed in educational television if it is to serve the needs of the schools. High quality pictures are much more important in a science demonstration than in *The Price Is Right.** In the second place, while UHF television stations do not have the range of VHF stations, they can have a greater effective range as educational stations than as commercial stations. It is not economically feasible to build really good television receivers for the general public. The schools, however, can erect a really high grade receiving antenna system to pick up television signals for distribution throughout the school. High quality preamplifiers with low noise factors can be employed and can be installed at the receiving antennas rather than in the television receivers. The use of high quality receiving equipment, especially antennas and preamplifiers, can extend the effective range of UHF stations. Such equipment is too expensive to sell to the general public in a highly competitive market, but it is not unduly expensive as part of the television receiving equipment for a school. The use of low-power on-channel boosters with highly directional antennas to extend service not throughout all of a given area but rather toward specific educational centers also offers good possibilities. It should also be emphasized that the educational television channels should be the lower UHF channels. Admittedly, these are not as favorable as the VHF channels, but they are much better than the highest UHF channels.

It may be said that this is all well and good as far as the schools are concerned, but it does not provide the adult educational or continuing educational service which is desired. It is true that a viewer wishing to receive programs from a UHF educational station would have to have either a UHF receiver or a UHF converter. It does not seem unreasonable to expect that such a person would be willing to make this investment. It is not realistic to expect that television programs for continuing education

---

* This problem of picture quality in educational television is of real importance. It has implications in other aspects of television than allocations—for example in studio equipment operation, in closed-circuit transmission, and particularly in television picture recording.

will at first be really popular. The people who are interested in such programs are intensely interested and would, in many instances, make the necessary investment, particularly if arrangements are made to spread the additional cost over a period of, say, several months. It must be remembered that, at least at first, programs for continuing education will still be carried on VHF educational television stations; and that as UHF educational television grows, the cost of UHF receiving equipment most certainly will be reduced, thus making UHF converters or receivers more attractive to those having a real interest in continuing education.

There is one further aspect to the recommendation that at least half of the UHF channels be permanently reserved for educational use. The possibility that all commercial television broadcasting be moved to the UHF region is considered to be slight. But suppose such a move were made. In this case, it would be all the more necessary that educational television should already have adequate space reserved for its use and that this space be in the lower part of the UHF television region.

It will be claimed correctly that an all-UHF educational television system will cost more than an all-VHF system. This, however, is one of the penalties which educational television must pay for arriving on the scene later than commercial television, which is already entrenched in the VHF region.

So far, no mention has been made of the possibility of new thinking which would lead to radically different types of television and to new transmission standards. Developments of this nature might possibly include some scheme for reducing the frequency band width required for the transmission of television signals. Such developments are devoutly to be wished. No economically practical schemes of this nature appear now to be in the offing. If such developments do occur, the entire allocation plan will be radically affected and entirely new assignments, of a nature not visualized now, will have to be developed. In the meantime, it is necessary to proceed on the basis of the present FCC transmission standards.

Likewise, no consideration has been given to the possible use of higher frequencies, in the microwave region or super high frequency region (3,000 to 30,000 Mc) for educational television. Such frequencies are of great value for point-to-point communication, but they do not appear to be suitable for broadcasting. If microwave frequencies were used for educational television, they might be adequate for some types of in-school service, but their use would make any type of continuing education service difficult.

Again, there has not been in this report any discussion of the use of outer-space satellites in television relaying and/or broadcasting. This, like airborne television, is a type of "extra-terrestrial" transmission which may very well be a significant factor in the not too far distant future. The FCC is currently inquiring into the needs of satellite systems for space in the frequency spectrum in its Dockets No. 13522 and 14024. Studies of the possible implications of such new types of operation in educational television should be made by those well versed in these new techniques. It should be noted, however, that the applications of these new techniques may be some time away. It would seem inappropriate to postpone action with respect to the reservation of an appropriate number of UHF channels for educational television until all new developments are fully explored. In the foreseeable future, it appears that the principal use of a satellite will be as a location for a relay station, or as a sort of super-service microwave relay tower, for the transmission of signals over great distances. Such a relay link could, for example, serve to interconnect television networks in widely separated countries. The signals from such a satellite relay station might, of course, cover relatively wide geographical areas; but the specialized and expensive receiving installations required to receive the signals would not make their use practicable in the home. In other words, a transmitter located on a satellite is expected to be, at least for a long time, strictly a relay station, not a broadcasting station. Thus, the use of satellites is not expected to have any immediate influence on the allocation of channels for educational television broadcasting.

The mention of satellite relay stations suggests the international interconnection of educational television networks. This certainly is an eventual possibility. In the nearer future, the needs of educational television in the neighboring countries of Canada and Mexico should be considered. From the point of view of allocations, it would appear probable that an allocation plan suitable for this country would also serve the needs of these neighboring countries. The only congested area, allocations-wise, probably would be the Detroit-Windsor area, and a plan based on the reservation of a sufficient number of channels to serve Los Angeles and New York should be capable of serving this area as well.

In all of this discussion of channels for educational television, it must be remembered that the basic premise is that educational television will grow and that its needs will be as great as those of commercial television. No consideration is given to sandwiching a few stations in here and there. If this were the basic premise, the conclusions would be different; but they would not serve the needs of educational television which are almost certain to develop in the next few years.

EDUCATION'S NEED FOR CHANNELS:
Report of the NAEB Survey

By Vernon Bronson
Mr. Bronson has been the Director of the NAEB Survey.

I. ALABAMA:

THE ALABAMA EDUCATIONAL Television Commission is now operating three VHF channels, interconnected by 12 microwave units. As of January 1961, the Commission applied for a construction permit to build another station in Montgomery. The Montgomery station would be on Channel 26. The immediate plan of the Commission is to establish an additional station in Mobile (UHF) and at least one station in the Tennessee Valley of northern Alabama. It has applied for and received reserved channels at nine additional locations. As rapidly as possible, in order to meet the demands for instructional service on the college level, as well as in the public schools, the Commission plans to double-channel the network. The present plans in Alabama indicate that they look forward in the next decade, or earlier, to a need of at least 30, and perhaps 36, channels to serve the state of Alabama in an eductional network system.

II. ALASKA:

Dr. Theo J. Norvy, Commissioner of Education in Alaska, writes:

It is unfortunate that television broadcasting is very limited in this state, primarily due to sparsity of population, as well as broadcasting problems. As you know, Alaska is a very mountainous state which poses special problems when it comes to delivering a picture. It may be that the technical difficulties will be overcome—then educational television would be a most welcome asset.

III. ARIZONA:

On April 5, 1961, there was a representative meeting of public school and college educators and representative citizens at Arizona State University to consider the needs of educational television in Arizona.

1. Television channels for educational purposes should be available in Arizona, in addition to the present stations in the following areas: Flagstaff, Safford, and Yuma.
2. At least two low-power UHF channels should be available to education in the Phoenix area and the Tucson area, so that KAET and KUAT would be able to move into multiple transmission as the need develops.

3. The two university stations at Tucson and Phoenix-Tempe should be linked so that they can exchange programs off the air at this time.

IV. ARKANSAS:

Arkansas has had an active legislative committee to study the educational possibilities of television. This commission has made a study during the current year and sponsored a bill in the 1961 legislature to establish an educational television commission for the State of Arkansas which would have the power to activate the reserved channels in Arkansas, and procure such additional channels as may be needed.

V. CALIFORNIA:

California at the present time has six educational reservations which have not been activated. On the other hand, the evidence presented by the schools and colleges for additional channels needed in the foreseeable future to meet the potential demand for educational facilities shows a need for an additional 32 channels for the State of California, distributed judiciously in the great clusters of population in the southern part of the state and in the central part of the state.

VI. COLORADO:

The University of Colorado reports that it is installing production facilities and closed-circuit television which is expected to lead to an early activation of Channel 12, which is now reserved for educational use, in Boulder. The University of Colorado indicates that it looks forward to a state-wide network which will eventually have a production center and closed- and open-circuit transmission facilities on the campuses of each of the seven state-supported institutions of higher learning.

A further indication of the recognition of the need for educational television in various areas of the state for future educational progress is the fact that the state legislature, at the 1960 session, passed an earlier act.

These various acts and plans are indications of future use of television channels for education in the state; and, coupled with the very effective school and community operation of Channel 6 in Denver, it indicates a potential demand for educational channels which must be given prime consideration.

VII. CONNECTICUT:

All colleges, universities, and school systems in Connecticut responding to the survey, with the exception of Yale University, indicated that they were planning to cooperate with the Connecticut Educational Television Corporation in the use of broadcast television. If the cooperative efforts for instructional use of broadcast television in Connecticut are successful, and meet the observed and potential needs, on the basis of minimum scheduling, there will be a need for at least six channels in Connecticut in addition to those now reserved.

VIII. DELAWARE:

Delaware has the peculiar problem of having to depend to some degree upon its neighbors for the development of such facilities as instructional broadcasting. Dr. George R. Miller, Jr., of the Delaware State Department of Education, says that Delaware is considering cooperation with the City of Philadelphia in its efforts to acquire Channel 12, now designated at Wilmington, for the use of education in the Greater Philadelphia area.

Statements from the leading educational authorities in Delaware indicate the attitude of eagerness and desire which is restrained by the geographical conditions of the state.

IX. FLORIDA:

The Florida Educational Television Commission has asked the Federal Communications Commission to reserve an additional 16 channels in Florida for the use of education. Florida originally had five VHF channels and four UHF channels reserved for education. The five VHF channels in the major areas of population and at the state universities have now been activated and are serving the school systems, colleges, and universities in the state. If the Federal Communications Commission grants these 16 additional reservations, this will provide Florida with a total of 25 channels to be activated in the general system of public education within the next ten years. However, this apparently will not in itself be sufficient. The response of the communities and the school systems throughout Florida, coupled with the official actions of the State Department of Education, and the State Board of Higher Education, and the State Educational Television Commission, indicates that the projected plans will require an additional 14 channels beyond that which was asked for by the Florida Educational Television Commission.

X. GEORGIA:

According to the report from the Governors' Conference on Education, the State Department of Education has established a program to provide in-school educational television service which eventually is intended to reach every classroom in the State of Georgia. This program is predicated on the development of a state-wide television network. A simple projection of these plans indicates a need for at least 18 additional channels in the state.

XI. HAWAII:

A study of the needs for educational television and potential program services is now being conducted in Hawaii. At the time of this report no definite action had been taken but it is expected that the activation of the four reserved channels in the Islands will be recommended. The channel in Honolulu is to serve as the prime station, and the three other channels on the other islands to act as satellite stations to carry the programs over as much of the entire state as possible.

XII. IDAHO:

If the state universities and the scattered schools are to be served, and the future educational needs of Idaho protected, then it is evident that several more channels must be made available for educational purposes in this state. A projection of future needs indicates that a minimum of nine additional channels will be required.

XIII. ILLINOIS:

Dr. Benjamin Willis, General Superintendent of Schools in Chicago, states:

> Many more uses could be made with more broadcast channels. The Chicago area needs as many as six channels for school use of broadcast television in the years ahead.

There have been two plans advanced for a primary network of educational television in Illinois.

In collating the assessment of the various educators in Illinois for future needs of educational television in terms of school schedules, varying levels of education and multiple channels, it appears that somewhere between 20 and 27 additional channels will have to be made available for Illinois if the future of the educational services is to be protected.

XIV. INDIANA:

Throughout the State of Indiana there is reported much interest but very little activity. Nearly all of the major educational institutions in Indiana seem to be somehow involved in the Midwest Project on Airborne, either as "coordinating centers," or as "demonstration schools," or as "resource institutions," or in some cases as all three.

Among the school districts there seems to be a very great hopefulness and future dependency on the Midwest Airborne Television Instruction Project. To what extent this hopefulness and dependency will continue to color the activity in activating the reserved channels is difficult to anticipate.

XV. IOWA:

Mr. David A. Dancer, Secretary of the Iowa State Board of Regents, writes:

> We are convinced that the present allocations of educational television channels

for Iowa are inadequate to serve the state as it should be served. We know that there is a need for additional channels, and for more financial support than is available at the present time.

XVI. KANSAS:

The State Legislative Council presented a plan for a Kansas State Network, designed as a basic service for the colleges and schools of the entire state, in its 1960 report to the legislature.

The minimum plan proposed for the State of Kansas uses five VHF channels with 1000-foot high antenna at maximum power, and one UHF channel using 1000-foot high antenna at maximum power.

The state legislature at its last session accepted this report in general, but could not find its way clear to provide any funds for the immediate activation of these channels. If the proposed six-channel network or any reasonable variation of the proposed six-channel network is put into operation, then in order to provide the multiple schedules necessary at the various levels of education, this network would have to be double-channeled within a short time.

XVII. KENTUCKY:

Following action by the state legislature, the Legislative Research Commission appointed an advisory committee on educational television. This committee was composed of educational, legislative, and civic leaders of the state.

After a study of the report on educational needs in the state, and consultation with local engineers, as well as engineers from the National Association of Educational Broadcasters and the Joint Council on Educational Broadcasting, the advisory committee recommended that a state-wide educational television network be established to *"enrich and upgrade the quality of education in Kentucky public schools."*

A technical and organizational plan for the establishment of such a network was devised and proposed. The proposal was approved by the Research Commission of the University of Kentucky, the State Department of Education, and other state agencies, and the Governor formally requested the Federal Communications Commission to allocate and reserve 10 specific channels to Kentucky for educational purposes.

XVIII. LOUISIANA:

According to Dr. J. B. Gremillion, Director of Research and Statistics for the State Department of Education, the Department believes that as more and better instructional programs are developed on television, more people will demand these services in the sections of the state not now being served by educational television channels. Dr. Gremillion says that plans are now being developed for extension of present facilities, and for activating the rest of the reserved channels. He further states that additional channels are needed in central, southern, and eastern portions of the state.

XIX. MAINE:

An educational television system has been recommended for the State of Maine. The educational community of the state is now organizing to develop such a system.

Dr. Phillip A. Annas, Executive Director of the Division of Instruction of the Maine State Department of Education, states:

> The private colleges are building an educational television station in Augusta and we are asking the legislature for funds to build a station at the University of Maine with translators in three other sections of the state.

XX. MARYLAND:

Dr. William M. Brish, Superintendent of Schools in Washington County, Maryland, with headquarters in Hagerstown, writes:

> Because of our experience with closed-circuit television, we have learned that broadcast television would add a dimension that would be profitable. It would be to include several small elementary schools in the program which are completely out of the circuit at the present time. It would also be possible to broadcast most of the adult education programs and perhaps the basic courses of the junior college program. By this means the present educational facilities in Washington County would be extended to numerous people. Furthermore, many cultural programs might be broadcast.

Dr. Daniel W. Zimmerman, Assistant State Superintendent of Schools in Maryland, states that while there are no plans at the present time to provide a state-wide system of educational television, there is a state-wide committee which has been participating in a study of the over-all need for educational television, and this committee has set forth a positive plan of use for educational television.

XXI. MASSACHUSETTS:

Hartford N. Gunn, General Manager of WGBH-TV, Channel 2, in Boston, which provides all of the educational television now available to Massachusetts, states in relation to the needs of the next ten years:

> We see the services extended to more groups within the community, plus multiple transmitters to serve a number of areas within the coverage of the high-powered transmitter; with unique local services that would not be justified for high-power wide area distribution. Eventual need will be for two complete state-wide systems, as well as the above mentioned.

XXII. MICHIGAN:

Dr. Lynn M. Bartlett, Superintendent of Public Instruction of Michigan, states that, while the State of Michigan is now in the process of conducting a state-wide study to establish a basis for a state plan of television development and utilization, he feels he can predict that strong recommendations for broadcast television expansion will result, whatever the details of the plans might be. He suggests that it would be extremely effective to have a VHF service for educational television covering the major population areas of the state, but that UHF service backing up any basic network and reinforcing instructional facilities throughout the state is essential.

XXIII. MINNESOTA:

The only channel activated at this time is Channel 2 in St. Paul–Minneapolis, which is owned and operated by a nonprofit educational foundation, but which services the colleges and universities and school systems of the entire area.

It is expected that Channel 8, in Duluth, will be activated in the near future; and Dr. Dean M. Schweickhard, Commissioner of Education, says that they are formulating plans to activate the station at Appleton in western Minnesota. Various educational interests are considering the establishment of a series of translators or repeaters to extend the utilization of the service of Channel 2 in St. Paul–Minneapolis.

Dr. Schweickhard further states:

We anticipate a greater demand for educational programming. Channels should be reserved for education in sufficient numbers to provide for future needs.

XXIV. MONTANA:

The Montana Educational Television Commission has drafted a tentative plan for a state network to provide the kind of basic system which it feels must be initiated and which it plans to follow up with the dual channeling.

The draft of the plan calls for a combination of high-power and low-power broadcast stations supplemented by a number of station translators to take care of the small isolated areas and the valleys which cannot be normally well reached by standard broadcast. The plan calls for linking the state colleges and universities at Missoula, Bozeman, Billings, Butte, Havre, and Dillon, as well as the state capital and the private colleges in the state, along with the two important junior colleges.

XXV. MISSOURI:

Dr. H. P. Wardlaw, Assistant Commissioner of Education, says that the Department of Education feels that many areas of adult education have need of television instruction at the present time, and there is a need to broaden the secondary education program in Missouri. Dr. Wardlaw feels that the demands for both in-school education and adult education by television will increase considerably in the ten years ahead.

The Assistant to the President at the University of Missouri emphasized that there were not enough broadcast channels available to education in Missouri and that this inhibited the planning for the development of broadcast television in that state. He said that the state government is interested in such development if channels could be made available; but it is presently involved in tax problems which prohibit any great amounts of financial help for such development.

XXVI. MISSISSIPPI:

Dr. James Tubb, State Superintendent of Education, says that:

We are definitely interested in developing educational television in Mississippi, but no definite plans are formulated as yet. A committee is at work on recommendations to make to the next term of the legislature.

XXVII. NEBRASKA:

Dr. Floyd A. Miller, Assistant Commissioner of Education for Nebraska, states:

The potential of educational television is such that every area of our instructional needs could be improved if we had state-wide educational television facilities. Recently the Nebraska Council on Educational Television developed a program which combined instruction in elementary science with teacher education in an effective manner. This is opening up a whole new field of endeavor. There is no doubt that the need for educational television will increase. Nebraska is a state of many small schools, some of which can never be properly organized into effective school districts, because of geography. Only by means of a state-wide educational television network can these schools obtain the advantages of the enriched instructional program which can be made available by this powerful new medium.

XXVIII. NEVADA:

Channel 10 in Las Vegas and Channel 5 in Reno have been reserved for education, but neither of these channels has been activated, at the present time.

Dr. Byron Stetler, Superintendent of Public Instruction of Nevada, feels that if the television-receiving facilities can be expanded and extended in Nevada, there will be use for educational broadcasting.

XXIX. NEW HAMPSHIRE:

Elementary and secondary schools have curriculum needs which can be served effectively through educational television, by bringing outstanding teachers, demonstrations, equipment, and materials, not normally available to our New Hampshire classrooms.

We need to extend our in-school service in New Hampshire to include services to primary grades, junior and senior high schools, and in-service teacher education. Our present station covers only 50 percent of the school population. We need a VHF channel reserved for educational purposes in the northern section of New Hampshire. The majority of schools not presently served by educational television are those small, understaffed, limited local-financed school systems.

XXX. NEW JERSEY:

Several state departments (such as the Department of Conservation and Economic Development) expressed a desire to use instructional television to develop their programs, particularly among the in-school population of the state.

Dr. Ernest E. McMahon, Dean of University Colleges and Extension, at Rutgers University, plans to "reach a wide general adult population with college level materials, in a variety of curriculum subjects."

XXXI. NEW MEXICO:

New Mexico has organized a Commission on State-wide Television for Educational Purposes (this is referred to as STEP).

The report from the STEP Commission by Dr. Claude Hempen, Director of the Commission, states:

New Mexico will utilize television for educational purposes in three ways:
1. *Open channel VHF broadcasting.* There will be four VHF television stations needed to adequately serve New Mexico at present.
2. *UHF low-power service.* Each of the institutions of higher learning will need from two to four UHF channels assigned for institutional use.
3. *Translator networks for the VHF outlets.* We will have 20–24 translators not including those necessary for the Indian Reservations.

XXXII. NEW YORK:

In 1952 the Regents requested and received, from the Federal Communications Commission, construction permits for ten UHF stations strategically located throughout the state. These stations were intended to serve as the nucleus of a state-wide educational network that would make it possible to serve the classrooms of the schools, as well as the homes of the state. However, the state government, controlling the funds of the Regents of the State University System, refused to go along, and the result was that the ten construction permits were never used.

The Regents are convinced that only through a systematic plan of state support can this medium reach the level of use in education which it deserves to attain. The Regents have proposed that the state proceed immediately to stimulate the further development and use of educational television in the state by:

1. Providing financial assistance to school districts for this purpose.
2. Contracting to assist state-approved local area educational television councils.
3. Activating a state-wide system of expanding educational television for use at college level education.

As of the writing of this report the New York State Legislature had not passed upon these recommendations.

Recently arrangements have been made to purchase Channel 13 in the New York City area for educational television purposes. If this purchase is consummated, it will undoubtedly be a large step toward the development of a total broadcast service for this area. In addition to this effort, the Federal Communications Commission is conducting an extended experiment with a special UHF station to see to what extent UHF can be adapted to large city usages where unusual amounts of physical and electronic interferences exist. From these two efforts may come a totally new kind of progress in the development of educational and instructional development of television in the New York City area.

XXXIII. NORTH DAKOTA:

Dr. M. F. Peterson, Superintendent of Public Instruction, of North Dakota makes the following statement:

> The people of North Dakota are progressive, and they see the need for educational television. Efforts are now in the planning and experimental stage, but the only way that educational and cultural needs in North Dakota can be met is through broadcast television.

North Dakota State University also said that broadcast television would help them relieve some of the pressures, particularly in the basic, high enrollment courses. They said at least 30 percent of the students come from a 25-mile radius, and broadcast television would allow them to serve many of these students at home.

XXXIV. NORTH CAROLINA:

The State Department of Public Instruction in North Carolina issued a statement that says:

> As is true throughout the country, Carolina is faced with an exploding school population. Numerous steps are being taken to provide quality education for this tremendous increase in students. Instructional television has proved itself in North Carolina as a teaching tool and increased use is necessary to help meet the increased needs of education. Recommendations have been made by the State Board of Education to strengthen and increase the present use of instructional television in the public schools, and to expand broadcast facilities. Most certainly additional facilities should be made available for educational purposes. Because television is the most powerful communication medium yet devised by man, it follows that a substantial protection be provided for its use in and by education.

XXXV. OHIO:

There are now four channels which have been activated, and the stations operate instructional programs on all levels of education, as well as for the general public. However, the community programming in Ohio has been extremely inhibited because of the fact that all the educational channels are in the UHF band, and the predominant service in Ohio is VHF. Therefore, the majority of available receivers in the communities are tuned for VHF reception only.

The Interim Study Commission recommended to the 1961 Legislature that legislation be enacted to create an Ohio Educational Television Network Commission, and to invest it with the authority and the funds to proceed with the establishment of a state-wide educational television network.

After a thorough engineering study, the interim commission report recommended in summary a plan for a single basic service for the state:

A total of 29 UHF stations, including six low-power translator-type stations, has been envisioned. In order to implement the plan fully it also would be necessary to request the addition of certain other UHF channels to the table of assignments of the Federal Communications Commission. Other UHF channels in certain areas would have to be changed by similar requests from non-reserved status to educational use.

XXXVI. OKLAHOMA:

Dr. E. F. Bryan, of the Oklahoma Department of Education, substantiates the need for educational television in Oklahoma. He points out that the demands are becoming greater each year as teachers and parents both become aware of the potential of using television for instruction.

Dr. Bryan states that the need is for more channels throughout the state and greater power, as well as for additional equipment.

XXXVII. OREGON:

Through the interconnecting of Channel 10 in Portland and Channel 7 in Corvallis, the General Extension Division of the System of Higher Education is able to provide continuing education and instructional services to 70 percent of the population of Oregon.

The administration of the educational system of Oregon is now planning to extend broadcast facilities to the Oregon College of Education and Southern Oregon College and Eastern Oregon College.

The Department of Education of Oregon has been given the responsibility for the development, coordination, and approval of all educational television programs for in-school viewing, for all elementary and secondary schools in the state; and also for in-service education programs for teachers. Present plans call for the provision for an in-school teacher service for grades kindergarten through grade 12, beginning with five hours weekly and growing to ten hours within two years. This service is planned on a state network basis.

XXXVIII. PENNSYLVANIA:

In the general survey in Pennsylvania, six colleges and universities indicated that they were now using instructional television in some form; 11 colleges and universities indicated that they were planning to use broadcast television, and 20 indicated that they were recognizing future need for the use of broadcast television in their planning. In the general survey of public school systems in Pennsylvania, 20 school systems indicated that they were now using instructional television and seven of the respondents indicated that they were planning to use instructional television.

Dr. Marcus Konick, of the Pennsylvania Department of Education, says that the State of Pennsylvania is currently developing a plan for full utilization of the full potential of television by the development of a state-wide network, and the maximum use of the present facilities which are on the air. Because of this he says that sufficient channels should be reserved for educational use in Pennsylvania and suggests, in addition to other things, that Pennsylvania should have at least a total of 14 additional UHF channels for the use of the state colleges alone.

XXXIX. RHODE ISLAND:

The Governor of Rhode Island recently established an educational television advisory committee to study the problems relative to the establishment of an educational television service for Rhode Island. Dr. Michael S. Walsh, Commissioner of Education for Rhode Island, says that they have instructional needs in the public schools for elementary science, teaching of foreign languages, both of which could be helped by the use of television. Dr. Walsh says that adult education needs to be met, to a great degree, by television programming.

XL. SOUTH CAROLINA:

Dr. Jesse T. Anderson, State Superintendent of Education for South Carolina, reports:

Although we have closed-circuit television in South Carolina, I have always been an advocate of broadcast television and I hope that some day we may eventually use the channels allotted to South Carolina. As for our needs, let me say that the three channels—one VHF and two UHF—would not cover the state. We have 1,418 schools: 614 white elementary, 269 white high, 389 Negro elementary, 146 Negro high. Our enrollment this year was in excess of 610,000 and estimates for the present year are 620,000. We expect an annual increase for the next ten years of 10,000 to 12,000. You can see from the above figures that it would be difficult to cover the state by closed-circuit television, and I have already stated three channels will not cover the state.

XLI. SOUTH DAKOTA:

Dr. M. F. Coddington, State Superintendent of Public Instruction, writes:

South Dakota is a rural state with few communities which are large enough to support an educational television station. For this reason little progress has been made in this field. We need educational television to supplement the rather limited instruction which is now available in many of our schools. We think that our only hope for adequate educational television coverage will be by means of a state-wide network.

XLII. TENNESSEE:

Dr. Joe Morgan, the State Commissioner of Education, writes:

There will be a need for expansion of television facilities which will increase the next ten years. The success of the educational television station in Memphis and the results of experimentation in a pilot situation in Tennessee schools and colleges has demonstrated the value of educational television and will insure its expansion in the future. There is a definite plan to extend the use of broadcast television and television channels should be reserved in sufficient numbers to meet the needs of the future in Tennessee.

XLIII. TEXAS:

Dr. Lee Wilborn, Assistant Commissioner of Education for Texas, writes:

Our needs for educational television service in the next ten years are much stronger than I have indicated in the formal response to your questions. School superintendents throughout our state are planning for some type of television service in almost all meetings I attend.

Dr. Wilborn further states that overcrowded classrooms throughout the state, three to four thousand qualified teachers lacking each year, and the urgency to share outstanding teachers and professors, are some of the problems that could be vastly improved by the use of broadcast television. The University of Houston issued the following statement:

It is our firm belief that the greatest single aid to education within the power of the federal government would be the reservation of a considerable section of the television broadcast spectrum, probably more than anyone is thinking about at this time.

Now, every time a subject is developed to the point where telecast seems profitable, a thirty-minute or one-hour slice of a channel is tied up for that one subject. In effect, then, when fourth grades of a broadcast area are receiving arithmetic, no one else in the area can receive anything else. As "materials" increase in number and variety, the pressure for simultaneous channels will mount and mount. In fact, unless they can mount, the school systems and colleges will be increasingly reluctant to stake much of their success on televised instruction.

XLIV. UTAH:

Within a short time, the four communities with reservations in Utah will be served. However, there are vast areas of the state still unserved.

Dr. H. Grant Vest, Director of the Utah Coordinating Council of Higher Education, writes:

The Coordinating Council of Higher Education anticipates an increased need for channel space and for extensive state-wide planning for educational television in Utah.

Dr. Wilbur N. Vall, State Superintendent of Public Instruction of Utah, says that the ultimate objective of the State Department of Education in so far as in-school television is concerned is a state-wide coverage through all of the multiple television systems that can accommodate the varying needs of individual districts, and permit them some selection.

XLV. VERMONT:

Dr. A. John Holden, Jr., Commissioner of Education of the State of Vermont, states:

> We have instructional needs which could be satisfied or enlarged by the use of broadcast television in such subjects as art, music, elementary science for schools and rural areas where special teachers are unavailable; advanced high school subjects such as art, mathematics, economics, especially for small schools and rural communities. There is need for programs for teachers, especially in the new mathematics and modern foreign languages for elementary teachers. We already have a severe shortage of teachers, especially in foreign languages, mathematics, and science. We believe the national demand for teachers in these areas will create a more acute shortage in rural communities of the future. The University of Vermont has a grant for a survey of the educational television needs of the state to activate one or more stations for Vermont. Our future extension will depend upon the results of this survey.

XLVI. VIRGINIA:

In Richmond, an effort has been made to establish a station in that area and superintendents in the surrounding counties have agreed to a one dollar per pupil funding system.

The College of William and Mary (which includes the College of William and Mary in Williamsburg, Richmond Professional Institute in Richmond and Norfolk Division, and two new junior colleges) is developing a video-tape exchange system with closed-circuit television installations on each campus.

Norfolk Public Schools in cooperation with adjacent county and city school systems in the Hampton Roads-Chesapeake Bay area are activating a station on Channel 15 to serve the schools and communities of that area.

Dr. Woodrow Wilkerson, State Superintendent of Public Instruction, states:

> We see a growing interest in Virginia in the use of television for instructional and educational purposes. This year 224 districts report participation in educational television compared to approximately 150 last year. Thirty-nine subjects are being offered compared to approximately 24 last year. Television is being used primarily for supplemental instruction, motivation, and enrichment.

XLVII. WISCONSIN:

There are two educational television channels on the air in Wisconsin—Channels 10 in Milwaukee and Channel 21 at the University in Madison.

Wisconsin, in the past, has taken the lead in educational broadcasting, and through the state council an effort was made in the early days of television to duplicate its radio network with an educational television network. However, up to the present time, the legislative support needed to provide funds and authority for such an educational television network has not been forthcoming. In the meantime, the development and experimentation on all levels of education are continuing.

XLVIII. WASHINGTON:

Washington has considerable difficulty in television transmission between the western part of the state where the bulk of the population lies, and the eastern areas of the state; but there are plans for the state-wide transmission for educational television to the extent that it is feasible.

XLIX. WEST VIRGINIA:

In the area of higher education there seems to be little concern with broadcast television in West Virginia.

Dr. John R. St. Clair, former State Superintendent of Public Instruction of West Virginia, feels that broadcast television can add to the general enrichment of all areas of curriculum, and can overcome present curriculum deficiencies. He also indicates the great need for the continuing in-service training of teachers.

There is evidence, by the contacts in West Virginia, that a lot of thinking has been done in relation to educational and instructional television; but little action has taken place.

L. WYOMING:

The Executive Assistant to the President, Mr. H. W. Benn, writes:

Wyoming needs educational television. With our sparse and scattered population, the use of this medium is particularly important in providing educational opportunities for the general public and in supplementing the instructional programs of our schools and junior colleges. State-wide multiple channel broadcasting is needed and there is a definite possibility that television teaching for our university students is also needed.

Dr. Velma Linford, the State Superintendent of Public Instruction for Wyoming, is an enthusiastic supporter of educational television. She says that it is needed in the state for in-service teacher education, for curriculum enrichment, and in isolated elementary and secondary schools, for continuing higher education, and for vocational education for courses outside of the schools. She feels that these needs are going to increase in the next ten years rather than decrease, and she explains that the only reason that the State Department of Education has not made other moves to develop broadcast television in Wyoming is the lack of financial resources.

EXCHANGE OF INSTRUCTIONAL TELEVISION MATERIALS: Report of the Nebraska Survey

By Wesley Meierhenry and Jack McBride

Dr. Meierhenry is Associate Dean of Teachers College, Mr. McBride Director of Broadcasting, University of Nebraska. They were co-directors of the Nebraska Study.

MUCH HAS BEEN SAID and written about the use of television in instruction. The rapidity with which developments have taken place, however, has made it very difficult to have a complete inventory as to the purpose to which television is being used for instruction at all levels. The rapid growth of the number of ETV stations along with the rapidly multiplying closed-circuit operations are among the factors which have made our accurate assessment of the status of instructional television very difficult.

Discussions with educators gave sufficient evidence, however, that televised instruction was expanding at a more rapid rate than had been true of any of the other media now used in instruction. The instructional power involved in the mechanism of television is not clear even yet, but the great impact that it does have is clearly recognized. It was for this reason, and others, that the United States Office of Education contracted with the University of Nebraska to conduct a project under the provisions of the National Defense Education Act, Title VII, Part B. The proposal for the study states the problem as follows:

There has been a great development of television programs for direct and/or supplementary instruction at elementary, secondary, and college levels. Programs have been developed in various parts of the country without reference to similar developments in other parts of the country. There has been a minimum of exchange of information on these materials and practically no exchange of the program themselves.

It would appear that there will continue to be a larger number and variety of subject-matter areas covered. In order to conserve time, energy, and money, it would seem urgent to study the present status of the field; to determine the likely future developments, and to recommend a plan, either national or regional, for some type of distribution system.

It was determined very early that the survey should be a national one, with contacts made in all of the states and further that individuals repre-

266

senting all levels of formal public and private education from the elementary, secondary, and college levels. A further criterion was that contact should be made with classroom teachers, administrators, television teachers, television specialists, personnel in state departments of education, executives of associations, both academic as well as professional, foundation officials, and employees of government. It was felt that if a "television policy" was to be developed it should be arrived at only after the most careful as well as thorough questioning of people who might be directly or indirectly related to its use. In order to accomplish these purposes, the study was divided into several phases of information-gathering, synthesizing of data, and summarizing each of which was interrelated.

The first was the appointment of a National Advisory Committee of individuals who were carefully selected in order to take into account the groups with a broad interest in education first of all, and in television secondly. The Advisory Committee included a major university president, a dean of a college of arts and sciences, a dean of a teachers college, the executive secretary of the chief state school officers, a superintendent of schools of a major school system, an experienced television administrator, an outstanding curriculum authority, and a person responsible for working directly with classroom teachers. This National Committee gave overall direction to the project before it began, during its operation, and reviewed and modified the recommendations at its close.

Ten regional consultants were selected to do interviewing in depth. The regional consultants were selected in such a way so that five of them were knowledgeable about and specialists in higher education. The other five were similarly active in the elementary and secondary fields. The use of the regional consultants brought years of experience and insight into the problems of instruction by television to bear upon the problems as identified in the survey. In addition, the consultants were aware of the leaders in instructional television as well as the educational leaders in the geographical areas in which they were located.

The regional consultants helped to develop the semi-structured interview device which formed the basis of the interviews. The regional consultants personally contacted 486 people and the interviews which they conducted were from several minutes to several hours in length. The purpose was to probe as deeply as possible into the thinking of many related to the educational enterprise concerning the present status of education and future developments including television in all of its forms. Following their exhaustive probings, the regional consultants were brought back together for summary reports and the development of conclusions and recommendations.

The co-directors of the study assumed the responsibility of contacting nineteen national organizations and groups for extensive interview sessions. The national groups contacted were among those which have participated in instructional television, or which represent groups which have an interest in either educational administration or classroom instruction or both.

In addition to personal consultations, information-gathering devices were developed which were directed to both open- and closed-circuit television operations. Returns were obtained from all 53 of the ETV stations now on the air and 88 out of the 222 known closed-circuit television operations. The return represented 100 percent of the former population surveyed while the latter represented 40 percent return.

Since much of the increase in televised instruction is likely to be in public elementary and secondary schools it was considered to be desirable to contact a wide sampling of such schools. The sample used was one drawn by Dr. Wilbur Schramm, Director, Institute for Communication Research at Stanford University. It provided for a coverage of 97 percent of all the public school enrollment in the country.

The procedures employed, therefore, included the advice, insights, and suggestions of outstanding educators who served on the advisory panel. The utilization of individuals as regional consultants who understood instructional television in all of its aspects was made for the guidance which they could give personally to the co-directors, but mainly for the penetrating and comprehensive interviewing assignments. Interviews were conducted in many places operating both open- and closed-circuit television stations, but in order to gain as complete a picture as possible, however, direct contact was made to all of the institutions with either of these two kinds of installations. Finally, information was obtained by the sampling of public school districts.

As information was tabulated from these many sources certain definite patterns began to develop, so that definitive conclusions could be reached and appropriate recommendations made. The whole process made possible the bringing together of an enormous mass of information never before gathered together and assembled. The gathering of this mass of information was made possible by both the depth and breadth of the information-gathering techniques.

During the 1958–59 school year, 569 public school systems and 117 colleges and universities in the United States used television for direct instruction in regular courses involving more than 500,000 school children and 100,000 college students. Figures are not available at this time for the 1959–60 school term but a substantial increase is expected to be reported. The 1961–62 school term likely will find a proportionately greater number of schools and students participating in the use of television for instructional purposes. This is evidenced by the increase in the number of participating schools, the increase of population in urban areas in which instruction by television is available, and the increase in the number of operating closed- and open-circuit broadcasting stations.

The data collected from the interview reports of educators at all three levels of education and from a sample of public school systems representing 97 percent of the public school enrollment reveal a definite receptiveness toward the use of television for instructional purposes and a very favorable attitude toward the use of recorded televised instruction. As this study progressed the need became evident for the dissemination of information concerning developments of programs of instruction for use on television and for the exchange of these programs. Further, it was indicated that educational institutions and organizations, both public and private, were duplicating efforts, and expending large amounts of money and talent in developing instruction for use on television without reference to similar developments of programs of instruction elsewhere.

Many excellent live programs of instruction are being presented via television but are not being recorded because of the lack of funds although the merits of recording the instruction are fully realized. It was felt that if more coordination and cooperation existed and programs could be exchanged which were applicable to the curricula, the community, the teachers, administrators, and students, the local school systems could provide a better quality of instruction and still maintain the individuality of their community and school system. Many school systems are recording their programs of instruction for their own use since it affords an opportunity to preview the instruction before presenting, to evaluate, to revise when necessary, to use repeatedly, to defray expenses through the possibility of wider dispersion, and to facilitate scheduling.

LIVE INSTRUCTION

The amount of instruction via television reported as being programmed *live* at the elementary-secondary, and college levels by the 53 ETV stations, and the 88 closed-circuit operations reporting for this study, has increased considerably the past few years. This growth is reported respectively in Table 1 as follows:

TABLE 1

Live Programming by 53 ETV Stations

Number of courses programmed *live*	1957–58	1958–59	1959–60	1960–61
Elementary	95	135	204	267
Secondary	82	111	132	145
College	79	91	161	157
Total	256	337	497	569

TABLE 1 (Continued)

Live Programming by 88 Closed-Circuit Operations

Number of courses programmed *live*	1957–58	1958–59	1959–60	1960–61
Elementary	26	87	115	71
Secondary	10	32	37	27
College	95	135	159	162
Total	131	254	311	260

Table 2 is a summary of the recorded televised instruction for elementary, secondary, college, postgraduate, and in-service education reported by the 53 ETV stations. This summary is believed self-explanatory with the exceptions of Column 5, *Types of Recording*, and Column 7, *Instructional Purpose*.

Column 5	Column 7
K—Kinescope recording	T—Total Teaching
V—Video-tape recording	S—Supplementary Instruction
F—Film recording	E—Enrichment Instruction
	R—Remedial Instruction

The ETV stations reported 199 recorded courses at the elementary level with 96 currently available for exchange. Seventy of the 103 recorded courses at the secondary level were reported as available for exchange as were 70 of the 135 recorded courses at the college level. Eleven of the 16 recorded courses for postgraduate and in-service education were listed as available.

A similar summary of the 83 recorded programs reported by the 88 closed-circuit operations is given in the major report as is each recorded course for each subject and grade level.

The reasons for the recorded courses to be listed as unavailable were not given on the information schedule used to survey the use and availability of recorded televised instruction; however, this information was revealed on some of the interview reports. Some of the reasons given, none of which seem insurmountable, were as follows:

The material was recorded for their own use, and at the time of recording it was not conceived that someone else could or would use the instruction.

Proper and adequate contractual and residual arrangements had not been agreed upon by the producer, teacher, holder of title, and others.

After reviewing and evaluating the instruction, it was apparent that adequate revision would be necessary before the holder of title would want to release the instruction.

Copies of the recorded instruction are not available for distribution because of the cost of duplicating.

TABLE 2
Summary of Recorded Televised Instruction
for Elementary, Secondary, College, and In-Service Teacher Training Use

Subject Area	Number of recorded courses in each subject area	Total number of lessons in all courses	Range of the number of lessons in each course	Average number of lessons for each course	Range of the length of lessons in minutes
Elementary Recorded Instruction (K-6)					
Science	53	1,101	3–128	20.7	15–30
Mathematics	11	171	3–69	15.5	14–30
Social studies	40	517	4–90	12.9	15–30
Language arts	28	760	6–189	27.1	15–30
French	9	698	15–128	77.6	14–30
Spanish	17	904	8–130	53.2	10–30
Russian	2	180	90	90	90
Music	28	413	1–72	14.7	14–30
Art	11	66	2–16	6	15–30
Total	199	4,810			
Secondary Recorded Instruction (7–12)					
Science	27	1,183	7–160	43.8	15–30
Mathematics	6	315	4–126	52.5	20–30
Social studies	31	511	4–128	16.5	15–120
Language arts	18	526	7–80	29.2	15–30
Music	4	64	15–60	16	8–35
Art	5	50	8–13	10	15–30
Others	12	161	4–36	13.4	15–120
Total	103	2,810			
College—Recorded Instruction					
Science	21	1,110	8–170	52.9	30–50
Mathematics	22	1,039	15–160	47.2	29–45
Social science	17	601	12–90	31.2	30–50
Language	33	1,043	4–87	31.6	30–50
Philosophy	14	571	30–90	40.8	30–60
Psychology	8	257	10–75	32.1	30–50
Business	11	424	10–82	38.5	29–50
Fine arts	3	98	20–48	32.6	30
Agriculture	2	79	34–45	39.5	45
*Education—(History of)	4	119	15–36	29.7	29–30
Total	135	5,341			
In-Service Teacher Training (Not classified as to grade unless specified)					
Total	16	278	2–42		25–45
Aggregate of Recorded Courses at all Levels of Instruction Telecast Over the 53 ETV Stations					
Total	453	13,239			

* One is a postgraduate course.

TABLE 2 (Continued)

Data from 53 Educational Television Stations

Types of recording			Number of courses with study guide	Instructional purpose				Ownership				Availability for use and exchange (with reservations)	
K	V	F		T	S	E	R	O	L	P	E	YES	YES
32	15	6	40	4	30	19	–	45	5	2	1	21	32
10	1	–	8	1	5	5	–	9	2	–	–	6	5
32	6	2	26	–	21	19	–	36	4	–	–	21	19
19	9	–	22	2	14	12	–	24	2	–	2	14	14
4	5	–	9	6	3	–	–	5	3	1	–	7	2
8	9	–	15	5	6	6	–	14	2	–	1	12	5
2	–	–	2	2	–	–	–	2	–	–	–	2	–
20	7	1	22	–	17	11	–	23	4	–	1	10	18
11	–	–	9	–	10	1	–	11	–	–	–	3	8
138	52	9	153	20	106	73	0	169	22	3	5	96	103
10	11	6	24	9	10	8	–	22	4	–	1	17	10
3	2	1	4	2	3	1	–	6	–	–	–	3	3
21	5	5	23	1	15	16	–	22	7	2	–	23	8
13	5	1	17	7	8	3	–	11	7	–	–	13	5
1	1	2	4	–	2	2	–	1	3	–	–	4	–
4	–	1	5	–	2	3	–	3	2	–	–	4	1
7	3	2	7	2	6	4	–	6	4	–	2	6	6
59	27	18	84	21	46	37	0	71	27	2	3	70	33
10	14	2	17	17	4	–	–	16	3	–	2	13	8
15	14	1	19	18	4	–	1	18	3	–	1	12	10
10	13	–	10	12	4	3	–	17	–	–	–	9	8
19	25	–	19	19	25	–	–	22	6	5	–	16	17
5	9	–	10	10	4	1	–	12	1	–	1	5	9
4	4	–	2	7	–	2	–	8	–	–	–	4	4
7	9	–	9	8	2	1	–	11	–	–	–	5	6
2	1	–	2	2	–	1	–	3	–	–	–	3	–
–	2	–	–	2	–	–	–	2	–	–	–	2	–
2	4	–	2	3	1	–	–	4	–	–	–	1	3
74	95	3	90	98	44	8	1	113	13	5	4	70	65
6	8	2	12	14	–	2	–	8	4	2	2	11	5
277	182	32	274	153	196	119	1	361	66	12	14	247	206

TELEVISION RECORDING EQUIPMENT

If recorded televised instruction is to be used widely, the necessary recording and play-back equipment must be available. Thus, it had to be ascertained what equipment, if any, was in use at the ETV stations and closed-circuit installations. Thirty-six of the 53 ETV stations reported film recording equipment available; 35 stations have kinescope recording equipment, and 50 have video-tape recording and play-back equipment available. Four stations reported having more than one video-tape recorder.

INSTRUCTIONAL TELEVISION AND THE PUBLIC SCHOOLS

In the preceding sections of Chapter IV emphasis was given to the transmission and recording of televised instruction. It is certainly necessary to have ETV stations and recording equipment, but it is possible that school systems might not utilize television even if available. It was essential, therefore, to obtain some picture of the extent to which public schools were now using televised instruction and the purposes it served. An information form was sent to public schools, according to a sample developed by Schramm as described in Chapter III, to gather facts about the present use of television for instructional purposes by the public school systems.

In the school systems categorized in Group 1, which have one-third of all the public school enrollment, instructional television was reported as being used by two-thirds of the districts that reported, as shown in Table 3.

TABLE 3

Public School Systems Using Television for Instructional Purposes

Group	Number of Schools Reporting	Using Television	Percent
1. 12,000 or more............ 162		110	68
2. 3,000–11,999 174		63	36
3. 150–2,999 140		22	16
Total 476		195	41

Assuming that the schools not reporting would have been using television to about the same degree as those who did reply, approximately 8,000,000 of the 36,000,000 pupils enrolled in public schools would have been in systems that reported they were making some use of instructional television. When the Groups 2 and 3 are similarly considered, it appears that another three to four million students were in schools in which television instruction was provided. Therefore, approximately one-third of the students are in schools using television and do represent potential receivers of television instruction if it were made available in one or more subjects at every grade level.

Reports from the 283 school systems not using television indicated a strong desire exists to use this medium for instruction, but broadcast and receiving facilities are currently unavailable. Thus, there appears to be a much greater likely use of television if and when television transmitters become more generally available.

The extent to which school systems are using recorded televised instruction is indicated in Table 4.

TABLE 4

Public School Systems Using Recorded Television Instruction

Group	Number of schools reporting using TV	Using recorded televised instruction	Percent
1. 12,000 or more.............. 110		61	55
2. 3,000–11,999 63		19	30
3. 150–2,999 22		15	68
Total 195		95	49

Almost one-half of the school systems reported using television are doing so with some pre-recorded materials. It is interesting to note that 55 percent of the largest schools (Group 1) are using one or more recorded instructional series where, presumably, the resources would make possible the greatest number of live telecasts.

School systems reported that recorded televised instruction was being utilized for total, supplementary, enrichment, or remedial instruction. A definition of each of these terms is indicated earlier in this chapter. Although not listed in Table 5, there were four recorded televised courses listed as in-service teacher education by schools in Group 1. Again, the larger schools made greater proportional use of television for direct instruction.

The summary of the reasons for using recorded televised instruction is shown in Table 6.

The use of television for the "improvement of instruction" was identified more frequently than all of the other reasons combined. The use of television to "decrease school costs" was checked by the least number of school systems.

Table 7 indicates whether those schools using recorded televised instruction reported in Table 4 were doing so from sources other than their own. Forty percent of all the school systems using recorded televised instruction obtained part or all of their material from sources outside their

TABLE 5

Type of Recorded Instruction

Group		Total	Instruction		
			Supplementary	Enrichment	Remedial
1.	12,000 or more	12	32	24	3
2.	3,000–11,999	7	9	2	1
3.	150–2,999	1	4	4	0
	Total	20	45	30	4

TABLE 6

Reasons for Using Recorded Instruction

Group		Increased enrollment	Improvement of instruction	Curriculum expanded	Reduce costs	Teacher shortage
1.	12,000 or more	4	32	19	1	4
2.	3,000–11,999	1	9	2	1	0
3.	150–2,999	–	4	4	1	1
	Total	5	45	25	3	5

TABLE 7

Public School Systems Using Recorded Instruction from Other Sources

Group	Number of schools using recorded instruction	Recorded instruction from other sources		Reasons for not using recorded instruction from other sources
		Number	Percent	
1.	61	26	42	Not available
2.	19	9	47	Not available
3.	15	3	20	Not available
Total	95	38	40	

system. Again, the larger school systems made more use of material produced outside their systems than did the small schools. The reason for not using recorded televised instruction was said to be "lack of availability of material."

The recorded instruction used from other sources was received from state departments of education, universities, other school systems, ETV stations, NETRC, and commercial enterprises. The respondents indicated that they received information about the existence of other recorded programs of instruction from ETV stations, the NETRC, state departments of education, and personal contacts. There was a definite willingness on the part of these people to use recorded instruction from other sources if it met the established criteria of their system.

The school systems indicated that they received little, if any, information on the sources of recorded televised instruction, and stated that a system that will provide complete up-to-date listings of available instructional series should be established. Thirty-six of the 246 school systems reporting on this item indicated that they were receiving information, whereas 210, or 85 percent, replied negatively.

Since public schools have been and, in all probability, will continue to be the largest users of recorded televised instruction, it was important to obtain their suggestions regarding the location and types of distribution centers. Table 8 summarizes this most important information.

TABLE 8

Exchange and Distribution Plan

Group		Regional Center	National Center	Commercial Center	State Dept. Center	County Center
1.	12,000 or more	99	40	9	7	2
2.	3,000–11,999	105	26	17	15	2
3.	150–2,999	69	8	8	1	2
	Total	273	74	34	23	6

The public school systems decisively favored the regional center exchange and distribution plan. There were a great variety of suggestions about the organization of regional centers, but the preferred plan was through established audio-visual instructional centers. It was the opinion that a separate television division should be organized within an audio-visual center that already had experience in serving the schools on a regional basis, or that could be expanded for regional service. Respondents stressed that the national and regional centers should be organized with educators involved and the needs of the consumer of instructional programming adequately recognized.

DISPOSITION TO USE TELEVISION FOR INSTRUCTIONAL PURPOSES

The exhaustive and thorough interviews conducted by the ten regional consultants, each an experienced specialist in the field of instructional television himself, clearly corroborated the findings and trends revealed earlier. As the study progressed it became increasingly evident that there was a need for the dissemination of information concerning developments related to the use of instructional television and the exchange of such programming. This need continues to increase in direct proportion to the activation and expansion of facilities and projects. It was clearly evident that the educational institutions and organizations, both public and private, have been needlessly duplicating many efforts and expending large amounts of money and talent in developing instructional programs without reference to similar developments elsewhere. During the course of their interviewing, the regional consultants frequently reported requests for an informational exchange, so that research findings and experiences could be profitably utilized, duplication avoided, and local programming strengthened.

There is consensus in the field that the limitations and restrictions of time, staff, facilities, and budget as related to local origination of instructional television programming are, even under optimum conditions, real and formidable. Given the use of certain quality recorded instruction, which in no way weakens, but rather strengthens the local program, the individual educational project could direct limited personnel and production funds toward fewer courses, thereby improving local live television instruction as well.

A wide range of opinions and attitudes toward all aspects of the use and distribution of recorded televised instruction was provided through processes described earlier. Upon analysis, however, certain additional trends and generalizations emerged primarily from the interviews conducted by the regional consultants, and can be summarized as follows:

1. There is real and increasing interest in the use and exchange of recorded televised instruction.

2. The school systems with the broadest experience in using television within the classroom are generally most amenable to recorded televised instruction and consider it a means of improving instruction.

3. Clearly defined functional and operational plans for an exchange system have not been agreed upon although the benefits to be derived from a workable system are fully realized.

4. Of those currently using instructional television, and potential consumers as well, there was considerable evidence of a willingness to support the reasonable financial costs of recorded instructional exchange and distribution.

5. Institutions hesitant to use recorded televised instruction will be less apprehensive when shown that quality materials will clearly improve their curricula and quite possibly at less cost than that necessary to originate such instruction locally. Evidence of this is revealed by the use of the series "Parlons Français."

6. The use of quality recorded instruction in an effective and efficient manner may help provide a breakthrough in traditional teaching methods.

7. As additional information is made available through publications, workshops, courses, meetings, and actual involvement in television instruction, the fear of the classroom teacher of being replaced is rapidly being dispelled. Television will not bring about technological unemployment to the teacher, but, used wisely and effectively, television will definitely improve the quality of instruction. In addition, television often permits the redeployment of educational facilities, resources and personnel in such a manner as to bring about additional educational services, smaller teaching groups, individual counseling, etc.

8. Recorded televised instruction for in-service teacher education will be utilized much more fully in the near future.

9. The state-supported colleges and universities, large and small, and the large private institutions are using television, or are willing to use it, and will consider using recorded televised instruction from other sources when it is superior to the instruction that they can provide or if it will strengthen their curricula. The small private institutions prefer to limit enrollment in keeping with resources, but some did reveal a willingness to investigate the use of television.

10. Schools at the elementary, secondary, and junior college levels are increasing enrollment and developing at an alarming rate as are the colleges and universities. Adequate staffing with competent people is a serious problem, and the use of recorded televised instruction from a parent organization, established institution, or other sources is foreseen as a means of providing future quality instruction.

11. While there is general recognition that the problems inherent in the establishment of a system of exchange and distribution are many and varied, to date few are able clearly to describe the total problem in all its complexity, let alone provide recommendations or solutions.

Those interviewed expressed a definite interest in recorded televised instruction if it were made available under a combination of the following conditions:

Recorded Televised Instruction Must:

1. be of good educational and technical quality.
2. meet the needs of the consumer.
3. be educationally sound.
4. be accompanied by a good teacher's guide and other necessary materials.
5. be produced by an experienced television teacher and crew, and the instruction must be tried and modified, if necessary, before being recorded and exchanged.
6. not be too expensive, and great profits above production costs should not be expected.
7. be constantly reviewed with provisions for revision and updating.
8. be superior to that produced locally.

FEASIBILITY AND ORGANIZATION FOR A SYSTEM OF EXCHANGE AND DISTRIBUTION

The amount of programmed instruction is evidence that a sufficient quantity of recorded televised instruction is available to warrant the development of pilot regional center and/or a national center for distribution. A minimum of necessary equipment is available for recording and play-back purposes and the public school systems are already utilizing a considerable amount of recorded televised instruction and are willing to use more. Although the need for quality recorded instruction was mentioned repeatedly, the data suggested that this quality would not improve measurably until some type of distribution system was initiated that would alleviate the necessity of this great amount of duplication of time, energies, and resources. Eliminating this unnecessary duplication of recorded instruction would afford institutions and organizations at all levels of education the possibility of expending equal resources and yet securing better material. This could be done by providing fewer programs but doing them well and using recorded series from other sources.

Support for the development of some system of distribution had been suggested previous to this study. ETV station managers confronted with a dire need for instructional materials have long clamored for the establishment of a system or systems of exchange. A seminar held in 1959 by the Division of Audio-Visual Instructional Service of the National Educational Association concluded with 13 recommendations for using television. One of these recommendations supports the exchange of recorded programs and reads as follows:

> We should initiate a means by which a voluntary exchange of video-taped resources can be made possible on a nation-wide scale. If local educational television stations are to exchange programs with other stations, school districts with other school districts, then there must be initiated a means by which this exchange of video resources can be made possible on a national scale. No individual school district can, or should, undertake to produce all of its television programming, any more than it can undertake the production of all its own films or other audio-visual materials. Each community has resources unique to its own area which could form the basis for a program series which could profitably be shared with many other communities. For example, a series of programs produced by the Detroit Public Schools on Greenfield Village Museum could be taped for use by many school districts; an Americana series featuring historic shrines throughout the United States and produced by local districts has already been mentioned earlier in this report; similar series on industrial and economic resources of a given area might also be exchanged. This would encourage local initiative in programming and yet be a means of making the unique resources of one area available to other areas.

It is that education has always been a local and state function in the United States. Because of this historic development each school system as well as each teacher within the system has been autonomous to a considerable degree. The United States does not have a national school system in the same way that many other countries, especially those of Europe, have insofar as common curricular content is concerned. As a consequence, local school systems adopt instructional materials for a variety of reasons including local application, philosophy of the school system, and the respect for the authors and producers of the material.

Because instructional television has implications for use where many school systems are involved frequently cutting across state boundaries, it is necessary to understand the unique interaction and status of the various academic and professional associations and organizations in this country. If these are not understood and taken into account it is possible to encounter almost complete rejection of programs by local educational institutions and the staff within them.

In higher education most of the organizations are academic and each related to a specific discipline or a part of a discipline. These groups are generally organized on a vertical basis to include the specialists in such fields as the American Psychological Association, American Library Association, and the Mathematical Association of America. The members of these organizations may have some interest in related disciplines but for status and professional reasons their major attention is given to the organization of their own subject-matter area. On college and university campuses, therefore, groups such as the American Association of University Professors and the Association of Higher Education of the NEA, which are horizontal in organization to include all disciplines, do not elicit the same kind of loyalty and support as do the organizations in the content areas.

When one moves to the secondary school level there are organizations which are both vertical and horizontal in nature. Such groups as the National Council for the Social Studies, the National Council of Teachers of English, and the National Council of Geography Teachers, are examples of vertical groups where the major emphasis is on content and subject matter. Other groups, such as the Association for Supervision and Curriculum Development, the Department of Audio-Visual Instruction, and the National Association of Secondary School Principals, are groups which are organized horizontally, which include individuals with all types of subject-matter background and where the major force which brings the individuals together is a professional one. At the elementary level most of the organizations are horizontal in nature such as the Department of Classroom Teachers, International Association of Childhood Education, and Department of Rural Education. It is true that many educators belong to more than one of these groups but the groups themselves give major attention to either content or professional matters.

If, therefore, a local school system is to be receptive to the use of a recorded televised course, for example third-grade arithmetic, it will desire to know if individuals with stature in the field of arithmetic, teaching methods, and in their professional associations have given their general approval to the course in addition to having it taught by a strong television teacher. The expertness of the teacher will not be sufficient alone to convince a school or group of schools that use should be made of the material.

For widespread success, therefore, it will be necessary to develop appropriate advisory committees representing the whole range of educational interests of the United States. Representation must include academic and professional interests, administrative and supervisory personnel, staffs of state departments of education, and classroom teachers. This group can give over-all direction to the development of sound policies of operation and identity the desirable areas for recorded televised instruction. Parenthetically, it should be noted that the Advisory Committee on this study were individuals with these types of interests and backgrounds. After the general areas are defined it will be necessary for the over-all committee to appoint subcommittees dealing with each content or subject-matter area. These sub-committees will have content specialists, instructional specialists, and representatives of the appropriate professional group or groups working with a television production team.

Other obstacles and problems are such matters as legal ones on certification of teachers, regional compacts of school districts, involvement of professional and academic societies to gain acceptance of recorded materials, and rigidity of the curricula to accommodate nationally prepared programs. The study has considered these various problems which were on the periphery of the main problem investigated and brought together materials and experiences which will help to point the way toward their solution. Against this background of study, gathering and synthesizing of data, the following conclusions and recommendations were made:

CONCLUSIONS

1. Considerable instruction is being presented locally at the elementary, secondary, and higher levels of education by means of both broadcast and closed-circuit television.
2. A backlog of recorded televised instruction is available for distribution.
3. The establishment of systems for the distribution of recorded televised instruction is urgently needed.
4. An increasing number of institutions, according to substantial evidence, wish to use recorded televised instruction.
5. Further study needs to be made to discover the best methods of utilizing recorded televised instruction in classrooms.
6. The dissemination of information concerning recorded televised instruction is needed.
7. Production and distribution of materials appropriate for use by tele-

vision should be continued by both commercial companies and educational institutions.

RECOMMENDATIONS

On the basis of the data and reports from representatives at all levels of education in the United States, the following recommendations are made concerning (1) policy decisions, (2) curriculum research, (3) personnel training, (4) production, and (5) distribution of recorded television instruction.

1. A nonprofit national center for recorded televised instruction should be established. The purposes to be served are as follows:

Purposes

a. The conducting and encouraging of surveys, analyses, and studies to determine which curriculum objectives can be served best by recorded televised instruction at the national level.

b. The encouraging and facilitating of the production of high quality recorded televised programs and supplementary materials to meet the curriculum objectives.

c. The conducting and supporting of organizations and institutions in experimenting with the utilization of recorded televised instruction.

d. The service as a cataloguer, disseminator, and distributor of recorded televised instructional programs and supplementary materials.

e. The facilitating of the selection and training of personnel for all types of instruction by television.

In order to accomplish the purpose of education at the elementary, secondary, and college levels, it is essential for the production and distribution center at the national level to fulfill the following:

Provisions

a. The establishment of a national advisory committee broadly representative of the various academic and professional interests in education. This committee should participate in the development of broad policies for the operation of the center and should encourage the acceptance of the material by both individuals and institutions. The national advisory committee would, in turn, appoint additional committees, or designate logical organizations, to develop individual course content for the production and/or distribution of materials.

b. The establishment, if within an existing national center, of a separate and distinct division dealing with recorded televised instruction.

c. The appointment as administrator of the division of someone who has interests and background in both television and education.

d. The establishment and maintenance of liaison and coordination facilities with regional distribution centers, as these develop.

The national center as designated should demonstrate that it possesses the following:

Characteristics and conditions

a. Experience in the production and circulation of materials at a national level.

b. Equipment and facilities which might be developed further at minimum cost.

c. Status as an institution of quality among educators, as well as among those interested in the medium of television.

d. Staff, either existent or available, experienced in both educational television and distribution of materials.

The reasons for national distribution are as follows:

Reasons

a. A need exists for complete information and evaluation of all recorded televised instructional programs now available for distribution to the nation.

b. Some subject-matter areas possess sufficient content similarity throughout the United States so that national distribution of locally produced materials would be feasible.

c. Many institutions wish to secure materials from such a national center.

d. This national center, with the assistance of such an advisory committee as has been described, could provide for nation-wide modifications in content and methodology, brought about by a rapidly changing society.

e. Available human and physical resources of an institution or a region could be shared by a great number of consumers.

2. Nonprofit regional production and distribution centers for recorded televised instruction should be developed. The *purposes* to be served are as follows:

Purposes

a. The conducting and encouraging of surveys, analyses, and studies to determine which curriculum objectives can be served best by recorded televised instruction at the regional and local levels.

b. The encouraging and facilitating of the productions of high quality recorded televised programs and supplementary materials to meet the curriculum objectives.

c. The conducting and supporting of organizations and institutions in experimenting with the utilization of recorded televised instruction within the region.

d. The service as a cataloguer, disseminator, and distributor of recorded televised instructional programs and supplementary materials.

e. The facilitating of the selection and training of personnel for all types of instruction by television.

In order to accomplish the purpose of education at the elementary, secondary, and college levels, it is essential for the production and distribution centers at the regional level to accept the following:

Provisions

a. The establishment of a regional advisory committee broadly representative of the various academic and professional interests in education. This committee should participate in the development of broad policies for the operation of the center and should encourage acceptance of the materials by both individuals and institutions. The regional advisory committee would, in turn, appoint additional committees, or designate logical organizations, to develop individual course content for the production and/or distribution of materials.

b. The appointment as administrator of the division of someone who has broad interests and background in television and in education.

c. The establishment and maintenance of liaison and coordination facilities with the national center as it develops.

The regional centers should be developed in the following manner:

Characteristics and conditions

Two pilot centers should be developed. One would probably be in an area in which state and local control of education rate as a very important factor, and which at the same time has strong intraregional social, economic, political, and cultural relationships. A second pilot center should be established in an area in which regionalism has received considerable thought and has achieved some development. This would be in an area in which the states, although conscious of their individual roles, have already experienced joint action in one or more projects because of the basic similarities among the people and the geographical area. The regional centers might well be located at educational institutions that are experienced in the production and distribution of well-planned and well-produced instructional materials on a state and regional basis.

Furthermore, there should be close cooperation and liaison between (1) the regional centers, and (2) each region and the national center. Overlapping membership on advisory committees might be one way of achieving and maintaining these close relationships.

The reasons for the development of regional centers are as follows:

Reasons

a. Schools, especially public schools, evidence a greater willingness to accept materials from a regional center.

b. Initial usage of materials will be increased because of personal relationships with the people involved.

c. Economies are possible because of (1) transportation and communication, and (2) probable joint use of equipment and facilities between regional and/or national centers.

d. Resources within a region could be shared by a greater number of consumers.

e. Similarities in subject content exist in many regions of the nation.

f. Separate listings of material appropriate for regional use are highly advisable.

PROBLEMS NEEDING FURTHER STUDY

This study has identified and considered other serious problems which need further attention if regional and national production and distribution of recorded televised instruction and supplementary materials are to be facilitated.

1. A variety of legal problems need further study. Foremost among these are the ones concerning compensation to television teachers for the re-use of materials. The use of commercially prepared materials on educational television programs also needs further study.
2. State and local laws affecting the use and distribution of recorded televised instruction need attention.
3. Further studies need to be made regarding costs in order to determine the economical feasibility of live and/or recorded televised instruction.
4. New industrial developments need to be studied constantly since they change dramatically such factors as cost, flexibility of scheduling, and facility of recording instruction.

FACILITIES FOR INSTRUCTIONAL TELEVISION

By C. R. Carpenter and L. P. Greenhill

Dr. Carpenter is Director, and Dr. Greenhill Associate Director, of the Division of Academic Research and Service, Pennsylvania State University.

INTRODUCTION

THE PURPOSE OF THIS CHAPTER is to describe systematically certain instructional functions and related television facilities. The descriptions are in language which, it is hoped, is understandable by educators; technical engineering language is avoided. Furthermore, the descriptions are limited to television activities and facilities which have become known fairly recently as *instructional television.* Instructional television is understood to refer to educational efforts using television which have as their purposes the production, origination, and distribution of instructional content for people to learn; efforts in which television is used as the principal or as an auxiliary medium of communication. This conception includes closed-circuit television, limited range broadcasts and even extended broadcast activities (e.g., the Continental Classroom and Airborne Television) which handle information specifically organized and produced for learning.

Learning is defined as changes in the behavior of individuals and members of audiences; changes which are related to the purposes of schools, colleges, universities, or continuing adult education. The scope of *instructional* television is more specific than that of *educational* television and very different from commercial television. In brief, instructional television is closely related to the work of organized formal educational institutions.

For the purposes of this chapter, television facilities are described from broadly functional points of view. The questions are: What are the instructional functions that are required and what kinds of equipment and facilities are needed to serve these functions? The problems arise of planning for and selecting *appropriate* facilities for defined instructional tasks. Facilities are considered, furthermore, not only to include cameras, microphones, control apparatus, cables, transmitters, and receivers, but also auxiliary equipment in studios, control rooms, and the reception environment or classrooms. Further extensions of descriptions include, for example, communication systems to permit interaction of students with teachers, with each other, and with other sources of instruction. Thus, facilities for instructional television are viewed as being assemblies of communication systems which mediate essential functions involved in teaching and learning.

When this viewpoint is accepted, it becomes necessary, in addition, to specify how existing and available facilities might be improved, and to suggest what new kinds of equipment need to be developed and made available for practical uses in creating favorable conditions for learning.

THE TEACHING-LEARNING CYCLE AND THE ROLE OF TELEVISION

The role of television when employed in education is viewed as part of a teaching-learning cycle. A generalized conception of this cycle consists of eight components: (1) There are organized units of information or content. (2) The information is made available on some medium (print, film, tape, as a demonstration with the teacher, etc.), for television origination and distribution. (3) The organized information is presented (displayed) in some mode and usually in several different modes. (4) The instruction is observed or perceived by persons who are expected and who themselves expect to learn. (5) The learners react to the presented materials. (6) Changes in behavior occur, i.e., learning takes place. (7) There is some kind of assessment of the learning by the learners themselves or by others. (8) Usually there are arrangements for reviews, practice repetitions, condensed summaries, associated with different kinds and degrees of "reinforcements" and "rewards." Thus learning of information is "integrated," remembered, and used.

A perspective of television exists when these basic components of the teaching-learning cycle are considered and the question is asked: Where does television fit appropriately into the cycle? Stated differently, which of the essential functions or components involved in the cycle can be performed primarily or in an auxiliary way by television equipment and facilities?

It is clear that all of the essential instructing and learning functions cannot be accomplished by television. For example, television cannot be a main means of collecting and organizing information. Television does not store information. It transmits it immediately unless linked with a source of information storage. Standard television systems cannot sense and record the learning responses of students unless supplementary communication systems are employed.

Essentially, television systems serve as mediators between sources of information to be learned and the people who would learn. The selection and preparation of the learning materials, their organization and arrangement for learning, and the choices of the kinds of modes of communication to use, i.e., print, commentary, photography (still or motion), real objects and people, are made prior to the activation of television facilities.

The straight line mediation functions of television are: (1) the electronic sensing of the information (encoding), (2) the transmission or distribution of the information to within the sensory reaches of people, (3) the representation of the information in such a way as to be within the visual and auditory sensory capacities and the conceptual abilities of the people who must perceive it in order to learn.

In one sense *instructional* television is a misnomer; television *per se* does not instruct, it does not educate, it does not learn. Television itself is a *tabula rasa*, a blank sheet or a clear channel. It is a potential mediator of instruction, it is an instrument, which may be used to provide some but not all of the conditions necessary for most kinds of learning to occur. It is a facility which makes it possible, but does not necessarily insure, that interactions occur between the information to be learned and the learner. Within the limits of functions which television facilities can be expected to perform, the effects on learning depend on how the facilities are used, by and for whom.

The general functions of instructional television, conventionally viewed, can be classified into three categories:

1. *Origination* of programs, video and audio, which have been produced or recorded for television in such a manner as to make it possible to handle them with television equipment.
2. *Distribution* of programs of instruction by cables, microwave, or broadcast used either singly or in combination.
3. *Presentation* of the instructional materials in some manner, either by television receivers or projected on screens accompanied by sound.

The main body of this chapter will describe the apparatus and facilities which are used in each of these three categories. Under each category, origination, distribution, presentation, and associated equipment will also be described.

KINDS OF USES OF TELEVISION IN INSTRUCTION

It may be useful at this point to describe briefly some of the main instructional-learning uses of television. Another way of stating this subject is to ask the question: What are the information handling potentials of existing television facilities relative to the provision of conditions which are necessary for learning?

Modes of information.—Television has the capability of handling information in several forms or modes. The two general modes are video and audio. These correspond in turn to the human sense modalities of seeing and hearing. The equipment for handling these different kinds of signals actually consists of parallel physical systems, involving video and audio wave frequencies. Furthermore, in general the video mode can accept such materials as real objects, persons and situations, pictorial and graphic representations, and a wide range of symbols including conventional printing. The pictorial-graphic images are "picked up" by television cameras and in due course presented on screens in *two* dimensions. Only limited use of three dimensional television has been made up to this time. The stereoscopic dimension is unnecessary for most kinds of learning.

Color is another mode-quality which can be mediated by color television systems. However, color systems are about three times as complex, expensive, and difficult to maintain as the corresponding image orthicon or vidicon black-and-white systems. The real advantage of color systems for learning most subject matter remains to be demonstrated. Furthermore, for most purposes the questions of color fidelity and its effects on learning require research.

The different modes of televised information in many combinations and patterns can be employed and used practically for a variety of instructional purposes. It appears desirable to outline and to give some examples of these practical uses because it is in terms of them, and at this level of definition, that educational administrators and teachers are most likely to make choices and decisions about the employment of television facilities in their school systems, institutions, or communities.

Extending instruction.—The principal use of television where systems have been in operation for several years is that of extending instruction. This is sometimes called the "instructor multiplier" function of television. Essentially, for this function, television is employed to originate instructional programs produced "live" by a single teacher or a teaching team, and through some kind of distribution system make the instruction available to students. A single source of instruction can be distributed for reception to any needed number of classrooms and auditoria of varying sizes in one or several classroom buildings in an area of space. Thus, one instructor or one originating source can serve many class groups in different rooms distributed over an area within an institution, city, or region. Therefore, the possibility exists by means of television to have one instructor perform the functions usually performed by many instructors.

There are several possible variations of this basic pattern. Multiple television systems, either in the same or different locations, can originate simultaneously a number of different programs of instruction. Also, depending on the kind and extent of the distribution system, the instruction can be made available to students or pupils in different schools of an area, community, city, or political subdivision. In an institution, instruction can be made available in buildings and spaces other than classrooms, such as libraries, student unions, dormitory lounges, and dormitory rooms. Furthermore, the single lecturer, team of lecture-demonstrators, panel, or other sources of instruction can be channeled into varied patterns to classrooms or to individual student study places. Thus, it can be seen that television may be used as a means of extending instruction or as an "instructor multiplier."

Demonstration magnifier.—Television systems can be used to magnify visual demonstrations, especially of small objects and microscopic specimens, to provide for students a close and clear camera-lens view. Similarly, sound can be picked up, distributed, and amplified for clear auditory perception. This facility provides for learners a necessary condition for the observation of materials and for learning. Advantages can be arranged compared with conventional lecture-demonstrations. In addition, the TV cameras can be put in positions for close viewing where only one or a few students could be placed and the demonstrations can proceed without interference from student observers.

Observatory television.—Experience has demonstrated the usefulness of even simple low-cost television systems for remote observational purposes. A television camera can be placed where it is dangerous for observers to be stationed. Observatory television is being used to show experiments where there are risks of explosions, for observing close-ups of operations in medical and dental schools, for observing patients, and, especially, persons in clinical psychological, psychiatric, and guidance interview situations. It can be used where the presence of observers might interfere with the events being observed. In education, observatory television is employed in classrooms for picking up authentic demonstrations or examples of classroom procedures and remoting them to teacher trainees for study and analysis. The presence of the observers in the classroom usually interferes with the normal procedures and this problem is solved by the use of television. Finally, it is possible by using mobile units and film or video-tape recording equipment to bring remote events into classrooms and laboratories for observational and learning purposes.

Distribution and presentation of recorded materials.—Television systems are proving very useful for distributing and presenting *recorded* instructional materials. With television chains for motion picture films and slides, with video- and audio-tape recorders, television systems are useful as a means of making available to students wide varieties of recorded programs. These materials are used as parts of programs which may also include "live" presentations, and the ease with which they can be "cut in" to live action instruction generally has the result of increasing the amounts of visual-graphic-sound recording materials used in teaching. Video- and audio-tape recorders provide a source of instruction and a ready means of storing, scheduling, and retrieving information. These factors make it practical to use television for repeating series of lectures or lecture-demonstrations. Thus, it becomes unnecessary for science instructors, for example, to repeat a number of times the same lecture-demonstrations to accommodate the students' class schedules. It is not improbable, finally, that most instructional films in schools and universities may be distributed and presented to classes by means of new arrangements of television systems, i.e., banks of film chains which can be used to distribute filmed materials on call to any connected classrooms.

Television and programmed instruction.—The current interests and developments in the area of programmed materials for teaching machines emphasize two problems for instructional television facilities: First, there is a continuing need to develop and improve lessons or courses for distribution over television, especially for the purpose of making maximum use of the potentials of this facility. Not only are the new types of lesson and course formats needed but new and imaginative production patterns should be created for using learning principles as a means of increasing the quality of televised instruction. Second, there exists the *possibility* that television systems may be used as teaching machines when supplemented by auxiliary "talk-back" or reciprocal communication systems from students, and by student-response recording devices. It seems reasonable to expect that by imaginative inventive efforts television systems can be used to apply the principles of programmed learning with a wide range of different kinds of instructional materials for large numbers of learners. However, in this connection there are many procedural and equipment problems that remain to be solved.

Conducting research.—Television systems with characteristics selected to be suitable as research instruments should not be overlooked. Such systems make it possible to design and conduct many kinds of experiments with more precision and control than would be true without them. For example, by using a closed-circuit TV system with a series of many connected classrooms or study conditions, the *same stimulus materials* can be presented *simultaneously* to students in a number of conditions, and thus, stimulus materials and time can be held constant while other conditions can be varied. Research often requires systematic and analytic observations without the observing interfering with the subject of study. Here, too, TV may be found useful. Furthermore, recordings of the necessary kinds can be made by other equipment. The different channels and modes of communication can be eliminated or added either at the point of origination or reception and large numbers of subjects can be used simultaneously in randomly composed treatment groups (1, 2). In conclusion, both regular and special television systems have extensive possibilities as instrumentation for research in the behavioral sciences and especially in communications and learning research.

GUIDE LINES FOR SELECTING TELEVISION EQUIPMENT

At the present time, in contrast to even the recent past, television facilities exist in a wide array of kinds and levels of equipment from which selection can be made to serve instructional requirements. The variations of most importance to educators are not those of brand names or manufacturers. Many companies produce very similar levels of equipment and similar component parts are used in the assemblies. The important variations under discussion relate to complexity, performances, size, operational requirements, and original and maintenance costs.

The image and stereotype which most people, even educators, have of television studios and systems reflect the large commercial image orthicon ("I.O.") installations. The stereotypes reflect a decade of promotional efforts, even in the educational field, for selling and installing standard commercial "I.O." systems. The vidicon-type systems which are simpler (though some models are complex), less expensive, and require less maintenance than "I.O." equipment have not been effectively promoted and are not generally well known enough. Profit margins have been small, hence the vidicon lines of television equipment have had less interest for manufacturers than commercial image orthicon equipment. However, the recent improvements in the sensitivity and quality of vidicon tubes and the proven usefulness of vidicon equipment are factors which are stimulating developments in the use of this line of television products.

These stereotypes, the lack of information, the existing and emerging varieties of acceptable and tested television facilities make difficult the selection of equipment for instructional uses. It may be helpful, therefore, to have stated some guide lines which educators can use in choosing television equipment for serving instructional purposes. The following are briefly stated guide lines or selection criteria:

1. *Appropriateness for functions to be served.*—The first task under this criterion is to define the uses which will be made of the television facility. Secondly, consideration should be given to how these uses might change over a period of the life expectancy of the equipment. (Antiquation rates are usually calculated for not less than five nor more than ten years.) The third step would be to become thoroughly acquainted with all of the kinds of equipment which exist or may fall within the range of instructional functions to be served, and, if possible, to visit installations which are performing functions similar to those for which the equipment is to be selected. Finally, there is the task of determining the "best fit" between the equipment and the uses to which it will be put.

FIGURE 1. 4 ½" IMAGE ORTHICON CAMERA

FIGURE 2. A PROFESSIONAL TYPE OF VIDICON CAMERA IN USE IN ZOOLOGY COURSE

FIGURE 3. VIDICON TELEVISION SYSTEM EMPLOYING PORTABLE CONSOLE

FIGURE 4. TV CAMERA ON METALLOGRAPH IS USED TO MAGNIFY METALLIC SPECIMENS IN METALLURGY COURSES

RADIO CORPORATION OF AMERICA

THE PENNSYLVANIA STATE UNIVERSITY

EASTMAN KODAK CO.

FIGURE 5. (Top) VIDICON FILM CHAIN WITH DUAL PROJECTORS AND MULTIPLEXER

FIGURE 6. (Center) TELEVISION KINESCOPE RE-CORDER

FIGURE 6b. (Bottom) RAPID FILM PROCESSOR WHICH USES DEVELOPING AND FIXING SOLU-TIONS IN VISCOUS FORM

FIGURE 7. VIDEO TAPE RECORDER FOR HIGH-QUALITY BROADCAST OPERATIONS

FIGURE 8. COMPATIBLE LOW-COST VIDEO TAPE RECORDER

ᴳURE 9. STUDIO AT EDUCATIONAL TELEVISION STATION WQED, PITTSBURGH, DURING ᴿESENTATION OF DRIVER EDUCATION COURSE

ᴳURE 10. SMALL CLOSED-CIRCUIT STUDIO FOR INSTRUCTIONAL TELEVISION CONTROL ᴬNEL FOR INTER-COMMUNICATION SYSTEM IS TO RIGHT OF INSTRUCTOR

FIGURE 11. 100 KW HIGH-POWER TV TRANSMITTER

FIGURE 12. 500 WATT LOW-POWER TELEVISION TRANSMITTER

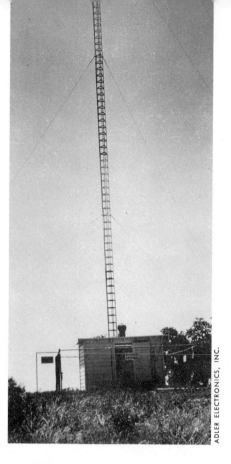

ADLER ELECTRONICS, INC.

FIGURE 13. TRANSLATOR INSTALLATION AT SAN SABA, TEXAS

FIGURE 14. HALLWAY OF CLASSROOM BUILDING SHOWING ARRANGEMENTS FOR INSTALLATION OF COAXIAL CABLE

THE PENNSYLVANIA STATE UNIVERSITY

FIGURE **15.** (Above) SMALL CLASSROOM WITH TV RECEIVER

FIGURE **16.** (Below, left) LARGE-SCREEN TELEVISION IN AUDITORIUM

FIGURE **17.** (Below, right) CONTROL PANEL FOR CLASSROOM INTER-COMMUNICATION SYSTEM

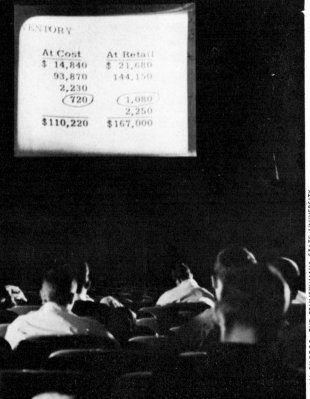

2. *Capital and maintenance costs.*—Usually in schools and educational institutions available funds set severe limits to choices of television facilities. Generally, also, there is a high correlation between original costs of the equipment and operation and maintenance costs. This relationship could be changed, although this is not now known to be the case, when transistorized equipment and printed circuits become generally available. Capital outlays of expenditures for equipment should be made with the full understanding of what installation and maintenance costs will be and how these are to be financed. Ideally a balance sheet should be prepared showing costs in relationship to the results of applications, i.e., the amount of scheduled uses of the system, the number of people served, and estimated effects in terms of achievable educational objectives as well as the relation of the costs of television to other competing expenditures. Thought should be given to relative costs of instructional television compared with other methods of providing similar instruction, and to the unique applications and results of using television.

3. *Flexibility and plans for change.*—Plans for instructional television should include arrangements for flexibility in origination, distribution, and presentation to students and audiences. The range and kinds of flexibility should, once again, be provided in relation to the uses to be made of the system assemblies. For example, multiple origination rooms might be needed. Some systems are movable, and mobile truck-mounted arrangements are possible. Patterns of distribution using cable, microwave links, channel translators, and direct broadcasts should be considered. Furthermore, changes in facilities are to be expected. Electronic equipment usually becomes antiquated rather quickly. Kinescope recorders which seemed to be essential in 1958 are considered to be antiquated in 1961. Generally, also, changes which occur tend in the direction of the systems becoming more and more complicated and compounded by adding components. *Successful* operations tend to expand and to be extended; unsuccessful ones tend to stagnate and become expensive burdens. Original plans should anticipate demands for more space, increased amounts of test equipment and maintenance apparatus and expanded uses of the equipment. The problems are constantly present of *regulating expansion relative to soundly justified developments.*

4. *Reliability of equipment.*—Television equipment should be selected in terms of reliability. Simply stated, *other things being equal, given several kinds of systems, the most reliable should be selected.* Equipment failures can affect very adversely programs of instruction. Regular, dependable operations are essential. This criterion relates to maintenance costs, requirements for engineering services, down-time, the need for duplicate stand-by equipment, as well as required major overhaul services. The

requirements for preventive maintenance work enter also as a factor. Rarely can educational agencies, which use instructional television, afford the levels or amounts of engineering skills usually found in commercial operations. At the present time, available kinds of television equipment and different components of systems, vary greatly in reliability and maintenance requirements. As viewed by educators, there is a great need for new designs to be built into equipment which will improve reliability and reduce the requirements for engineering skills.

5. *Simplicity.*—The selection of facilities should be done with reference to another principle: *Of several alternative systems, the simplest or least complicated one, which will perform the needed instructional functions, should be selected and used.* Technical qualities of images which meet engineering standards are more likely to exceed the requirements for learning meaningful materials than to fall below these requirements.* The excess above the necessary level of quality is expensive to purchase and to maintain. Once again it is emphasized that the equipment's performances should be *matched* closely with the instructional jobs to be done. For example, the employment of a standard full-scale commercial system for observatory television uses could only rarely be defended. Recordings of instruction for analysis of methods and techniques of teaching can be done equally as well by a $9,000 or a $25,000 kinescope recorder. Match the machinery to the job.

This admonition works both ways. On another level, that of producing and recording high-quality instructional materials for national or international distribution, the very best studio and control room equipment is required, even though complex and expensive, and this must be operated with great precision. Otherwise the wastage of rejected tapes may soon consume the differential between moderate-cost and high-cost television facilities.

It should be realized that the initial costs of television facilities may be a small percentage of all operating costs over a period of ten years, that the production and presentation of instruction is expensive, and that equipment failures and production faults are, proportionately to original equipment costs, very costly.

6. *Professional assistance.*—It is very likely that educators will need to have the services of competent and experienced professional people in

---

* This statement does not apply to the present-day audio systems of television. Generally, the sound quality available in standard television receivers is below what is needed for classroom or group "viewing" and listening. Loud speakers are too small and are often side mounted rather than front mounted. Auxiliary speakers must be used for audibility and this is especially desirable for such programs as music appreciation and language learning.

the planning of television facilities and in the selecting of the most appropriate kinds of equipment to serve defined needs. Sales engineers who represent manufacturers can provide essential and useful information. It is to be expected, however, that they will recommend the products of their own companies. Professional television engineers who are consultants and are not committed to a special brand of equipment may be needed. Of equal importance would be educational television consultants who would advise on functional and operational problems with emphasis on the instructional processes and objectives.

To a very large degree each instructional television installation is a special case and requires special designs and arrangements. It is on these special adaptations that professional advice will be most needed.

PLANNING BUILDINGS FOR INSTRUCTIONAL TELEVISION

Two developments are occurring simultaneously in American education: (1) There is under way a great program of construction of new buildings for educational uses at all levels and this construction of buildings will probably continue and expand during the next decade. (2) There is a great ferment, exploration, and development in the technology of education. These two trends urgently need to be coordinated and synchronized. Many of the new technological developments such as learning laboratories, audio distribution systems, radio, individual learning devices (e.g., teaching machines), and certainly instructional television require for their effective use buildings that are especially designed in some respects to accommodate them. Unfortunately, too few architects of educational buildings have been informed adequately by educators or engineers of the special needs in buildings for new educational facilities and equipment. Fortunately, the Educational Facilities Laboratories, Inc., has sponsored a number of design projects which have yielded published reports of value on these problems and some have given special attention to the use of instructional television (3, 4).

It is probably not an overgeneralization to state that every new educational building that is projected now and in the future should be planned to accommodate appropriate kinds of technical equipment and facilities and included among these is television. The present and possible future needs for facilities should be part of the statements of functional specifications for buildings and, in turn, should be designed into the structures of the buildings. The same emphasis should be given to planning for the uses of mechanical, electrical, and electronic instructional-learning apparatus as is given to planning for a library and for conventional instructional materials.

For the special case of instructional television, several basic questions should be asked and answered: 1. If it is assumed that television will be used, then the first question is: How will television be used, for whom and to what extent? 2. Will the building need course production space and facilities? 3. Will it need originating and control room space and facilities? Or, 4. Will the building receive only instructional programs by cable, broadcast or both, and present them to students? The asking and answering of these questions will then set the stage for specific program and building planning.

In most situations at the present time specific answers may not be possible. Here again several general guide lines could be helpful to the planners.

There are key concepts which may govern building designs:

1. *Flexibility.*—Space arrangements should permit modifications without undue cost and effort and with maximum convenience or ease for the use of needed facilities.

2. *Multiple-use.*—Space can be so designed as to make possible a range of different uses. For example, classrooms, laboratories, libraries, auditoria, cafeteria and dining halls, dormitories and lounges can be reception points for video and audio channels of information (using headsets where necessary) and at other times serve conventional functions. Also, lecture-demonstration rooms, some laboratories, auditoria and stage areas, music rooms and art studios can be so designed as to make it possible to originate and record or variously distribute television programs to and from them.

3. *Expansibility.*—Provisions should be made in the design and construction of buildings for expansion, especially when it is impossible to estimate accurately the amount of space and facilities that will be needed. The experience of successful instructional television installations has been that, beginning with one originating room, at least a second and frequently a third originating room are soon needed. The same expansion possibilities exist for equipment. Beginning with a two-camera system as a minimum for a moderate-cost operation, it is quickly found to be necessary to add a film chain for films and slides, and a fourth bench-mounted camera for graphics, still photographs, titles, and superimpositions or special effects. The successful use of one video-tape machine apparently creates the need for another. Therefore, provisions should be made for possible expansions. Ideally, the maximum development should be visualized, and then beginning where one must, a step-by-step development plan and schedule should be projected.

4. *High utility.*—Television facilities are expensive. Building designs and installation plans should be such as to permit, encourage but not hinder, the highest possible utilization rate. This means usefulness for different purposes, when they are appropriate, consecutive or continuous sched-

uling daily and weekly, and service for the greatest possible number of students. The adequacy of buildings, availability of space, lack of interference with other activities, distribution and reception capacities of systems all relate to the desirability of high utility. Television is a mass medium and has an enormous potential for distributing instruction to large numbers of people. Building arrangements and other conditions should support the utilization of these potentials.

In planning new buildings for television there are critical points which need special attention: (1) Adequate electrical power should be available for the TV systems, control rooms, lighting, and air conditioning. (2) Control rooms should have visual access through glass into originating rooms. (3) Adequate storage space for parts, electronic maintenance areas, and space for the preparation of instructional materials should be available nearby. (4) The course coordinators ("producers") and engineers will need office space and desks or benches. (5) Space for running cables must be provided. This will require more space than is usually estimated, especially when reciprocal communication connections with classrooms are provided.

The modification of existing buildings for television facilities presents many problems and compromises. Here the general objective should be to have designed a model arrangement and then do as much as possible to approximate this model. Many instructional television systems are poured into existing buildings, rather than planned into them, with consequent great handicaps to effective operations.

LOCATION OF TELEVISION FACILITIES AND RELATION TO POSSIBILITIES OF USES

The location of TV-originating facilities in an institution, school system, or area may have important effects on the kinds and extent of uses to which the installation will be put. Ideally, originating facilities should be located in buildings or building complexes where they are most useful, where resources for programming are available, and where audiences or classes can be served. If distribution is to be by cable, originating facilities should be located at a place from which minimum cable runs are required to reach reception points. Usually this will mean a central location in the area served.

If, within an area, program originations must be arranged at several separate locations, then a closed-loop cable layout will make it possible to feed signals into the distribution system at a number of origination points and to distribute programs to all connected reception points. Coaxial cables can carry six or more different channels of information. This multi-channel capacity of coaxial cable is a great advantage in school, college, and university television. The need for a number of channels at the same time becomes acute as courses are added and recorded and more "live" programs are used.

The route from studios to reception places may include buildings other than classrooms and laboratories. The right kind of television facilities can make it possible to use many kinds of spaces for instruction, when they are not otherwise committed. Lounges, dining areas, auditoria, and residence halls can be used during some hours of the day for instructional purposes. Distribution systems should be planned to take advantage of these possibilities.

The general and widespread conception of an instructional television facility is that of a large, centralized, originating complex of studios, control room, space for engineering and production. However, the availability of low- and moderate-cost systems and compatible auxiliary components makes possible decentralized installations. At the Pennsylvania State University, for example, vidicon professional systems are installed wherever they can be justified by use potentials and can be accommodated in buildings. In 1961 three complete instructional closed-circuit systems are in operation and in the fall of that year each will operate on a full schedule. A fourth independent system will be added in an education building now under construction. Two of the origination systems are interconnected and also feed programs by cable to a 1200-seat auditorium where instruction is presented on a large screen (15′ × 12′) by means of an Eidophor projector. This decentralized pattern of operations might well be considered for many institutions as an alternative to a centralized origination facility. Each of these plans, and other intermediate plans, has advantages and disadvantages which should be considered by agencies when planning television installations. The principal advantage of the decentralized pattern of operation is that television facilities are installed where they are needed, and this seems to encourage the acceptance and use of the systems. They are a part of the regular academic facilities. The principal disadvantage relates to problems of operating and maintaining separated facilities. Additional stocks of spare parts and test equipment may also be needed. In some situations a combination of centralized and decentralized facilities may be desirable. For instance, broadcast and recording facilities might be centralized, while closed-circuit operations might include several decentralized systems. All may be interconnected.

ORIGINATION EQUIPMENT

TELEVISION CAMERAS

As was pointed out in the previous section, the equipment needed to originate programs for instructional television can vary greatly according to the functions it is required to serve. This equipment can range from elaborate, rather expensive, image-orthicon television systems with film projectors and broadcast quality video-tape recorders as may be required for a large educational television station, to a simple self-contained industrial type of vidicon camera which might be required for the remote observation of phenomena or activities or the magnification of demonstrations.

In between these extremes are the professional and semi-professional vidicon cameras which are capable of serving less rigorous broadcast and closed-circuit requirements. A careful analysis should be made of the functions to be performed, the conditions of use, the kinds of operating and maintenance personnel who will be available, and the potential budgetary support. With the help of a competent engineer, these factors should be carefully weighed and an appropriate system designed to meet each specific situation.

In the following section some general suggestions will be made concerning the types of television camera equipment that will be needed to meet the needs of several major classes of functions (5).

FULL-SCALE PROFESSIONAL BROADCASTING OR THE RECORDING OF PROGRAMS FOR SUBSEQUENT BROADCASTING

For a full-scale educational television station or production center which is to produce high grade video-tape recordings for broadcast purposes, and if adequate funds are likely to be available for purchase of the equipment and for its operation, and if adequately trained engineers are available to operate and maintain the equipment, and if low lighting levels are likely to be encountered, then it would seem advisable to use the highest quality and most advanced television cameras available. At the time of this writing such cameras would be those employing the 4½″ image orthicon tube as the photosensitive pickup unit. These cameras have the highest resolution and lowest noise, stable circuits and high sensitivity which permit the origination of good pictures with relatively low light levels (10 to 50 foot candles of light incident on the subject). (See Figure 1.)

At least two such cameras with associated control and monitoring equipment, power supplies, synchronizing generator and switcher would be needed. Lenses and camera pedestals of matching size and quality would also be required. Such a basic dual camera chain would cost about $60,-000.* It would provide the ultimate in picture quality at the present state of development. During the past ten years or so the standard television camera employed by commercial and educational broadcasters has used

---

* This price does not include other necessary equipment such as audio, film chains, spare units, lighting, etc.

the 3″ image orthicon tube. In the opinion of the writers, this has now been superseded by equipment using the 4½″ image orthicon tube, and the latter equipment would appear to be justified if the requirements and conditions outlined above should prevail.

MODERATE-COST EQUIPMENT FOR BROADCASTING
AND CLOSED-CIRCUIT TELEVISION

Where the function to be served is that of originating instruction in a studio for distribution to multiple classrooms over closed-circuit systems, or where broadcasts are to be originated that do not require the highest possible technical quality, and where modest budgets are available and somewhat less skilled operating personnel than would be required for a full-scale professional broadcasting operation, then moderate-cost professional vidicon cameras would be appropriate.

Such cameras, at the present stage of development, are capable of 600 line resolution or better (using Electronics Industry Association's test chart), and, if well designed, have stable circuits. They require 200 to 250 foot candles of light on the subject area to produce pictures of high quality, and they may be operated by relatively unskilled personnel without serious risks of damage. However, as for all television cameras, adequate engineering competence should be available in order to maintain the systems at high performance levels.

Such professional vidicon camera systems are the type most widely used for originating instruction to be presented in multiple classrooms over closed-circuit television, and at the time of writing they are now being used for broadcasting by a limited number of educational institutions. It seems possible that this number will increase as a result of substantial improvements that are being made in vidicon tubes and cameras and the increased availability of information on their performances. (See Figure 2.)

A basic professional vidicon camera system employing two cameras, appropriately scaled camera pedestals, lenses, camera control consoles, power supplies, monitors, switcher, and standard synchronizing generator would cost from $15,000 to $20,000.* In some of the less expensive models, the controls have been simplified and the control console made portable. Such units would be most appropriate for closed-circuit applications in public schools and small colleges (Figure 3). Maintenance and operating costs of such equipment are much lower than that for image orthicon cameras because of the low cost and long life of vidicon tubes. The principal disadvantage of these systems is that they require from five to ten times as much light as image orthicon cameras to produce optimum quality pictures. However, such lighting levels are not difficult to achieve in small studios.

---

* This figure includes only basic camera equipment.

LOW-COST CAMERAS FOR MAGNIFYING DEMONSTRATIONS
AND FOR REMOTE OBSERVATION OF ACTIVITIES

A third major category of functions involves the magnification of small objects or demonstrations in an auditorium or large classroom, or the remote observation of events in situations where highly mobile and flexible camera coverage is not needed (e.g., the observations of interviews, or the use of a television camera on the microscope to permit viewing by groups of students).

For such applications a single camera equipped with one or more lenses or a "zoom" lens would be adequate to originate a picture. Such cameras may be completely self-contained. They may, if necessary, be remotely controlled and some models may be equipped with a built-in viewfinder. Such a camera with lens or lenses and tripod may cost from $700 to $4,000 depending on specific requirements. Usually such cameras do not employ standard EIA synchronizing pulses* and are not compatible with more elaborate systems. They are, however, used independently in many installations with a high degree of success (see Figure 4).

EQUIPMENT FOR TELEVISING FILMS, SLIDES, AND PRINTED MATERIALS

Important sources of information for television instruction are sound and silent motion pictures (usually 16mm), slides (usually 2″ × 2″), and printed materials.

Typically, films and slides are televised by means of a film chain (see Figure 5). This usually includes a vidicon camera, one or more 16mm projectors designed for television use, a slide projector, and a multiplexer which permits one television camera to pick up images from two or three projectors. The film chain is generally remotely controlled from the control console and has its own monitor as a part of this console.

Whether one or two film projectors are used and whether these are heavy duty or regular duty will depend on the volume of films to be presented over the system. Generally speaking, the 16mm projectors are designed for use with television systems and have a special pull-down mechanism to reduce flicker. In a few instances where extremely limited budgts were available, some closed-circuit systems have used standard classroom 16mm projectors with the shutter removed. The image from this projector is projected onto a small rear projection screen (16″ × 12″) and is picked up directly by a vidicon studio camera.

It is also often convenient for a television teacher to use a similar arrangement for the televising of 2″ × 2″ slides. The slides are projected onto a rear projection screen in the studio and are televised by a studio camera. This arrangement makes it possible for the teacher to point to

---

* These pulses conform to standards established by the Electronic Industries Association.

specific areas of a slide, and it permits the camera to move in for close-up views of parts of the slide. Slides and film-strips (3½″ × 4″) can be televised in a similar fashion.

In some educational television studies a "telop" is used as a part of a film chain for the presentation of opaque pictures. In other instances flat pictures are mounted on "flip cards" or a bulletin board and are televised by means of the studio camera.

In televised instruction it is often desired to televise title cards or to superimpose printed words over a live scene. If these kinds of materials are to be presented frequently it is desirable to have an additional camera (usually a vidicon camera) to pick up flip cards and title cards. This camera may be mounted in a corner of the studio or in the control room. It would have a control console and monitor as a part of the main video control console and would be connected with the switcher along with the studio cameras and film chain. Thus, the director or television coordinator can view the output from each camera on its own monitor and can select the appropriate picture by the use of the push buttons or fader on the switching unit.

TELEVISION RECORDERS

An important capacity of a television system may be the ability to record and store instructional presentations for re-use or exchange with other educational institutions. During the next few years it seems reasonable to expect that there will be a considerable increase in the use of such recorded instruction.

Recorded instruction is also useful for self-evaluation by television teachers, for study and analysis by student teachers, and for research on instruction. As costs of recording are reduced it is probable that recorded televised instruction may be used for individual review, or for individual and home-study purposes.

At the present time there are two principal methods available for recording the pictures and sound that make up a television presentation. These are recording on film, commonly referred to as kinescope recording, and recording on magnetic tape, generally known as video-tape recording.

Film recording.—Film recording is accomplished, at the present time, by photographing the television image from a special picture tube (a kinescope) by a special camera (see Figure 6). The sound may be recorded simultaneously on the same film, or it may be recorded synchronously on magnetic tape for later recombination on motion picture film.

Currently, film recording has the advantage that the end product (a 16mm film) can be used on a regular classroom film projector as well as on a television film chain. Neither the equipment nor the film is as expensive as video-tape recording. The main disadvantages are that kinescope recording requires carefully controlled television images for recording and photographic laboratory processing with very precise control. At the present state of development kinescope recording is a process which is not easily or quickly mastered. Furthermore, there is a delay while the film is being processed between the time of recording and the time when the film is available for use. Nevertheless, even the kinescopic recorders now available can serve many important functions of instructional television. It is the view of the writers that engineering research and development on kinescopic recorders should have been continued even after the advent of video-tape recorders.

As with television cameras, there is also a range of types of kinescope recorders at various prices. The more expensive models are intended to meet or approximate broadcast standards. The less expensive ones are suitable for recording programs which will be re-shown on closed-circuit systems or on standard classroom projectors.

A recent development in 16mm film processing equipment, the Viscomat, which uses chemicals in viscous form, will process, wash, and dry film in approximately one minute after it has entered the machine. This type of equipment, which enables educational institutions to process their own films or kinescope recordings to good commercial standards, may eliminate some of the disadvantages of delay involved in the earlier kinescope recording and processing techniques. The equipment is designed to be used as an integral part of a television film recording installation. It is estimated that this new rapid processor will be available during 1962 and will cost about $12,500. This advance emphasizes, once again, the need to continue the development of kinescope recording equipment. It should be pointed out here that at present estimated prices, a kinescope recorder plus rapid film processor would amount to approximately the same cost as one of the moderate-cost video-tape recorders.

Magnetic tape recording.—The development of video-tape recorders has created new possibilities and practices in the recording and re-use of television programs. Such recordings have high quality and the pictures and sound may be played back immediately after production. In many installations it is becoming standard practice to pre-record programs on video tape. This facilitates scheduling of personnel, makes for more efficient use of studio space, and may actually reduce studio space needs.

The video-tape recorders initially developed were designed for broadcast use. They record both picture and sound on a 2″ wide magnetic tape.

The availability of video-tape recorders in most educational television stations has permitted the recording of many courses, principally at the elementary and secondary levels, and the exchange of this recorded instruction among different school systems is developing and may be expected to expand greatly in the future. Such broadcast quality video-tape recorders for black-and-white recording cost between $50,000 and $60,000 at the present time, and many educational stations find they need two such recorders, one for recording programs while the other is being used to play back recordings for broadcast (see Figure 7). Some would like a third recorder to mount in a mobile unit for remote pickups. Recorders can be used advantageously for repeating course materials, like lecture-demonstrations in chemistry, when this repetition is required for large numbers of students in different time schedules.

The recording of courses has been restricted to a large extent by the cost of recording tape. Tape costs alone for a semester or a year-long course would be between $10,000 and $15,000 at present tape prices. These may soon be reduced. Such recorded courses would have to be re-used a number of times to justify the investment, although the signals can be erased and the tapes used again.

Where the recordings are not to be broadcast, somewhat less rigorous requirements exist and there has been much interest among users of closed-circuit television systems in the development of a video-tape recorder that would be comparable in terms of prices with vidicon television systems and which would use less expensive tape, or would make existing standard 2″ video tape go farther.

Recently two U.S. manufacturers have announced the availability of video-tape recorders which will sell in the $18,000 to $25,000 price range, and which are designed for closed-circuit television applications (see Figure 8). One Japanese video-tape recorder has also been announced to sell in the $10,000 price range. These recorders all use 2″ tape, but some of them run the tape at half the usual speed, thereby cutting tape costs in half. At present it is too soon to give an evaluation of these machines which should have extensive field testing under regular conditions in educational institutions. However, it is clear that substantial reductions of costs of video-tape recorders and of the cost of making recordings can be expected, and this should open up the way for the widespread use of recorded televised instruction in schools, colleges, and universities, and for other uses which may lead to the improvement of instruction.

As with television camera equipment, the purchaser of video-tape recorders should give careful thought to operating requirements, specialized personnel, maintenance costs, and needed test equipment.

MOBILE UNITS

A desirable facility in an advanced instructional television installation may be a mobile unit which can go to remote locations to televise events or phenomena of educational importance. Such a mobile unit may be very elaborate and would include a large truck equipped with a complete television system (including two or more cameras, control consoles, audio facilities, etc.), a video-tape (or film) recorder, and perhaps a power generator. If live simultaneous broadcasts are to be made, the unit would also have a microwave or cable connection with a studio or transmitter.

At a more modest level of operation, the mobile truck could use the same camera equipment and video-tape (or film) recorder that are used in the studio. Such equipment would be designed for easy portability— all units being on casters and easily disconnected and reconnected. Thus, the equipment could be rolled out of the studio and control room, mounted in a truck, and taken to the remote location in the matter of a few hours.

Some television installations have chosen to have camera control units permanently mounted in a mobile unit and to use this unit as a control room for cameras operated in the studio. Under these circumstances careful attention has to be given to temperature control in the mobile unit if it is to be so employed for year-round operation.

AUDIO ORIGINATING EQUIPMENT

Audio is an important component of the television signal and because of the complexity of equipment for the picture component, sound equipment is often given inadequate attention.

Equipment for originating sound involves microphones of various types, microphone holders, audio-tape recorders, occasionally disc equipment, motion picture and video tape sound sources and a control console which permits the control of levels, and amplification, where necessary, of several sources of sound.

Microphones.—For instructional television, whether for broadcast or closed-circuit, where the presentation is by one or two people, individual chest ("lavalier") microphones are generally worn. These should generally be dynamic-type microphones of low impedance (50 or 150 ohms) and of good quality. Under some circumstances a "wireless" microphone of a similar type may be useful. This frees the instructor from the cable that connects the microphone to the control console. In other situations table microphones may be needed.

Sometimes where a group of people are to be covered a single highly directional microphone may be used on a boom which permits the microphone to be placed near the speakers and rotated to favor each speaker as necessary.

For some sound, such as pre-recorded announcements or music, good quality audio-tape recorders may be needed. These should be of the type designed for professional rather than home use. The audio control console permits adjustment of the level of each sound input, and should be equipped with a volume indicator. For an elaborate installation it may be capable of handling eight or more inputs. For a smaller installation a console that handles three or four inputs may be adequate. The console should have good frequency response and low distortion characteristics and care should be taken to see that all impedances are properly matched.

LIGHTING EQUIPMENT

Special lighting equipment is essential in practically all television installations except perhaps for the situation where television is being used for the remote observation of classroom teaching demonstrations. In these circumstances the existing room illumination would be used (preferably at least 50 foot-candles of even incident light over the room).

For a major broadcast studio a variety of spotlights and floodlights would be needed ranging in wattage from 500 watts to 2,000 watts. The number of lighting units and their type and wattage would depend upon the number of sets to be illuminated, the type of sets, and the kind of television cameras being employed. Television lighting for image orthicon cameras generally ranges from 50 to 100 foot-candles (read at the subject with an incident light meter). At the present time vidicon cameras require 200 to 300 foot-candles of illumination on the subject. The convenience of lighting an area is aided by having a number of lighting units available. These are usually suspended from a lighting grid located 12 to 15 feet above the floor, and each lamp is powered from a separate outlet. Each outlet may be on a separate switch at a switchboard or, in an elaborate installation, a plug board and dimmers may be used.

In any event, adequate power should be available to serve the number of lights to be used, and the circuit loads should be carefully balanced and protected by circuit breakers.

The quality of a television picture is greatly affected by both the amount and the arrangement of the lighting. Skilful use of back light or cross light, for instance, will greatly increase the depth dimension of a picture and improve its contrast.

In a very simple installation where a single small vidicon camera is used to magnify demonstrations or small objects, two or three internal reflector floodlights on portable stands may suffice.

TEST EQUIPMENT, TOOLS, SPARE PARTS

One of the costs frequently overlooked or underestimated in installing and operating a television system is the equipment, tools, and parts needed for repair and maintenance of the system. It is impossible to specify a single list of test equipment for television installations. What is needed will be a function of the complexity of the system, the level of performance to be maintained and the skill of the engineers who will do the maintenance.

The advice of a competent television engineer should be sought, and the annual operating budgets should include some funds for additional items of test equipment and tools.

It is generally essential to have adequate stocks of spare parts on hand to maintain electronic equipment. Vacuum tubes and the photosensitive pickup tubes are the largest items; capacitors, resistors, connectors, and transformers are also needed. The stock on hand will be a function of the size and complexity of the system, the immediate availability of spare parts from local suppliers, and experience with the kinds of component failures that will be likely to occur in a given system.

Experience indicates that a rough guide to the annual amount to be budgeted for replacement parts would be about 10 percent of the original cost of the equipment.

In planning a system, thought should also be given to the purchase of certain spare equipment units. Again, the actual spare units to be obtained would be a function of the complexity of the total television system. Certain units are critical to the operation of many television systems and a failure in such a unit (for example a synchronizing generator) could put the entire system out of operation.

In noncritical applications there is less need for the duplication of equipment for such insurance purposes.

OFF-THE-AIR RECEPTION SYSTEMS

For many public schools and some colleges it is likely that the main source of instructional television programs will be the reception of off-the-air signals from a broadcast transmitter. In areas near a powerful transmitter, reception may be obtained through the use of a small television antenna for each receiver. When many receivers in different classrooms spread throughout a school are to be served it is usually necessary to install a central high-gain antenna and a cable system to carry the signals to each receiver. Such a cable system could also be used to distribute instructional programs from other sources—such as television cameras, video-tape recorders, and television film chains. These cable systems will be described in more detail in the section of this report concerning distribution of television signals.

DISPLAY DEVICES FOR ORIGINATING TELEVISED INSTRUCTION

Equipment for originating televised instruction should include a range of display devices for use in the studio by the television teachers. These may include demonstration tables (with water, power, gas, etc., if necessary), bulletin boards for mounting pictures, easels for displaying title cards, books, etc., chalk boards, flannel boards, newspad easels, possibly a prompting device, overhead projector for large transparent overlays, and suitable furniture and backgrounds. Some of these display devices may be purchased from commercial sources. Other items may have to be made especially for a particular installation. A rear projection screen and slide projector are also useful studio equipment. Other auxiliary items may include equipment for making 16mm films and slides, devices for printing title cards, and facilities for editing film.

SPACE FOR TELEVISION ORIGINATION

This section will consider the space requirements and functions to be served by buildings which will house the equipment and personnel who originate instructional television programs. There is no single ideal plan that will fit all situations. The space that will be needed will be determined by the functions to be served, the volume of programs to be televised or recorded, and the kinds of equipment that will be used. Available funds usually are another determining factor which results in compromises.

When planning building facilities for origination of television programs it is usually desirable to seek the guidance of people who have planned and operated similar facilities and, if possible, to visit such facilities.

Space for several different levels and types of operation will be outlined in the section that follows:

FACILITIES FOR AN EDUCATIONAL BROADCASTING AND/OR PRODUCTION CENTER

The largest amounts of space and the most elaborate building facilities are likely to be needed for a full-scale professional broadcasting operation or for a production center which will produce high quality video tape or film recordings to meet professional broadcast standards.

Such a center would require at least one studio of 60' × 40' with a ceiling 15' to 18' high to permit the mounting of lighting grids 12' to 13' above the floor and to aid in dissipation of heat from lights. (See Figure 9.) A second studio perhaps 40' × 40' in area would be very useful, especially if "live" programs are to be broadcast in immediate succession. These studios should be given suitable acoustical treatment, should have solid, smooth floors, and should be air conditioned to prolong the life of the equipment and to provide reasonable comfort for personnel who may have to work under intense light for an hour or more at a time. Care should be exercised to see that the air conditioning system does not introduce extraneous noise into the studios. The studios should also be well shielded from sources of outside noise.

In addition to supports for the lighting units, the studios should have adequate electrical power available for lighting, and outlets for television cameras and microphone cables. Adjacent to the studios should be the control room. Preferably the control room should permit visual contact with the studio through double-glass windows, although this is not absolutely essential. The control room in a major studio should be large enough to accommodate the monitors, switching equipment and audio console, and the personnel who will operate them. A small booth for an announcer located next to the control room may also be desirable.

Adequate air-conditioned space near the studio is also required for the master and engineering control room. This area should be large enough to permit the installation of equipment racks in accessible locations. These racks contain power supplies, synchronizing generators, video patch panels, distribution equipment, some test equipment and tape recorders, etc. They generally are in standard units 22" wide and 7' high and should be accessible from the front and rear. The camera control units are also installed here, although in some stations they are found in the control room where the director is located.

In the control room or adjacent to it space is required for the film chain or chains and one or more video-tape or kinescope recorders.

These areas should also be air conditioned for heat dissipation and to prolong the life of the equipment. A raised floor or a floor with recessed channels should be provided to facilitate the installation of interconnecting cables. Other engineering space requirements would include a shop for repair and testing of equipment, spare parts storage, and office space.

Space is also required for program production activities. Such space would include rooms for the preparation of graphics materials of various types, and the storage of scenes and properties, films, and video tapes. Areas where production personnel can work with instructors or where instructors can work alone on the development of course materials are highly desirable. Office space, a reception area, dressing rooms, toilets, and an observation room where visitors may observe television programs should also be provided.

It is advantageous if such a large activity can be located at a central point where it is easily accessible to those who will use it, and where parking space and access by motor vehicles is possible.

SPACE FOR MODERATE COST CLOSED-CIRCUIT TELEVISION ORIGINATION FACILITIES

A closed-circuit television system to be used by schools or universities will require less elaborate facilities than will a professional broadcast operation. Space will be needed for the same general functions but the areas can be smaller. For one thing the smaller and more compact vidicon television cameras are more likely to be used. Secondly, less ambitious presentations will be undertaken and smaller studios will be required. With these reservations in mind some suggestions will be made concerning space needs.

Studios. — A minimum size for a studio for closed-circuit television origination is 25' × 30'. An area of 30' × 40' would be preferable. Ceiling height should be 15' with a minimum of 12'. Lighting grids, power outlets for lights, and acoustical treatment will be needed (see Figure 10). For many institutions a second studio of the same size and situated alongside the first one will be desirable for continuous "live" instructional presentations. The same cameras and control room can serve both studios. The use of pre-recorded instructional presentations on video tape may reduce or eliminate the need for the additional studio.

Control rooms.—A control room for a small closed-circuit installation should be about 20' × 25' in area. It would house video and audio consoles, monitors, equipment racks, and film chain. An additional area should be provided for repair and maintenance of equipment, storage of spare parts, and housing of video-tape or kinescope recorder if one is used. The studio and control room should be air conditioned.

Preparation space.—Space for preparation of graphics materials and storage of instructional materials and offices for personnel are also needed.

SPACE FOR DEMONSTRATION-MAGNIFIER USE OF TELEVISION

When a simple, single camera television system is used for the remote observation of events or to magnify demonstrations in a large classroom or auditorium, the equipment is usually located in the room where the activity is performed. If this kind of work is anticipated, power outlets for camera and supplemental lighting should be provided, and provision made for the placement of the camera in the auditorium so that it is not obtrusive. Ducts for carrying cables to receivers and power outlets for the receivers would also be needed. The kinds of cameras envisaged for such activities use 115 volts, and a standard 15-ampere electrical outlet should be adequate for the camera equipment, with separate outlets for lights and receivers.

DISTRIBUTION OF TELEVISION SIGNALS

This section will discuss the problem of getting television signals from the point of origination of the instruction to the classrooms where the televised instruction will be viewed and heard.

There are three principal methods of distributing television signals at

present: (1) by broadcast, (2) by coaxial cable, and (3) by microwave links. The first method is sometimes referred to as open-circuit; the second and third are often called closed-circuit because the signals can be received only by receivers which are connected to the cable or microwave system.*
Requirements of each of the systems will be discussed briefly.

BROADCAST DISTRIBUTION

High power.—The broadcasting of instructional television programs requires a transmitter and a channel on which to broadcast. In some instances, instructional programs are broadcast over commercial television transmitters but usually there are severe limitations on available time.

The availability of television channels and the assignment and supervision of their use is under the control of the Federal Communications Commission. Such channels may be Very High Frequency (VHF) (Channels 2–13) or Ultra High Frequency (UHF) (Channels 14–83). A number of channels have been reserved for educational use. Any educational institution interested in acquiring the use of such a broadcast channel should consult one of the companies which specialize in legal work with the Federal Communications Commission, and should engage a qualified engineering company to carry out the surveys that are required. Additional assistance in planning can be obtained from such agencies as the National Association of Educational Broadcasters and the National Educational Television and Radio Center.

If it is assumed that a channel has been granted, a transmitter of appropriate power, a tower, antenna, monitoring equipment, and a building to house the equipment will be needed. A site and adequate source of power for the transmitter will also be required.

It may be necessary to connect the transmitter with the television studio by means of one or more microwave links. These are also subject to licensing and approval by the Federal Communications Commission.

Without having full details of power, location, etc., it is impossible to estimate the costs of high-power transmitter facilities, but they are likely to be between $150,000 and $300,000 (see Figure 11).

Low power.—Where it is necessary to cover a fairly limited range (say a radius of 12 to 25 miles) it is possible to use a low-power transmitter (100–1000 watts power). Low-power transmitters are commercially available at moderate cost. The total cost for transmitter, appropriate antenna, and a small tower should not exceed $25,000 to $50,000 (see Figure 12).

---

* Television programs may, of course, be "distributed" in the form of video tape or film recordings. For many purposes this is an efficient and excellent method of getting televised instruction from one place to another.

NEED FOR MULTIPLE CHANNEL BROADCASTING

One of the difficulties confronting broadcast television is that the broadcaster in a given location is usually limited to a single channel. Where good use is made of instructional television programs the time available on one channel soon becomes completely absorbed. In some cities in the United States a second educational channel is already in use, and this trend can be expected to continue. However, the time will undoubtedly arrive when additional channels will be needed to provide for additional courses.

One approach to solving this problem could be to use several low-power television transmitters with limited range. A group of, say, four such low-power transmitters could serve a city with a wide range of courses of instruction at various levels.

EXTENDING THE RANGE OF BROADCAST TRANSMITTERS BY CHANNEL TRANSLATORS

Sometimes it is necessary to extend the range of a television transmitter to certain areas. This may be the result of "shadowing" because of mountains, or because there are scattered clusters of population beyond the range of the transmitter.

The use of channel translators is one way of accomplishing this objective (see Figure 13). A channel translator is a low-power television repeater which is fed by a high-quality receiver. The translator is located on the fringe of the range of the broadcast signal. It picks up this signal, converts it to another channel, and rebroadcasts it. Another translator may pick up this signal and relay it farther. Such devices afford the possibility of extending instructional television into remote areas at moderate cost. A 10-watt UHF channel translator costs about $3,000. Antenna, tower, and housing of the unit would bring the total cost up to about $6,000.

In other situations the signal from an educational broadcast station may be picked up by a well-placed antenna of a community antenna system and fed to receivers over a cable system.

AIRBORNE TELEVISION DISTRIBUTION

In an effort to spread several channels of high-quality instruction over a large area the Midwest Program of Airborne Television Instruction will broadcast instruction over a large area on several channels simultaneously from an airplane circling at 23,000 feet. In a few years, it seems probable that programs might be relayed by satellites in orbit around the earth, and it is not too early for educators to visualize the possibilities and requirements of this method of diffusing instruction.

CLOSED-CIRCUIT TELEVISION

Closed-circuit television refers to the procedure whereby the television signals are distributed from the origination point to the reception points by means of coaxial cable.

The closed-circuit system may cover a substantial part of a state as is proposed in South Carolina; it may cover a county as in Washington County, Maryland; it may cover a city as in Corning, New York; or it may be confined to a campus or single building as in many institutions of higher education.

The cable system may be installed by a telephone company and used by the educational organization on a rental basis, or it may be installed, owned, and operated by the educational institution itself. In some cases it may be installed and operated by a community cable company.

Distribution of television systems over cable may be done in two ways:

(1) *Video system.*—Video and audio frequencies may be distributed on separate cables. Such an arrangement is often used in television studios where distances are short and maximum detail is required in the pictures. It has the disadvantage that only one program at a time may be transmitted on the cable, and special video monitors and audio systems are needed.

(2) *R.F. system.*—The video and audio frequencies from the camera and control consoles may be fed into an audio-video mixer and used to modulate a radio-frequency carrier wave. This mixer is a small transmitter and sends the picture and sound signals over a coaxial cable on one of the VHF channels (2–13).

The main trunk cable may be tapped at various points and signals fed to regular broadcast receivers. The advantages of this system are that several signals (at least six) may be transmitted over the same coaxial cable simultaneously and received by tuning the receivers to the appropriate channels. Secondly, the signals are easily amplified and the system can readily be extended. Thirdly, regular television receivers may be used. The principal disadvantage is that under normal conditions, with standard receivers, the resolution from an R.F. system is not as high as that obtained from a video system with special video monitors. However, picture and sound from a well-designed R.F. distribution system should be equivalent to good off-the-air reception.

An R.F. distribution system should be designed and installed by a company which specializes in such work if good results are to be obtained. Amplifiers must be well designed and carefully selected, and the signal strength at the various outlet-points must be within certain tolerances.

In planning the system a decision should be made as to whether the channels to be used will be confined to 2–6 or whether they will also be in the 7–13 channel range. These considerations will determine the kinds of amplifiers that will be needed.

When a building or campus is planned for the possible use of closed-circuit television, provision should be made for duct space for installation of coaxial cables. Furred-down ceilings with removable acoustical tile in hallways and classrooms will greatly facilitate cable installation. Conduits are not normally necessary within buildings except between floors to permit vertical cable runs. (See Figure 14.)

Where signals from a broadcast transmitter are to be received and distributed within a building or institution, a good antenna site should be selected and high-gain antennas used. If the broadcast signals are UHF they will need to be converted to VHF for distribution over the cable system.

MICROWAVE

The use of microwave links not only affords a way of connecting transmitters to form a network for the sharing of programs; they may also now be used by educational institutions to link campuses or buildings together in a closed-circuit system. Microwave transmission is likely to be used when the distances are great. Cable will probably be advantageous when the distances are short and when several programs must be distributed simultaneously.

FACILITIES AND EQUIPMENT FOR PRESENTING TELEVISED INSTRUCTION

The use of television for instruction has focused attention on needed functional requirements for classrooms to an extent that was never achieved by other teaching methods. Fortunately the demands made by television also improve classrooms for other teaching methods and materials. Many good suggestions will be found in the report *Design for ETV*. (3)

Seeing.—It is essential that students be able to see television pictures properly. This means that there should be adequate control of internal and external room illumination. For internal illumination fluorescent or incandescent lighting units mounted flush with the ceiling are desirable. The lighting units should be on two or three different circuits so that the level of illumination can be reduced for television viewing and increased for other types of activities. If the classroom has windows, there should be control of light from external sources. Venetian blinds running in channels are commonly used. Receivers should be mounted in such a way as to provide unobstructed vision and good visibility of details in the pictures.

Experience has shown that the television receiver should be mounted in the corner of the average small classroom on the side nearest the windows to reduce reflections, and at a height to make it clearly and comfortably visible. This height usually is about 5′6″ from the floor to the center of the picture. (See Figure 15.)

A maximum viewing distance will need to be adopted as a standard if people of normal vision are to read small details in the picture. A maximum viewing distance equal to 12 times the screen width has been widely used, and visual materials are prepared and televised in such a way as to be legible from this distance. Thus, no student should be seated farther than about 20 feet from a 21-inch television receiver, or 22 feet from a 24-inch receiver.

Generally, square rooms are better than long narrow rooms, but in the latter several receivers may be used if necessary to stay within the maximum viewing distance standard.

Hearing.—It is also essential that students be able to hear the sound clearly. This not only means that the television system should have a good-quality audio system, but the need for acoustical treatment of classrooms is also indicated. It would appear that the best acoustical treatment is a soft floor covering such as carpeting. This covering not only reduces reverberations, but it stops most unwanted noises at their source. Studies have shown that suitable carpeting is economically feasible. A less desirable alternative is treatment of the ceiling and rear wall with acoustical tile. Headsets for individual students are another alternative which has not yet received the attention it deserves.

Ventilation.—Many classrooms are poorly ventilated and improperly heated. Large windows contribute to excessive heat rise in summer and heat loss in winter. Circulation of air is often inadequate and this may result in lack of alertness of students.

Adequate air circulation and reasonable temperature control are essential in classrooms. In some climates this may mean air conditioning; in others good mechanical ventilation systems will be adequate. It may be desirable to eliminate windows from classrooms.

Seating. — Functional, durable seating is also essential. The seats should be placed so as to give the students a good view of the television receiver. They should have adequate work surfaces for note-taking.

Color.—Color may play an important role in the classroom learning environment and attention should be given to its appropriate use.

Large rooms.—In many schools and colleges it is necessary to use cafeterias and auditoria for television viewing. In these large spaces multiple receivers on stands or a large-screen television projector may be used.

Attention to acoustics, control of light, and seating is especially important in very large classrooms. Rear projection may be advantageous in some situations.

TYPES OF TELEVISION RECEIVERS AND METHODS OF SUPPORT

Most schools and colleges are using standard commercial television receivers in the 21-inch, 23-inch, or 24-inch picture sizes. These may be table model or console receivers. They are usually mounted on special stands to raise the receiver to the desired height and to provide mobility. The greatest deficiency of most table models is in the quality of the audio which is often of low output through small loud speakers. Console model receivers are usually somewhat better in this respect, but there is much room for improvement in the audio systems of most television receivers. Commercial models are generally purchased because mass production makes it possible to buy them at more favorable prices than most of the special classroom receivers that are now available. There is little doubt that we shall see the development of improved receivers for classroom television when the volume of sales warrants it and educators demand improvements. Improved arrangements are needed for mounting receivers in some situations, such as special wall brackets, or ceiling suspension mounts.

In any event, it is a good investment to buy high-quality receivers made by reputable manufacturers.

The necessity for maintenance of television receivers should not be overlooked. This may mean carrying a stock of spare tubes and other parts and of having a person available to make repairs and adjustments. Also spare receivers should be available on each floor of each building so that in the event of failure another receiver can be quickly substituted. The use of receivers which incorporate "plug-in" sub-assemblies may facilitate maintenance.

In some circumstances it may be advantageous to contract with an outside company to carry out the maintenance on receivers.

PROJECTION TELEVISION

Projection television receivers offer an alternative method of providing television pictures in a large auditorium. The sound must be provided over a separate audio system.

Some projection television systems work on the principle of projecting the picture from a small, very bright cathode ray tube through a lens system onto a screen. Generally, such receivers must be operated in almost total darkness to obtain a picture of adequate contrast. This situation can be improved by using a rear projection screen which is mounted in the auditorium in such a way that an image is projected on it from the rear. Under these conditions a higher level of ambient illumination may be tolerated in the room. Television projectors can be obtained for as little as $4,000 or as much as $25,000 or more.

A recent Swiss development, the Eidophor television projector, works on a different principle. This projector throws a very bright, sharp image onto the screen. The image is of sufficient brilliance that a good deal of room illumination can be tolerated without serious degradation of the picture. (See Figure 16.)

This use of projection television may make it possible to use auditoria for effective instruction in a way that would be impossible without the availability of this kind of equipment.

FACILITIES FOR STUDENT INTERACTIONS AND RESPONSES

Communication facilities and particularly those which fall into the classification of "mass media" provide for the uni-directional flow of information, instruction, and stimulus materials from a source to individuals, singly or in groups. The media which can be so classified are newspapers, journals, radio, motion pictures, teletype, and of course television. Simply stated, the messages or information are originated, distributed, and presented in some form to people. Additional auxiliary facilities, efforts, and arrangements are required to provide for *reciprocal communications* from readers, listeners, viewers, or learners which will influence and *regulate* the kinds, rates, and flow of the communication. In brief, the media of communications are mainly uni-directional—one way—and this is not always adequate for instruction.

Ideally, conditions for learning resemble intense and engaging conversation: a person speaks, another responds; the interactions are both *progressive* and *reciprocal*. Of all the telecommunication systems, the telephone most closely provides the means for progressive reciprocal communication, usually for two and rarely for more than a few people simultaneously.

There is another related concept: The essential conditions for learning include *interactions* between the learner and the information or materials to be learned. The effectiveness of learning, i.e., the quality and quantity of learning, importantly depends on the intensity, persistence, precision, and extensity of the learning interactions of individuals with the informational or instructional content.

Furthermore, modern views of learning generally agree that controlled reaction of students to learning materials requires knowledge of the appropriateness or inappropriateness, correctness or incorrectness of students' learning responses. Certainly there are many other conditions which are variously described in psychologies of learning which are necessary to and affect learning, retention, and the uses of new information. However, the basic requirements stated briefly above emphasize two main points: (1) Television facilities, as presently conceived and operated, have limitations in providing several important and essential conditions for effective learning. (2) Supplementary or auxiliary facilities and supplementary instructional and learning activities are needed in order to arrange for these conditions.

The focus of this discussion is on what auxiliary facilities are needed to supplement television systems when these are used for instructional purposes. The task of providing supplementary instructional and learning activities is another story. (6)

Television systems provide a superb means for an instructor to talk to students as a person "in the large," even to very great numbers dispersed in space. The problem is to have a means for students to "talk back" to the instructor when this is appropriate and in the interest of the greatest learning for the largest number.

After six years of trial-and-error work at Penn State on equipment development and on a search for components of equipment, it is now possible and practical to provide in each study location or classroom, and for all such locations that are simultaneously in use in an institution for the same instruction, a means for any student to signal the instructor that he has a question or comment. When the instructor is ready to accept the comment or question, he can invite the student to respond. The instructor, in turn, can reply to the student. All students in the different classrooms can hear the student and hear and see the instructor replying over television. Furthermore, the instructor can take the initiative and query or set a problem for the reaction of any particular student in a television section composed of many classrooms and hundreds of students.

This type of auxiliary audio intercommunication system is used with each of the three vidicon professional installations now in full-time use at the Pennsylvania State University (Figure 17). The Case Institute has experimented with interclass communication systems which include both audio and video exchanges. (7) This complex arrangement, which requires a pickup camera in each student class location, would seem to have limited but important practical applicability and future developments are possible.

Several years of very favorable experience supports the recommendation that reciprocal audio communication facilities should be installed *and* *used* as supplementary equipment with all closed-circuit instructional television systems.* The cost will be in the range of $2,000 to $3,000 but the potential usefulness of the equipment justifies the investment.

When television instruction is being distributed over large areas, either by cable as in Washington County, Maryland, or by broadcast as in Chicago City Junior College, Illinois, student to teacher or conference telephone circuits could be used in conjunction with television to provide a means for "feed back." Radio transmission might also be employed in some situations where broadcast channels are available.

The procedures described above may involve *immediate* or delayed reciprocal communication between instructors and students. Delayed exchanges can be arranged by notes, correspondence, conferences, telephone calls, and tests or examinations.

Another essential condition for learning which needs to be provided in instructional television is the opportunity for each student to make responses to the presentations and to be informed of, or have a means of judging, the correctness of his responses. In addition, it is desirable in some instructional-learning situations to have permanent records of student responses. These requirements can be met, mainly, by developing and using a range of different teaching techniques in the production and presentation of televised instruction. For example, emphasis can be put on raising questions, stating issues, defining conflicts and controversies, requiring students to make judgments or inferences from a body of evidence or demonstrations, etc., then providing time for students to make and record their responses and, finally, giving them a basis for assessing the quality or correctness of their performances. These and many techniques and formats of teaching known to be effective can be creatively developed for engaging students actively, intensively, and precisely in interaction with materials to be learned. Many of these conditions can be arranged and controlled within the potentials already built into television facilities. Indeed, it seems possible to develop instructional television facilities into most effective "teaching machines" for implementing the principles of programmed learning.

The need remains to be met for equipment which will record the individual responses of large numbers of students simultaneously and provide permanent individual records for immediate or delayed analysis. There is presently a resurgence of interest in equipment which will serve these functions. Some of these "classroom communicator" and response-ana-

---

* A system of this type called the "Telequest" is manufactured by Community Engineering Corporation, State College, Pa.

lyzer facilities are being produced to function as integral parts of television systems in both broadcast and cable distribution arrangements.* The demand and encouragement of educators for those who are developing new educational products will speed up this development of new equipment.

In summary, what has been said in this section is: (1) that the straightforward linear presentation of information as in the case of pure lectures or even lecture-demonstrations over television does not meet all of the required conditions for learning; (2) that complementary facilities and activities may be necessary; (3) that audio "talk back" systems exist and can be used; (4) that known and proven techniques of instruction for accentuating student interactions with subject matter need to be used more extensively than they are; and (5) that the available means of recording learning responses of students where large numbers are being taught over television need and deserve further development.

NEEDED DEVELOPMENTS IN TELEVISION FACILITIES

Suggestions have been made in this chapter previously about many improvements that are needed in television equipment for use in instruction and education. It is hoped that these suggestions have been noted.

The question might reasonably be raised now of what are the needed developments for the future improvement of instructional television equipment and facilities.

Origination improvements. — It has been suggested that the 3-inch image orthicon equipment may be replaced by 4½-inch image orthicon cameras. This would provide a new level of quality performance in terms of sensitivity, resolution, stability, and reliability at some increase in cost. The requirements are met for the most exacting standards for video tape and perhaps other kinds of high-quality productions and recordings. Developments should be pressed for further improvements in vidicon tubes and cameras. Especially, sensitivity might be increased and thus permit good quality of pictures with lower light and heat levels than are now required. The further development of vidicon color tubes is awaited. Transistorized cameras might become standard while reliability is improved and maintenance costs reduced.

It is possible that the development of moderate-cost kinescopic recording equipment was interrupted prematurely by the advent of video-tape recording equipment. Kinescopic recordings using 16-mm. sound film stock, either with or without rapid processing, would supplement impor-

---

* The Teletest device developed by Corrigan and Associates of Garden Grove, California, is an example.

tantly vidicon installations for many purposes. The film can be projected on 16-mm. projectors and these are widely available.

Relatively few schools, colleges, and universities can easily afford to purchase and operate $50,000 video-tape recorders, however useful and desirable they may be. As has been noted, the development of recorders for less than half this cost, and the reduction of the amount of tape needed by at least one-half, may be a most useful development. These products are already in sight. Future possibilities exist for relatively very low-cost video-sound recorders which may be useful and feasible for small group or even individualized applications. As with TV cameras, the needs exist for a *range of different levels of recording equipment* which can be fitted to different kinds of instructional requirements. A central problem is that of providing adequate and appropriate but not unnecessary quality of recordings and doing this at bedrock costs. Reliability and simplicity of operation and maintenance are important factors. Completely new types of recording processes, as for example those employing thermoplastics, are likely developments.

There would seem to be need for developing TV-originating equipment for many kinds of origination problems. Some examples are "picking up" and "remoting" of print, graphics, photographic materials, and objects from libraries to points of use, the development of equipment for improving science laboratory instruction, and the application of TV systems with auxiliary mechanisms in engineering and technical training. Special microscopes and other optical systems when adapted to television cameras make it possible to show objects greatly magnified to as many students as need to observe them wherever located. Thus, the use of television in science education could replace some kinds of traditional equipment.

Finally, equipment systems need to be developed which will increase the feasibility of originating simultaneously as many channels of video and audio instruction as may be required by educational curricula programs and students, perhaps using computers as control mechanisms. The large number of applications which are possible even in a single school system or institution of higher education make necessary a multiplicity of originations. Therefore, equipment system designs must be developed which include "live" and recorded originations. The problem here is to develop compatible multi-programming systems which satisfy functional requirements but which employ as many common components as possible and are relatively simple to operate.

Distribution.—Even though much progress is being made toward improving distribution systems, new developments are needed. Relatively economical but entirely adequate coaxial cable has been developed, but its production and distribution is restricted, and therefore this type of cable is not available for purchase by educational agencies. The costs of installing or renting cable distribution systems need to be greatly reduced, if possible, by new and simplified equipment. Here again the different methods and equipment for distributing programs, i.e., full-power broadcasts, limited-range broadcasts, microwave links, channel translators, and cable, need to be designed into compatible systems for serving the definable educational functions. The general problem is to distribute selected instructional materials to people where and when these study materials are needed and to do this with the greatest possible reliability and economy of cost and effort.

Ground-based distribution systems may be superseded in some situations where multi-channel and wide-area coverage is demanded. The Midwest Airborne Project has been planned and is being conducted to explore many new possibilities. Communication satellites, now in the experimental stage, may become operational in the next decade. These will make it possible to relay programs over wide areas of the earth. Intercontinental broadcasts of educational and instructional materials are becoming technical possibilities. These future prospects, however, should not displace efforts for the effective utilization of immediately available ways of distributing instructional materials such as the film and video tape network distribution of the National Educational Television and Radio Center with its affiliated educational stations, regional and state tape networks, or even the use of commercial networks (e.g., The Continental Classroom).

Presentation.—Two developments are occurring in the area of televised presentations: First, the designing and producing of small picture tubes, 6″ to 8″, used in conjunction with transistorized TV receivers for individual and small group (two or three individuals) close-up viewing, and second, large-screen projecting of television images. Small TV receivers, equipped with earphones when needed, will make it possible to individualize instruction of learners widely dispersed in study spaces. Large screen television projection will increase the acceptability and feasibility for presenting instruction to classes or audiences which vary in size from several hundred to two or three thousand. New electronic tubes which intensify light reportedly up to 100,000 times are being demonstrated.

A development which is long overdue is the extensive production of better all-channel TV receivers. As the demands for broadcast channels come to exceed the limits of the number of very high frequency (VHF) channels that are available and it becomes increasingly necessary to use ultra-high frequency (UHF) channels, the needs for all-channel TV receivers increase. Furthermore, developments in receivers are needed to make them more suitable for classroom uses: e.g., unitized component construction and the improvement of audio components and speakers. However, many classrooms where receivers must be used are so inadequate acoustically that for good sound reception it may be necessary to provide earphones for students. This would seem to be especially desirable in instruction which requires excellent sound quality as in language and music instruction.

Finally, surely there are many development possibilities for reciprocal communication and recording systems from reception points back to points of origination.

GENERAL LONG-RANGE DEVELOPMENT*

A conference under the auspices of the National Academy of Sciences in September 1959, identified some of the capabilities that education may expect of its instructional apparatus in the future. Among them were:

1. The capability of capturing, in dim or subdued light, black and white or color images, whether static or moving, and of reproducing them almost immediately.

2. The capability of interlinking the classroom master screen (or screens) and those at the individual pupil's desk with outside transmission sources, such as closed-circuit or commercial telecasts or the output of documentary libraries.

3. The capability of transmitting high fidelity, stereophonic sound synchronized with motion picture and television images.

4. The capability of making tape recordings of the entire class, of subgroups of students, or of any single student from his own desk.

5. The capability of connecting the assortment of class and individual television-type viewing screens with a central library from which films, book pages, or documents can be reproduced, upon demand, and without delay.

6. The capability of using more imaginative laboratory and specimen collections: tri-dimensional objects displayed by the best museum techniques and changed to fit the topic currently being taught in each class.

7. The capability of a modular approach to the design of instructional system components, so that as much or as little of the system as needed in a particular instance, can be bought first. Subsequent acquisition of other apparatus items in the total system could thus be achieved with maximum compatibility of components, plus over-all economy.

8. Easy access to low-cost publications in miniaturized form; such as Minicard, Microcard, Microprint, Microfilm, etc.

---

* Quoted from Hauf, H. D., Koppes, W. F., Green, A. C., and Gassman, M. C., *Designs for Learning*, Vols. I and II, Rensselaer Polytechnic Institute, Troy, N.Y. 1961.

Among other developments and trends that have been suggested are:

1. The development of large, flat, wall-mounted television receivers based not on a tube principle, but on a wire-sensitive grid. The receiver will not be limited in size by tube design, but can cover an entire wall, and possibly replace projected television. The unit will be flat and easily incorporated into a wall containing other viewing surfaces.

2. Economical color television. One of the basic drawbacks to current television usage is the lack of color. This is of particular concern in sciences where the color of fluids, organisms, and materials is so critical. Economical color television will open up whole new areas for educational television usage.

ADDITIONAL REFERENCES

1. See for example: Carpenter, C. R., Greenhill, L. P., et al. *An Investigation of Closed-Circuit Television for Teaching University Courses. Report No. 2.* The Pennsylvania State University, University Park, Pa. Spring 1958.
2. *Research on the Communication Process.* Division of Academic Research and Services, The Pennsylvania State University, University Park, Pa. October 1960.
3. *Design for ETV.* Educational Facilities Laboratories, 477 Madison Avenue, New York. 1960.
4. Hauf, H. D., Koppes, W. F., Green, A. C., and Gassman, M. C. *Designs for Learning,* Vols. I and II. Rensselaer Polytechnic Institute, Troy, N.Y. 1961.
5. Valuable sources of additional information are: Brugger, John R. *A Survey of Television Equipment and Facilities Used for Purposes of Instruction by Public Schools, Colleges and Universities.* Board of Education, Washington County, Hagerstown, Md. 1960.
6. See *Interaction in Learning: Implications for Television.* Division of Audio-Visual Instructional Service, National Education Association, Washington, D.C. 1959.
7. Lewis, Philip. *Educational Guidebook.* New York: McGraw-Hill. 1961.

VII. APPENDIX

A NOTE ON THE HISTORY BEHIND ETV

By Richard B. Hull

Mr. Hull is Director of Telecommunications, The Ohio State University.

IN 1932 A SMALL CLUSTER of people on a Midwestern university campus witnessed what were probably the first educational television programs to be broadcast anywhere. They were presented over W9XK, an experimental station developed by the State University of Iowa electrical engineering department. Using a "scanning disc" system instead of a picture tube, the station between 1932 and 1939 transmitted more than 400 programs including lecture courses in art, shorthand, engineering, and botany, as well as drama and other entertainment.

By 1946 there were only six regularly authorized, nonexperimental television stations in the United States with 6,500 receivers. By 1948 there were 40 commercial stations in operation and 600,000 receivers in use. The Federal Communications Commission predicted 400 stations by 1950 and a coast-to-coast television network by 1952. In spite of its technical imperfections and the high cost of receivers, television captured the public imagination in a way no other medium of communication had been able to do. Even then there was little doubt in the minds of radio manufacturers, broadcasters, and advertisers that television would become the dominant medium of the future. Education, however, did not share this vision. It had not pursued the potentials implicit in the Iowa experiments of 1933. Whether television had any role in education, much less the nature of the role, remained to be determined.

The year 1948 found five U.S. educational institutions seriously involved with television and television planning. The State University of Iowa had applied to the Federal Communications Commission for permission to construct a station. Its sister institution, Iowa State College (now Iowa State University), had received a construction permit from the FCC. Kansas State College was operating an experimental station on Channel 1, since removed from the broadcast band by the FCC. The University of Michigan and American University in Washington, D.C., equipped with studios of their own, were producing programs for broadcast over commercial television station transmitters, and other new developments were under way.

In February 1950, WOI-TV at Iowa State College began regular program operation as the 100th television station in the United States and the first nonexperimental educationally owned television station in the world, culminating a planned development begun by President Charles E. Friley in 1945.

Syracuse University had constructed television studios, was producing a full array of programs for release over commercial station WSYR-TV and had instituted the first formal degree program for the professional training of television students.

Michigan State University had begun systematic experimentation in closed-circuit television instruction and planned to build its own station. Other institutions were making plans, some tentative and some definite, to get into this field.

The 1951 Federal Communications Commission allocation hearings which were to result in nation-wide reservation of television channels for education, and a revolution in American educational methods, were about to begin—a precursor to a remarkable series of events.

In April 1952, as a result of those hearings, the Federal Communications Commission established a new kind of broadcast entity, the noncommercial educational television station, and reserved 242 channels in the broadcast spectrum for use by the educational establishment. In July 1952, Kansas State College applied for permission to construct one of these new stations but was unable to proceed and a later applicant was to have the distinction of being first on the air. KUHT, jointly licensed to the University of Houston and the Houston Board of Education, became the pioneer educational noncommercial station on May 12, 1953.

Eight years later there were 62 educationally owned television stations on the air, 57 of them holding noncommercial licenses. Twenty-eight more such stations were under construction or in advanced stages of planning. A "fourth network," NET, a service of the National Educational Television and Radio Center had been developed to meet the needs of this new dimension in education. NET counted 53 of these stations as affiliate outlets, claimed 10,000,000 regular viewers and a potential national audience in excess of 26,000,000 people. Alabama, Florida, and Oklahoma were operating state-wide television networks. WGBH in Boston was the key outlet in a projected regional network which would link East Coast cities from Philadelphia to Montreal. KTCA-TV in Minneapolis had completed similar plans for a six-state network in the central Middle West. Kansas, Nebraska, Maine, and Ohio had engineered state-wide network plans, and the Southern Regional Educational Board in Atlanta proposed a microwave system which would link each of the educational stations and all of the four-year colleges in a 16-state area.

The growth in educational television and broadcast networks was matched by an even more rapid but less costly development in closed-circuit television installations totaling more than 300, Armed Service facilities excluded. Cable and microwave systems were widely employed for special laboratory applications, the observation of university lectures and demonstrations (notably in medical schools) and for the formal instruction of regularly enrolled students on all levels. Installations ranged in size from simple room-to-room one-channel cable connections in a single school building to multiple-circuit systems, complete with studios and video-tape recording equipment. In Anaheim, California, for instance, an entire city school system was linked together; in Washington County, Maryland, the entire county system; at Ohio State University, the entire campus; and in central Texas a cluster of institutions with the University of Texas at Austin as the central point.

By 1960–61 a student body, estimated at 3,000,000 in 7,500 secondary and elementary schools, was receiving televised instruction from noncommercial educational television stations, while an additional 1,500,000 were utilizing closed-circuit television for the same purpose. In higher education, more than 400 institutions throughout the United States had offered credit courses for well over 250,000 registrants on and off campus. "Continental Classroom" on the National Broadcasting Company television network had been watched by at least half of the Nation's science teachers.

Culminating this period of explosive growth was a new development in a different dimension, the Midwest Project for Airborne Television Instruction. Headquartered at Purdue University, MPATI was financed by the Ford Foundation and by corporate grants from Westinghouse and other companies. MPATI had equipped two DC-6AB transport-cargo planes with UHF transmitters, video-tape reproduction equipment, conducted a nation-wide teacher talent search and begun beaming programmed instruction to elementary, secondary, and college students throughout Indiana and its five bordering states.

At the same time the Federal Communications Commission and the National Aeronautics and Space Administration had granted the American Telephone and Telegraph Company permission to orbit a series of satellites on which a new world-wide communications system would be based, a development with even more far-reaching implications for education.

Educational broadcasters could now view these developments from a new perspective which included: nearly a decade of research in instructional television; the passage of Title VII of the National Defense Education Act which for the first time provided federal funds for research in the new media (radio, television, films, teaching machines, etc.); and a pending bill in the Congress originally introduced by Senators Bricker and Magnusson designed to subsidize the growth of television transmission facilities in the several states. Thus with considerably more assurance than existed three decades ago, they had begun tenuous discussions of education's role in the unfolding age of space communications.

These remarkable developments had their roots in a 30-year history of educational involvement with broadcast communications beginning in 1917 when the University of Wisconsin constructed 9XM, the nation's pioneer educational radio station, relicensed in 1921 as WHA.

In 1926 a group of educational broadcasters at the National Radio Conference, called by Secretary of Commerce Herbert Hoover, formed the Association of College and University Broadcasters headed by Robert C. Higgy, manager of WOSU at Ohio State University. First official action of ACBUS was a plea to a conference of state governors for a permanent reservation of radio frequencies for education. Simultaneously, the organization began efforts to secure funds for a professional headquarters, a national program facility, and Washington representation before the Federal Radio Commission, predecessor organization to the Federal Communications Commission.

In 1931 Ohio's Senator Fess backed the new National Committee on Education by Radio in an effort to reserve 15 percent of all radio frequencies for education, and in 1934 Dr. Arthur G. Crane, University of Wyoming president, addressing the annual meeting of the National Association of Educational Broadcasters (successor to the ACBUS), called for government action to reserve 25 percent of the radio spectrum for educational use and the creation of a nation-wide "public service network" whose coverage would parallel that of the Columbia Broadcasting System and the National Broadcasting Company. Crane's hope was that nonprofit and noncommercial stations would make up the matrix of the network; he would also permit commercial stations to have access to the educational and public service features which the new national program enterprise would provide.

During the period from 1920 to 1930 schools, colleges, and universities constructed at least 176 radio stations—perhaps as many as 200 according to some authorities. Properly speaking, a great many of these stations were not educational broadcasting endeavors, but experimental projects in transmission technology sponsored by departments of electrical engineering and physics. By the mid-thirties, following the economic crash of 1929, only 35 of these stations remained. Significantly, most of the survivors were located on Land Grant College campuses where a commitment to off-campus education and to programs of extension education was a chartered obligation of the institution under the Morrill Act which created them. Equally significant was the survival of station KBPS, the Board of Education station in Portland, Oregon, established to serve the city public schools.

Commenting on this attrition in educational station numbers, C. M. Jansky, a leading radio-television engineer and designer of the original 9XM at the University of Wisconsin, pointed out, "The pioneer (in educational radio) was the engineer and not the specialist in education or the educational administrators . . . leading educators never looked upon their stations as major activities (in their institutions)."

Exceptions to the rule were a hard core of state universities in the Midwest whose station managers comprised the leadership in the National Association of Educational Broadcasters, which later spearheaded the effort to reserve television channels for education. One of these institutions, Ohio State University, sponsor of the annual International Institute for Education by Radio, founded in 1930 by Dr. W. W. Charters, Director of the O.S.U. Bureau of Educational Research, provided throughout these lean years the platform where hundreds of educational broadcasters met to discuss the issues in broadcasting, to refine their concepts of radio's role in education, to begin plans for televised education, and to continue their struggle for a place in the sun. Here were conceived and argued the two differing but inextricably related concepts of the broadcaster and his role in education: (1) broadcasting as an instrument of general culture providing an alternative national program service for the mature adult and the out-of-school child; and (2) broadcasting as a systematized and sometimes total tool of formal education. These were the concepts which, in differing forms, were to be argued for the next two decades.

A list of educators, civic leaders, educational broadcasters, and organizations almost too numerous to mention helped to sustain these efforts toward the development of responsible broadcasting, to develop what some called "serious radio," and ascertain the specialized applications of this medium to the needs of formal education. The Payne Fund, the Rockefeller Foundation, the National Committee on Education by Radio, the Association for Education by Radio, the Land Grant College Association, the U.S. Office of Education, and some members of the Federal Communications Commission itself were consistently involved in the pursuit of these goals; the roster would include every member and officer of the National Association of Educational Broadcasters, and finally, the Institute for Education by Radio provided the continuum and the forum which never allowed these issues to be dismissed. Even during World War II, when most of these efforts came to a halt, the Institute continued its annual meetings in Columbus, Ohio.

With the end of the conflict and the emergence of FM, a new electronic process devised by Major E. H. Armstrong for broadcasting sound, educational broadcasting underwent a rebirth and in the words of Dr. Charles Siepmann had its "second chance."

The U.S. Office of Education, the National Association of Educational Broadcasters, and the other national educational groups, encouraged by the Federal Communications Commission, successfully petitioned for educational reservations in the new FM spectrum, thus achieving a precedential decision which established the right of education to its fair share of U.S. broadcasting frequencies.

In 1948 the National Association of Educational Broadcasters retained Cohn and Marks as its Washington, D.C. legal representatives, saw its membership grow to 95 educational institutions with 50 stations in 31 states, and embarked on a preliminary exploration of television in education.

By 1948 the Federal Communications Commission had licensed 1,761 AM (standard broadcast) stations, 290 FM (frequency modulation) stations, and issued 134 authorizations for standard television stations. Of these, seven were licensed to operate, 33 were actually in operation pending final licensing, and two experimental stations were operating commercially under special permission. Television receiving sets were being produced at the rate of 58,000 per month.

New applications for television stations had begun to flood the Commission. It soon became apparent that the original allocation plan for television would not serve the demand. Consequently, the Commission held preliminary hearings to begin development of a new nation-wide television allocation plan. While some educators hoped this plan would reserve channels for educational use, the Commission clearly gave no evidence of such intentions. Meanwhile the vast majority of American educators had expressed little interest or concern about this new electronic medium.

Concerned at this apathy in American education, the National Association of Educational Broadcasters called a special "caucus" at the 1948 meeting of the Institute for Education by Radio and heard C. M. Jansky propose a plan for educational reservations in the Ultra High Frequency (UHF) spectrum, an unoccupied area of the electronic spectrum, which might serve as a "hedge" for the predictable but still unfelt needs of most of American education.

If an observer were to try to define a single time and place where the educational broadcasting movement finally "found" itself, the year would be 1949 and the site, Allerton House, the University of Illinois continuing education center. Dr. Wilbur Schramm, dean of the university communications division, a long-time observer and constructive analyst of "serious broadcasting," concluded that educational broadcasting had reached a critical stage in its development; decisions made now would probably determine its pattern of success or failure for the next two decades.

Schramm, enlisting the aid of the Rockefeller Foundation and the support of Dr. George Stoddard, university president (later to become chairman of the board of the National Educational Television and Radio Center), brought together 30 educational broadcasters from Canada, Great Britain, and the United States. Here, finally, these men began to develop a real synthesis of purpose and to spell out a practical working philosophy which could be widely understood and supported. Here, too, many of the individuals who subsequently fought for educational television channel reservations and became key figures in the educational television movement, met each other for the first time. The functional plans for a nation-wide educational radio broadcasting network were developed at this seminar, and later these same concepts provided the basis for a nation-wide educational television network and program center.

Meanwhile the Federal Communications Commission had released the long-awaited plan for a new nation-wide television allocation system, a proposal which, as had been expected, made no provision for educational needs. The Commission then imposed a "freeze" on any additional television station construction pending completion of hearings on the new allocations plan and issuance of a final allocations order and report. In 1950 there were 108 television stations in the United States, only one of which, WOI-TV at Iowa State College, was licensed to an educational institution.

The only dissenting opinion in the Commission's proposed allocations plan was voiced by Commissioner Freda Hennock. In a history-making plea for the reservation of television channels to meet the present and future needs of education, Commissioner Hennock provided the legal and moral platform on which the educational establishment was subsequently to act; she also became the "mother protector" image of the educational television movement, perhaps its most widely known advocate and an effective champion of almost fanatic zeal. Typically through her efforts, the American Association of Mayors became interested in educational television as an important factor in the late emergence of educational television stations in many communities.

The Commission, having heard testimony in support of its new allocations plan, then established a late summer deadline for the filing of protest petitions. Unhappily, the date coincided with the time when activity in most educational institutions is at its lowest ebb and when most educational administrators are vacationing. However, Cohn and Marks, attorneys for the National Association of Educational Broadcasters, at the request of its president, immediately filed a petition asking for permanent educational reservations in the Ultra High Frequency (UHF) television spectrum, a position promptly supported by co-filings from the Association of Land Grant Colleges and Universities, the Association of State University Presidents, and by the National University Extension Association. Ohio State University's president, Howard Bevis, and Dr. I. Keith Tyler, alerted by the National Association of Educational Broadcasters, worked rapidly and under great difficulty to secure these supporting petitions in time to meet the Commission deadline.

In late 1949 efforts to reserve television channels for education were finally achieving substantial momentum. The United States Office of Education had filed its own petition with the Federal Communications Commission asking that Very High Frequency (VHF) as well as Ultra High Frequency (UHF) channels be reserved for education, and the National Education Association joined in this plea. The issues now were no longer hypothetical ones. Exploitation of the UHF band in an indefinite television future was one thing. Actual and immediate designation of commercially valuable VHF channels for educational use was quite another, and a kind of structured opposition from some areas of the commercial broadcasting industry began to develop.

By 1950 there were a number of supporting national educational groups preparing petitions for educational television reservations. Some of these statements were contradictory in terms of goals and procedures. The differences were sharp enough in some cases so that their public voicing might well have negated a common educational effort. One group, for instance, held out for nonprofit educational television; another for noncommercial educational television; and some for both. In October the president of the National Association of Educational Broadcasters and Dr. Franklin Dunham, Radio Chief of the U.S. Office of Education, called a joint meeting which succeeded in reconciling these differences and resulted in the formation of the *ad hoc* Joint Committee on Educational Television, subsequently to be formalized under the auspices of the American Council on Education. The group voted unanimously to petition the Federal Communications Commission for an educational television reservation plan based upon the concept of nonprofit as well as noncommercial educational television broadcasting stations. Ultimately this point of view was overruled by Telford Taylor, special attorney for the Joint Committee on Educational Television, who with Commissioner Hennock, shared the belief that any "nonprofit" concept would "muddy" education's appeal before the Commission and complicate educational television's future relations with business, industry, labor, and philanthropic foundations.

Proponents of the "nonprofit" plan believed that many sparsely populated areas of the country offered at best only marginal commercial opportunities to prospective commercial television applicants. Yet, here in many cases lay the area of greatest need for television service, both educational and commercial. If the nonprofit concept were to be accepted, responsible licensees such as municipalities or educational institutions (who might thus write off part of their operating expenses) could be encouraged to build stations whose primary goal was public service. However, the concept of the "noncommercial" educational station was presented in the Commission hearings as the only alternative.

Throughout 1950 and early 1951 these various educational groups focused their attention on problems of finance and strategy. The National Association of Educational Broadcasters led by George Probst, Director of the University of Chicago "NBC Round Table," and Seymour Siegel, Director of WNYC and the Municipal Broadcasting System in New York City, began a national fund-raising campaign. These men, the WOI-TV director, the WGBH director, and the NAEB officers, held conversations with C. Scott Fletcher, president of the newly created Fund for Adult Education, an independent organization established by the Ford Foundation. Fletcher and the Fund, keenly aware from the outset of the educational potentials of radio and television, immediately saw six areas of desirable supporting activity which could forward and sustain this endeavor: (1) establishment of a permanent agency such as the Joint Council on Educational Television in Washington to represent education before the Federal Communications Commission; (2) a series of research studies to monitor existing programs on commercial television collecting data for Federal Communications Commission hearings; (3) special subsidized programming for the NAEB radio network to demonstrate the quality levels possible in properly financed educational productions; (4) supported program experimentation at WOI-TV to create new television program formats and develop syndication practices for any national educational television network which might ultimately emerge; (5) a national citizen's committee which would tap business, labor, industrial, and civic leadership; and (6) a national educational television network.

During 1951 and 1952 an almost dizzying series of events took place. The Fund for Adult Education provided interim and then full-scale support to the Joint Committee on Educational Television now formally organized under the American Council on Education. The Federal Communications Commission announced hearings on a new allocation plan which would assign 209 Ultra High Frequency and Very High Frequency channels for educational use, a signal for the Joint Committee on Educational Television to launch a full-scale offensive. The National Association of Educational Broadcasters, through the Lowell Institute, received Fund for Adult Education support for a massive radio program production and study grant which was supervised by William Harley of WHA. The association also undertook a national monitoring study of commercial television program fare headed by Dr. Dallas Smythe of the University of Illinois. WOI-TV, under another grant from the Fund for Adult Education, began experimental educational television production for national distribution. The National Association of Educational Broadcasters, under a grant from the Kellogg Foundation, established a national headquarters at the University of Illinois, put its radio tape network on a professional basis, initiated coast-to-coast educational radio programming, and began the series of professional institutes and seminars which were to provide much of the personnel for the new educational television development. The Joint Committee on Educational Television led by Ralph Steele, its executive secretary, planned, coordinated, and conducted the presentation for the reservation of television channels on behalf of the educational establishment before the Federal Communications Commission, providing that body with 838 petitions on behalf of educational television reservations from institutions of higher education, city boards, and state departments of education, public service and civic agencies. The American Council on Education enlisted the support and counsel of a comprehensive cross section of U.S. educational, business, communications, and governmental leadership in the precedent-making "Educational Television Programs Institute" held at the University of Pennsylvania. The National Citizens Committee on Educational Television, headed by Robert Mullen, its executive secretary, representing more than 100 leaders from business, industry, and labor, was established in Washington, D.C., and a new educational television network program facility, "the fourth network," titled the National Educational Television and Radio Center, was legally incorporated in the State of Illinois, both under grants from the Fund for Adult Education.

High point of 1952 occurred when the Federal Communications Commission issued its Sixth Report and Order which reserved for the educational establishment a total of 242 television channels (80 Very High Frequency and 162 Ultra High Frequency). Shortly thereafter, Kansas State College became the first institution to apply for an educational noncommercial station and in 1953, KUHT at the University of Houston began telecasting programs (1) for the adult and out-of-school child, and (2) programmed instruction for students registered at the university.

All of these events marked the beginning of a new era in American education. The FCC had finally established a new nation-wide television allocation plan; created a new kind of broadcast entity, the "noncommercial educational television station"; and reserved 242 channels (now increased to 267) for exclusive noncommercial educational use by schools, colleges, universities, and nonprofit educational television corporations.

The Commission had insured the development of special cultural and educational television services throughout the nation in an action as significant and far-reaching in its implications as the Morrill Act of 1862 which created the Land Grant College system in the United States.

These decisions by the Commission represented the culmination of an organized effort by citizens and educators, begun more than three decades before. These groups had now staked out a permanent educational claim in a new medium which they repeatedly called "the most important invention since printing," and which, Dr. George Stoddard, Chancellor of New York University, describing the educational television movement, defined as "a new social institution, *not* a supplement to existing institutions."

In 1961 the multiplicity of purposes, activities and differing types of technical installations which the term "educational television" served to describe, did not lend itself to easy generalization.

Education is a complex of processes and purposes. Television is a technical facility with the capacity to transmit sound and sight images. It may be used by many elements of education for a variety of purposes whose requirements may and do differ greatly.

At first, this new term meant broadcasting. Its focus was the educational television station and its purpose to provide an alternative national television program service characterized by its attention to news, information, public affairs, general education, and cultural entertainment. It was conceived within the framework of public as well as educational policy. It was to be directed to a free-choice audience of mature adults and out-of-school children. The vision and the financial support of the Fund for Adult Education made possible the organizational structures, the facilities, and the personnel whose joint efforts had made the first stages of this concept a reality by 1955.

The "broadcast development" in turn provided the basis for the whole "instructional television" development which the Fund for the Advancement of Education, a separate but related agency of the Ford Foundation, beginning in 1955 so significantly pioneered by underwriting experiments and demonstrations in the systematic and regular use of television as part of the daily instruction in schools and colleges. More than 50 colleges and universities, 250 school systems, and better than 300,000 students have been involved in these studies, studies which have consistently demonstrated television's formal teaching potential.

Educational television's potential benefits to U.S. citizens are almost immeasurable. They could now be viewed in terms of alternative program choice, opportunities for formal and informal adult education, out-of-school children's programming, as a method of meeting the new quality and quantity needs of schools and colleges in terms of formal instruction. This whole development had coincided with American education's crisis in a dramatically fortuitous way.

The problem no longer is whether to use ETV as a teaching instrument. The new questions are rather "where" and "when," "for whom" and "how often," and "in what context."

The total educational television effort had dramatized and spotlighted many of education's problem areas in a variety of ways other than its broadcast uses. In one way or another, educational television had involved the whole educational establishment, had made television a major consideration in education's future planning, whether the educational television station was to become its focus or not.

The total educational television movement—its broadcast aspects, the point-to-point development and the special applications of television in education—began to emerge just as the first effects of rapid U.S. population growth were making themselves felt.

If some population experts are correct in their projections—given no atomic war, a constant birth rate, and the maintenance of present living standards—the next 40 years will see an increase in the number of people and their wants and needs which can literally overwhelm the resources and facilities in all areas of endeavor—educational and otherwise.

Existing demands will be multiplied by the sheer weight of human numbers and new demands in every field of need and endeavor will appear. A labor force, whose numbers are limited and whose ranks include the professor, will have to employ every resource of technology to amplify, multiply, and distribute its effort if the present standards of living and education are maintained, to say nothing of meeting the new demands.

In a society whose future depends not only upon an increase in the supply, but in a fundamental upgrading of its scientists and engineers— a society which must somehow secure from the arts and humanities a type of leadership which could make technology a means to an end instead of an end in itself—the agencies of education face their most basic challenge. These concerns are basic in the mind of every educator who has seriously examined educational television in any of its several roles—the inexorable need to step up quantity, the even more fundamental need to improve quality in education. In the search for solutions to these problems, television clearly has great potential and the search in 1961 is well under way.

A NOTE ON ETV AUDIENCES

By Wilbur Schramm

Dr. Schramm is Director, Institute for Communication Research, Stanford University.

THIS IS AN INTERIM REPORT on the NETRC study of educational television audiences.

During the course of this research, six audiences were sampled and studied closely. These included (a) the audience of a state ETV network whose three stations cover most of the state; (b) the audiences of two well-established community-owned ETV stations; (c) the audiences of two university-owned ETV stations, one station broadcasting on VHF, the other on UHF in a community where all the commercial stations are on VHF; and (d) the audience of a school board-operated ETV station. These represent all the distinctive types of educational television station, and are spaced widely around the country.

In addition to these, studies have been made, within the last year, of the Boston ETV audience (by Pool and Adler), the Minneapolis audience (by Carter and Troldahl), and the Champaign-Urbana audience (by Parker). All three of these used the same measure of "regular" viewing as did the NETRC study, and much the same sampling procedure. Thus, in addition to six communities (and eight stations) in the NETRC survey we have three more communities where the audiences were measured about the same time and in about the same way, for comparison. These represent about 20 percent of all existing educational television stations in the United States.

How were the studies made?

In each case, the studies were made in about the same way. A large sample of telephone homes in the viewing area was drawn by random methods from available telephone lists. Relatively brief interviews were conducted by telephone with individuals at all these numbers that could be reached. These interviews served to establish how much use the individual makes of the educational station, how much use of television generally, and enough about his characteristics to test a series of hypotheses about viewers of ETV forming a more highly educated, publicly more active, culturally more advanced, group. From these telephone lists, subsamples were then drawn at random of about 300 viewers and 100 non-viewers, and these individuals were interviewed in their homes. The purpose of the home interview (which lasted nearly an hour) was to find out more in detail the pattern of listening to ETV, to find out in depth what the station means to its viewers, and, so far as possible, why they view it, and in general to ascertain how people relate themselves to educational television and how fully it meets different needs.

The telephone interviews, then, served as a gross measure of audience size and a rough test of some of the main hypotheses about the nature of the audience. The home interview was a study of the audience in greater depth.

How large are the ETV audiences?

Three well-established and skillfully programmed community-owned stations in this country have shown they can attract nearly one out of four adults in their viewing areas to tune in once or oftener each week. The definition of a "regular" viewer used in these studies is an individual who views at least once a week and can remember a program to prove it. These three stations—and I think they will not be offended if their identities are revealed—are San Francisco (KQED), Pittsburgh (WQED), and Boston (WGBH). So far as we know, these are the largest ETV audiences. The other stations in our study draw from 3 to 15 percent, as this table shows:

Station	Ownership	Site	Band	Viewers Regular (Percent)	Occasional (Percent)	Nonviewers (Percent)	N
A	Community	Large city	VHF	24.0	39.8	36.1	1,749
B	Community	Large city	VHF	24.0	37.6	38.4	4,187
C	Community	Large city	VHF	20.9	31.3	47.8	9,140
D	University	Small city	VHF	15.4	29.2	55.4	1,204
E	Schoolboard	City	VHF	13.3	32.1	54.6	3,280
F	State	State network (three stations)	VHF	10.5	28.6	60.9	4,773
G	Community	City	VHF	9.7			3,157
H	University	City	VHF	9.4	37.0	53.6	3,290
I	University	City	UHF	2.3	10.9	86.8	1,930

The audiences vary greatly. If it were possible to imagine an "average" ETV audience, on the basis of these figures, we should have to think of a community in which about 15 percent of the adults view the station at least once a week, and another 30 or 35 percent view it less often. Half the potential audience is untouched.

But there is no *average* audience. Audiences vary greatly with the kind of programs and with the educational and cultural level of the community. It may be that the community-owned stations, being dependent on broad support, learn to program for larger audiences. Stations A, B, and C, in the table, are much older than Station G, and have had longer to learn their programming job. On the other hand, Station I has the unenviable task of broadcasting *UHF* educational programs in a community where all the commercial stations are broadcasting on *VHF*. Only about 15 percent of sets in this community are equipped to receive UHF. Even so, the regular viewers who do stick with Station I on UHF are extraordinarily faithful and interested, and actually spend more time on ETV than the regular viewers of any other stations in our list.

Are ETV audiences changing in size?

In every case where we have an earlier study made in a way that is at all comparable with these late studies, we find that the audiences are growing. On Station B, for example, we have four previous measures. On Station E we have a study made a little less than three years ago. The best inference to be drawn is that the audience of E has nearly doubled in that period, and the audience of B has increased more than 50 percent.

How much do viewers view?

On the average, regular viewers view three or four programs a week. They tend to be extremely selective—to know when a program they want is scheduled, to turn to it, and then to turn off the set. Comparatively seldom do they see even two ETV programs in succession, and almost never do they tune in the ETV station and "let it run," behavior which is more common in commercial television viewers.

In time, they average between one and one-half and two hours a week on ETV, as this tabulation indicates:

	Regular Viewers		Occasional Viewers	
	M	F	M	F
Station A	1:13	1:59	:43	:39
Station B	1:49	2:13	:34	:39
Station F	1:07	1:20	:20	:21
Station H	1:39	1:39	:28	:24
Station I	2:59	3:15	:34	:37

It will be noted that the UHF viewers (Station I), few though they are, give more time than VHF viewers to their educational station. Apparently only the truly interested viewers are motivated enough to view regularly on UHF.

Analysis of the data has not proceeded far enough to permit the making of program ratings, but some idea of what these are can be drawn from preliminary figures on Station E. These are percentages of regular viewers who saw each of these programs on the ETV station during a test week:

Program	Men	Women
	%	%
Ragtime Era	32.1	28.2
Open End	35.7	21.8
Redman's America	19.6	11.5
Decision	16.1	10.3
Your Income Tax	10.7	15.4
Spanish (Monday night)*	10.7	15.4
Invitation to Art	8.9	11.1
Challenge	5.4	14.1
Written Word	10.7	6.5
Eastern Wisdom	12.5	5.1

Now these are not precisely program ratings; they are percentages of the 13.3 percent of adults in the station area who regularly view the station. Thus, if Ragtime Era reaches about 30 percent of these regular viewers, it must have a program rating in that community of about 4. This is good for educational programs, especially when one considers that some additional viewers, outside the regular list, may also have been drawn to it. Commercial audience surveys have several times shown programs like Open End achieving a program rating of about 10 on certain educational stations. But most of the programs on the list just given would appear to have a program rating between 1 and 2, and most studies have found that a rating of 1 is about par for an educational program.

The important aspect of these figures is that some educational programs do far better than par. As the resources and skills of educational stations grow, it should be possible to break par oftener.

What kind of audiences has ETV?

All kinds of people are in the ETV audience, but the group is heavily skewed toward more highly educated people; people who go to lectures, concerts, and meetings; people who read books; people who are politically active and tend to be opinion leaders—in other words, a cultured, active, and probably influential audience. Here are a few illustrative figures:

---

* This audience is larger than for other grade school televised classes because a number of parents are cooperating with a Denver-Stanford experiment that requires them to view, with their children, an evening repeat of the day's class.

	Regular Viewers		Occasional Viewers		Non-Viewers	
	M (Percent)	F (Percent)	M (Percent)	F (Percent)	M (Percent)	F (Percent)
Have some college education						
Station B	63.6	63.7	44.9	40.9	28.3	20.2
Station F	49.6	60.8	31.9	26.0	16.0	13.5
Station H	65.3	58.0	50.2	45.4	38.2	27.0
Have read how many books "since last summer"?						
Station B	5.6	9.0	3.6	4.5	2.0	2.3
Station F	5.1	3.8	1.7	1.6	0	0
Station H	5.7	4.4	2.5	2.6	1.7	1.3
How many magazines read regularly?						
Station B	3.3	3.2	2.9	2.6	.6	.9
Station F	3.5	3.3	2.3	2.5	1.6	1.5
Station H	4.0	3.9	2.9	3.4	2.6	2.6
Have attended concerts this year						
Station B	27.6	30.9	20.4	20.5	13.5	10.4
Station F	17.6	20.2	13.3	12.2	7.7	10.5
Station H	28.1	34.5	17.2	22.4	8.9	9.9
Have attended lectures this year						
Station B	33.8	32.8	22.5	18.2	15.5	12.3
Station F	34.0	25.7	20.9	13.3	8.3	9.3
Station H	41.3	26.9	18.4	16.3	13.1	8.8
Have attended discussion group or evening course this year						
Station B	28.5	30.9	16.4	27.3	10.8	9.9
Station F	30.1	26.4	20.6	16.9	11.7	8.4
Station H	28.1	29.4	18.4	17.5	11.5	8.0
Have attended civic meeting this year						
Station B	34.2	39.7	22.5	15.9	24.3	18.9
Station F	56.2	49.8	40.2	41.8	33.8	32.2
Station H	39.7	43.7	28.0	28.8	21.5	18.7

In some places this pattern is seen in an extreme variant. For example, in the case of Station D, which is in a small university city, half the viewers were professional people, and one quarter of the viewers were professors or in the families of professors. It would have been interesting to carry that study beyond the borders of the city, to see what kind of audience the station attracts in a region where there are fewer professors. But on the other hand, every audience has deviants. Every ETV audience includes a number of persons with so little education that one wouldn't expect to find them there. Every ETV community contains a number of highly educated persons who don't view ETV and some who are not only highly educated but also go to concerts, read books, and are politically active—and *still* don't view ETV. These deviant groups are being intensively studied at this moment, and a report on them will come later.

One interesting deviant group is in the male audience of Station A. The female audience of that station fits the typical pattern—high education, cultural and public affairs interest, and so forth—but the male regular viewers are actually lower in education than the male occasional viewers or non-viewers. This is apparently because Station A did an excellent and intensive job of putting university and professional athletics on the air. This attracted male viewers who otherwise would not have been in the ETV audience, but made little difference in the female audience. Now the interesting thing to find out is whether these male viewers have learned to like *other* ETV programs besides athletics.

It is worth noting that families with grade school children are more likely to be in the audience than families with either younger or older children. Knowing that children in a given family tend to view ETV if parents do, and vice versa, we can guess that ETV is doing its best job for children of grade school age.

One more detail: Viewers of ETV are likely to spend *less* total time on television than are non-viewers. Therefore, ETV is usually substituted for, not added on, commercial TV time.

Why do they view?

One of the main questions being analyzed at the moment is the motivation for viewing ETV, and the gratifications that result from viewing it. Undoubtedly there are a number of different patterns of motivation and gratification involved. In the audience are doubtless some refugees from the parts of commercial television they don't like, some seekers after self-improvement, some intellectually curious persons, some aesthetically hungry persons, and so forth. It will be possible to tell more about these patterns shortly.

Meantime, however, it has become clear that ETV does look quite different to its regular viewers from the way it looks to others. And commercial TV looks different through the eyes of people who also view ETV. Here are two examples, from semantic differential tests:

	Said *ETV is fun*	*CTV is fun*
	(Percent)	(Percent)
Viewers of ETV	43	32
Non-viewers of ETV	11	65

The same reversal will be seen in the responses to questions as to how satisfying the two kinds of TV are:

	Said *ETV is satisfying*	*CTV is satisfying*
	(Percent)	(Percent)
Viewers of ETV	84	30
Non-viewers of ETV	23	52

Here is a table made up from free responses to the question of what viewers think are the reasons why the persons they know are attracted to ETV. Asking the question in this way is likely to bring out a less self-conscious and less biased answer than asking viewers why *they* view.

	Rank Order of This Reason Among Viewers of Station		
	B	F	H
General self-improvement: intellectual curiosity, the wish to learn and to consider ideas in general, rather than learning a particular skill	1	1	1
Specific self-improvement: the wish to learn a particular skill or craft that will be useful	3	2	2
Enjoying the programs—not self-improvement, but enjoyment	2	4	4
Reaction against commercial TV — against violence, commercials, and so forth	4	5	3
Wish to get something good for children on TV.......	5	3	5

Of course, these are very general statements, and we shall know much more about them when the analysis is complete. Yet there is a general trend in the answers, and it fits with what we know of the audience in other ways. ETV tends to attract all these kinds of people, and for all these and other reasons.

Why is it that non-viewers *don't* watch? We asked viewers why they thought those among their acquaintances who were non-viewers did not view. The answers, like those just given, require a great deal of further study and interpretation, but they are also interesting and, for the most, logical and convincing. The reason most often heard is that people are accustomed to thinking of the TV set as a source of entertainment; they are in the habit of using it that way, and don't like to "shift gears" and use it for learning, which means work rather than entertainment. The second and third reasons were about tied. One was that some people just don't know enough about ETV; it isn't advertised enough; people aren't exposed to it on all sides as they are to commercial TV. The other was that some people just don't like ETV programs; they feel these programs are sometimes dull, and sometimes not quite professional quality as they are used to seeing it in commercial TV, and sometimes require a degree of effort that is out of proportion to their rewards. A fourth reason given is related to what has just been said: that some people are a bit lazy about tackling education on the air.

Let me hasten to say that no one is so naïve as to think that these stated reasons are necessarily the real or complete reasons. But they give some of the flavor of the extraordinarily rich material which is now being analyzed, and which, we hope, will allow us to describe and understand educational television's audience more fully and deeply than ever before.

EDUCATIONAL RADIO: ITS PAST AND ITS FUTURE

By Harry J. Skornia

Formerly president of the National Association of Educational Broadcasters, Dr. Skornia is now a professor, teaching radio and television, in the College of Journalism and Communications at the University of Illinois. He was asked to write about the lessons to be learned from the history of educational radio, and the probable future importance of educational radio in the period when educational television is looming so large.

IN ALL TOO MANY TREATMENTS of educational media and methods these days, educational radio is mentioned in a postscript or minor position. The present writer believes that as solid a record of accomplishment as that of educational radio over the past 40 years needs no apology. The present treatment therefore will likely disappoint all who expect a defense or apologia for radio as an instrument of education.

In view of what already available evidence proves that radio can do— in many cases better, in other cases only more economically and faster— than other media, we believe that radio is one of the most important weapons in our arsenal for the combating of ignorance. This belief applies both to the United States and to the the world situation. It is my honest belief, for instance, that we are not getting the best possible mileage and service out of the combinations of media now available to us; and that television, especially, but in some cases other media as well, is frequently being wasted on things which radio can do better.

We shall later have occasion to examine in greater detail radio's supplementary or "team" role—its use with all other media, and with teaching machines. At present, however, it is sufficient to stress that, although words, pictures, print, and other symbols are all essentially media of communications, they are not interchangeable. When they are substituted, one for another, significant changes occur in results and products. Research is only now awakening to the need for studies into the unique biases and roles of the various media in anything like an adequate approach to the real meanings to our society of these media. We have come a considerable distance since we believed that we had nothing to worry about from media except content.

In the United States we have too often, I fear, come to consider two very different factors or characteristics as if they were the same. I refer, of course, to quantity and quality. The "best" program on television—even by many educational broadcasters' standards, I fear—has come to be considered the one that attracts the largest audience. The presence of a host of "stars" on a program makes it a "better" program—i.e., one of better "quality" than a simple program with few or no celebrities. A "showman" is "better" than a professor. By these standards a full or crowded screen or lots of movement or action is "better" than the simple, the stark, or the modest; the fast is better than the slow, etc.

Equally relevant here is the conviction that seems to prevail in education as well as in commerce that communication through more than one sense is "better" than that exercised through only one sense. Seeing a newsman read the news is preferred by many to merely hearing him read it. Generally, because it is more attracting or "entertaining," even educators are likely to fall into the cliché that television is "better" in such a case, that they "get more out of it." The possibility that television may in fact be poorer or *less* effective, depending of course on what you want done, is rarely heard or hazarded. To pursue this point a bit farther, sound film is generally simply accepted as "better" than silent film or slides; color than black and white; a globe than a flat map, etc.

In such cases we may be confusing attraction and interest with impact. For interest and attraction are not necessarily related in any direct way to learning—which is the use we are interested in. As the editors of the *Yearbook of Education* (1) point out: "This is no doubt correct with regard to casual observers and more or less passive spectators. Yet doubts remain. Simply to add further stimuli not relevant to the message being transmitted may seriously interfere with interpretation and understanding. A moving film of a steam engine is not necessarily improved, as a teaching aid, when the sound of whistles and the clang of piston rods is added. While granting that television is more *attractive* to audiences than sound-radio, we must not assume that it is always to be preferred in the classroom."

A shotgun may be better for certain uses than a rifle. But we often may not want that many pellets in the game.

Some media may widen the perspective like a wide-angle lens, when what is needed is to pinpoint one aspect or factor or quality, or at least one of them at a time. For certain jobs a nail is better than a knife, besides being more economical. Dispersal rather than concentration sometimes characterizes multi-sensory effects—whereas education requires concentration and focusing more often than not. We often forget this, since entertainment often gains by the vagueness that broad shots can so well provide.

Someone in the commercial broadcast industry once said that in radio we have "a rifle for shooting down large minorities." While I do not like the rather ruthless businesslike concept, it is true that radio does help education over the one big hurdle it has in the use of what have been all too readily labeled "mass" media—the need for *individual* listening and attention which genuine education always requires.

In recent years, in fact, radio has tended to become a medium listened to by one person per set, on an individual basis. It has moved out of the living room in which social "dispersal" often prevails, to the bedroom, the kitchen, and the study where people, alone, are likely to be in a more "concentrating" mood. In this respect it is closer to reading or the teaching machine than any of the other media currently in use. In this respect, therefore, radio is in an almost ideal position to attract and serve individual interest groups which education everywhere must always identify and recognize, since "mass education" is in many senses a contradiction in terms.

Otto Neurath, the distinguished Austrian scholar, once said that "the best teacher is he who is best at leaving out." In this sense, the various media need to be examined with regard to the extent to which they do what is required, without doing so much more than is needed that they erase what was accomplished—or doing what the student himself must do if learning instead of merely exposure is to take place.

For the first 20 or so years, as several scholars have observed, the phonograph was dedicated to bell-ringers, musical saws, the dialogues of comedians, etc. It is not altogether certain that television and radio may not still be at that stage. Certainly radio has not yet even begun to provide that service to education of which it is capable. Significant breakthroughs undoubtedly still lie ahead in the uses of radio as well as those of the other media now available to education. In several respects the nature of these breakthroughs is being suggested by uses being made of radio abroad more clearly and imaginatively than in the United States. The uses of the electronic media in newly emerging countries without the fulcrum of literacy which is available in most Western nations reveals the promise of radio in ways which the United States has all too superficially explored and frequently dismissed.

Before we turn to some of these uses of radio, on behalf of education in other nations, however, let us take a brief backward look at the history of educational radio in the United States.

Historical background, United States educational radio

The first educational radio station in the United States, WHA, the University of Wisconsin, began a regular broadcast service on or about January 3, 1921, following some two years of operation on an experimental basis. During the next four years 175 licenses were issued for other so-called "educational" radio stations. Most of these licenses were issued to the engineering departments of schools of various types, or to speech,

English, or other departments, indicating a "blind man and the elephant" concept of the role of this new medium and its place in the educational institution.

By 1926 nearly half of these stations had disappeared with hardly a trace. During the 15-year period from 1921 to 1936, according to Harold E. Hill's *National Association of Educational Broadcasters: A History* (2) and S. E. Frost's *Education's Own Stations* (3), a total of 202 broadcast licenses were issued to educational institutions. One hundred sixty-four of these were revoked or allowed to expire during this period, leaving only 38 licensed stations of this type by January 1, 1937.

Secretary of Commerce Herbert Hoover held Annual Radio Conferences throughout the early twenties from 1922 through 1925. At the Fourth Annual Radio Conference, in 1925, the decimated group of educational broadcasters, finding little support and sympathy at the hands of either the government, the press, their commercial brethren, or educational administrators, banded together into a mutual protective association called the Association of College and University Broadcasting Stations (ACUBS). This organization in 1934 changed its name to the National Association of Educational Broadcasters, hereafter referred to as the NAEB.

In the bitter struggle for available frequencies in the twenties and thirties, educational radio found it had some friends in Congress, a few in education, but almost none in the industry or the regulatory agencies involved, which were already then taking on the coloration of the industry regulated. Hill's study quotes Paul Segal of WOW, Omaha, opposing the application of WCAJ, of Nebraska Wesleyan, which was successfully crushed out of existence: "Our contention is that as a matter of principle educational programs should be given by stations having regular listening audiences—WOW desires to take the responsibility of rendering this service to the public." (4)

The magazine *Radio Guide* of those days declared, regarding the direction of Congress in the 1934 Communications Act, requesting the newly created FCC to study the feasibility of setting aside specific frequencies for education, in its editorial of September 15, 1934: "Americans do not want education thrust down their throats or into their ears. You can't force education on a nation. There are types of educational programs to which the public does respond, and these programs are available today. The National Broadcasting Company devotes more than 20 percent of its time to highly educational features. The Columbia Broadcasting System runs a little higher." (5)

Broadcasting magazine was generally inclined to question the need for separate frequencies for education and particularly to question the motives of educational broadcasters. The same was true of the National

Association of Broadcasters (NAB) which on more than one occasion took positions which could hardly be called friendly to education.

As education was moved from one untenable position and from one undeveloped portion of the spectrum to the other, and as more stations were forced out of existence by the costs of litigation and other obstacles, Dean A. M. Harding of the Extension Division of the University of Arkansas declared: "The men [of the FRC, predecessor of the FCC] merely cut off the arms, legs, and head of an educational station and then allow it to die a natural death." (6) He was referring to what appeared to many educational station operators as repeated evidences of discrimination against them. In reply to repeated suggestions by Congress for reservations on behalf of education—from a bill by Senator Simeon Fess of Ohio in 1931 which proposed to reserve 15 percent of all channels for education through the years until 1938 when the first (UHF and therefore not "regular" or "standard") frequencies were finally set aside for education in what was later to be the FM band, the FRC, the FCC, and the industry provided little encouragement or help for education in the use of the electronic media. Commerce, "free enterprise," freedom from regulation, and freedom from government activity in education characterized this period, and there were few inclined to challenge the belief that the use made of radio by commerce was a proper use, if not indeed the only thinkable use.

Had leading educators of the United States in greater numbers called for such reservations, or themselves been more enthusiastic about radio in education, this situation undoubtedly would have been different. It is therefore difficult to condemn opponents of educational reservations without at the same time regretting the absence of more voices within education itself on their behalf.

Fortunately there were a few who were concerned and who spoke up. In 1931 the Payne Fund had made a $200,000 grant which made possible the creation of what was to be called the National Committee on Education by Radio (NCER). That educational radio, frequency reservations, and efforts on behalf of the use of these media for education continued at all was undoubtedly due very greatly to this grant and the efforts of people it interested in a new aspect of education.

In March of 1940, S. Howard Evans, Executive Secretary of the NCER, declared: "Future developments in this [FM] field might make possible an educational broadcasting chain which would lessen the burden on individual stations so that they could concentrate on quality rather than quantity." (7) This called to mind the earlier proposal made in Iowa City in September 1935 by Dr. Arthur G. Crane (President of the University of Wyoming and Chairman of the Radio Committee of the National Association of State Universities) for a separate, publicly owned network, to which 25 percent of available frequencies would be assigned. Such a network would, he suggested, be operated by the federal government, which would be advised by a system of boards made up of individuals "selected as carefully as are judges." (8) This was the most ambitious proposal on behalf of education and public ownership of stations in the electronic spectrum until Walter Lippmann, in October of 1959 in his syndicated column called for a publicly owned federal television network. During the forties some gains were made. Educational radio began to grow again, though many of the new stations were still of the ten-watt FM variety, largely student-operated.

In 1949 and 1950, thanks largely to the efforts of then Dean of Communications at Illinois, Dr. Wilbur Schramm, grants to the University of Illinois were secured from the Rockefeller Foundation to make possible what are now referred to as the First and Second Allerton Seminars. From these meetings of educational radio station managers and program planners emerged the philosophical and program idea bases of educational broadcasting as we know it today and which finally began to unfold in the 1950's. For the first time a unique and distinctive role was recognized for educational broadcast media. The first major breakthrough was near.

In quick succession other philanthropic foundations became interested, and contributed. Nineteen hundred and fifty-one brought a quarter million dollar grant from the W. K. Kellogg Foundation to the NAEB to make possible the creation of a central office for the NAEB on behalf of educational broadcasting and the launching of an "educational network" by tape—the world's first "educational" network as such. Later Kellogg grants supported these efforts for a total of 11 years, on a declining grant basis, as the NAEB and the network became increasingly self-supporting.

In the same year, 1951, the Fund for Adult Education provided the first of several grants to the NAEB amounting to over a quarter of a million dollars to develop outstanding programs for distribution by the NAEB's tape network. The growing numbers of stations which followed both of these grants attest to the debt owed both the Kellogg Foundation and the Fund for Adult Education by American education. Until the National Defense Education Act of 1958, which made some provision for modest expenditures on radio projects, no significant grants were made for radio after the Kellogg and FAE grants mentioned above. With the advent of television, radio went into eclipse. In some cases the plundering it experienced—for budget, personnel, and ideas was total, and some stations were closed down because "radio was dead," as several television promoters declared. In other cases radio merely saw itself reduced to the barest of subsistence budgeting.

The 1950's were lean years for radio, and only with the dawning of the sixties did a solid resurgence of interest in radio begin to manifest itself here and there.

Fortunately, as will be seen below, the situation was somewhat better in various other parts of the world, to which television was to come later or in a different form.

Without the support of the Payne Fund, the Rockefeller Foundation, the W. K. Kellogg Foundation, and the now defunct Fund for Adult Education, which operated on funds from the Ford Foundation, there would today probably be no educational broadcasting in the United States deserving of attention—if indeed there would be any at all.

With the launching of the NAEB Tape Network in 1951, and the opening of the NAEB's permanent offices at the University of Illinois, which provided generous support under Dean Schramm's direction, educational radio was finally securely launched, with reserved frequencies, at least, in the FM spectrum. Television frequencies were to come later; as this is written, efforts are still being made to secure some portion of the AM or standard radio band on a reserved basis for radio as well.

Radio in education outside the United States

While Marconi's miracle invention was in the United States being taken over largely by commerce and entertainment, as if radio were by nature solely or principally an instrument of pleasure and a tool of salesmen, other countries were having their own experiences.

In *The Listening Schools*, a BBC publication, K. V. Bailey quotes Mary Somerville regarding the first broadcast she ever heard in a school: a talk on music by Sir Walford Davies. "Things happened in all of us, in the children, in their music-loving teacher and in me. Beauty could now (through radio) enter every home and every classroom! After the broadcast we made our own music—and then, far into the night, she (the teacher) and I talked of what this brave new medium of communication might mean to the schools." (9)

In Britain, between the first broadcast to the public in 1920 and the granting of the BBC's first charter in 1927, radio had grown up in a quite different way from the path it followed in America. It was, in Britain, looked upon as a public service. The famous "Kent Experiment," carried out in 1927 and published by the Carnegie United Kingdom Trustees in 1928, brought in a strong and favorable report on radio's usefulness to education—especially in radio's role of supplying "something that cannot be supplied by ordinary methods." As Mr. Bailey relates: "A contribution to the education of young children was at the beginning of the nineteen-thirties an experiment in school broadcasting. At the end of the decade it was an achievement." (10)

In 1929 the Central Council for School Broadcasting was established. School radio—as an enrichment and supplement to other procedures— was a success in Britain. It has ever since continued to be widely used.

In view of interference problems which early plagued the BBC's standard broadcast outlets over which the school programs were broadcast, VHF, the British equivalent of our FM, won early appreciation for its clarity and freedom from interference.

Besides regular school uses of the radio in Great Britain there are others which deserve mention. In 1939 the first programs teaching English by radio were broadcast by the BBC. Today such broadcasts go to 61 countries in 35 languages, for elementary and secondary level lessons around the world. Today, too, quoting R. C. Steele in the 1960 *Yearbook of Education,* "The BBC, which broadcasts some three million words a year to the schools alone, must be the greatest single provider of educational material in the world." (11)

In India educational broadcasting has been practiced since 1929. Even before the organization of All-India Radio, schools were being serviced by radio at both the elementary and secondary levels.

To mention only a few of the more important uses outside the United States following World War II, United States consultants urged the creation in Germany, Austria, and Japan of Schools of the Air. Many of these were patterned on such schools of the air as those of Wisconsin and Minnesota. By 1948 all major German and Japanese stations were operating such Schools of the Air. Teaching manuals and procedures were soon appearing which in many ways excelled those of the United States. For by this time in the United States itself, television's advent and glamour were seriously interfering with the growth of educational radio. This problem seems never to have been as serious abroad as in the United States.

One by one, increasingly distinguished uses of radio in education appeared: in France, the Scandinavian Countries, the Low Countries, Germany, Austria, Italy, India, Japan, Jugoslavia, and the Middle East. As this is written, several countries which have used time on existing broadcast systems are planning the development of separate educational networks. Robert Lefranc, reporting on plans for France, for instance, writes: "A new national radio network is being planned in France, a network which will be exclusively devoted to educational purposes." (12) Plans in various African and Asian countries call for intensive uses of radio which will dwarf efforts made so far in the United States. Sir Patrick Renison, Governor of Kenya, in his dedication speech for the new Broadcasting House in Nairobi in late 1960 is quoted as having declared: "While many Africans may still be unable to read and write—they are accustomed by long tradition to listening—radio can, at this juncture, fill the vacuum better than any other medium of communication in bringing people out of the darkness of ignorance into the light of knowledge." (13)

The NAEB, as Contractor for the International Cooperation Administration, is, as this is written, sending the first members of qualified teams to selected African nations for the establishment of radio as a "bridge" desperately needed to meet the educational and literacy needs imposed by the coming of self-government.

In such new countries, where literacy and a heavy investment in print-based materials do not exist, the social and educational balance resulting from the use of the electronic media challenge far more basic attention than has so far been given to the use of these media in the United States.

Let us take as a brief case history one instance of the use of radio on behalf of education in an underdeveloped country—Colombia, South America. This development is excellently reported in the 1960 *Yearbook of Education* by Señor Pablo M. Ozaeta. It describes the activities, during the past several years, of Radio Sutatenza, operated under Catholic auspices. Perhaps the greatest single problem attacked by this station was illiteracy. Under the inspired and crusading leadership of Father Salcedo, however, far more has been done than teaching illiterates to read.

Señor Ozaeta reports that "the greatest methodological difficulty was to change the listener into the student. Radio was apparently unable to take the place of the teacher. But it was noticed that a man who could only just read and write was able to act as an intermediary between the radio teacher and the students without himself teaching anything." (14)

Radio, it should be noted, is not used to do the various tasks *alone*. And why should it in an age when other media needed are available?

A few results of this project:

1) Eight hundred letters a day are received from individuals who, a year ago, were illiterate.

2) Using Radio Sutatenza, the Ministry of Education has conducted teacher-training courses for teachers, 86.3 percent of whom previously had had only four years of primary schooling. Sixty-five hundred teachers have so far passed examinations which conclude the four-year teacher-training courses given.

3) Thirty-eight percent of the soldiers called up are illiterate. They are taught to read and write in 75-lesson series. Similar special programs for the prisons have likewise been most successful.

4) Twenty-two thousand five hundred houses had been remodeled or improved as a result of these radio-based rural education efforts.

5) One hundred eight-four thousand seven hundred vegetable plots, to relieve vegetable and dietary deficiency, are traceable to radio's catalyzing efforts and leadership.

6) Some 2,030,450 trees have been planted in a reforestation project initiated by the radio station.

7) Nearly 4,000 aqueducts have been built—each serving from 10 to 12 families to a whole village.

8) Over 2,000 athletic fields were built and over 3,000 basketball teams had been formed by 1958.

9) Twenty-eight thousand cesspits and 14,000 roads and bridges have been built; over 15,000 rural workers had learned to vaccinate domestic animals, etc., by 1958.

10) "A series of farm booklets, at the price of one egg each, will shortly be published every week." (15)

Such is the success story of radio in one remote area.

It is when one has an opportunity to study examples of this sort that one becomes ashamed of the lameness of so many efforts in the use of radio —in cooperation with any or all other tools, in what might be called "over-privileged" or "over-developed" countries, like the United States.

Some uses of radio in education

After the purposely brief and general look we have taken at the history of educational radio in the United States and elsewhere, let us seek to assess its value—not merely in terms of past accomplishments, which are substantial—but also in terms of unique potential and proved ability.

J. C. Carothers has written: "When words are written they become, of course, a part of the visual world. Like most of the elements of the visual world, they become static things and lose, as such, the dynamism which is so characteristic of the auditory world in particular." (16)

With the invention of radio and television, we told ourselves, we had new instruments with a unique characteristic: they did not have a backlog or accumulation of materials crying to be re-used. Such an accumulation, insisting on being amortized, is a conservative force so powerful that it often renders progress either impossible or so slow that the potential revolution which these media made possible becomes the slow march of "too little, too late."

Radio did not have this albatross around its neck. But then came the use of records and tape recorders. With the use of these archive, library, and other media materials—and we are not here saying such use is bad— radio, like television, becomes something different from the "live" medium we thought it would be. The electronic media suddenly became laden and leaden with all the accumulated ballast of the *old* media—an accumulation of generations—from book-based ideas as to how to use these non-lineal media to the inheritance of union copyright and other problems which we thought belonged to other fields. We thought we had a window on the world, a telescope. We found we had a microscope, instead, in all too many of the uses of these media.

Undoubtedly the NAEB Radio (by tape) Network has given the United States much that is desperately needed, which our nation would not otherwise have. But, as one suggestion for the use of radio, how about a return to those functions, for radio, which capitalize on its peculiar qualities of immediacy, intimacy, and stimulation to the kind of achievement illustrated by Radio Sutatenza?

In an interesting brief monograph, Canadian scholar Alan Thomas says: "Neither country (United States or Canada) has accepted radio and television as distinct media. . . . As long as broadcasting is regarded as a means of contributing to other forms of art, then there will remain a conflict between the artistic productions of radio and television and established culture." (17)

Interested as we are in improved and increased selective uses of radio along lines already familiar, we are even more interested in suggesting and exploring uses which capitalize more fully on radio's own unique capabilities and qualifications rather than merely its efficiency as a transportation or pipeline facility of the common carrier type which it has so largely been to date.

Let us turn now to what might be some such uses. Dr. Kenneth Harwood in an as yet unpublished manuscript (18) of a study of the accomplishments of sound broadcasting during the past 30 years, raises some interesting questions. "When sound broadcasts are freely selected by individual listeners, informative effects appear to be produced most often by lyrics of popular songs, news reports, popular drama, and other presentations that are not perceived by general audiences to be directly and seriously informative in intent," he states. We have been aware of the defenses which many people erect against "speakers," "education," "politicians," etc., whereas they remain vulnerable to programs not so labeled, which shape them far more. But the question raised here goes even further. Should the *real* message, or capsule, or trigger for action, be put in popular song form? Or spots? Perhaps before we exclaim in outrage we should at least experiment a bit with techniques of this sort. In respectable educational hands they need be neither obnoxious nor high-pressure. How *is* educational content best transported or translated?

Another observation by Dr. Harwood: "Sound broadcasting of announcements may accomplish substantial informative purposes. Both recognition and recall are aided by repetition of very brief messages." Perhaps "programs" alone as we have conceived them, are not yet quite what we need?

Or how about the use of various sounds instead of words for providing commentary, stimuli, or other effects? "In addition to setting mood, music without words may provide a more incisive commentary than any verbal statement. The sound broadcaster who wishes to make complete informative use of the medium . . . should . . . make more of music than a filler of backgrounds or transitions." It would appear that stereo and other areas are less peripheral and nonintellectually relevant than many broadcasters and educators alike have assumed: Is another look perhaps justified? Music is "content" in effect, after all, in many respects, it would appear.

The more we learn about these media, the more we learn that their effects are not merely hit-or-miss. There are specific "best orders," for example, in which to present materials by more than one medium. The printed version of certain types of material should precede the aural version, we find, for example—while the contrary applies in other situations. Some of these "laws" of learning by the various media may be surprising, but they do appear to exist and to be discoverable. Those responsible for the use of radio in education would do well to engage qualified scholars to help guide them in their discovery and application.

Flying by "the seat of the pants" may have been adequate once. With jets and missiles now involved, it no longer is. The same applies to radio programming. Much of what we "know" is simply not true. What was true ten years ago, before the cross-bombardment of radio by television and vice versa, and of viewer-listeners by both, again is no longer true. The impermeability factor of viewers and listeners is changing with every passing year. There are no permanently right answers in many areas of communication today.

Many stations now being planned, I fear, will look very inadequate in a few years, when satellite-based world coverage is a reality. Some of the program and educational approaches now being discussed will appear even more anachronistic in a world that is becoming one whether we like the term "one world" or not.

Democracy depends as much on the free flow of vital and new information today as a city or nation depends on water, if it is to survive. The intellectual thirst, or drought, of a nation, is less apparent than that for water. But it is no less real. It shows up in crime, boredom, standards of values in public and business life, delinquency, tastes, and the like. Radio is and will remain the medium of mass communication through which the public will receive its first (and therefore usually most lasting) information and impression of what is occurring. Whether taken as simple diversion or not—and much of what we absorb is so taken—does not reduce or alter the power and permanence of radio's effects, particularly its unintended ones.

That many educational stations do not see themselves as crucially central to this function—not merely as stations, but as the sacred and indispensable channels to the people of their institutions and resources, is perhaps one of the most shocking aspects of educational station operation. If education does not "correct" the images now seen almost solely through the polarized and rose-tinted glasses of commerce, who will?

Let us not count unduly on print to correct this picture. With newspapers shrinking in number and diversity, the balance is no longer adequate. The breakdown which some scholars are beginning to point to in the dominance of our world by print and even verbalism begins to take on meaning. A distinguished American educator used to refer to "those d—— black marks (print, the alphabet) to which children all over the world are forced to devote the major portion of their youth." This age is past. Today what youths learn to do and believe reaches them largely through the electronic media. For education to abdicate these media—leaving them to commerce, is both dangerous and a violation of educational responsibility. And we refer especially to radio. For the electronic miracle tools of radio and television to have been used in such a way as to allow the people to become as out of touch with the concepts of democracy as they apparently have, is not only a story of misuse of the media by those who use them; it is an indictment of those who *should* be using them: *viz.,* educators.

To have these media used to make spectators instead of participants of us can be fatal in a democracy. Education must move itself into a more central position of influence with reference to the use of these media. It cannot do this itself while remaining a "spectator."

In the area of news we have come to believe many clichés. An hour-long documentary, it is often alleged, is an excellent contribution by the networks, especially if they spent a great deal of money on it. Yet in many cases such programs are little more than a hodgepodge of fractionalized impressions. Educational significance can be illustrated by educational radio as well as by television, by the use of simpler techniques, and more qualified authorities. The "heap of stuff" which hypnotizes us into nodding in approbation does *not* often meet the needs of people who learn from whatever they see. Education must do better.

At times education must take issue with the urgings of the commercial media which would keep John Q. Public in his consumer role, and immobilized before his television set. Education traditionally is intended to *activate* man, not to immobilize him. Let it so do in this instance. To those who would raise the question as to whether such a suggestion is not unrealistically naïve, we would ask: How sick, how close to disaster, must a country become before such behavior by social institutions is not only accepted but expected? This time, we feel, is already here.

For years news and continuity specialists have pointed out that, in radio, ideas must be *simple,* or people won't understand. Some *ideas,* however, are themselves challenging or complicated—and can't be reduced to one-syllable words. A large part of the problem can be resolved only by educating people to understand ideas, some of which *are* tough, rather than skipping what can't be made easy, and making the rest simple enough for a child to follow. It is time that education made clear the responsibility of the listener to rise (with assistance) as well as the responsibility of the broadcaster to stoop. Otherwise we shall all be down on the floor with the kiddies when there are things requiring more serious consideration. The obligation not to become song-and-dance specialists is one that education *must* keep in mind in radio as well as in television.

Malcolm Muggeridge in *Encounter* has expressed the hope that by taking over the *Police Gazette* type of news function, television might free newspapers to resume what might again be called serious journalism. I would express the same hope for radio. To quote Mr. Muggeridge: "Thus it might be that the television cult will rescue journalism from the triviality and sensationalism which have so corrupted it in recent years. It might force journalism to return to an earlier and better tradition by, as it were, siphoning off the excrescences, the cheese cake, the gossips, the melodramatic overplaying of news stories, simply because of the unhappy chance that, in this field, television is unbeatable." (19)

The challenge to radio is at least as great as that which Mr. Muggeridge sees to the press. Let us hope that, using the specialists which most universities have as resources, news and public affairs in our nation can be given new meaning by educational stations. Today, according to studies by our good friend Leo Lowenthal, nine out of ten celebrities are show people. With serious efforts education should be able to help and guide our nation to redress this balance.

One of the principal errors in approach to the use of the media has been, perhaps, to ask what each medium can do—by itself. Nowhere has this been more obvious than in radio. And nowhere has it been more harmful in striking that balance in education and information which the presence of a multi-media complex makes available.

It appears by now that radio's greatest value is in service *in conjunction with other media.* Concern for the ability of radio as a medium, or television, for that matter, to do things by itself as a medium has made for imbalance, competition, and lack of perspective on the task rather than the tools, which can only be a disservice to education. It is time that a truce was called on this ridiculous attitude. What is important is not what *radio* can do but what it can *help* do. In some cases it will be a primary medium. In other cases it will be secondary, or co-equal with another or several others. It is in this context that the best balance would seem to result. Dr. Harwood points out, with reference to learning, that "those who listened, and then read, showed notably greater changes than those who read and then listened." In such cases, why should both not be used together or in tandem? If they are more efficient than television, why should they not still be used even in the presence of television? Radio, then, is best when used in conjunction with such other procedures and materials as teachers' efforts, maps, books, pamphlets, group discussions, etc. Indeed radio may be uniquely useful in many such functions. The concept needed, it would appear, is one which we might call the "concert," almost the "symphony," approach. There are times for solos, indeed. But for the great burden of education today, an orchestration of media can best bring results. It is in that role, rather than as a "solo instrument," that radio seems at its best.

When seen in this way, we can legitimately expect of radio certain specialized tasks which it is unfair to expect of it if we expect it to be a jack-of-all-trades. Many more men make good "second men" than corporation presidents. So with radio.

Dr. Grant Fairbanks of the University of Illinois has found that we can double the rate of comprehension of spoken words from 140 words per minute to 280, without difficulty. In fact, because the mind goes wool-gathering if the rate is too slow, speeding up frequently *improves* comprehension. What kinds of possibilities does *this* offer regarding the use, as lecturers, of teachers who, when they speak directly, are so slow as to be dull? In such cases would a time compressor, applied to the tapes, be more valuable and rewarding than speech lessons, applied to the teachers? If the informative efficiency of a unit of time can be increased so markedly by such an approach, is radio not uniquely useful in providing one of the tools and approaches needed, without, however, assuming responsibility for doing the entire job? Perhaps a printed version of the material is also indispensable. If so, let us not hesitate to use it, for such duplication is often not repetition but reinforcement. Such uses, if carefully controlled, are not mere gadgetry. They represent imaginative uses of the media—each being used for its best contribution—following which it may retire from its solo bit to its position in the orchestra again.

There are, of course, scores of uniquely valuable uses of radio on behalf of education. The discussions of three distinguished American university presidents with their Soviet counterparts in 1957 is one example of imaginative use of the medium. But the range is limitless. As Dr. Harwood has said, "The gamut of topics upon which sound-broadcasting has been demonstrated to produce measurable informative effects includes almost every conceivable category of knowledge. It follows from these demonstrations that the choice of topics for sound-broadcasting needs to be governed more by what is appropriate than by what is possible."

In the annual reports of the Philadelphia Public Schools, we have read of the superiority of radio for various types of music programs and other classroom uses in which the students must engage in activity instead of merely passively listening.

James Schwalbach, distinguished professor of art at the University of Wisconsin, in reply to my request for his own statement of his experience in teaching art by radio, says: "At the present time, I feel that the skill of teaching art education by radio is sufficiently advanced and tried so that we do an excellent job of stimulating the imagination of the youngsters to do creative expression. Radio is adept in this because it is able to help youngsters to re-visualize their own experiences with events that have happened to them in the past—either actual events or fictitious events. Also, radio has the advantage of being able to develop a situation which gives, in a way, a primary stimulus to the imagination. I am thinking here of the use of a dramatic production. The use of music for stimuli sometimes falls in between, since music, when listened to, will help youngsters recall experiences which they have had, themselves, or will tend to give youngsters a new experience.

"The advantage of radio over television is that the reliance upon the voice and the sound alone puts the burden upon the youngster to recall his *own* creative interpretation of the stimuli. This is a very important fact in art. I think, in the future, television will be able to do this, but at its present state, it has not been too successful. The very presence of a pictorial symbol or image tends to overpower some of the youngsters' own creative experiences and tends to be a device which the youngsters tend to imitate or copy. Also, the fact that an image to be used must be looked at (and at the same time you view it, you have some difficulty doing work of your own), while a verbal image may be listened to and the youngster can be creating at the same time, provides another advantage of radio. Therefore, while I do not sell the future of television short, I feel that at the present time radio is more effective in the field of creative expression than is television." So much for Dr. Schwalbach's experience, which deserves consideration and reflection.

In such areas as family problems, religion, the teaching of languages, history, citizenship, consumer education, recreation, news and public affairs, music, and a score of others, I believe radio also has unique contributions to make to the pattern of everyday living. It is especially superior in areas in which visuals interfere at the time, in cases where print and television are too slow or too expensive, or when events are too visual or too immediate for print media.

As a means of tapping available resources economically, in the staffs of universities and colleges, the United States and education have a "stable" of talent greater than that of any networks or publishing ventures or collections of groups, or probably any other nation. I believe that radio has not yet found its true role in the transforming of these latent resources into dynamic forces. My appeal is for it to be so used—at adult as well as lower education levels. I believe *educational* radio should provide positive leadership in helping to discover and develop this new role. In the fields of dissent and controversy, responsible, authoritative practices will succeed in an educational framework which people trust. In such areas, educational radio must lead and pioneer courageously, not merely coexist with the intolerably neutral approaches which characterize all too many commercial efforts even in recent months.

We hear that teen-agers have been "stolen" by radio and disc jockeys as pied pipers. Is there any reason why educational radio cannot compete for the attention of teen-agers outside the classroom? If so, let educational radio recognize such minorities and, blending them into its programming, build for tomorrow with the tools at hand. In such an effort no one need be ashamed of educational radio.

Research still needed

We have suggested above a few general approaches to the uses of radio that we believe will serve education. Many more need to be developed. But they must grow out of research and experimentation.

One of the tragedies of the last few years is that most potential donors of educational research funds have been "vamped" by television. Radio as a poor relative has suffered greatly in what has been less real research than an effort to prove that television, for example, can do virtually anything—more cheaply, more efficiently, and with fewer teachers and less space than was possible before. These seem to me to be negative contributions. A greater service to education would have resulted, we believe, if:

1) such research had been more "open-ended" and basic, and
2) if it had *not* concerned itself with the media separately. Joint uses should be considered far more than most projects now provide.

Dr. Harwood declares that "Many of the questions that were posited decades ago remain to be answered because the number of apparently pertinent questions is large and human abilities are limited. Some of the questions need to be answered differently again and again as society and knowledge change." It should also be remarked that findings valid in a pre-television age are not necessarily valid after television has come of age. The effects of the cross-bombardment of the various media are such that neither any of the media nor any individuals now alive can escape any one medium's effects by avoiding that medium. The ricochet of the media today leaves no avenue or channel of communication unpermeated.

Today, too, we have tools not available at the time of earlier radio research; candid, polaroid, and infrared photography, inconspicuous and economical recording devices, and many others.

Radio and television as tools of education are now "respectable" in increasingly wide educational circles. The conditioning to modesty of earlier days does not necessarily apply everywhere today. Personnel available to use these tools are generally better trained than in the days of early "radio research" or pioneering. We are finally beginning to have enough people in educational broadcasting who are well trained, so that we can begin to speak of a "profession."

Our own conviction, of course, as has been suggested earlier, is that "research" into how to make education cheaper and easier is not what is needed. Hard work is not necessarily good. But learning and education would seem usually to require discipline. This never comes easily. Easy work is not necessarily better than hard work, either. Learning and wisdom are still among the important products which we as educators have to offer. They are unfortunately, as qualities go, not "soft goods" which can be "turned out" rapidly and easily. Neither can they be "injected painlessly," in all too many cases, for education is less a product than an attitude or habit.

Hence, except as it may be useful for studying subliminal effects, or for achieving such objectives as rote learning, it would appear that research might concern itself less with such dramatic and showmanlike practices as "sleep-learning," intended to make it possible to get rich quickly and easily, educationally, and more with more basic educational problems intended to show how radio might help improve the quality and efficiency of education without reference to how "easy" it can be made.

There are scores of aspects of radio use for education which deserve further study. A good many are listed by Dr. Harwood in his forthcoming study.

Much research to date does not, in fact, deserve that designation. It has often been largely the gathering of statistics, or it has consisted of gross studies likely to lend themselves to argument; or "directed" studies in which objective, unintended effects have little or no opportunity to be reported—as has been true of "market research" for many years.

Perhaps one important reason for the absence of more real research is the lack of support for it by the commercial industry. In exchange for the millions which the networks and stations have earned in profits through the years, it is discouraging to see their niggardly support of basic research in radio and television. To our knowledge no other industry has shown such lack of leadership and such a lack of support. It is our hope that this situation will soon be changed and that radio research, and research that is not necessarily "steered" from "dangerous" findings, will again yield to honest searches for truth in the public interest.

The research and experimentation called for, of course, include studies in the technical areas as well as in learning. Facsimile, stereo techniques, multiplexing, and many other applications of radio and FM must some day be recognized, studied, and used for the efficiency and economy which they can contribute significantly to education's arsenal of instruments for the combating of ignorance and prejudice and the activating of democratic man—intellectually, spiritually, and physically.

The type of research needed, however, requires at least two additional types of support and implementation, if it is to be successful:

1) Educational broadcasting must be recognized and approached as a true and exacting profession involving adequate background study, specialized training, and skills and standards which practitioners will not violate for money or private advantage.

2) Courses in the evaluation, criticism, and discriminating use of these media must be introduced into the schools of the United States at high school or lower levels, with more advanced counterparts in our colleges and universities. Electronic fall-out may be as serious as radioactive fall-out. What the electronic media are doing to human beings, on the assumption that their effects are known, or neutral, or harmless, may some day kill us. In the complex of research and experimentation needed to support such courses, and to produce qualified critics, teachers and professionals, radio and television, and all other media must be studied together, rather than in the isolated way in which television and teaching machines, particularly, have so far been studied.

Conclusion

To quote Dr. Kenneth Harwood: "It appears clearly possible to inform children, adolescents, and adults through sound-broadcasting, to effect approximately as much learning through use of sound-broadcasting as through face-to-face discourse, to inform upon almost every conceivable topic through sound-broadcasting, to stimulate imagery and provide suggestion, to contribute to change or maintenance of opinion and attitude, and to promote initiation, continuation, or completion of social or individual actions. Affective acknowledgment of these kinds of possibilities may never cease to require some further demonstrations of them, but the intellectual facts of their existence are public."

Thus Dr. Harwood summarizes the result of his study of the uses of radio for instruction over the past thirty years. Because television provides much more entertainment and is, to many, more interesting, we sometimes forget that interest and learning are not necessarily synonymous. They may be opposite in some respects. We sometimes get so "carried away" that we "forget to remember" or "fail to notice." This seems to be one of the disadvantages of television, as compared to radio, which we must guard against.

In addition to the potentials of radio which are not yet fully explored, television has brought about so complete a change of radio's role and a change in the nature of the radio audience generally that wholly new evaluations are now needed.

It is unlikely that education will ever be "popular" in the same sense that the "popular arts" are. Entertainment is still both a valid and popular function of virtually all media. But decision-making, new ideas, leadership, and other aspects of democratic life generally depend not on a mass, but on leaders to propagate and explain and "popularize" them. We should neither insist nor expect that educational radio and television should be "popular" in that sense. If they are available to and used by those who need them and want them, like other minority services which are indispensable—they will be fulfilling their function.

At the same time I believe educators have been too modest in their concepts of the role of educational radio. I do not believe it needs to be an "economy annex" to television. In most senses these media can be more nearly equal than they now are. Just as there may now be UHF Educational Television Annexes (to VHF services) for in-school uses, so there is no reason in an age of such specialization why there can not be radio transmitters which might carry, for example, nothing but college and university lectures. In an age when retrieval of materials is such a problem, and when it is distribution rather than the production of materials of education that is the bottleneck, there are secondary uses of radio, such as this, which can legitimately be made. But this should not obscure the peculiar gifts of radio for intimacy and immediacy—freedom from commitment to materials which are to be "re-used." This freedom can give it the most unique and significant role in education and society today—leaving more nearly to films, books, and all the other media those permanent, library, and status-quo-preserving conservative pressures which, of course, we can not escape and would do well to preserve as history's lessons. But I do not believe radio and history should mix.

Funds, top-level government support, and educational recognition of its effectiveness can, and will, I am convinced, eventually "put radio over the top" educationally. But if this is to happen, more vigorous efforts will be needed than the frequently milquetoast-like, timid efforts most characteristic to date among educators.

Education should not be satisfied until it has at least as efficient a communications system as industry and commerce in the United States. Is there any reason why the public's educational station should not be the *finest* one in its area—instead of the disgraceful, understaffed, out-of-date eyesores and toys now too often the lot of schools that operate them?

Teaching machines will undoubtedly enormously free teachers from routine drill-work, taking over this learning and practice function. Television can uniquely do many parts of the job—with specific demonstrations and many more procedures. But each medium, including radio, still is only *part* of the arsenal available to education. The latter should remain indivisible, bigger than any medium. Perhaps one of education's greatest needs today is for media specialists who can objectively evaluate which parts of the tasks before us can best be done by which media. With the approaching shortages of teachers and space and funds, radio and all these other media should, in fact, safeguard and help preserve and renew the highest goals of education.

The educational administrator who makes the decisions of which media a school is to install and use has a terrible responsibility. History will judge him to no small extent not only by how progressive he is in using new tools and techniques, while preserving valid objectives for education; it will judge him also by how wasteful, or how discriminating and imaginative he is in what he asks for, and how he uses what he can secure to advance the cause of education in the United States. Within that framework the history of communications progress in education is likely to inquire especially into that economical, unique, and readily available medium: educational radio.

NOTES

1. *Communication Media and the School: The Yearbook of Education*, 1960. Joint editors: George Z. F. Bereday and Joseph A. Lauwerys. London: Evans Brothers Ltd., and New York: World Book Co., Editors' Introduction, pp. 12–13.

2. Harold E. Hill, *National Association of Educational Broadcasters: A History*. Published by National Association of Educational Broadcasters, Urbana, Illinois, 1954. Mimeo. 46 pages plus appendices.

3. S. E. Frost, Jr., *Education's Own Stations*. Chicago: University of Chicago Press, 1937.

4. Hill, *op. cit.*, p. 8.

5. *Ibid.*, p. 21.

6. *Ibid.*, p. 12.

7. *Ibid.*, p. 28.

8. *Ibid.*, p. 22.

9. BBC, London, 1957, 164 pages plus appendices, p. 26.

10. *Ibid.*, p. 35.

11. *Yearbook of Education*, 1960, p. 305.

12. *Ibid.*, p. 375.

13. *The Multiplier in Technical Cooperation*. Published by ICA (International Cooperation Administration), Vol. III, issue No. 12, November-December, 1960, p. 19.

14. *Yearbook of Education,* 1960, p. 558.

15. *Ibid.,* p. 564.

16. "Culture, Psychiatry, and the Written Word," *Psychiatry,* November, 1959, p. 311.

17. Alan Thomas, *Audience Market, Public: An Evaluation of Canadian Broadcasting.* University of British Columbia, Department of University Extension, April 1960. Occasional Paper No. 7. Mimeo. 23 pages.

18. Dr. Harwood kindly made his manuscript of his study of Informative Sound Broadcasting available to the author. This study was done under a joint project of the NAEB and the National Project for Agricultural Communications at Michigan State University. Currently under revision, portions of this study are scheduled for publication during 1961. Our thanks to Dr. Harwood for access to his excellent study is hereby acknowledged.

19. *Encounter,* December 1959, p. 16.